THE STUART COURTS

THE STUART COURTS

EDITED BY **EVELINE CRUICKSHANKS**
FOREWORD BY **DAVID STARKEY**

First published 2000
This edition first published 2009

The History Press
The Mill, Brimscombe Port
Stroud, Gloucestershire, GL5 2QG
www.thehistorypress.co.uk

British Library Cataloguing in Publication Data.
A catalogue record for this book is available from the British Library.

ISBN 978 0 7524 5206 7

Typesetting and origination by The History Press
Printed in Great Britain

To Patrick O'Brien of the Institute of Historical Research
and Chantal Grell of the Université de Versailles,
without whose help and encouragement
this volume of essays would not have been produced.

CONTENTS

List of Contributors

G.E. AYLMER was Master of St. Peter's College, Oxford until 1991. He published *The King's Servants, The Civil Service of Charles I 1625–1642* (1961 and 1974) and *The State's Servants; The Civil Service of the English Republic 1649–1660* (1973) and other books on Seventeenth Century history. He was a member of the Editorial Board of the History of Parliament 1968–1998 and its Chairman 1989–1998. He died in 2001.

ANDREW BARCLAY is a Research Fellow with the 1640–1660 section of the History of Parliament Trust. His recent publications include articles on the Court of William III, the 1661 Edward's Crown and Oliver Cromwell's protectoral Household. His monograph on Cromwell's early political career is forthcoming. He is the Treasurer and Secretary of the Society for Court Studies and Treasurer of the Jacobite Studies Trust.

TOBY BARNARD is Fellow and tutor in history at Hertford College, Oxford. His recent books include *A New Anatomy of Ireland* (2003); *Making the Grand Figure: lives and possessions in Ireland, 1641–1700* (2004); and *Improving Ireland? Projectors, prophets and profiteers, 1641–1786* (2008). He is a Fellow of the British Academy and an honorary member of the Royal Irish Academy. From 2006–2009 he has held a Leverhulme senior research fellowship, working on a study of the cultures of print in Ireland between 1680 and the 1790s.

EDWARD CORP is Professor of British History at the University of Toulouse. His publications include *The King over the Water; Portraits of the Stuarts in Exile after 1689* (National Galleries of Scotland, 2001), *A Court in Exile: the Stuarts in France, 1689–1718* (Cambridge University Press, 2004, forthcoming in paperback), and *The Jacobites at Urbino: an Exiled Court in Transition* (Palgrave Macmillan, 2008). He is currently working on a similar study of the Stuart Court in Rome and Bologna, 1719–66, for Cambridge University Press.

EVELINE CRUICKSHANKS has worked on the volumes of the History of Parliament 1660–1714 and edited most of the 1690–1714 volumes. She has written on Toryism and Jacobitism in the reigns of George I and George II and edited several collections of essays on Jacobitism. Her latest book (in collaboration with Howard Erskine-Hill) is *The Atterbury Plot* (Palgrave Macmillan, 2004). She is a Fellow of the Institute of Historical Research in the University of London.

NEIL CUDDY has published a series of essays on Stuart politics and the Court, notably on James I's Bedchamber by David Starkey et al (1987) and most recently on 'Salisbury's 1610 Great Contract' in Cliff Davies's festschrift 'Authority and Consent in Tudor England' (eds. George Bernard and Steven Gunn, 2002). He is preparing for publication a book on court politics and parliaments in James I's reign.

DAVID LINDLEY is Professor of Renaissance Literature at the University of Leeds. He has published on the court masque, on music and poetry, and on the scandalous history of Frances Howard. Most recently he has edited Shakespeare's *The Tempest* for the New Cambridge Shakespeare (2002) and written *Shakespeare and Music* for the Arden Companions to Shakespeare series (2005). His edition of eleven Jonson's masques will form part of the Cambridge *Ben Jonson*, forthcoming in 2002.

ARTHUR MACGREGOR was, until his retirement in 2008, a Senior Assistant Keeper in the Department of Antiquities at the Ashmolean Museum, Oxford. He has served as Director of the British Archaeological Association and of the Society of Antiquaries; currently he is a Vice-President of the Royal Archaeological Institute. In addition to his archaeological interests he has published widely on the history of museums and collecting, most recently with a book, *Curiosity and Enlightenment. Collectors and Collections 1500–1800* (2008). He is editor of the *Journal of the History of Collections.* He is preparing a book on the relations between man and the animal world since the Norman Conquest.

LORRAINE MADWAY received her Ph.D. in History from Yale and a MS in librarianship and archives from Simmons College in Boston. She is the Curator of Special Collections and University Archivist at Wichita State University Libraries in Kansas. She is also a lecturer on archives in the History Department at Wichita State University and the library school at Emporia State University. She has delivered papers in Europe and the USA on topics related to the Courts of Charles II and Cromwell and on topics related to her scholarly interests in archives and collective memory, film, and Jewish history.

NICK MEYERS is a senior lecturer in the Department of English and American Studies at Paul-Valéry University, in Montpellier, France. In recent years, he has published articles on such subjects as the question of law, justice and kingship in Montaigne's essays, the problem of the Elizabethan succession, and the vision of the interplay of chance and providence in the writings of Pierre Mathieu and John Foxe. He continues to work on issues of kingship, statecraft and authority, but has begun to make incursions into the field of travel literature in the Early Modern period. He is a member of the Institut de recherche sur la Renaissance, l'Age classique et les Lumières, a CRNS accredited research centre, and is assistant editor of *Cahiers Élisabéthains*.

HUGH OUSTON read history at Christ Church, Oxford and undertook research under Hugh Trevor-Roper into the intellectual life of late seventeenth-century Scotland. He has made a career as a history teacher in Scottish schools and is currently the headmaster of Robert Gordon's College in Aberdeen.

MURRAY PITTOCK is Bradley Professor of English Literature at the University of Glasgow, and formerly held chairs at the universities of Manchester and Strathclyde. His research on national identity, Jacobitism and Romanticism has had an international impact; his most recent work on Jacobitism includes a second and comprehensively revised edition of *The Myth of the Jacobite Clans* and a co-edited collection on *Loyalty and Identity: Jacobites at home and abroad*, both to appear in 2009–10.

SIMON THURLEY has written widely on the architecture of the English Court. He is currently Chief Executive of English Heritage and Chairman of the Society for Court Studies.

BRIAN WEISER is Assistant Professor at Metropolitan State College of Denver and reviews editor for *H-Albion*. He is the author of *Charles II and the Politics of Access* (2004) and of several articles on the representations of Charles II. He is currently researching economic thought in the reign of Charles I.

JEREMY WOOD is Associate Professor of Art History at the University of Nottingham. He has published a number of essays concerned with the study of Italian Art by Northern artists working in the seventeenth century, Rubens and Van Dyck in particular, as well as various aspects of the history of collecting. In 2002 he was curator of the exhibition 'Rubens: Drawings on Italy', which was held at the National Gallery of Scotland in Edinburgh. He is author of Volume XXV (2) of the *Corpus Rubenianum Ludwig Burchard*, which is focussed on Rubens copies and adaptations after Italian art, the first section of which, on Raphael and his school, will appear in 2009.

SONYA WYNNE completed a doctorate 'The mistresses of Charles II and Restoration Court politics, 1660–1685' in 1997 and subsequently took part in radio programmes and art exhibitions on Charles II's mistresses, The 'Painted Ladies'. After working for the History of Parliament Trust and Oxford University Press, she returned to New Zealand, the country of her birth.

FOREWORD

David Starkey

I am delighted to welcome this volume of essays on the Stuart Court.

Court studies is a comparative newcomer to the world of historical scholarship, and this is particularly true in the English-speaking world. In Continental Europe the near universality of absolute monarchy meant that courts, whether you loved them or loathed them, had an inescapable importance. At home, however, the dominant school of 'Whig' historiography saw the use of Parliament as the central thread of British history. This made the Court not only unimportant but somehow un-English as well.

'Whig' history drew its strength from the Victorians' own confidence in their present. Inhabiting, as he did, the best of all possible constitutional and political systems, it became the nineteenth-century historian's duty to explain how such perfection had come about. And Victorian political theory, as Walter Bagehot shows, reduced the monarch to an empty shell: sometimes 'hidden like a mystery and sometimes paraded like a pageant'. Instead, Parliament was all.

Historians are now questioning Bagehot's picture of the marginality of Victoria's monarchy, and hence that of the Victorian Court. More important, however, is the fact that none of us shares his sublime confidence in the perfection of British parliamentary institutions. On the contrary, we doubt them as we doubt all the other principal features of the Bagehotian constitution: the Church, the monarchy, the United Kingdom itself.

There are many drawbacks to this sudden deflation of national self-confidence. But one unquestioned gain is that we can view our past afresh. History is only on the side of the winners if the historian thinks he is a winner too. And we no longer do. So, freed from the shadow of the Westminster Parliament, the blighting tradition of constitutional history and the churning, progressive juggernaut of the Great British success story, a thousand flowers have bloomed. Many of these have been humble, workaday plants. Local history, the history of women, that of the everyday life of ordinary families and communities, have all been studied as never before. But there are more exotic blossoms as well, of which the history of aristocracy and royal courts are the most important. A hundred years ago, at the height of the Victorian age, W.S. Gilbert put the case for the classes against the masses:

Hearts just as pure and fair
May beat in Belgrave Square
As in the lowly air
Of Seven Dials.

Gilbert wrote satirically. But it is time to take the argument seriously.

And we should do so on the same grounds that we take the poor, the dispossessed, the foreign and the deviant seriously. We now take for granted (sometimes too much for granted) that women, blacks, Muslims or gays have their own culture and that they must be addressed in terms of that culture. The same is true for that infinitely more alien world of aristocratic and court culture.

This volume is a testimony to the fact that this approach is beginning to take hold. It contains a selection of the papers delivered at a conference in 1994 on the seventeenth-century Court, which was held at the Institute of Historical Research, University of London, under the auspices of the Institute of Historical Research and the Université de Versailles. It combines studies of festivals and finance, of building and dining, of patronage and the pornocracy of Charles II's mistresses, as well as a careful overview of the changing place of the Court in the politics of Britain.

These themes seem extraordinarily diverse and it is tempting to divide them into the serious and the insubstantial, propaganda on the one hand and the real business of politics on the other. But this is to relapse into the categories of the old historiography. In the Court, there was almost no distinction between form and substance: a procession was a political statement, a Council meeting, a ceremony (with the *placement* organised according to the same rules as the procession). Only with Bagehot's world do we come to the distinction between the efficient and the dignified exercise of power, with the Crown and Court belonging to the latter.

I have written this Foreword in a personal capacity. But could I end by inviting everyone who reads this volume on the seventeenth-century British Court and is excited by it to join the Society for Court Studies? Our aim is to develop the court studies of every country and every century. For the Court is an obstinate beast that survives the best attempts of levellers and democrats to render it extinct. By analysing it we understand not only remote ages but our own.

David Starkey
London
January 2000

LIST OF ABBREVIATIONS

Places of publication are London unless otherwise stated.

AAE	Archives des Affaires Étrangères
Aylmer, *King's Servants*	G.E. Aylmer, *The King's Servants: the Civil Service of Charles I*, 2nd edn 1974
BN	Bibliothèque nationale de France
Bucholz, *Augustan Court*	R. Bucholz, *The Augustan Court: Queen Anne and the Decline of Court Culture*, Stanford, CA, 1993
CBR	Guiffrey, J. (ed.), *Compes des Bâtiments du Roi sous le Règne de Louis XIV*, Paris, 1891
Chandaman, *Public Revenue*	C.D. Chandaman, *The English Public Revenue 1660–1688*, Oxford, 1975
CJ	*Journal of the House of Commons*
Colvin, *King's Works*	H.M. Colvin (ed.), *The History of the King's Works*, 6 vols, 1951–82
CPA	Correspondance Politique Angleterre
CSPD	*Calendar of State Papers Domestic*
CTB	*Calendar of Treasury Books*
EHR	*English Historical Review*
Evelyn, *Diary*	*The Diary of John Evelyn*, ed. E.S. de Beer, 6 vols, Oxford, 1966
GEC	G.E. Cokayne, *The Complete Peerage*, ed. Peter W. Hammond, Stroud, Sutton Publishing, 1998
HC 1660–1690	*The House of Commons 1660–1690*, ed. B.D. Henning, Secker and Warburg for the History of Parliament Trust, 3 vols, 1983
HJ	*Historical Journal*
HMC	Historical Manuscript Commission
LJ	*Journal of the House of Lords*
Lockyer, *Bukingham*	Roger Lockyer, *Buckingham, The Life and Political Career of George Villiers, First Duke of Buckingham 1592–1628*, 1981
Orgel, *Illusion of Power*	Stephen Orgel, *The Illusion of Power: Theater in the English Renaissance*, Berkeley, CA, 1975
Parry, *Golden Age*	Graham Parry, *The Golden Age Restor'd: the Culture of the Stuart Court 1603–42*, Manchester, 1981
Peck, *Mental World*	Linda Levy Peck, *The Mental World of the Jacobean Court*, Cambridge, 1991

Pepys, *Diary*	*The Diary of Samuel Pepys: A New and Complete Transcription*, eds R. Latham and W. Matthews, 11 vols, 1980–3
Russell, *Parliament*	Conrad Russell, *Parliament and English Politics 1621–1629*, Oxford, 1979
Sharpe, *Criticism and Compliment*	Kevin Sharpe, *Criticism and Compliment: The Politics of Literature in the England of Charles I*, Cambridge, 1987
Sharpe, *Personal Rule*	Kevin Sharpe, *The Personal Rule of Charles I*, New Haven, 1992
Smuts, *Stuart Court*	R. Malcolm Smuts (ed.), *The Stuart Court & Europe: Essays in Politics and Political Culture*, Cambridge, 1996
Starkey, *English Court*	D. Starkey, D.A.L. Morgan, J. Murphy, P. Wright, N. Cuddy and K. Sharpe (eds), *The English Court from the Wars of the Roses to the Civil War*, 1987
Strong, *Henry, Prince of Wales*	Roy Strong, *Henry, Prince of Wales and England's Lost Renaissance*, 1986
Thurley, *Royal Palaces*	Simon Thurley, *The Royal Palaces of Tudor England*, New Haven, 1993

INTRODUCTION*

Eveline Cruickshanks

In the seventeenth century the royal Court at Whitehall had a greater importance and continuity than Parliament at Westminster as the main centre of fashionable social life and the focal point of politics and administration. The Palace of Whitehall was a jumble of courts, galleries, halls and about 1,400 rooms built at different times. Though the topography was often inconvenient, it had the advantage of bringing the monarch, the members of the Household, the ministers and chief courtiers in close proximity and easily accessible to one another. The Court consisted of three divisions of the Household, as Neil Cuddy explains: the Board of Greencloth, 'below stairs' under the Lord Steward, the Chamber under the Lord Chamberlain, and the Bedchamber under the Groom of the Stole (originally Stool). The Household operated at full strength only when the King occupied one of his royal palaces. The Court, however, was wherever the King and Queen were and there were administrative difficulties (though Elizabeth I's successors were less ambulatory than she was) when it moved to Newmarket, or to Winchester after 1683. The medieval tradition of magnificent hospitality continued. James I and Charles I were expected to clothe and feed members of their entourage. Communal dining was a central part of the life of the Court and court tables to feed the Household and many others was one of the largest items of expenditure until 1662 when it was reorganised. Purveyance, which enabled food and goods to be purchased below the market price, was unpopular, but James I's attempt to change the system in the Great Contract of 1610, to obtain a parliamentary grant in lieu of Purveyance, failed[1] and magnificent hospitality continued until Charles I abandoned London in 1642. The prime reason for going to Court, however, was not free meals, but the search for fashionable pastimes. Magnificence took other forms, such as the giving of precious metals, jewels and rich clothes, which made a court a splendid spectacle.[2]

In the later years of Elizabeth I's reign, her popularity had waned and her parsimony and procrastination could no longer conceal the administrative and financial malfunctioning. Without regular taxation, a standing army or a navy of any size, the monarch's power was more apparent than real. There was a

* I am grateful to Katharine Gibson for comments on the contents of this introduction.

breakdown between the cost of government and the royal revenue and Conrad Russell has depicted Charles as poverty-stricken.[3] Many of the men in Parliament were parochial in outlook and their disputes with the Crown were less over high principles and constitutional causes[4] than unwillingness to pay realistic taxes or to take any responsibility for their actions.

James VI of Scotland, Mary Stuart's Protestant son, cousin of Elizabeth and great grandson of Henry VIII's sister Margaret, ascended the English throne as James I in 1603. He came with the advantage of an assured succession, having two sons already. Murray Pittock shows the strength and variety of the Scottish court culture over which James presided. He was a scholar king, wily, witty and gifted, yet accessible and on familiar terms with his subjects. James's court culture was deeply influenced by Renaissance traditions, as Elizabeth's had been.[5] James was interested in church music and he appointed Thomas Hudson, an Englishman who had lived in France, as Master of the Chapel Royal. This explains his later leanings towards Anglican ceremonial and his readiness to defy the Kirk's strictures. When James went to London much of Scottish court culture moved with him and by 1625 Scottish culture had been completely anglicised. Yet James remained more closely in touch with Scotland than any of his successors, with the exception of James II as Duke of York. Ben Jonson's masque *Hymenaei* of 1606 represented the union between England and Scotland. James encouraged dynastic alliances between the English and Scottish aristocracy, which were celebrated in court masques.[6] The masque was the dominant mode of entertainment at the first two Stuart courts, an extravagant fusion of dance, drama, music and a theatrical spectacle. It displayed the magnificence of the Court, and foreign ambassadors and diplomats vied for invitations.[7] Chapman's *The Memorable Masque*, the subject of David Lindley's essay in this volume, was probably devised by Prince Henry to celebrate the marriage of Princess Elizabeth and Frederick, Elector Palatine. Presented to James by two Inns of Court, the masque is an apologia for the Virginia enterprise, stressing the strong missionary nature of its colonial activity rather than the quest for gold, which had proved non-existent there in any case. The masque was designed to appeal to those who applauded the Protestant alliance and who were anti-Spanish. It is an interesting example of its use as a critique of sections of the Court.

James I and Henry IV of France were often compared: new kings in unfamiliar kingdoms. Henry's entry into Lyon, one of the most important towns in France described here by Nick Myers, presented him as Hercules, with a blend of mythology and history, replacing war and rebellion with peace and plenty. The central theme was that only he could drag France out of the quagmire into which it had sunk. James's entry into London, the only full-blown pageant of the reign, projected him as monarch of four nations – England, Scotland, Ireland and, theoretically, France – guided by the hand of God. This was a much more magnificent occasion than Elizabeth's entry and was seen to herald a new golden age.[8] James was warmly welcomed. He enjoyed his popularity and the greater affluence of an English monarch, while his Scottish friends made the most of new career possibilities in England. In an attempt to gratify both English and Scottish suitors, James's pension list swelled to over £100,000, or nearly a third of Crown revenue.[9] James asserted the doctrine of divine hereditary right as part of the ancient constitution, which imposed duties as well as rights on the King. He personally supervised the Authorised Version of the Bible of 1611 and was much given to theological discussions with his chaplains and other clerics. The Anglican Church, which claimed primitive purity and apostolic descent from St Augustine, tended to interpret history as providential. James I took his role as head of the Church very seriously and professed to value the title of Defender of the Faith above that of King.[10] It is much to James's credit that he encouraged John Donne, who was a Catholic, to take Holy Orders, became his patron and appointed him one of his chaplains. In the pulpit Donne addressed James both as the Image of God and as a sinful man.[11] Easy of access and ready of speech, under a mask of tomfoolery, James possessed the sense of dignity of kingship which his son and grandsons also had. But it was not long before his homosexuality and partiality to Buckingham and other favourites engendered criticisms of his being dissipated and self-indulgent. James drank heavily and his Court was riotous and disorderly at times On the other hand, Roger Lockyer has argued that Buckingham was trying, rightly, to prevent Habsburg domination of Europe, though he lacked the financial resources to prevent it.[12]

The two leading pastimes of European monarchs in the seventeenth as well as in the eighteenth centuries were *la gloire* and *la chasse*. Fortunately for his finances, James, who was a pacifist, had no ambition to lead armies in person. A weakness in the legs he shared with his son Charles made his gait awkward. He compensated by being a superb horseman and devoting himself to hunting for which he had a passion and which made his Court ambulatory at times. To the pleasures of the chase and the killing of vast quantities of wild animals, as Arthur MacGregor shows, he added cockfights, bull- and bear-baiting, tastes he shared with the majority of his subjects, of course.

Charles I had been brought up in the shadow of his elder brother, Prince Henry, who before his premature death had been lauded as the ideal of Protestant chivalry.[13] More recently, historians have argued that the mental horizons and social environment of the Stuart courts was European rather than purely English or British.[14] The first monarch to be raised from birth in the tenets of the Church of England, Charles I tried to bring out its splendour and dignity. Obsessed with order and decorum, he took a strong moral stance.[15] From his accession in 1625, he placed an even greater emphasis on the divine right of kings than his father had. The series of paintings by Rubens on the ceiling of the Banqueting House in Whitehall sought to justify the divine right of kings, mixing

Christian images with those of Roman emperors. In court masques James I was portrayed as a royal Solomon, praised for his wisdom, prudence and magnanimity, while Charles preferred the role of royal knight, inspired by the beauty of his wife to purge the realm of vice and discord.[16] Van Dyck portrayed Charles both as a hero and an emperor, a chivalrous knight whose most important battle was not against foreign enemies but against evil on behalf of virtue.[17] Charles's masques, in which he and his queen participated, emphasised the name of Britain, stressing his special status as a British monarch and Scottish courtiers were invited to take part.[18] As Charles could not afford to wage war after the disastrous La Rochelle expedition and governed without Parliament during the years of personal rule, the olive branch rather than laurels became his metaphorical symbol. Though Buckingham, until his death in 1629, was allowed to behave as extravagantly as ever, Charles's reign was not racked by scandals as James's had been. Kevin Sharpe believes that Charles was driven to the personal rule of the 1630s by the failings of Parliament and that his ambitious programme of reform in Church and State was more successful than previous historians have allowed.[19]

Charles I succeeded in shaping a court culture which embodied the highest ideals in art and politics.[20] In all things Charles sought to foster order and virtue. Sharing James's dislike of the anti-episcopal stance of the Puritanical party, he believed in the reality of the 'no Bishops, no Kings' cry. Charles, though a devout Anglican, was attracted to the rituals and ceremonies of the Catholic Church. Anglican Church music, one of the glories of English civilisation, owes much to Charles and Laud. Laud in fact argued for the suppression of Catholicism, while he and most bishops defended the royal prerogative, as the High Anglicans did after the Restoration of 1660. This together with his patronage of Archbishop Laud and embracing Arminianism, which defended free will and denied the Calvinistic doctrine of predestination, led the sectarians to accuse him of trying to reintroduce Popery.[21] His quest to achieve one uniform order of religion in his three kingdoms, however, led to rebellion in Scotland and Ireland.[22] In other respects, prominent parliamentarians and monarch shared a common culture and code of honour. Part of that code, duelling, was violent, as was much in that society. Presbyterians were prominent duellists in Charles I's reign[23] as were, for instance, the Presbyterian Whartons in Charles II's.

Charles I's marriage with Henrietta Maria, daughter of Henry IV, was a diplomatic coup by European standards, but it misfired as France would not give Britain assistance against Spain, and this brought severe criticisms from his subjects. Theirs was a love match and a model Christian marriage, but in her open profession of her Roman Catholic religion, she was less discreet than Anne of Denmark's, James I's queen's, secret worship had been. Caroline masques depicted Charles as the embodiment of heroic virtue and Henrietta Maria as Divine Beauty or Love, particularly in *The Triumph of Love*, produced by Inigo

Jones in 1634.[24] Caroline drama was neither escapist nor servile, though criticisms of the Court were more likely in works produced outside it.[25] The cult of platonic love flourished round the Queen. Charles, who was an enthusiastic reader of Shakespeare, had a genuine enthusiasm for the theatre and built a new Cockpit Theatre in Whitehall, while Henrietta Maria brought the taste of the Parisian *Precieuses* from the *Hotel de Rambouillet*.[26] She was responsible for introducing French musicians at Court. Whitehall in the 1630s was a place of gallantry and sophistication.

From the time of his accession Charles, who was in sympathy with the Baroque culture of Europe, had established a network of agents familiar with the court culture of Spain, France and Italy to bring art treasures and artists to England, as Jeremy Wood shows. Their greatest triumph was the purchase of the Duke of Mantua's collection in 1627 for £15,639 through Nys, who was apparently a Venetian merchant.[27] Charles, who brought Rubens, Van Dyck and Jordaens to England, was the greatest connoisseur of the arts who ever occupied the throne. He was assisted by members of the royal Privy Chamber such as Endymion Porter and Sir Kenhelm Digby who had the reputation of being good connoisseurs of paintings. Charles appointed Inigo Jones as Surveyor, the first man possessing a knowledge of Renaissance architectural theory, whose art expertise made the royal collection the finest in England.[28] Many of the statues of Charles I were destroyed during the Interregnum, but Le Sueur's statue, now in Charing Cross, survived and is one of the oldest equestrian statues in London. Van Dyck's paintings depicted Charles as a king on horseback. Charles made an enormous contribution to the fine arts in England. These acquisitions were made on what was a shoestring, costing less than tapestries and carpets but were nevertheless denounced as extravagant by some historians, particularly Americans brought up in a culture of Protestant dissent, seeing in it also a tendency to absolutist ideology and Neo-Platonism.[29] Nor did they bring much credit to him with his subjects, many of whom were not only philistines, but iconoclasts. A more valid criticism is that few of those who might have appreciated them had a chance to see his great collection, which was made more accessible, ironically enough, when it was sold and dispersed after his death.

Charles brought the more rigid etiquette of the Spanish Court to Whitehall. His perfect good manners and gentle nature, however, were known only to a small inner circle and he lacked the common touch which his father and his eldest son had. He was of a retiring disposition, suffered from a stammer and kept his plans to himself. Faced with the unprecedented circumstances of the Civil War, he appeared double-faced at times, which led John Morrill to describe him as 'inaccessible, glacial, self righteous, deceitful'.[30]

Ceremonies and rituals were more important in the seventeenth century than now. Nobles entered the King's apartment not in confusion but each according to rank and according to his appointed place. The King's right to regulate behaviour and show his esteem for certain individuals was a form of power.[31] Charles was preoccupied with regulating the Order of the Garter, especially its religious aspects, and he insisted that the Knights should wear their Garter badge, the embroidered red cross of St George on the left side of their cloak.[32] Charles sought to establish a well-regulated court as a shrine of virtue and decorum. Charles had not been granted tonnage and poundage for life as his father and Elizabeth had and he could not emulate other European rulers in building royal palaces. He had wanted to rebuild the Palace of Whitehall along more rational, classical and ordered lines, twice the size of the Escorial, which he had seen in 1623, but could not afford to do so.[33] Instead, he built smaller edifices, such as the Queen's House at Greenwich, the new theatre in Whitehall and chapels for his wife at St James and Somerset House.[34]

At his execution in 1649, Charles's dignity and pathos won a posthumous victory. He was consecrated as Charles the Martyr, the only saint of the Church of England. By turning Charles into a Christ-like figure, the Cavaliers managed to associate the Regicides and their Puritan allies with the scribes and the Pharisees who clamoured for the crucifixion.[35] Earlier, contemporaries had seen a likeness between Van Dyck's portrayals of Charles and Christ and this cult was promoted by Marshall's famous engraving at the beginning of the *Eikon Basilike*, published in 1649.[36] The cult of Charles the Martyr and the keeping of 30 January, the day of his execution, as a solemn feast continued from the Restoration until the nineteenth century. It was such a powerful symbol that at the time of Bishop Atterbury's plot in 1722, the 2nd Duke of Leeds commissioned a spectacular series of canvasses to depict the life of Charles I in order to advocate 'the restoration of our only true and rightful king James III'.[37]

After the Civil Wars, political chaos and army rule, and twelve years of exile for Charles II, the Restoration of 1660 was greeted with immense joy, as a new dawn. Its anniversary, 29 May 1661, Charles's birthday and the date of his entry, became a major feast in the calendar. The splendour and significance of his coronation on 23 April, St George's day, following a triumphal procession through the City the previous day, discussed here by Lorraine Madway, left spectators speechless. The coronation was an essentially religious ceremony, illustrating the centrality of the Church of England, for which Charles I had died, and William Juxon, Archbishop of Canterbury and Gilbert Sheldon, Bishop of London organised the ceremony. Charles was depicted as a new King David and was portrayed as slaying the dragon of rebellion and rescuing the people from chaos.

Charles II was much more accessible and convivial than his father had been. Though his was a limited monarchy, he continued the charismatic aspect of divine right by touching over 100,000 people with the king's evil (scrofula), a greater number than any other monarch. He eschewed the elaborate and static formality of the Court of Versailles under Louis XIV and spoke contemptuously of the King of Spain, who 'will not piss but another must hold the pot'. Endowed with great personal charm, he was always courteous and affable and doffed his hat to people of all ranks in Whitehall, just as Louis XIV did at Versailles. He would receive suitors and ambassadors with his hat on, so that they could keep theirs on too.[38] One should not overemphasise the informality, however, for, as Simon Thurley explains, Charles redesigned Greenwich as a ceremonial gateway to the kingdom in which to welcome foreign ambassadors and important visitors. Yet Charles valued his privacy and, on the French model, retreated into a new 'private' Withdrawing Chamber and Bedchamber some distance from the former Privy Lodgings at Whitehall. The withdrawal did not lead to tranquillity, however, as his informality with his intimates and voracious sexual appetites led his Court to be described as 'a cross between a brothel and a beargarden'.[39] His beloved spaniels were everywhere, even in the royal Bedchamber and his Queen, Catherine of Braganza, had a miscarriage in 1668 when a pet fox jumped on her belly. Amid it all, he was faced with a financial deficit, for even the ultra-loyal Cavalier Parliament had not wished to make him financially independent by voting a revenue adequate to run the administration, the minute army or the navy (to which, under an air of nonchalance, he devoted much time), let alone wage a successful war.[40] He gave up Purveyance in exchange for a parliamentary grant. To make ends meet, Clarendon determined to reform the diets because of the vast Household arrears and the growing cost of hospitality, as Andrew Barclay shows. By 1663 all but a handful of court tables had been replaced by boardwages for all but the most senior servants. Wholesale reform failed, however, because it was not extended to the Queen's Household and her Portuguese servants or the Duke of York's, so that a shortfall between revenue and Household expenditure persisted.

Yet, after the years of exile, hardships and privations, Charles would not curb his search for pleasure, indulging in hard-living, gambling and flamboyant *maitresses en titres*. Lady Castlemaine was installed in Hampton Court Palace and her ruthless quest for wealth proved expensive. The Duchess of Portsmouth had apartments in Whitehall more luxuriously furnished than the Queen's. Between 1670 and 1677 Portsmouth received £36,073 in royal gifts, while Nell Gwyn, 'the Protestant whore', received £7,938 only. French historians have studied the influence of royal mistresses extensively, while their more puritanical English counterparts have tended to underrate them, but things are changing. Courtiers looked to the mistresses rather than to the Queen as a way of influencing Charles.[41] As Sonya Wynne writes, courtiers counted the number of times the King visited them as a barometer of favour. Since cards were played there, it provided opportunities for privileged conversations with the King at the Duchess of Portsmouth's, especially for the French ambassador Barrillon. Nancy Klein Maguire attributes real political and diplomatic power to Portsmouth, who was attacked by Whigs in Parliament as 'the lewd Babilonish Dalilah'.[42] Mistresses were even capable of influencing parliamentary elections and grants of land in Ireland. Wynne argues, however, that their power should not be overrated as the King was very secretive and did not consult ladies in great affairs of state. Whig historians have tried to blame Charles's financial problems on extravagance and moral laxity, but these did not make a great financial impact.

Charles's Court was the last truly splendid and entertaining court in English history with a ball or a play every other day.[43] Charles was the patron of Samuel Cooper, Peter Lely, John Riley, John Michael Wright, Antonio Verrio, Grindling Gibbons, Dryden and Purcell. The cult of Charles II was a secular cult, popular and spontaneous. He was the most painted king in modern British history, with over 900 copies of his portrait, many commissioned for the great houses as a way of showing allegiance. Towns and ports erected many statues of him, Grindling Gibbons's Roman statues for the Royal Exchange and the Royal Hospital Chelsea being notable examples.[44] Charles was responsible for introducing French taste in music and gardens designed by or in the style of Le Nôtre. He lacked Louis XIV's financial resources but he was able to restore the artistic and cultural patronage of the Court after the hiatus of the Interregnum and made it a potential source of profit, power and prestige for all who frequented it.

Access to the King was vital for all sections of society. As Brian Weiser argues, Charles II's accessibility extended to those presenting petitions, then a principal means of obtaining redress for grievances or initiating legislation in Parliament. Gerald Aylmer examines patronage in the widest sense, looking at patron and 'intermediary', those who procured jobs or rewards of all kinds. Grooms and other members of the Bedchamber were superbly placed to act as brokers, but they did not exercise decisive influence in making appointments. Charles II was criticised for being too easy-going and good-natured, but these characteristics account for his relative success as King and ruler. His freedom of manoeuvre was limited. Unable to restore forfeited estates to Royalists, he tried to compensate them with Household offices. One example was Sir Theophilus Oglethorpe, whose family had incurred the greatest losses during the Civil Wars, and his wife, Lady Oglethorpe, a clever and beautiful woman, who lived a virtuous life at Charles's Court.[45] Appointments in Ireland, in the diplomatic service, the upper ranks of the Church and the law as well as the army and navy remained wide open to direct royal intervention and the influence of intermediaries was eagerly sought. There was continuity too. Two of the staunchest and most prestigious of the Royalists remained in office throughout the reign: Ormonde, Charles II's companion in exile, as Lord Steward and John Granville, Earl of Bath as Groom of the Stole and as Lord Warden of the Stannaries, where he looked after the revenue from the Duchy of Cornwall. The lst Duke of Ormonde was three times viceroy of Ireland between 1643 and 1685 and, as T.C. Barnard explains, he entrusted the government of Ireland to leading Irish noblemen. Dublin Castle was invested with new grandeur and refurbished with a good deal of Ormonde's own property. Two chairs of state were installed in the Presence Chamber and the Castle became the focus of Court society, as well as Kilkenny Castle and Ormonde's other properties, which were used for official duties. The success of the viceroys, however, was measured by their ability to convert the Irish deficit into a surplus and, as Simon Thurley writes, money from the Irish customs was used to revamp Windsor Castle in the 1670s. It was not until the 1670s and 1680s, after years of living beyond his means, that Charles introduced retrenchment, and French and Italian music became casualties at this time.[46] Yet in 1683, as Simon Thurley shows, Charles began to build Winchester, his very own palace and country seat, far from factious London and Whig-dominated Newmarket.

As Duke of York, James, Charles's brother and heir, had his own Court in London. In 1679, however, during the Exclusion crisis, Charles removed him by sending him to Scotland. At Holyrood Palace James created the first Scottish Court since 1603. As Hugh Ouston explains, he was sent to ensure Scottish loyalty at a time of crisis. He was surprisingly successful and the Church of England saw his achievement as a proof that it was safe in his hands. The Scots were delighted to have a member of the royal family among them and James ensured that the political classes became courtiers. About 114 members of his Court followed him to Scotland. Princess Anne, James's second daughter, visited Edinburgh and all enjoyed the court theatre which was new to Scotland's capital. James secured Scotland for his brother and did much to ensure his own peaceful succession to the throne.

In the reign of James II patronage of the arts continued, as he commissioned works from Kneller, Verrio, Gibbons and Gennari (whom he later employed at St-Germain-en-Laye). In the early part of the reign there were frequent balls and James attended more plays proportionately than any other living monarch. It was also a more formal court than his brother's, as he restored much of his father's emphasis on ceremony and etiquette. It was also a more moral court from which duellists, drunkards and men who kept mistresses were banned. James set an example in 1686 when he sent away his own mistress, Catherine Sedley, whom he made Countess of Dorchester. He had a well-deserved reputation for being frugal and able in matters of financial management, as he showed when he cut his Household by a third, paid his servants regularly and left virtually no debts, unlike Charles II or William III. What isolated him and his Queen, Mary of Modena, was their Roman Catholic religion. He had a Catholic chapel designed by Wren, where mass was celebrated in public. Some courtiers attended, but many went instead to Princess Anne's Anglican chapel.[47] James's policy of religious toleration to all Christians and Jews and the giving of office to Dissenters and Roman Catholics alienated the Anglican majority in England and the Episcopalians in Scotland, his natural supporters. It gave William of Orange the chance to invade England. In exile in the Palace of Saint-Germain-en-Laye after 1689, James reduced his Household still further, but there was continuity as a substantial number of his and an even greater number of the Queen's Household accompanied them in exile. This small Court, which represented legitimacy and Royalism, was a splendid example of a Baroque court with extensive patronage of the arts. The changes in etiquette for access to James, dictated by the different topography of St Germain, as Corp shows, sheds new light on conduct at Whitehall before 1689.

In the reign of William III court life declined even more rapidly. William restored the Household to its pre-1685 size, but paid his servants infrequently and its administration was often in chaos. Members of the old Royalist families who had stood by the Stuarts in darkest times were purged and replaced by Whig supporters, some of them republicans. William did not like his English subjects and even less his Scottish ones and he retreated to Hampton Court or his newly purchased Kensington Palace. He disliked balls and would not have understood English plays. For a good part of the year he was absent on the Continent, leading the British and Dutch armies in the Nine Years' War. In contrast his Queen, Mary II, James's eldest daughter, was affable and gained popularity before her death in 1694.[48] The burning down of the Palace of Whitehall in 1698, marked the end of a way of life, of a type of court culture and the end of an era.

Notes

1. Pauline Croft, 'Parliament, Purveyance and the City of London, 1589–1608', *Parliamentary History*, IV (1985), 12–15.

2. R. Malcom Smuts, 'Art and Material Culture of Majesty', in Smuts, *Stuart Court*, pp. 86–112.

3. Conrad Russell, 'Parliamentary History in Perspective 1604–1629', History, LXI (1976), 6; and Russell, *Parliament*, p. 423.

4. See John Morrill, *The Revolt of the Provinces: Conservatives and Radicals in the English Civil War 1630–1650* (London, 1976). There is a good synthesis of the controversies surrounding Charles I's reign and the origins of the Civil War in Michael B. Young, *Charles I* (Basingstoke, 1997).

5. Roy Strong, *The Cult of Elizabeth: Portraiture and Pageantry* (London, 1977); Orgel, *Illusion of Power*.

6. Smuts, *Stuart Court*, p. 70.

7. See David Lindley (ed.), *Court Masques: Jacobean and Caroline Entertainments 1605–1640* (Oxford, 1995).

8. See Peck, *Mental World*.

9. Smuts, 'Art and Material Culture', in Smuts, *Stuart Court*, p. 89.

10. Parry, *The Golden Age*. See also Kenneth Fincham (ed.), *The Early Stuart Church* (Stamford, 1993).

11. Parry, *Golden Age*, pp. 238–9.

12. Lockyer, *Buckingham*.

13. Strong, *Henry, Prince Henry of Wales*.

14. Introduction, Smuts, *Stuart Court*. See David Howarth, *Images of Rule: Art and Politics in the English Renaissance 1485–1649* (London, 1997).

15. Sharpe, *Personal Rule.*

16. See R. Malcom Smuts, *Court Culture and the Origins of a Royalist Tradition in Early Stuart England* (Philadelphia, 1987).

17. Roy Strong, *Van Dyck, Charles I on Horseback* (New York, 1972), pp. 49, 70.

18. Martin Butler, 'The Early Stuart Masque', in Smuts, *Stuart Court,* pp. 64–85; D.J. Gordon, '*Hymenaei*: Ben Jonson's Masque of Union' in Stephen Orgel (ed.), *The Renaissance Imagination* (Berkeley, 1975), pp. 157–84.

19. Sharpe, *Personal Rule.*

20. Smuts, *Court Culture,* and Orgel, *Illusion of Power.*

21. See Kenneth Fincham and Peter Lake, 'The Ecclesiastical Policies of James I and Charles I', in Fincham (ed.), *Early Stuart Church*; Julian Davies, *The Caroline Captivity of the Church: Charles I and the Remoulding of Anglicanism 1625–41* (Oxford, 1992); Nicholas Tyacke, *Anti-Calvinists: the Rise of English Arminianism* c. *1590–1640* (Oxford, 1987); and Caroline Hibbard, *Charles I and the Popish Plot* (Chapel Hill, 1979).

22. See Conrad Russell, *The Causes of the English Civil War* (Oxford, 1990) and *The Fall of the British Monarchies 1637–42* (Oxford, 1991).

23. Caroline Hibbard, 'The Theatre of Dynasty', in Smuts, *Stuart Court,* pp. 156–76.

24. Parry, *Golden Age,* pp. 164, 193–4.

25. See Martin Butler, *Theatre and Crisis 1632–42* (Cambridge, 1984), and Kevin Sharpe, *Criticism and Compliment.*

26. Parry, *Golden Age,* pp. 203–4.

27. Ibid., pp. 215, 217.

28. Smuts, *Court Culture,* pp. 122–5.

29. Orgel, *Illusion of Power,* pp. 49–52, 87–9.

30. 'What was the English Revolution?', *History Today,* XXIV (March 1984), 12. See also Morrill, *The Nature of the English Revolution* (London, 1993).

31. Smuts, 'Art and Material Culture', in Smuts, *Stuart Court,* p. 89, and Smuts, *Court Culture,* p. 188.

32. Roy Strong, *Van Dyck,* ch. 4, and John Adamson, 'Chivalry and Political Culture in Caroline England', in Kevin Sharpe and Peter Lake (eds), *Culture and Politics in Early Stuart England* (Basingstoke, 1993), pp. 162–97.

33. Kevin Sharpe, 'The Image of Virtue: the Court and Household of Charles I 1625–42', in Starkey, *English Court,* pp. 213, 230.

34. Smuts, *Court Culture,* p. 126.

35. Ibid., p. 289.

36. Roy Strong, *Van Dyck,* p. 30.

37. Ibid., p. 34.

38. John Miller, *Charles II* (London, 1991), p. 31.

39. Ibid., pp. 95, 97.

40. Chandaman, however, in *Public Revenue,* argues that by the 1670s Charles's revenue should have been adequate.

41. Ronald Hutton, *Charles II* (Oxford, 1992), pp. 186–7, 335.

42. Nancy Klein Maguire, 'The Duchess of Portsmouth, English Royal Consort and French Politician, 1670–85', in Smuts, *Stuart Court*, pp. 247–73.

43. Bucholz, *Augustan Court*, p. 15.

44. Katharine Gibson, *The Cult of Charles II*, Royal Stuart Paper XLVII (1995).

45. Eveline Cruickshanks, *The Oglethorpes, a Jacobite Family*, Royal Stuart Paper XLV (1994). *HC 1660–1690*, Vol. 3, pp. 170–1.

46. Bucholz, *Augustan Court*, p. 21.

47. Ibid., pp. 23–5.

48. Ibid., pp. 26–33.

1

FROM EDINBURGH TO LONDON: SCOTTISH COURT WRITING AND 1603

Murray Pittock

James VI and I, as Jenny Wormald perceptively remarks, is a king on whom history conferred two characters, not merely two titles: the wily, gifted, loved and successful Scot of Edinburgh gives place to a dissipated, filthy and self-indulgent alien monarch, overflowing with favouritism and excrement in England's capital. That this is so, Dr Wormald argues, owes as much if not more to differing court cultural expectations, as to the circumstantial spite of Sir Anthony Weldon. James was a king with two courts as much as two kingdoms. That this self-evident fact is worth attending to, is due to the eliding of Scottish into 'British' culture practised by our inherited historiography, and unwittingly underlined by those patriot critics who, in seeing the 'GB' of 1603 as initialising Great Betrayal, implicitly yield to assumptions of the poverty and vulnerability of the northern kingdom. In this chapter I seek rather to emphasise not only the strength and variety of Scottish court culture before 1603, but also its survival after that date, and the importance of that survival for Scottish literature itself.[1]

Edinburgh's court in the sixteenth century was not lacking in the features of Renaissance cosmopolitanism. Sir David Lindsay's characterisation of James IV as 'myrrour of humylitie/Lode sterne and lampe of libiralytie . . . of his court, throuch Europe sprang the fame' was a piece of nostalgia in step with the 'panegyrics in both Scots and Latin' that 'establish the monarch as a personification of virtue' at the centre of the Court, the persistence of which after regal union is seen in the greetings poured out in *The Muses' Welcome* of James to Scotland in 1617 (though by this time, Scots has been replaced by English: the panegyrists seem conscious of the King's 'British' status). Yet this high cultural idealisation of the monarch had its demotic counterpart in the accessibility and familiarity of the King, and the closeness between King and people long remarked on in Scotland, of which James V's incognito travellings and reputed contribution to folksong was only the most recent example. This paradoxical doubleness of iconography and intimacy could not be reproduced in an England that viewed James VI's familiarities as coarse derogations from the image of Tudor sovereignty. The King's description of himself as 'your Dad, James R' on letters to favoured subjects is first found in correspondence with the Earl of Huntly in the 1590s: in England, it could raise revulsion.

Likewise the adoption of friendly personae such as the 'Sandy Mow', by which James denominated himself Alexander Montgomerie's poetic apprentice in the 1580s, would have been gross abdications of dignity in London. After 1603, James's easy relations with his Scottish court fools (he was one of the last to keep such) in his new capital was only one of many indications of the preservation of Edinburgh court *mores* in his new kingdom.[2]

This dimension of familiarity in Scottish court culture is of particular significance, and will be returned to. But on a European scale, Scotland's high culture was also a powerful force, operating systems of patronage through the 'sufficient surplus of wealth' held by Crown, aristocracy, Church and towns, in much the style (if on a limited scale) of those in place in Italy. The poetry of William Dunbar, the establishment of the Chapel Royal in 1501, the music of Robert Carver written for it, and the choral skill required for pieces such as his 'O Bone Jesu' were, like James V's role as king of love and the drama of Sir David Lindsay, earnests of an achievement within a Scottish nation whose proud history was marked abroad in the writing of its humanist scholars such as George Buchanan, whose 'Epithalamium on the Marriage of Mary and the Dauphin' boasted that '*Sine milite Scoto/Nulla unquam Francis fulsit victoria castris*' (without the Scottish soldier, no victory ever shone in French camps). At the same time, this cosmopolitanism (which seems to have helped the rapid dissemination of Reformed ideas) existed in the context of an early move towards native speech, both for patriotic reasons (as in Bishop Gavin Douglas's translation of the *Aeneid* into Scots) and administrative use: 'much earlier than in England, vernacular became the language of government in Scotland'. This vernacular, perhaps never universally identified as a tongue separate from English despite Douglas's aim to 'kepand na sudroun bot our awin langage', became much more closely identified with its sister speech after the Reformation.[3]

Whatever damage the Reformation did (and Mary tried to limit it, particularly in the Chapel Royal), in 1567 James inherited many of the features of earlier court culture. Music had been badly injured through its association with the ecclesiastical establishment (for example, 'on 19th May 1563, John Hamilton, subchantor of Glasgow, was tried for assisting at Mass along with forty-seven others'), but even here the King inherited significant resources in his own Household, and sought to bolster the institutional status of music as soon as he came to maturity, paying particular attention to the song schools. Less tangibly, he may have inherited from his mother an interest in music (though not perhaps her skills in singing or composition, if she is responsible for the 'Galliards which bear her name') and significant poetic gifts. Mary was 'brought up in the company of . . . Ronsard, to whom she dedicated one poem of her own', and her verse can show a definitive clarity in its feeling passion, as in this plea from captivity:

> O Domine Deus! Speravi in Te;
> O care mi Jesu! nunc libera me,
> In dura catena, in misera poena, desidero te; . . .
> Adoro, imploro, ut libera me!

Beside her political and personal failings, Mary was the unfortunate victim of a Reformation typology which discovered in Elizabeth a new type of the Virgin, 'in earth the first, in heaven the Second Maid', who in the rhetoric of 'apocalyptic monarchism' was 'the Woman Clothed with the Sun' from Revelation, a near 'goddess' in George Buchanan's words. Mary was, despite her name (or because of it, given Elizabeth's predecessor) all too readily seen as an antitype: the Whore of Babylon, Spenser's Duessa – a literary characterisation which James VI understood and disliked.[4]

Son of Duessa as he was, and baptised a Catholic, James was not demonised, and his claim to the English throne was from the beginning more credible than his mother's. George Buchanan's *genethliacon* on James's birth prophesied that he would be the 'child, for whom the oracles of former prophets promise a Golden Age. . . . Now the Saxon race will not oppress the Scots nor the Scot in enmity oppress the Saxon.' Buchanan's praise of his royal master in 1566 is not unlike the English welcome that greeted him as Arthur restored thirty-seven years later, though the English guests present at Buchanan's rich court masque in celebration of James's birth took offence 'when the satyrs wagged their tails at the audience, "fancying that it was done in their derision"'. They perhaps need not have worried, as when the poet laureate of Mary's reign and James's regency wanted to insult people he could be less than subtle, as these lines on Pope Julius II testify, barbed as they are with evidence of Buchanan's unique gifts as a theological controversialist:

> Your father was from Genoa, your mother from Greece, and the waves of the sea gave you birth. How can you be good? Italians are false, Greeks liars, and no-one can trust the sea. You alone have each of these things in you.

As official laureate, 'the deaths of friends, colleagues and court figures kept Buchanan busy with the composition of epitaphs', while 'annual celebrations at court seem to have demanded a poetic response. . . . From 1566 . . . editions of Buchanan were coming off the press almost annually, and his reputation as the grand old man of Latin literature was firmly established.'[5]

After 1570, Buchanan was also tutor to the young King. Eventually the tutelage he underwent would spur James to remark that 'they gar me speik Latin or I could speik Scottis', but there is no doubt that it was effective, and the King's learning was remarked on by visitors to the Court, increasingly prosperous with the decline of Marian strife lamented by Sir Richard Maitland in his 'Satire on the Age' ('Quhair is the blythnes that hes bein/Bayth in burgh and landwart sein'). Under the Regent Morton, Scotland 'recovered with great rapidity from the disastrous consequences of prolonged civil strife; and in 1574 her sudden increase in wealth and comfort struck the English ambassador with astonishment'. Within a few years, 'the court of James VI succeeded in re-establishing Scotland as a cultural centre of importance'. Undertaking this task, James's chief efforts were directed towards music and poetry: arts often conjoined, as for example in Andro Blackhall's settings of Alexander Montgomerie's poetry.[6]

James was at the heart of a move to restore music as fully as practicable to the significant status it had held prior to 1560. There were elements of tokenism, perhaps, but what emerges is nonetheless a programme. In 1579 'a most important statute was passed for encouragement of Sang Schools', earnest of developing reform. By 1586, the process outlined showed a degree of commitment to the musical *status quo ante*:

> He [the king] is weill myndit as he hes already begun, that the said art [of music] salbe restorit partlie agane within this realme be providing sic personis as hes some entres in the art, and will gif their mynd and labouris thairto to the prebendareis and chappellenries of the Collegis and Kirkis that were foundit and erectit of auld to be served be musicians.

Musicians such as James Lauder and Andro Blackhall served to provide artistic (and in some cases clerical) continuity with the Marian Court. Given James's later leanings towards Anglican ceremonial, the appointment of the Englishman Thomas Hudson as Master of the Chapel Royal may not have been without significance. Hudson, 'a person of some account', has been adjudged to have 'over a period of some thirty years had the ear of the king'. Court music in Scotland was in any case witnessing something of a drift towards English models.[7]

Some of James's musical restoratives were perhaps eased by the fact that crypto-Catholicism was present among apparently conforming kirkmen in the King's circle, and indeed it was by no means always hidden, the English Ambassador noting after the Ruthven Raid that 'the King was now surrounded by nobles most of whom were Catholic'. James's willingness to restore the Marian Archbishop of Glasgow to his see, and the King's frequent cat and mouse games with the Catholic interest, were parts of the same pattern. The ornate and extravagant ceremonies in the Chapel Royal and Stirling Castle attendant on the baptism of Prince Henry in 1594 were tokens of a defended and preserved Renaissance high culture in Scotland. Likewise, the more demotic aspects of Jacobean monarchy found a place for the King's musical interest: James's pipers, 'skirling in front of him' en route to 'Dalkeith Church' and the 'bawdy songs and

. . . bawdy tales' of 'his own special court-jester' were in defiance of Kirk strictures, as indeed was the 'latitude' surrounding court minstrelsy, especially in the inclusion of such minstrels in the offices of the Chapel Royal itself.[8]

As alluded to earlier, court music was conjoined with poetry, a feature of the time common to high and folk culture alike: this was long before Allan Ramsay became 'the first man in Scotland to indulge in the pernicious malpractice of printing the texts of ballads without their tunes'. There was a cultural partnership in these arts as there was between high and folk aspects of Scottish court culture itself: ballads were known at Court, and James IV and V were familiar with folk culture, the latter indeed being supposed the author of 'The Gaberlunzie Man' in reference to his tour of his subjects in beggar's disguise. For James VI, however, the marriage of register and form seems to have been better celebrated at the higher level. The famous Castalian band of the 1580s placed a high cultural emphasis on the Court's activities. Apollo was the leader of the original Castalian band: so James was of his poetic group, which included Alexander Montgomerie, Robert and Thomas Hudson, William Fowler, John Stewart of Baldynneis, William Alexander, the future Earl of Stirling, and Robert Ayton. The King's Apollonian role invited an intensification of the iconography of Stuart monarchy, and the band did not disappoint him of the sun-king image his leadership invited. As Montgomerie put it: 'can golden Titan shyning bright at morne,/For light of torches, cast a gritter shaw?' James would have liked to think not, so despite his poetic deference to such as Montgomerie ('Beloved Sanders maistre of our art'), redolent of the intimate and democratic aspects of the Court, the King claimed the obedience of his poets not to rank alone, but by becoming their determining theorist in his distinctly Scottish literary theoretical tract *Reulis and Cautelis*, which he attached to the modestly titled *Essayes of a Prentise in the Divine Art of Poesie* (1584).[9]

The Castalian band's title may also hint at a more immediate political realm that that of Parnassus. The Scots 'band', descriptive 'of a sworn brotherhood in league for violent action', was what James and his mother had both faced, the King most recently in the Ruthven Raid of 1582–3. In this sense, the Castalian 'band', being 'a brotherhood of peaceful, constructive *making*', may be a name indicative of a courtly rebuttal to the pressure Protestant associations had been bringing to bear on the throne. Within the band, figures such as Montgomerie were strongly linked to Marian agitation. His *Cherrie and the Slae*, to read which has been said to be 'to experience something of the enduring culture of Europe', may well be an allegorical celebration of Catholicism, the fruit provided by God 'Quha did myne helth to me restoir,/Being sae lang tyme pynd', and who might do the same for Scotland. Though later embarrassed by Montgomerie's pro-Catholic activities, James's own *Lepanto* disturbed Scottish opinion by praising the Catholic Don John of Austria, though the poem dutifully concludes with an attack on Rome.[10]

Castalian poetry's European dimension must have made such an appreciation of the community of Western Christendom more than likely. Montgomerie and Thomas Hudson both had a background in France, and through these and 'the perfect French scholarship of the King, the Castalians had access and indeed recourse to . . . the new poetry of France' (more generally, James planned to render 'great European masterpieces into Scots', a task on which a start at least was made). The influence of the Pleiade was marked in James's own literary theory, and the strong French backdrop to Castalian practice is itself a natural cultural link given the long-standing alliance of the two countries gloried in by Buchanan in the poem quoted above. Ronsard himself had, as a boy, been 'a page in the train of Madeleine of France when she married King James V in Paris on New Year's Day 1537', and shortly afterwards travelled to Scotland. The reliance on French sources was (perhaps more self-consciously than would have been the case in pre-Reformation Scotland) 'part of the Castalian desire to emphasise the difference between their practice and that of England'. In the context of the band's 'major poetic aim, the task of making Scottish writing once more revered at home and abroad', James's own *Reulis and Cautelis* was a critical statement emphasising Scotland's readiness to make its unique contribution to the Renaissance'. The King's theory combined cosmopolitan influences with a nationalist poetic manifesto (dedicated 'to the docile bairns of knawledge') studded with peculiarly Scottish poetic terminology (most of which has not stuck, though James may have been the first in Britain to use the term 'quadrain' (quatrain)). Assessing the text, Gabriel Harvey wrote that it contained

> The excellentest rules & finest Art. that a King could learne, or teache, in his Kingdom. The more remarkable, how worthie the pen, & industrie of a King. How mutch better, then owr Gascoigne's notes of instruction for Inglish Verse & Ryme.

This high opinion can still stand to some extent: James was attempting in *Reulis and Cautelis* to create a native theoretical tradition, differentiating its 'sundrie reulis' from those of English poetry through adoption of the definitions of Continental writers. His limitations include a powerful addiction to prescriptive theory, common enough at the time, but a serious constraining factor in the context of a poetic circle so intimately centred on its kingly critic. The result was an 'over concern with manneristic perfection', which Professor Jack has argued is found elsewhere in Europe in 'societies of high cultural attainment', notably Italy, and Italy is an apt comparator for Scottish systems of patronage at this time.[11]

James VI presided over and to an extent directed an integrated court culture. The contextualisation of music, poetry and song was part of the maintenance, restoration and defence of a royal zone of artistic patronage, where 'panegyrical sonnets' would laud in the King 'the ideas of his divinity (Apollo), lyrical genius

(David) and benevolent patronage (Maecenas)'. Whether overtly or implicitly, James was continuing to move the iconography of Stuart monarchy towards the idealisation surrounding Elizabeth south of the border. Dressed in Castalian duds, Apollonian James was Astraea's rival. After 1603, the increasing emphasis on Minerva rather than Astraea as a feminine model for royal identity built on the Castalian praise of the King as gifted 'with Minerva's spreit', in biblical terms a Solomon. The praise of James's poetic band had, like that of Buchanan at the King's birth, contained a foreshadowing undertone of destiny that, in Montgomerie's words, 'His brand all Brytan to obey sall bring'. Part of the high praise given James was due to an in the end misplaced Scottish optimism that he would, in becoming Britain's first ruler, bring the auld enemy the gifts of the north, and remain a specifically Scottish ruler in the English capital. It was of course truer to say, as Henry VII had done, that the greater would always prevail over the lesser.[12]

Yet for all this cultus, 'the peculiarly personal quality of Scottish kingship', could still be noted by an English visitor such as Sir Henry Wotton in 1601/2. Less than two years later, as James journeyed south, a discommoded Scot, on noting how 'obsequious and submissive' James's new subjects were, girned that 'this people [the English] will spoil a gud king'. This dimension of Scottish court culture had been perhaps best expressed in literary form in the 'flyting': a poetic competition in personal invective which has been linked with Provençal 'débat' and other Continental sources as well as the Gaelic tradition. Its depth of intimate revelation and public insult was probably 'read aloud in full court', as when Montgomerie displaced Sir Patrick Hume of Polwarth as Court poet in the 1580s. The degree of familiarity required by the form was not commensurate with the dignity of the English Court, and it is no surprise that flyting does not appear to have accompanied James across the border. Intensely oral and conscious of its audience, flyting's appropriation of the vast power of the Scots language for insult led to a closeness to folk vernacular: it is perhaps no coincidence that the new laureate Montgomerie took up his place in the 'chimney neuk', traditional seat of the folk cultural tale-teller. Flyting was not centrally a court form: hence we read of the 'flyting on the Hie Gait' at Peebles in 1570, or 'public flyting . . . on the calsay' at Elgin in 1596. As a court entertainment it bore marks both of vernacular rootedness and of the energy that springs from it, as in this excerpt from the flyting that won Montgomerie the laureateship:

> Vyle venemous viper, wanthriftiest of things,
> Halfe ane Elfe, halfe ane Aipe, of nature deny it,
> Thou flait with a countrey, the quhilk was the Kings;
> But that bargan, unbeast, deare sall thou buy it.
> 'The cuiff is weill waved, that twa hame brings.'

This proverbe, faile pelt, to thee is apply it:
First spider of spyte, thou spewes out springs;
Yet, wanshapen woubet, of the weirds invyit . . .
. . . war facit nor ane cat.

When James moved to London, much of Scottish court culture went with him (save for a staff at the Chapel Royal). The absence of such distinctly Scottish forms as the flyting at the English Court after 1603 is surely one aspect of the idea that James betrayed his 'awin tung' after the move to London, and that he and his circle ceased to write in Scots, in so doing vitiating their patriotism. Certainly, the language question is one of the central themes in patriotic criticism: the other being the neglect of Scotland brought on by the opening up of new opportunities in the south. Ambitious Scots now had the possibility of a career in England as apparently never before: there were only fifty-eight Scots in London in 1567, the year James came to the throne in Edinburgh. Indeed, the themes of ambition and linguistic betrayal can be united in the need the Scottish court circle and its hangers-on felt to conform to the London standard, the universal speech of Puttenham's gentlemen. The tongue as well as the manners of James's new kingdom conspired to 'spoil a gud king' on this reading.[13]

The patriotic emplacement of 1603 as a linguistic nemesis for Scottish court writing has been challenged on a number of counts. Firstly, it has been argued that the paradigm which advances the Scots tongue as the measure of Scottish national literary identity in the sixteenth and seventeenth centuries is flawed, especially at a time when so many of the educated wrote Latin. Secondly, it can be argued that whatever the nationalist dimension of *Reulis and Cautelis*, James and his Castalians cared more for prosodic than linguistic separatism: the King's preface virtually says as much, and his famous sonnet critical of Sir William Alexander for writing after the English fashion seems to bear this emphasis out. In any case, 'most of the Castalians were already writing thinner Scots than their predecessors', and thus the linguistic issue pre-dates 1603. The near-absence of good models for Scots prose (as opposed to verse) rendered the language vulnerable, and it was weakened still more in a Reformation which leant towards the use of English and English publishing. This in turn advances a third argument: that the damage had already been done. Catholic apologists attacked Knox in the sixteenth century for his preference for English. Ninian Winzet wrote 'Gif ye, throw curiositie of novations, hes foryet our auld plane Scottis, quhilk your mother lerit you, in tymes coming I sall wrytt to yow my mind in Latin, for I am nocht acquyntit with your Southron.' Similarly, in 1581 John Hamilton 'declared it treasonable to copy the Southern speech . . . "Giff King James the fyft var alyve, quha hering ane of his subiectis knap suddrone . . . declarit him ane traiteur; quhidder valt he declare you triple traitoris, quha not only knappis suddrone in your negative confession, bot also hes causit it be imprentit at

London in contempt of our native language"'. Likewise, in 1582 Queen Mary suggested to Mendoza that English Jesuits should not be sent to Scotland 'as they are foreigners . . . and do not understand the language'.[14]

These three points are not consistent. It is clear that Scots was *a* patriotic paradigm before 1603, but that by the latter sixteenth century this status was already subject to sectarian debate. With the Presbyterian Kirk already publishing in London, it is hard to see James's passage south through a thunderstorm which cleared when he crossed the border as a cultural watershed. Indeed, it may even be suggested that the sectarian divide in Scottish politics posed serious underlying problems for James's Renaissance, despite the King's attempts to paper over these difficulties both before and after 1603 (as with the ascendancy of the Catholic (but conforming kirkman) Seton and James's own policy on ecclesiastical government). The vision of the realm's community and clerical and royal legitimacy was fragmenting. In this context, James's own translation of his *Basilikon Doron* and the Anglicising revisions of poets such as Alexander and Ayton were straws in the wind rather than catalystic betrayals. Increasing cultural contact with and awareness of English writers such as Sir Philip Sidney and Henry Constable (who contributed 'a prefatory sonnet' to the King's *Poetical Exercises* of 1591) was in any case nothing new: and the accompanying linguistic drift was amply explained by the emerging theocracy in Scotland, itself developing in a culture where the vernacular had a long history of primacy. The linguistic gulf between English and Scots was far less than between either and Latin, even though defenders of Scots such as Winzet might exaggerate the political difference between them. Any hope of the King's 'kepand na sudroun' was vanishing long before he took a customarily deep draught of his *deoch an doruis* on leaving for England in the spring of 1603.[15]

Nonetheless, the Court's arrival in London completed the process. Printing was now the central means of distributing authoritative language, and here the change was rapid. English metropolitan printers, used to local forms and the question of standardisation ever since Caxton's encounter with 'eggs' and 'eyren', took the same attitude to Scots. After all, though Scots was a language by the standards that differentiate the Scandinavian tongues, such a definition was a matter of degree rather than kind in an early modern state with wide linguistic variations within itself: it was noted in the 1520s that Scots speakers could pass themselves off as northern English should the need arise (which would be hardly surprising in ears used to neither). By 1617, with 'interpreters declared no longer necessary at the port of London, because English and Scots were now "not so far different but ane understandeth ane uther"', a further change seems to be remarked on. Perhaps this was due to middle- and upper-class Scots adjusting their speech as their country grew closer to England: if so, it was paralleled in Scottish printing. Here, before 1560, English forms do not appear; between 1560 and 1580 18 per cent of books have them (again, the indication that the

Reformation is the real watershed in linguistic patriotism). By 1580–90 it is 57 per cent, 1590–1600 68 per cent, 1600–10 78 per cent and 1610–25 93 per cent. These figures suggest an anglicising process virtually complete by 1625: significantly, it is one which had gathered pace well before regal union. If Scots was being displaced from printing, Court and commerce, it was well on its way to the 'chimney neuk', not that of the laureateship Montgomerie had won, but the domestic surroundings of oral vernacular.[16]

I will argue, however, that three kinds of Scottish court writing survived the physical and linguistic court flit (to leave aside a fourth, the bardic culture of the Gaeltacht, which deserves its own treatment). Firstly, there was the writing of Scots who moved there with the Court, such as Sir Robert Ayton, William Fowler and Sir William Alexander, latterly Earl of Stirling. By the nature of their transition, they wrote in English (something of a poetic achievement, particularly perhaps in Ayton's case) or in hyper-corrected Scots (for example, Alexander's substitution of 'must a space' for the quite acceptable 'must a while', in an attempt to eradicate the Scots 'whiles'). By the nature of their transition also their distinctive voice did not outlast them (save attenuatedly, as in Ayton's influence on the Cavaliers).[17]

Secondly, there were those writers who stayed in Scotland or returned there, such as Drummond of Hawthornden and Alexander Craig (who returned to Scotland in 1608, holding London to be 'this Abydos where I duyne and die': in 1621 he became MP for his home county of Banff). Drummond, 2nd Laird of Hawthornden, son of James VI's Gentleman Usher and nephew to the Castalian William Fowler, had a background ideally suited to becoming a poet at the Edinburgh Court, had it still existed. As it was, he is a poet of that culture's relocation from Court to castle and college which is characteristic of writers of the second and third groups. Drummond's praise of retreat in his poetry ('What sweet delight a quiet life affords,/And what it is to be of bondage free'), as well as being a theme most suited to a Horace with an absent Maecenas, foreshadows the topoi of Scottish Jacobite poetry, as expressed, for example, in the work of Alexander Robertson of Struan. Another figure in this group, William Mure of Rowallan, continued in castle culture the links between music and poetry found in the Edinburgh Court (and which indeed continued in London in the interaction of Ayton with Dowland and Campion). Later, Rowallan turned Covenanting partisan and 'the titles of the delectable French songs in the family music-book' were blotted out. Mure did, however, revive 'the custom of flyting' in his anti-Catholic sonnets.[18]

Many of the figures of castle culture, such as Craig, Duncane Burnett, William Stirling of Ardoe and Alexander Forbes of Tolquhon, were the products of the north-east of Scotland: and this background is also that of many of the third group of surviving courtly writers, the Scoto-Latinists whose distinctive hold on the culture of Aberdeen and its hinterland ended only with the death of James

Melvin in 1853. There was a strong bias in such writers towards 'the Episcopal persuasion': indeed, by the seventeenth century, Scoto-Latinity and Episcopalianism were cultural yoke-fellows. This part of Scotland was also the Lowland area where Catholicism was sustained longest and revived most quickly, with the development of seminaries and mass confirmations by the early eighteenth century. At the heart of this distinct cultural zone, Aberdeen produced, in Sir William Geddes's words, 'a singularly cultured group of scholars, such as no other city in Scotland, or even in the British Isles, could match at the period when they appeared'.[19]

After 1603, foremost among this group of writers was Arthur Johnston, doctor to both James VI and Charles I, rector of the University of Aberdeen and sometime Professor of Logic and Metaphysic at Sedan, who in 1633 dedicated 'a specimen of a version of the Psalms' to Bishop (later Archbishop) Laud, and was subsequently taken under Laud's patronage. Far from being a follower of the London Court, however, Johnston's verse (while very pro-Stuart) has a strongly patriotic flavour: for example, his lament of 1626 'On the Rupture of the Peace Between France and Scotland' draws attention to 'the grant of citizenship in France to every born Scot', a right not withdrawn until the Entente Cordiale three centuries later. Similarly, Johnston's lines on Sir William Alexander, Earl of Stirling, show a native pride:

> As soon as he of Menstrie saw the Thames, he became a confidant of the throne, but I wish he had withdrawn thence to other, though far ruder, climes. Even in the bleak land of Scotia the Muses can live. So Naso lived in Scythia, and Orpheus in cold Thrace. The Court is a clime unfavourable . . . the abode of Circe, imposing spells of silence . . .

Here the Scottish holder of British court office obliquely laments in learned phrase the absence of Scottish court life. It comes as no surprise to find that in a poem such as '*De Pluvius Anglicanis et Scotia Serenitate*', Johnston celebrates the fact that it has been raining in England for two months. To quote Francis Kinaston's translation:

> Twice hath bright Cynthia wan'd; twice fill'd her round,
> Since England with continuall raine lies drowned;
> While Spring here withers, Scotland doth behold
> Dayes without cloudes, skies azure, sunnes of gold.[20]

Other writers in this tradition include Thomas Dempster, professor at Bologna, knighted by Pope Urban VIII and Historiographer-Royal to King James, William Blackhall, John Forbes, second son of the Episcopal Bishop of Aberdeen and James Kennedy, who in 'Aeneas Britannicus' welcomed Charles II home in terms similar to those adopted in *Astraea Redux* by the English court writer, John Dryden.[21]

It has been said of the Scoto-Latinists, in particular of Arthur Johnston and the author of the scatological *Polemo-Middina*, written in a mixture of Latin and Scots (who may be Drummond of Hawthornden) that they were: 'though scarcely members of the "folk" . . . often much closer to the realities of life and day-to-day human contacts than were their contemporaries who wrote in English'. This observation points in an interesting direction. For the court-connected writers who remained in or identified with Scotland, 1603 marked the beginning of a divorce between the intimate and iconic functions of Scottish kingship. In Nick Myer's terms, the degree to which advice was hidden in praise is accentuated. The poems marking James's return in 1617 in some part bear this out: the iconic remoteness and glory of his London monarchy is emphasised, and the approachable egalitarian qualities of the specifically Scottish monarchy can be seen in displaced form as the cries of a woman against her abandonment: 'a direct complaint on behalf of Scotland. She, for [Thomas] Craig as for Drummond, becomes a neglected lover.' The 'sun' image of Apollonian James no longer holds out the promise of a 'Golden Age' in which the new British monarchy 'would predominantly mirror Scottish values'. Horace cannot always praise the Augustus who brings 'back the light, good leader, to the land' with the same verve when the visit is temporary: instead, the image becomes that of a withdrawn love: '*Triste solum sine sole*'. Scotland is strongly feminised in keeping with Scoto-Irish monarchical myth: 'the widow of King Fergus who had outlived all her later husbands' was now abandoned by her latest mate. Drummond's 'Forth Feasting' strikes such a note, soon to become far more familiar in the abandoned lover songs of the Jacobite tradition in Scotland, or the Irish *aisling:*

> Ah! why should Isis only on thee shine?
> Is not thy Forth as well as Isis thine?
> Though Isis vaunt she hath more wealth in store,
> Let is suffice thy Forth doth love thee more . . .

Drummond's introduction of 'the vocabulary of a lady lamenting her fickle, departed love' then emerges into clearer view: 'When in her arms she doth thee fold . . . Loath not to think on thy much loving Forth.' The elements of Augustan celebration are disturbed and undercut by this theme: Scotia's intimacy with her icon has turned to the beginnings of reproach.[22]

What in Drummond's poetry is an uneasy subtext, elsewhere and later becomes conjoined in alliance with the folk/vernacular traditions of abandonment and betrayal (as in the ballad 'Lord Dunwaters', for example). The castle culture which retained minstrels, musicians and perhaps ballad-singers after the Court had departed Edinburgh was (as was the burgh culture of the north-east, rooted in the richest folk area in Scotland) a natural meeting-place for folk and high culture, as the Court had once been. Poets like Robert Sempill (and even Ayton) return in the seventeenth century to folk models: for example, the latter's '"Elegie on Habbie Simpson" . . . looks forward in tone and form to the eighteenth-century vernacular revival, thus providing a fitting bridge to . . . later movements.' An intensely iconised and celebratory court verse concentrated on the new London Stuarts shifted its tone from complimentary awe to pathetic gratitude when they ventured north of the border (a feature later seen in the intensely Jacobitised visit of George IV in 1822). At the same time, the familiar and intimate qualities of Scottish monarchy, lost in London, were displaced into a poetic expression of betrayal and abandonment, joined to a longing for restored intimacy. This could be an undertow in any celebration or be a statement standing freely, as it was in any case more likely to have to do after 1689. The rural lairds and their patronage circulated this poetry of a familiar king voiced in familiar terms, thus helping to feed the cross-class alliance which was a major dimension in Jacobitism. Charles Edward Stuart, feminised as a type of the nation itself in his portrayal in woman's dress on Stuart glassware, was the only one of his dynasty to renew the displaced intimacy of 1603: perhaps as a result he received the most intensely personal literary welcome from the poetic tradition, courtly and vernacular, left behind in Scotland (as in 'Hail Glorious Youth!' or the 'Bonnie Highland Laddie' cycle). He cultivated this, for such terms were already familiar from his father's day, as in this poem by Alexander Robertson, Major-General in 1745:

> THOU, JAMES of my Heart!
> Who art ne'er in the Wrong,
> Why dost thou not part?
> I have mourn'd for thee long.[23]

Scottish court writing did survive 1603, its distinct qualities helping to create that close interchange between high and folk traditions which became characteristic of Scottish literature itself. Well into the twentieth century, the folk tradition and Scotland's relationship with the Stuarts were themes which clung to Scottish writing as close as any lover, fearing to be abandoned, might.

Notes

1. Jenny Wormald, 'James VI and I: Two Kings or One?', *History*, LXVIII (1983), 187–209; Sir Anthony Weldon, *The Court and Character of King James* (London, John Wright, 1650).

2. Sir David Lindsay, 'The Testament and Complaynt of our Soverane Lordis Papyngo', in Joan Hughes and W.S. Ransom, *Poetry of the Stewart Court* (Canberra, London and Miami, ANU Press, 1982), p. 1; National Library of Scotland MS 14239 (*Muses Welcome*); R.D.S. Jack (ed.), *The History of Scottish Literature Volume 1: Origins to 1660* (Aberdeen, Aberdeen University Press, 1988), p. 2; John

Purser, *Scotland's Music* (Edinburgh and London, Mainstream, 1992), p. 122; Henry George Farmer, *A History of Music in Scotland* (London, Hinrichsen Edition Ltd, n.d.), p. 178; Jennifer Wormald, *Court, Kirk and Community: Scotland 1470–1625*, The New History of Scotland 4 (Edinburgh, Edinburgh University Press, 1991 (1981)), p. 151; Matthew P. McDiarmid, 'The Scots Makars and the Ballad Tradition', in J. Derrick McClure and Michael Spiller (eds), *Bright Lanternis: Essays on the Language and Literature of Medieval and Renaissance Scotland* (Aberdeen, Aberdeen University Press, 1989), pp. 14–23 (14).

3. Wormald, *Court*, pp. 56, 58, 59; Hughes and Ransom, *Poetry of the Stewart Court*, p. 5; M.A. Bald, 'Contemporary References to the Scottish Speech of the Sixteenth Century', *Scottish Historical Review*, 25 (1928), 163–79 (164); Helena Mennie Shire, *Song, Dance and Poetry of the Court of Scotland Under King James VI* (Cambridge, Cambridge University Press, 1969), p. 3; R.D.S. Jack, 'Of Lion and of Unicorn: Literary Traditions at War', in R.D.S. Jack and Kevin McGinley (eds), *Of Lion and of Unicorn: Essays on Anglo-Scottish Literary Relations in Honour of Professor John MacQueen* (Edinburgh, Quadriga, 1993), pp. 67–99 (89); for choral skill, see Arthur Oldham, 'Scottish Polyphonic Music', *Innes Review*, 13 (1962), 54–61 (58). Duncan Shaw, 'Adam Bothwell: Conserver of the Renaissance in Scotland', in Ian Cowan and Duncan Shaw (eds), *The Renaissance and Reformation in Scotland: Essays in Honour of Gordon Donaldson* (Edinburgh, Scottish Academic Press, 1983), pp. 141–69 (143).

4. John McQuaid, 'Music and the Administration after 1560', *Innes Review*, 3 (1952), 14–21 (15); Purser, *Scotland's Music*, pp. 103, 111; *Poems of Alexander Montgomerie and Other Pieces from Laing MS. No. 447*, supplementary volume, ed. George Stevenson (Edinburgh and London, William Blackwood and sons and sons, 1910), p. lxii; Frances Yates, *Astraea* (London, Routledge & Kegan Paul, 1985 (1975)), pp. 30–1, 41, 42, 60, 67, 78; David Norbrook and H.R. Woudhuysen (eds), *The Penguin Book of Renaissance Verse 1509–1659* (London, Allen Lane, Penguin Press, 1992), p. 20; Philip J. Ford (and W.S. Watt), *George Buchanan, Prince of Poets* (Aberdeen, Aberdeen University Press, 1982), p. 108.

5. Ford, *George Buchanan*, pp. 105, 106, 107, 108, 111, 163; Purser, *Scotland's Music*, p. 108; R.D.S. Jack (ed.), *A Choice of Scottish Verse 1560–1660* (London, Sydney, Auckland, Toronto, Hodder & Stoughton, 1978), p. 12.

6. R.D.S. Jack, 'Poetry under King James VI', in Jack (ed.), *History of Scottish Literature Volume 1*, pp. 125–39 (125); Jack, *A Choice of Scottish Verse*, p. 36; T.F. Henderson, *James I and VI* (Paris, Edinburgh, New York and London, Goupil & Co., 1904), p. 13; Purser, *Scotland's Music*, pp. 113–15.

7. McQuaid, 'Music and the Administration after 1560', 14–21 (16); Farmer, *A History of Music in Scotland*, pp. 122, 139, 227; Wormald, *Court*, p. 187; Shire, *Song, Dance and Poetry*, pp. 57 ff., 72, 73.

8. The Revd David McRoberts, 'Provost Skene's House in Aberdeen and its Catholic Chapel', *Innes Review*, 5 (1954), 119–24; cf. William Forbes-Leith SJ, *Narratives of the Scottish Catholics under Mary Stuart and James VI* (Edinburgh, William Paterson, 1885), p. 190 ff.; Shire, *Song, Dance and Poetry*, pp. 93, 111, 138; R.D.S. Jack, *Montgomerie* (Edinburgh, Scottish Academic Press, 1985), p. 11; Farmer, *A History of Music in Scotland*, pp. 128, 133–4.

9. Francis Collinson, *The Traditional and National Music of Scotland* (London, Routledge & Kegan Paul, 1966), p. 134; Wormald, *Court*, p. 186; McDiarmid, 'The Scots Makars', p. 14; Jack, *Montgomerie*, pp. 1, 3, 7; 'Poetry under King James VI', 125; David Irving (ed.), *The Poems of Alexander Montgomerie* (Edinburgh, James Ballantyne & Co., 1821), p. 69; James Craigie (ed.), *The Poems of James VI of Scotland* (2 vols, Edinburgh and London, William Blackwood and sons, 1955), pp. 3, 65 ff. ('Ane Short

Treatise, Conteining Some Reulis and Cautelis to be observit and eschewit in Scottis *Poesie*'); Shire, *Song, Dance and Poetry*, p. 96.

10. Shire, *Song, Dance and Poetry*, p. 98; Ian Ross, quoted by Jack, *Montgomerie*, p. 107; Jack, 'Poetry under King James VI', 133; *Montgomerie*, p. 60; Craigie, *The Poems of James VI of Scotland*, p. 197 ff.

11. R.D.S. Jack, 'The Scottish Sonnet and Renaissance Italy', unpublished Ph.D. thesis (2 vols, University of Edinburgh, 1967), Vol. I, pp. 28–9; Jack, *A Choice of Scottish Verse*, pp. 13, 21; Shire, *Song, Dance and Poetry*, pp. 55, 96, 160; Craigie, *The Poems of James VI of Scotland*, pp. xxxiii, 66; A. Walter Bernhart, 'Castalian Poetics and the "Verie Twichestane Musique"', in Dietrich Strauss and Horst Drescher (eds), *Scottish Language and Literature, Medieval and Renaissance*, Scottish Studies Vol. 4 (Frankfurt, Verlag Peter Lang, 1986), pp. 451–8 (451).

12. Jack, 'Of Lion and of Unicorn', p. 93; Shire, *Song, Dance and Poetry*, p. 225; *Montgomerie*, p. 67; Madge Dresser, 'Britannia', in Raphael Samuel (ed.), *Patriotism: The Making and Unmaking of British National Indentity* (3 vols, London and New York, Routledge, 1989), Vol. III, pp. 26–49 (30 ff.).

13. Wormald, 'James VI and I', 189–90; Priscilla Bawcutt, 'The Art of Flyting', *Scottish Literary Journal*, 10:2 (1983), 5–24 (7, 11, 14); *Montgomerie*, pp. 76, 113; Jack, *Montgomerie*, pp. 26–7; Farmer, *A History of Music in Scotland*, p. 178; cf. Jack, 'Of Lion and Unicorn', *passim*; cf. Charles Roger (ed.), *The Poems of Sir Robert Aytoun* (Edinburgh, Adam & Charles Black, 1844), p. xxxix.

14. Jack, *Montgomerie*, p. 7; Jack, 'Of Lion and of Unicorn', pp. 74 ff.; Jack, 'Poetry under King James VI', p. 137; M.A. Bald, 'Contemporary References', 164–6.

15. Wormald, *Court*, p. 192; *Poems of Alexander Montgomerie* (1910), pp. lvii–lx; Maurice Lee, Jr, 'King James's Popish Chancellor', in Cowan and Shaw (eds), *Renaissance and Reformation*, pp. 170–82; Shire, *Song, Dance and Poetry*, p. 225; Forbes-Leith SJ, *Narratives of the Scottish Catholics*, pp. 284–5.

16. Wormald, *Court*, p. 192; Bald, 'Contemporary References', 178 and M.A. Bald, 'The Anglicisation of Scottish Printing', *Scottish Historical Review*, 23 (1926), 107–15 (115); cf. Michael Spiller, 'Poetry after the Union, 1603–1660', in Jack (ed.), *History of Scottish Literature Volume 1*, pp. 141–62 (142 ff.).

17. L.E. Kastner and H.B. Charlton (eds), *The Poetical Works of Sir William Alexander, Earl of Stirling* (Edinburgh and London, Scottish Text Society, William Blackwood and Sons, 1921), p. 12; Jack, 'The Scottish Sonnet', pp. 394–5; Rogers, *Poems of Sir Robert Aytoun*, p. xliv; cf. William Gillies, 'Gaelic: the Classical Tradition', in Jack (ed.), *History of Scottish Literature Volume 1*, pp. 245–61; Derick S. Thomson, 'True Seventeenth-Century Bardic Poets: Niall Mór, Cathal and Niall MacMhuirich', in Adam J. Aitken, Matthew P. McDiarmid and Derick S. Thomson (eds), *Bards and Makars: Scottish Language and Literature: Medieval and Renaissance* (Glasgow, University of Glasgow Press, 1977), pp. 221–46.

18. Wormald, *Court*, p. 186; L.E. Kastner (ed.), *The Poetical Works of William Drummond of Hawthornden with 'A Cypress Grove'* (2 vols, Edinburgh and London, Scottish Text Society, William Blackwood and Sons, 1913), pp. xvi, xl; Jack, 'The Scottish Sonnet', pp. 399–400, 402, 439, 509, 542–7; Shire, *Song, Dance and Poetry*, p. 214.

19. Shire, *Song, Dance and Poetry*, p. 207; Bruce Lenman, *The Jacobite Risings in Britain 1689–1746* (London, Eyre Methuen, 1980), p. 225; *Musa Latina Aberdoniensis*, ed. Sir William Duguid Geddes LLD. (Aberdeen, New Spalding Club, 1892), p. vii; James MacQueen, 'Scottish Latin Poetry', in Jack (ed.), *History of Scottish Literature Volume 1*, pp. 213–26 (221); cf. *'The Aberdeen Doctors', The Aberdeen*

Journal: Notes and Queries IV (1911), 286–7, 290–1, 297–9; 'State of Religion, etc, in Upper Deeside Two Centuries Ago', *The Aberdeen Journal: Notes and Queries*, IV, 145–6.

20. *Musa Latina*, pp. xix, xxiii, 180–1, 219; *Musa Latina* (Vol. II, 1895), pp. xv, xviii, 241; MacQueen, 'Scottish Latin Poetry', pp. 222.

21. *Musa Latina Aberdoniensis III: Poetae Minores*, ed. William Watt Leade (Aberdeen, New Spalding Club, 1916), pp. 20 ff., 38 ff., 82, 167 ff., 173; Jack, 'Of Lion and of Unicorn', 93.

22. Wormald, *Court*, p. 193; Jack, *History of Scottish Literature Volume 1*, pp. 3, 9; *idem*, 'Of Lion and of Unicorn', pp. 92, 94; MacQueen, 'Scottish Latin Poetry', pp. 222; George Eyre-Todd (ed.), *Scottish Poetry of the Seventeenth Century* (Abbotsford Poets, Glasgow and Edinburgh, William Hodge & Co., n.d.), pp. 205, 206; Horace, *Odes* IV:v; Michael J. Enright, 'King James and His Island: an Archaic Kingship Belief', *Scottish Historical Review*, 55 (1976), 29–40 (37); cf. Edwin Morgan, 'How Good a Poet is Drummond?', *Scottish Literary Journal*, 15:1 (1988), 14–24 (20).

23. Jack, *A Choice of Scottish Verse*, p. 16; Alexander Robertson of Struan, *Poems* (Edinburgh, 1749).

2

HERCULE GAULOIS, GREAT BRITAIN'S SOLOMON – MYTHS OF PERSUASION, STYLES OF AUTHORITY

Nick Myers

The relationship between the monarch and his image is a complex one. Apart from his own efforts to shape it into the most persuasive forms possible, he must accommodate the models proposed by those who are both ill-intentioned and well-intentioned – in either case, their interpretation of good government is never entirely predictable or controllable. the poet Osip Mandelstam died in a Siberian labour camp for having painted a less than flattering portrait of Stalin in one of his poems. But it is not given to many monarchs, at any time or in any place, to exercise the kind of control over the representation of power characteristic of that regime.

The image of kingship that emerges is therefore composite. In a stable monarchy, the makers of kingly images can be assumed to share a common cause. Yet, outside the very rare totalitarian regime evoked above, there will always be room for interpretation as to what the King should be and do, and even the basest flatterer exercises his right to it.

There is, too, the question of the past and its weight. Signally, the monarch is burdened by it. Unless the monarchy is elective, the past, expressed in terms of lineage, is precisely what legitimates the monarch, along with the axiom – valid for any society permeated by a belief in Providence – that the King is God's choice. In terms of imagery this means that the monarch inherits a garb that never fits him perfectly, although he does his best to make it fit him more or less. For the Renaissance monarch, the two great repositories of images – the 'wardrobes', as it were – are of course the Bible and antiquity. No two monarchs go to them for exactly the same resources, for even where the same image is chosen, it is never made to signify in exactly the same way.

A final point to be made among these preliminary comments: absolutism is, in the early seventeenth century at least, perhaps nothing so much as a form of rhetoric, and to say so is by no means to deny it its potential effectiveness. The rhetoric of absolutism is what the linguists call 'performative' – or it would like to be. This can be expressed another way, more simply: when A says to B that he is so powerful that he does not need to persuade him, he is adopting a form of persuasion, and insofar as B is in fact persuaded, A is exactly as powerful as he says he is – neither more nor less.

All the above is a way of giving a certain qualification to James Stuart's 'stile of Gods', which has given rise to much comment in recent years.[1] Historians have been willing to characterise both James's and Henry IV's reigns as absolutist, and indeed to see them as part of a general tendency affecting most, if not all, of Europe throughout the century. One thing, perhaps, can be agreed upon: whatever absolutism as a theory and a practice might mean in the three decades or so that are touched on here – roughly, from 1590 to 1625 – and setting aside the very real question of institutional differences on either side of the Channel, it does not afford anything remotely like the variety practised by Henry's grandson at the other end of the seventeenth century. This is not the place to go into the dynamic historical process by which the one leads through many a rough patch, to the other.[2] More modestly, I want to look very selectively at some of the ways in which Henry IV and James I are painted – and paint themselves – larger than life. In stating their authority, it may be taken as given that they are also creating it.

In 1595 Henry made a royal entry into Lyon. Paris had fallen to him the year before, but under very different circumstances. Lyon had in fact come over to the Royalist side in what seems to have been a spontaneous popular uprising as early as 1593. Amid scenes of great rejoicing, the silk capital's stocks of white silk were sold out as the inhabitants rushed to express their symbolic allegiance to the Crown, and Henry issued an edict thanking the Lyonnais for their fidelity.[3] It is worth remembering that Lyon had been, in the first half of the century, the economic dynamo of the kingdom.

The main record of the entry comes down to us via the lawyer Pierre Matthieu, who played a leading role in designing it and wrote up the whole event on Henry's express command.[4]

The central aspect of any royal entry is that the civic space presents itself to be 'read' – one might say deciphered – by the monarch, like a text that reveals itself as the monarch casts his eye over it. Specific features of the city, along with its overall identity, are presented as submissive to the royal presence as if, indeed, they had only been waiting for that moment to arrive in order to fulfil their destiny. The monarch makes 'sense' of the city, in more ways than one. At the same time, the city makes sense of him: it reads him back to himself, in a series of tableaux and incidents that freely mix recent royal biography, distant semi-mythic national history, Graeco-Roman mythology, all with a view to demonstrating that his triumph is the only possible outcome of time itself, that everything past and present has been converging on it. As Henry arrived in the Vaise district of the town, he was confronted with a painting that showed a lion crawling, slowly being revived from the ravages of fever by the rays of the sun.[5] The symbolism neatly packages an allusion to Antiquity along with the reference to the troubles that had so recently laid low the fortunes of Lyon and beyond it, the whole of France. This theme – that the King alone had had the capacity to drag France out of the quagmire into which she had sunk – is repeated in many different ways in the entry.

Elsewhere, the changes are rung on the theme of the city of Lyon and the animal that is its emblem. A painting represents the city as a beautiful woman, dressed in the King's colours, inviting the King to 'wipe your warlike sweat on my breast'.[6] Still another variation has the lion abasing itself before a cock with splendid plumage, just as the city has submitted to the monarch, since it was believed that the cock drew its strength from the sun.[7]

As everyone knows, the lion itself features royal qualities, and as such is exploited in a niche showing one vanquishing a hydra while another pours honey into a morion.[8] The onlooker would have had no difficulty in grasping the allusion to Henry crushing rebellion and then replacing the force of arms with the blessings of peace. The theme is developed with the image of a lion offering its own hide to Hercules, thus demonstrating that the French lion, unlike the Nemean one, submits to a superior regal power of its own free will. This was not *too* gross a distortion of what had been happening all through the summer and autumn of the previous year, as the cities still in Leaguer hands fell one by one.[9]

The symbolic bestiary is exploited in two other ways. A globe, which is usually taken to represent both the world and fortune, is surmounted by an eagle about to take flight. Above the eagle is a statue of the King bearing the palm. Below the whole ensemble one reads, blazoned in the royal colours, gold on azure, the single word 'Altius'.[10] The eagle was, of course, a familiar symbol in numerous emblem books of the time, with many different associations.[11] The configuration here is virtually a commonplace, indicating that the monarch overcomes the vicissitudes of fortune through his virtuous qualities, the emphasis being placed rather on moral fortitude than on brute power or force. Curiously, Matthieu's commentary assigns a quality much more commonly associated with the pelican, as he notes that the eagle's will and pleasure is to die upright and to pierce its own side in order to nourish its young ones with its blood.[12] The idea that the defining characteristic of the good monarch was that he be prepared to give everything, including, if necessary, his own life had been put forward in 1576 by the political theorist Jean Bodin in his *Six Livres de la République*:

> When I speak of a good and just king, I am speaking rather in relation to his people, than of a Prince of heroic virtues, or of a model of wisdom, justice, piety, who is perfectly blameless, free of vices, for such perfection is all too rare; rather I call a king good and just when he puts every effort into being such, and one who is ready to expend his wealth, his blood, his life for his people; as did Codrus or Decius, who, on being informed that victory could only be gained through their death, on the instant sacrificed themselves.[13]

Certainly Henry had been prepared to play this role on many occasions, such as the one in 1585 on which he begged the then King, Henri III, to give him permission to meet the Duke of Guise in single combat in order to determine the fate of the nation. The French historian Denis Crouzet has recently argued that the idea of Henry's sacrifice became an inevitable condition of salvation for France and that the assassination in 1610 had not merely been prefigured but actually rationalised by royal propaganda for many years prior to it.[14] It does not seem probable that either the King or his entourage felt that such an eventuality would prove to be literally necessary but, as can be seen in the case of Elizabeth, the theme certainly had immense affective, galvanising force as a source of unification around the figure of the monarch.

The other image that was invoked from the symbolic bestiary was the legendary phoenix, common, of course, in royal iconography of the period, but peculiarly resonant in the circumstances of the Lyon entry. For at least one of the Arabian bird's traditional attributes – self-renewal – fitted Henry's trajectory nicely, but may also be taken to evoke the prestige of the monarchy as an institution, which had reached an all-time low in the years 1588 and 1589 with the humiliating exclusion of Henri III from his own capital on the Day of the Barricades, followed by the unedifying assassination of the Guise brothers, arranged by the Valois king at Blois. Under the first of the Bourbon kings, the monarchy as an institution and as an idea underwent a rebirth.

The theme of Hercules has been touched on and we may now return to it. One of the first scenes presented to the visiting monarch showed Hercules between two pillars killing the monster Geryon. What is being evoked here and elsewhere in the pageantry is a kind of double Hercules, the one that we are familiar with, who performed the twelve labours, among which was to recover Geryon's flocks. In the Greek tradition this Hercules had had to choose between virtue and pleasure when a young man. This choice is perhaps not totally unrelated to that which had faced Henry during his years in the gilded cage at the Court of Catherine de Medici, before he made the final break, escaped to Guyenne and began the long years of more or less constant campaigning in the field that finally brought him to the throne. The picture is, however, more complicated than this. Exploiting the legend that Hercules had wandered into France on his way back from Geryon's kingdom, the humanists of the early sixteenth century had created a national version of the hero as founder of various royal lines, among which was the Foix/Navarre one.[15]

In emblem books of the period from Alciati onwards this version of Hercules was commonly represented as having golden chains connecting his tongue to the ears of a crowd of what were, presumably, his subjects. The message is clear: the ideal monarch charms, as it were, his subjects' obedience. He does not force it from them.

In its broadest aspect, the programme of the humanists was part of a movement both to establish the pedigree of the French language as against Latin and Greek – that is, as a vehicle for eloquence in the noblest sense – but also to contribute to pride in national identity itself. Every one of the Valois kings from Francis I onwards had been identified with the homespun Hercules, and on the way the standard kingly qualities of justice and prudence had accrued to his image. Moreover, the attributes of the winged messenger of the gods, Mercury, had become fused with him to the point where he was often represented furnished not only with the familiar club but also the *caduceus*, which signifies, of course, peace, eloquence, and reconciliation. In any case it is fair to say that in the iconography surrounding Henry, where Hercules is present, Mercury is never far away. This allows the creators of panegyric to represent the dual qualities of Henry's style of kingship, qualities amply attested to by all the more serious historians of the reign: namely, his extraordinary ability to carry the day by feat of arms on the one hand and, on the other, where mere feat of arms was not enough, his skill in winning over to his side both moderate Catholics and erstwhile fanatics connected to the League by pardoning his enemies and identifying his destiny with that of the community as a whole.

The cult of Henry as Hercules was taken to its limit in the Avignon entry of 1600 designed for Marie de Medici, which Henry was supposed to attend but failed to. He is nevertheless everywhere, in his allegorised form.[16] The Jesuit André Valladier, who was principally responsible for designing the entry, explains his chosen theme of the Hercules figure in the following terms: 'As we have seen and see every day, not only the French people, but even foreign nations, captivated and, one might say, fettered by the merciful and affable nature of the King, follow him as if bewitched.'[17] One notes the ambiguity here – the notion of being virtually ravished by the King's powers – but also the forlorn hope that was pinned on Henry, more or less seriously, that he would somehow provide a rallying point for the Europe that had been divided by the Reformation.

Enough has perhaps now been said to fix the main features of Henry's image. It is time to turn to James I – and VI – to examine the way in which he was viewed at the start of his reign.

A major difference between the way the two monarchs were received respectively is determined by the fact that, putting it simply, the English had a much hazier notion of who James actually was. Even before he succeeded to the throne, and thus long before his coronation at Chartres, Henry had a history that was intimately familiar to his subjects, and this is reflected, of course, in the literature and the iconography. Not the least reason that drove the English crowds to flock to see their King as he came down from Scotland was undoubtedly curiosity about a virtually totally unknown factor. Their desire to acclaim is mixed with a desire to observe the King's every gesture. Even before James reached London, John Savile commented about the King's presence at Theobalds: 'I have heard many grey heads speake it, that in all the meetings they have seen or heard of, they never heard or saw the tenth man was there to be seen that day betwixt Enfeeld and London.'[18] For the gawping crowds James was a novelty, not simply as a Scot, but also as a male, adult successor to the throne, with a family in tow, for such an event had not been witnessed in living memory. David Bergeron is undoubtedly right to emphasise that a large part of the capital of good-will from which James initially benefited was based on the fact of there being such a family, with the succession already assured, and this was reflected in the speech of the Genius of the City made during the London entry the following year.[19] Perhaps the sentiment most in evidence was one of relief that disaster had been avoided and that the succession had passed off calmly. One versifier wrote:

> Peace did [Elizabeth's] raigne begin, peace it maintain'd:
> . . . Peace she hath left behind; which, no way stained
> With bloody warre, rejoyceth England's heart.[20]

In France, Thomas Pelletier wrote a congratulatory tract in which he commented that all of Europe had been looking on after Elizabeth's death and expecting England to become, as he put it, 'a theatre filled with the most horrible and bloody tragedies which one could expect in an entirely disordered and ravaged state', and yet, instead of the tempest, there had appeared, to everyone's relief, a pure, shining sun.[21] The metaphor is well worn but the fear was no less real for that. Pelletier gave credit for the peaceful succession to the Queen and above all her Council, and contrasted it explicitly with Henry's in France, where, as he puts it, their 'Mars had had to open the way to peace at the point of the sword.'[22]

Something that *was* known about the new monarch was that he was a writer who took himself seriously as such, and this was latched onto in some of the panegyric. Savile wrote:

> 'Mongst all estates Poets have cause to sing
> King James's welcome; for hee doth excell
> As his Lepanto and his Furies tell,
> In Poesie all Kings in Christendome.[23]

The theme of James as the king of the book – with all that this implies – is the central definition of his style of kingship and it recurs at regular points throughout the reign. One only has to think of the way his collected works were presented to the world in 1616 – an unprecedented gesture for any monarch – or the statue of him, enthroned, book in hand, on the Tower of the Five Orders at Oxford. There seems to be no doubt that the new reign raised high expectations of all kinds, some of which were incompatible. John Chamberlain, in alluding to James's symbolic gesture of clemency in having Southampton and Sir Henry

Neville released from the Tower, wrote sarcastically of the unreal optimism which pervaded the times, 'these bountiful beginnings raise all men's spirits, and put them in great hopes, insomuch that not only Protestants, but Papists and Puritans, and the very Poets, with their idle pamphlets, promise themselves great part in his favour',[24] James himself was to come close to recognising that he had perhaps not been measured enough in his liberality in the early years of his reign when he told Parliament in 1607, 'My first three years were to me as a Christmas, I could not then be miserable.'[25] It should be added that in that particular context James was defending himself against the charge that he had been overly generous to the Scots in his entourage. However, at the time of James's royal entry into London, such Anglo-Scottish jealousies were not yet on the horizon, and the designers of the pageant were prepared to acknowledge, if only in symbolic terms, a general reconciliation of traditional enemies through the person of the monarch, and the creation of a new entity, something called Britain. Let us look, briefly, at the kind of king which is reflected back to James that day.

James's role as head of the four monarchies – four in theory, three in reality – was emphasised. In a somewhat forced conceit of symmetry, he is advised to rule each according to the virtues taken to be proper to kings. Scotland has already been set in order in both Church and State according to the prudence of the King; Ireland, always a source of potential rebellion, will require a firm sort of justice; France, the monarch is told in an obscure way, will bring out his fortitude 'when necessarie reason of state shall bend your majestie's Counsells to that enterprize'; England, however, being a reasonable sort of place, will only require temperance and moderation. Elsewhere in the speech James is welcomed as the realisation of the Platonic ideal: the philosopher king.[26] This was echoed by the speech at the Italian community's arch, where it was emphasised that the people were most happy where both philosophy and a philosopher king reigned. As in the case of Henry, and indeed naturally enough, the pageant designers seized on actual characteristics of the King, and by shaping them to the overall theme of peace and plenty and representing them in allegorised terms turned them into virtues amply fitted to the requirements of the kingdom he had inherited. God's plan for his Israel had ensured this. Divine Providence was featured in the Dutch pageant as a woman pointing to heaven, at her feet the words '*Provida mens coeli*'; just below this scene the imperial crown crossed by two sceptres made it clear that the union was an integral part of the plan.

As in the case of Henry Bourbon, it was felt necessary to legitimise the new monarch by presenting him as the outcome of a distant and legendary past which had seen the birth of an incipient national identity. Thus, a variation on the theme of unification was to present it in terms of *re*unification; in this version, James was hailed as a second Brute, the king who was supposed to have come from Troy to found Troynovant – new Troy – on the banks of the Thames. The

Scottish King, however, was seen as having come down from the north in order to put together the fragments of Brute's kingdom, to prove himself a wiser king than the original by repairing the damage he had done. This is developed by Anthony Mundy for his London pageant of 1605 when he writes:

> . . . the three virgin Kingdomes seeme to reprove [Brute] for his over-much fond love to his sons, and deviding her (who was one sole monarchy) into three several estates . . . our second Brute . . . by whose happye comming to the Crowne, England, Wales, and Scotland, by the first Brute severed and divided, are . . . re-united and made one happy Britania again.[27]

Jonathan Goldberg has argued that James's characteristic style was Roman and imperial. Certainly on the day he entered London and throughout the reign the classical style was thoroughly exploited, in particular through references to Augustus and the Virgilian idea of the golden age. Henry Petowe developed the theme in his poem 'England's Caesar', written to celebrate the coronation.

The Scottish King's culture, however, was just as thoroughly biblical as it is was classical, and it is not easy to see that there is an imbalance between the two modes of allusion in representing him, either in the London entry or elsewhere. In James's own addresses to Parliament, he took evident pleasure in citing biblical authorities to buttress his own. In doing so, he was no doubt seeking to give accreditation to his Protestant affiliations to those in Parliament who may have been worried about a certain slackness characteristic of the monarch in furthering the Protestant cause abroad. To return to the London pageant, the most obvious tendency in the symbolic vocabulary is a free and supple movement back and forth between the two styles of representation. This is, incidentally, just as true in the case of Henry's Lyon entry and all the others. One doubts that it would have seemed natural for an educated Englishman or Frenchman to think in any other way. The Dutch arch in London gives a particularly clear example of this tendency, with the portrayal of the two 'kings' Solomon and Apollo, representing alternative aspects of James himself.[28]

The London entry has seemed worth dwelling on since it was really the only full-blown pageant of the reign. For whatever reasons – whether because they were costly affairs or because, as is often claimed, James had a horror of the crowds involved on such occasions – there were no others of anything like comparable scale.[29] Moreover, like Henry's entry at Lyon, it featured virtually all the images and traits taken to typify the monarch throughout his reign. It has to be emphasised – and we have seen – that many such images applied to both kings, with, of course, an appropriate contextualisation and validation in either case. Henry can, plausibly, be presented as a second Augustus; so can James. In both cases, what links them is the hope and optimism generally visible at the beginning of a reign. There are, though, limits to this interchangeability.

For obvious reasons, James will not be compared to Mars – although Mars turns up in the royal iconography as being subdued by the mere presence of the *Rex pacificus*; in the case of Henry, by contrast, the comparison was a commonplace.

We are now in a position to make an intermediate summary. All monarchs are initially presented as being providential, but some, to paraphrase George Orwell, are more providential than others, because they unite around their person a community whose existence is either really or potentially threatened. In this sense, Henry and James can reasonably be compared. They were both seen as having come through considerable personal dangers because they had been protected by the hand of God. In both cases, despite the fact that they were the only realistic candidates for the throne, the succession was a delicate affair, particularly so in the case of the first Bourbon. In other respects, it is rather the contrasts which should be emphasised: Henry is seen as the warrior king, the king on horseback, who has to make war in order to win peace: James, enthroned in wisdom, brings peace in order to avoid war. In even more abstract terms, it is evident that Henry is presented in terms of mobility – he is the king who goes everywhere, sees everything, plays every role, almost like a Gallic Prince Hal. In the account of the days leading up to his death which Matthieu dedicated to Marie de Medici, the historian noted:

> the promptness and vivacity of his mind, which moved even faster than his eyes, and penetrated things which could only be guessed at. . . . A chair had been prepared for him, but the joy that was in him made him leap up from it . . . changing his position from one moment to the next, and always talking either about what he could see, or about what was happening . . .[30]

James, by contrast, is immobile, but this is a strength, a form of steadfastness and equitable judgement – the King seated on his throne also sees everything, but because the world comes to him. In a letter of 1614 Donne wrote of the Court, 'all is created there, or relates thither'. The Court is the centre of the world, and the King sits at the centre of the Court, sifting, weighing, now giving, now taking away, James plays Solomon to Henry's David.

In the manner of their dying kings are epitomised. As we know, the vaunted peace which was taken to be the signal achievement of both James and Henry did not last, indeed could not last in a Europe profoundly divided by the religious schism. At the time of his death Henry was preparing to go to war with Spain for one last time. In the assassin Ravaillac's fevered mind, this was the justification for his gesture, for it was the proof that the King had never really converted to the true Catholic faith in his heart. By the time of James's death, the Thirty Years' War was well under way, and James's son-in-law had been long since turned out of the Palatinate by the imperial forces.

In his funeral sermon for James, Bishop John Williams gave the most complete exposition of James as Solomon that we have, and in so doing picks out the features of the reign. In a reference that was to prove darkly prophetic, Williams points out that, towards the end of forty years of peace, Solomon's kingdom, too, was being threatened by enemies.[31] One might add – although of course Williams doesn't – that although Solomon, according to the Lord's promise, was allowed to sleep in the bosom of this fathers, his son was very shortly faced with a rebellion because, as the Bible states, 'all Israel saw that the king did not hearken to them'.[32]

James is praised rather for his Solomonic eloquence, the eloquence that, as all the mirror-for-princes literature of the period from Budé onwards agrees, is just as vital a part of the monarch's make-up as his liberality, justice, and mercy. Williams notes:

> Those speeches of his in the parliament, starre chamber, councell table, and other publique audiencies of the state . . . doe proue him to bee the most powerfull speaker, that euer swayed the scepter of his kingdome. In his style you may obserue the Ecclesiastes, in his figures the Canticles, in his sentences the Proverbs.[33]

This might be thought to be merely the kind of inflated praise typical of funeral orations. If, however, one makes allowances for the Bishop's highly stylised assessment, there does seem to be some basis for it in fact. Many years previously, in private correspondence and before James had come to the English throne, Sir Henry Wotton had noted the King's love of debate and considerable discursive powers.[34]

The Bishop instances the ways in which the King had been preserved from danger including, of course, the Gowrie conspiracy and Gunpowder Plot, in order that he 'might appear in the world . . . a Monster, as it were, of the Diuine Prouidence'.[35] Specific aspects of James's ecclesiastical, domestic and foreign policy are enumerated approvingly – his maintenance of Church discipline through episcopalianism, his policy of peace which had encouraged trade abroad and manufacturing at home, the untroubled border with Scotland, the securing of Ireland through the Ulster plantation,his role in Europe in which, according to Williams, he 'held the ballance'.[36] His virtues as a writer are not forgotten. Williams rejects the parallel with the legendary Brute, preferring to claim that, as Solomon was the first king to reign over all Israel, so James is the first 'ouer all this island'.[37] Manifestly, the terms in which his reign were presented a the outset remain perfectly stable throughout it. In sum, he is seen as having fulfilled the contract expected of him. Such, at least, is the point of view of a bishop, speaking before the son and heir Charles. We are familiar with vastly more hostile assessments by contemporaries or near-contemporaries, which it is no part of my brief to assess here. As he had reigned unspectacularly, so he dies. As Williams describes it: '[with] his lords, and servants kneeling on the one side, his archbishop, bishops, and other of his chaplaines on the other side of his bed, without any pangs, or conuulsion at all . . . Salomon slept'.[38]

For Nicholas Coeffeteau, chaplain to Henry, it was naturally harder to fit the King's passing into the divine scheme, except as a punishment visited on the people for their sins. As he preached in his funeral oration – only one of many, incidentally, which were delivered in France in a national outpouring of grief – 'we have become fatherless orphans, and our mothers are as widows'.[39] Coeffeteau finds in the princes of antiquity with whom Henry had so often been compared in other respects – Alexander, Julius Caesar – fitting examples demonstrating the inconstancy of human affairs, which bring down the mighty in the moment of their highest felicity. It is the Bible which affords the most telling parallels. In the manner of his coming to the throne, Henry is compared, once more, to David for we are told, 'although he was the son of a King, he was not for all that pampered like the children of Princes or even the rich: but as in Sparta, [where] the youth were accustomed to the most exacting exercises'.[40] Like David, he has to overcome the contempt of his enemies and their refusal to recognise his title as King. Once firmly established on the throne, Coeffeteau wishes us to see Henry as another Solomon, for the quickness and the solidity of his understanding. In the manner of his death he is the pious descendant of David and Solomon, Josias, struck down by an Egyptian archer as he rides to battle in his chariot, although Coeffeteau is at pains to emphasise – and this is the only completely false note in the extended parallel – that the Bourbon monarch died in the middle of the peace.[41] The final word is David's warning to the great ones of this world – though like Gods, they will die like men, and fall like one of the princes.[42]

The absolute final word, though, on Henry the Great, as he came to be known, should be given to Agrippa d'Aubigné, his companion in arms through so many campaigns and the poet who, more than any other, immortalised his image in his epic poem *Les Tragiques*. At the end of his history of the period, *L'Histoire Universelle*, he presents the following epitome of the reign in lines which are really too beautiful to be quoted in anything other than the original:

La main large de Dieu, qui par cinquante annees
En deluge versa tant de graces donnees,
Du berceau condamné l'iniuste mort chassa,
Qui de ses doigts porta les tendons de l'enfance,
Vn bouclier au massacre, aux prisons delivrance,
La victoire aux combats, à la fin se lassa.

The hand of God grows weary, even of kings.

TAILPIECE

There is a life after death, at least for the great ones of this world. It is called apotheosis. Both the British and French sovereigns were lucky enough to be elevated posthumously in this manner by the skills of the greatest allegorical painter of the Baroque era, Peter Paul Rubens. The central panel – and the first to be sketched in Rubens's scheme – of the Banqueting House ceiling at Whitehall is of course the Apotheosis of James I, and the pivotal representation of the vast Medici cycle which Marie de Medici commissioned in an unprecedented move – for what she had eulogised was her entire life as queen and regent – was the painting known as the *Death of Henri IV* and the *Proclamation of the Regency*.[43] Rubens in his usual efficient way assimilates all the qualities most commonly associated with the dead kings and brings them all together in dynamic allegorical form. The requisite symbols of reconciliation and triumph abound in both cases. The caduceus is held over the seated James's head, as *putti* relieve him of his earthly crown in preparation for the heavenly crowning by the victor's laurels which Henry already bears as he is whisked away to join his 'companions' Hercules and Mercury in paradise.

We need not linger to gloss every figure of these crowded, agitated paintings in which Rubens mixes the allegorical and the historical, the topical and the timeless in his inimitable fashion, one which now, perhaps, we find a little bewildering. The Catholic artist and diplomat came to deal with the Banqueting House commission several years after he had dealt with the considerably trickier one of the Luxemburg Palace. One needs to make allowance, certainly, for a difference of intention which translates itself formally into the fact that Henry has to share the space very exactly with his widowed queen and Rubens consequently chose to divide the scene by using the earthly trophy and Mercury's wand direct above it, whereas James is the undisputed star of his own apotheosis. What needs underlining, though, is simply that although the two paintings share so many symbolic features, the treatment reveals two different accents which are, I suggest, the local accents of history itself. James's relatively tranquil, seated posture is, as we have seen, both indicative of the temperament of the man and the fact that he and his reign come and go in a regular and uninterrupted unfolding of events. History, as Rubens would have us see it, flows smoothly into eternity.

The Medici cycle apotheosis is, by contrast, strikingly violent. There is a notable tension between the expression of Henry's face – acquiescent, apparently placidly accepting that this, after all, was to be his fate – and the position of his body, limbs flailing as if he had been untimely ripped from the womb of history, which, of course, he had. Saturn points heavenward with his sickle to indicate that Henry's time is up, but Henry looks away from him. What we witness is a rupture in history, something the artist would have us think of as unresolved. In textual terms, one might say that the Banqueting House image submits to closure; the Luxemburg Palace one resists it.

Notes

1. See particularly Jonathan Goldberg, *James I and the Politics of Literature* (Baltimore, 1983) pp. 28 ff.; also Jenny Wormald, 'Basilikon Doron and the Trew Law of Free Monarchies: the Scottish Context and the English Translation', in Peck, *Mental World.*

2. There is fine recent synthesis of this thorny issue in Richard Bonney, *L'Absolutisme* (Paris, 1989). See also Roland Mousnier's *La Monarchie Absolue en Europe* (Paris, 1982).

3. J.A. de Thou, *Histoire Universelle* (The Hague, 1740), Vol. 8, p. 370. Matthieu (see n. 4) wrote 'Lyon . . . par sa fidelité s'estoit acquise le surnom de fille aisnee de sa couronne . . .'.

4. Pierre Matthieu, *L'Entrée de . . . Henri IIII . . . en sa Bonne Ville de Lyon* (Lyon, 1595).

5. Ibid., p. 23.

6. 'Grand Roy qui commandez aux forces comme aux coeurs/Essuyez dans mon sein vos guerrieres sueurs.' Ibid., p. 32.

7. Ibid., p. 39.

8. Ibid., pp. 39–40. I take a small liberty here. Matthieu writes 'un Lyon qui versoit une *ruche* d'abeilles dans un morion'. 'Honey' fits the verb much better and is clearly what is meant. The helmet was commonly represented as having itself been transformed into a hive by the peace-bringer.

9. Cf. Janine Garrisson, *Henry IV* (Paris, 1984), pp. 187–8.

10. Matthieu, *L'Entrée . . . Henri IIII*, pp. 30–1.

11. See for its political associations Alain Boureau, *L'Aigle – Chronique Politique d'un Emblème* (Paris, 1985).

12. '. . . l'Aigle vole plus haut que les autres oyseaux, le plaisir duquel est de mourir debout et se brecher le flanc pour faire viure les siens . . .'.

13. *Six Livres de la République*, Book 2, ch. 4 for the original. This and all subsequent translations are my own.

14. 'Les Fondements Idéologiques de la Royauté d'Henri IV', in D. Crouzet, *L'Avènement d'Henri IV – Quatrième Centenaire* (Pau, 1990). In many respects Crouzet's work, especially his state thesis, *Les Guerriers de Dieu* (Paris, 1990), is the most provocative and fruitful contribution to our understanding of sixteenth-century France to have appeared in decades.

15. For this whole discussion I am heavily indebted to M.-R. Jung, *Hercule dans la Littérature Française du XVIe Siècle* (Geneva, 1966), and Corrado Vivanti, 'Henri IV, the Gallic Hercules', *Journal of the Warburg and Courtauld Institutes*, 30 (1967), 176–97.

16. André Valladier, *Labyrinthe Royal de l'Hercule Gaulois Triomphant* (Avignon, 1601).

17. Quoted in the original French in Vivanti, 'Henri IV', p. 186.

18. Quoted in J. Nichols (ed.), *The Progresses of James the First* (4 vols, New York, 1967, reprint of 1828 edition), Vol. 1, p. 139.

19. David Bergeron, *Royal Family, Royal Lovers* (Columbia, Missouri, 1991), p. 68; for the Genius's speech see Stephen Harrison, *Arches of Triumph* (London, 1604).

20. Nicholas, *The Progresses of James the First*, Vol. 1, p. 10.

21. Thomas Pelletier, *Dicours Politique à Tres-hault et Très Puissant Roy Lacques Premier* (n.p., 1603), p. 4.

22. Ibid., p. 8.

23. Nichols, *The Progresses of James the First*, Vol. 1, p. 144.

24. Ibid., p. 52.

25. C.H. McIlwain (ed.), *Political Works of James I* (Cambridge, Mass., 1918).

26. Nichols, *The Progresses of James the First*, Vol. 1, pp. 130, 132.

27. Ibid., pp. 568–9.

28. Ibid., p. 350.

29. For a study of the pageants of the reign see David Bergeron, *English Civic Pageantry 1558–1642*, (Columbia, Missouri, 1971).

30. Matthieu, *Histoire de la Mort Déplorable de Henry IV* (Paris, 1611), pp. 14–15.

31. John Williams, Bishop of Lincoln, *Great Britain's Salomon, a Sermon Preached at the Magnificent Funerall of the Most High and Mighty King, James* (London, 1625), p. 39.

32. 1 Kings 12:16.

33. Williams, *Great Britain's Salomon*, p. 41.

34. *Life and Letters of Sir Henry Wotton*, ed. L.P. Smith (2 vols, Oxford, 1907), Vol. 1, p. 314.

35. Williams, *Great Britain's Salomon*, p. 45.

36. Ibid., pp. 57, 60–1.

37. Ibid., p. 63.

38. Ibid., pp. 72–3.

39. Coeffeteau, *Oraison Funebre Prononcée en l'Eglise de S. Benoist*, collected in *Les Oraisons et Discours Funebres . . . sur le Trespas de Henry le Grand* (Paris, 1611). Quoted sentence on p. 235.

40. Ibid., pp. 237–40.

41. Ibid., pp. 245–6, 249.

42. Ibid., p. 253.

43. My thanks are due to Dr Elizabeth McGrath of the Warburg Institute for pointing me in the right direction as far as this section is concerned. For the genesis and development of both the Banqueting House ceiling and the Medici cycle in which the apotheosis of Henry IV figures see Julius Held, *The Oil Sketches of Peter Paul Rubens* (Princeton, 1980). I have also found illuminating D.J. Gordon's 'Rubens and the Whitehall Ceiling', in Stephen Orgel (ed.), *The Renaissance Imagination* (Berkeley, 1975). Detailed commentary on the Medici cycle and the *Death of Henri IV* and the *Proclamation of the Regency* which forms part of it may be found in R.F. Millen and R.E. Wolf, *Heroic Deeds and Mystic Figures* (Princeton, 1989).

3

COURTLY PLAY: THE POLITICS OF CHAPMAN'S *THE MEMORABLE MASQUE*

David Lindley

'Masques were essential to the life of the Renaissance court; their allegories gave a higher meaning to the realities of politics and power, their fictions created heroic roles for the leaders of society'.[1]

Stephen Orgel's formulation is one with which few critics would now argue. Indeed, his brief but powerful essay, published in 1975, marked a shift in the nature of the attention accorded to these elaborate, often obscure and always ephemeral entertainments. In earlier years it had been the study of the sources of the genre, or elucidation of the arcane symbolism of individual masques, or consideration of the part they played in the evolution of theatrical practice, which most occupied critics.[2] But in the last quarter-century it has been consideration of the strategies by which writers from Jonson to Davenant encoded in their masques an idealised picture of the royal Court which has been the starting point for most critical commentary. Increasingly, scholars have teased out the specificities of the ways in which individual works addressed the particular circumstances that surrounded their performances, and have thereby located them ever more precisely in the political world of the early seventeenth century. But even here there has been some shifting of emphasis in the most recent writing about the genre. Where for Orgel in 1975 the masques of James and Charles 'express the developing movement toward autocracy',[3] and are to be regarded as direct expressions of the royal will, many critics now would see them as more problematically implicated in the shifting allegiances and political debates of the period.[4]

This change of emphasis, from a view of masques as simply reduplicating the royal voice to a recognition of their place in courtly negotiation, has derived from careful attention to aspects of these works that earlier critics tended to overlook. The first such feature is signalled by Chapman's observation in his introduction to *The Memorable Masque*, that 'all these courtly and honouring inventions (having poesy and oration in them, and a fountain to be expressed, from whence their rivers flow) should expressively arise out of the places and persons for and by whom they are presented'.[5] It is the double focus on performer and audience that is important here, and critics have picked up on the sense that the meaning and implication of particular masques might be read very differently by different sectors of the Court in order to disrupt too monologic a reading of these events. For though all masques were commissioned works, some might be sponsored by individual noblemen (as Francis Bacon financed masques both for the marriage of Frances Howard and Robert Carr and for the Palatinate marriage), and therefore have functioned as tools of personal advancement. A significant number of masques were produced at the request of members of the royal family other than the monarch – in particular, the series of early Jacobean masques in which Queen Anne took a direct part,[6] and those Caroline masques which were directly sponsored by Henrietta Maria.[7] And, as I shall be arguing, it is extremely likely that Prince Henry took a significant part in the devising of at least some of the masques for the marriage of Princess Elizabeth. The Inns of Court had a tradition of Christmas festivity and themselves sponsored a number of masques at Court, including *The Memorable Masque*, the central focus of this paper.[8] The possibility therefore exists that the agenda of any particular work might be determined by the interests of the particular sponsor, and be offered to the monarch not simply as inert praise of the royal will, but as advice or caution, or as embodying a specific political agenda not necessarily identical to that of the sovereign.

In this respect, the masque draws upon its heterogeneous ancestry, itself a further complication of too univocal a reading of the genre. It is, of course, true that part of the tradition it encompassed was that of courtly Christmas celebration, and that it therefore functioned simply as the occasion for sociable dancing and feasting to follow. At the same time it served, through its costliness, elegance and the elaboration of costume and scenic device, to declare the magnificence of the Stuart Court, especially to the foreign ambassadors who jostled for invitations to the presentations. But at the same time it had the potential to draw upon a long history of panegyric shows which offered advice to the monarch. In Elizabeth's reign many of the civic welcomes staged for her in the early years were surprisingly blunt in adjuring her, for example, to sustain the Protestant faith, and the Earl of Leicester's Kenilworth entertainment of 1575 was designed 'with one aim in mind: to encourage Elizabeth to marry him'[9] – advice which so irritated her that she left several days early. As Helen Cooper remarks, her response indicated clearly that the Queen 'was not the principal spectator but the principal actress and the principal character'.[10] There was, of course, an important difference between Elizabethan, Jacobean and Caroline shows, in that while James never himself danced, Charles was the main participant in those masques which he commissioned. Inevitably it is more difficult to embody advice to the monarch in a work where he is himself the principal performer, but even in the later period it was possible, as Carew demonstrated in *Coelum Britannicum*, to articulate some critical distance from royal policy, however much that criticism is contained and folded back into the work as a whole.[11] Most famously, the work to which Carew's masque might be construed as a response, Shirley's *Triumph of Peace*, presented by the Inns of Court, set out to remind the King of the unpopularity of 'projectors', and in so doing 'pleased the Spectators the more, because by it an Information was covertly given to the King, of the unfitness and ridiculousness of these Projects against the Law'.[12] Even a masque like *Salmacida Spolia*, the final masque of the period, has recently been seen as embodying a far more complex political message than older critics imagined.[13]

Indeed, the question of how far this most courtly of genres could yet embody dissent or resistance has become one of the most important arenas of critical debate. Jonathan Goldberg argued that 'poets who entered politically sensitive areas . . . found their own consciences put in question. They were forced . . . either to speak openly and, possibly seditiously, or to speak opaquely and, seemingly, loyally', and concluded that they ended up using 'James's own strategy of equivocation against James, relying on his self-deception to keep him from understanding the implications of that language'.[14] It seems, though, very unlikely either that James and Charles themselves were not well enough aware of the tradition of education through praise to be capable of hearing the subtext of a masque's argument, or that those who commissioned and those who wrote the masques believed that they were wasting their time in proffering a point of view distinct from that of the monarch. One should not overstate the case, however. As Martin Butler has judiciously put it:

> Monarchs expected to be advised as well as praised, and the humanist tradition of *laudando praecipere* licensed panegyric as an arena in which counsel might be offered, in which discreet criticism could be advanced, or in which analogy and oblique allusion could be employed to insinuate a commentary on topical events. And yet the risks were considerable and the advice was unlikely ever to be unconstrained by the limits of tact.[15]

Nonetheless, Butler's contention that 'reverence and reform – the power of the king and the education of that power – constituted the two poles on which the Caroline masque moved, and the structure of the masque consisted in the dialectic between them'[16] is true also of the earlier Jacobean masques and, I wish to argue, of Chapman's *The Memorable Masque*, staged as the second of the court entertainments for the marriage of Princess Elizabeth and Frederick, Elector Palatine.

Jonson was, of course, the dominant writer of masques for the Jacobean Court, but yet in his *Conversations with Drummond of Hawthornden* he is reported as saying that 'next himself only Fletcher and Chapman could make a masque'.[17] Despite this magisterial endorsement, however, the general critical opinion of *The Memorable Masque* has not been generous. Even at the time, Chapman found it necessary to justify himself angrily against 'insolent objections made against the length of my speeches and narrations' (1. 188), and recently Graham Parry has commented that 'The thematic content of this masque was slender, its success consisting mainly in sheer extravagance of costume and excellence of dancing', and concludes that 'Chapman's invention here creeps very close to the ground indeed.'[18] Earlier critics, D.J. Gordon and Jack Reese, produced defences of the masque, largely on the grounds of its iconographic richness and coherence.[19] In this paper, however, I am not concerned directly with the Platonic symbolism of the work, important though it undoubtedly is in answering Jonson's demand that masques should be 'curious after the most high and hearty inventions to furnish the inward parts, and those grounded upon antiquity and solid learnings'.[20] Rather, I want to take Chapman's own cue for interpretation in the already quoted observation that his work, like others in the genre, arises 'out of the places and persons for and by whom they are presented'. Looked at from this perspective, I will argue, the work conducts a negotiation between the monarch who was its prime audience, the lawyers who were its presenters, and Prince Henry, who almost certainly played a significant part in the devising of this, as other festivities for the marriage, before his untimely death. At the same time I want to suggest that the business of 'reading' this masque is altogether less straightforward than it might at first appear, and that Chapman self-consciously draws attention to the possibility of varied interpretation within the text itself.

In the masque's narrative Plutus, the god of riches, appears first. He has fallen in love with Honour, and has thereby been released from his traditional iconographic blindness. He has determined to pursue Honour to her home in the British Court. He is quickly interrupted by the fantastic figure of Capriccio, a 'man of wit', himself in pursuit of riches, informing us that Plutus is accompanied by a 'troop of the noblest Virginians' (1. 306) who, 'hearing of the most royal solemnity of these sacred nuptials', have arrived to participate in the celebrations. But before these Virginian masquers are revealed, Capriccio presents an antimasque of baboons, his own 'acceptable service' for the marriage (1. 375–6). His 'low induction' dismissed, the masquers are then gradually revealed in a mountain of gold and, after a series of songs instructing them in obedience to James, they descend to offer worship to the King and to the couple; then, as is customary, take out the ladies of the Court in the communal dancing of the revels.

The topicality of the subject of Virginia for a masque in 1613 is obvious enough. The second and third charters had been granted to the Virginia Company in 1609 and 1612. Both of the lawyers whom Chapman mentions in his dedication, Sir Edward Philips and Henry Hobart, were involved with the company, the latter as a member of the Council. The company, furthermore, had sponsored an unprecedented flood of published propaganda for their colonial enterprise between 1610 and 1612. A striking feature of this material, and one, as we shall see, particularly relevant to the masque, is its insistence upon the missionary nature of colonial activity, and its playing down of the hope of immediate wealth. Indeed, the first clause of the 1609 charter insisted on the evangelical purpose of the company: 'The principall effect which we can desier or expect of this action is the conversion and reduccion of the people in those parts unto the true worship of God and Christian religion.'[21] In this it is quite different from the tracts of the 1590s, where dreams of gold, and hopes of an anti-Spanish empire prevail, or at least are translated into the imagery of a religious crusade. A typical note in the sermon literature is Crashaw's adjuration to 'remember the end of this voyage as the destruction of the devil's kingdome, and the propagation of the gospel'.[22] John Parker states that: 'To a degree never again equalled in the history of British overseas expansion the appeal was most forcefully made by preachers, with a message essentially religious.'[23] Various reasons could be adduced for this heavy religious emphasis, but perhaps the most obvious was the conspicuous failure of substantial riches to arrive from the new colony. In 1607 Sir Walter Cope sadly reported to Salisbury:

> Thys other daye we sent you newes of golde. And thys daye, we cannot returne yow so much as Copper. Oure newe dyscovery ys more Lyke to prove the Lande of Canaan then the Lande of ophir.[24]

A number of writers turned the absence of gold in the colony into a moral test for would-be subscribers and explorers. Robert Johnson, in his *Nova Britannia*, warned:

> wee must beware, that . . . bitter roote of greedy gaine be not so setled in our harts, that beeing in a golden dreame, if it fal not out presently to our expectation, we slinke away with discontent, and draw our purses from the charge.[25]

Crashaw similarly argued:

> we heere see the cause why no more come in to assist this present purpose of plantation in *Virginea*, even because the greater part of men are unconverted and unsanctified men, and seeke meerely the world and themselves and no further. They make many excuses, and devise objections; but the fountaine of all is, because they may not have present profit.[26]

It is important to stress that these arguments were produced in a context where some at least worried about the motivation for colonisation, and the legality of it. (Rather too easily do some literary critics assume that the colonialist ideology was uniform and unchallenged.) Their voices are not easily heard, for they tend to appear only as the enemies cited in apologists' tracts. Johnson, for example, wrote that:

> some obiect, we seeke nothing lesse than the cause of God, being led on by our owne private ends, and secondly how we can warrant a supplantation of those Indians, or an invasion into their right and possessions.[27]

B.J. Sokol and Mary Sokol have recorded striking testimony to the anxiety of the legality of the Virginia enterprise in the fragmentary record of a private meeting in 1609 discussing the possibility of publishing a written justification of the plantation. They conclude:

> The meeting decided not to publish a justification, because if they did they would be 'putt to defend our title' which was not as yet 'publiquely quarreled'. If it was, they could show at least as good a title as the Spanish, but they would also have to show a title absolutely 'good agaynst the Naturall people'. Some members clearly thought this presented problems and therefore publishing a justification for planting could present unnecessary provocation.[28]

Chapman's masque reduplicates the emphasis of these treatises on spiritual rather than material benefit and, at the same time, attempts to answer characteristic anxieties about the justice of the colonial enterprise by figuring as one of its presenters of the masquers, Eunomia, a 'virgin priest' consecrated to the Law. The work can therefore be seen simply as an apologia for the Virginian enterprise, entirely complicit with official propaganda and endorsing its characteristic strategies. At the masque's opening, for example, we are to imagine that Plutus, the god of riches, 'being by Aristophanes, Lucian, etc. presented naturally blind, deformed, and dull witted, is here by his love of Honour made see, made sightly, made ingenious, made liberal' (11. 239–41). Plutus is not sought out, but arrives voluntarily, uncompelled, drawn only by the honour of Britain. In just the same way the Virginian princes unproblematically present themselves at Court as a free tribute to its glorious reputation. Unlike the few Amerindians who had actually been brought to Britain, they turn up out of the goodness of their own hearts – comfortably re-echoing the colonists' frequent assertion that these people 'are easie to be wrought to good, and would fayne embrace a better condition'.[29] Compulsion and conquest, together with any anxieties about the rights of the 'Naturall people' are simply effaced. This is then underscored by the way in which the masque emphasises the centrality of Law, since, as Chapman puts it, 'none should dare access to Honour but by virtue, of which Law being the rule must needs be a chief'. Appropriate enough to the profession of the presenters, this emphasis also serves to lay to rest arguments about the legality of colonisation.

The two most significant elements which underline the way Chapman dramatises the contemporary propaganda of the Virginia Company, however, are the presentation of Capriccio in the antimasque, and the specifically religious flavour of the main masque. Capriccio irrupts into the scene obviously and nakedly in pursuit of gold, having managed to pick up a few scraps from the feet of Riches. He is a 'wit' and a fantastic traveller, dressed 'half French, half Swiss', and his company of baboons in their Neapolitan suits are called by him 'accomplished travellers'. (The image of the vain traveller 'aping' foreign fashions is frequent in the satirical literature of the period.) Just such travellers were unfavourably compared with the true explorer by Johnson, in his second treatise, *The New Life of Virginea*, when he berated the 'wits of England, whereof so many of unsetled braines betake themselves to plots and stratagems at home, or else to wade from coast to coast, from England to Spaine, to Italy, to Rome, and to wheresoever they may learne and practise any thing but goodnesse'.[30] From this perspective, Capriccio and his baboons function as antitype of the true colonist who, in the propaganda of the period, should be free of personal greed and determined to work for his reward – the kind of labouring or skilled person that the Virginia Company demanded in its publicity. Indeed, it was precisely the presence of such idlers as Capriccio in the Jamestown settlement that had frequently been invoked as a peril to its success.[31]

In the masque itself the Virginian princes appear in a 'mine of gold' at line 495, but they only descend to the dancing place at line 580. In between, the Virginian priests, called 'Phoebades', sing two hymns to the Sun, which are each systematically answered by 'other music and other voices', redirecting their prayer into a praise of the 'Briton Phoebus', King James, the true God's true representative. Where the Phoebades begin their hymn with the words 'Descend, fair Sun', the answering song begins 'Rise, rise, O Phoebus', and this pattern of point-by-point conversion of their imagery is carried throughout. The purpose and direction of this exchange is made clear when, at its end, Eunomia baldly speaks to the 'masquers set yet above':

> Virginian princes, ye must now renounce
> Your superstitious worship of these Suns,
> Subject to cloudy darkenings and descents,
> And of your fit devotions turn the events
> To this our Briton Phoebus, whose bright sky,
> Enlightened with a Christian piety,
> Is never subject to black Error's night,
> And hath already offered heaven's true light
> To your dark region; which acknowledge now.
> Descend, and to him all your homage vow. (ll. 568–77)

Though we had been informed that the Virginians had set out in order to honour the marriage, it is made abundantly clear that what is really at stake is their willingness to do homage to the King himself.[32] Chapman thereby dramatises the ideological thrust of the Virginia propaganda. The conversion of the Phoebades in the masque can be paralleled in many treatises which insisted that the Amerindian religion was not really very far from Christianity, and that the Indians were therefore susceptible and keen to embrace the gospel. But Chapman's easy modulation of one priesthood into another sits uncomfortably by the side of instruction to Sir Thomas Gates to seize all Virginian priests and 'deal more sharply with them, and to proceede even to death with these murtherers of Soules and sacrificers of gods images to the devil'.[33] So, too, one might be more than a little impatient with the religious insistence of masque and propaganda alike, when one encounters assertions like Crashaw's 'if wee intend Gods honour, and the conversion of soules, God will assuredly send us great profit, which we may take lawfully and thankfully as his blessing',[34] or like the author of *A True Declaration*'s complacent assurance that we 'by way of marchandizing and trade, doe buy of them the pearles of earth, and sell to them the pearles of heaven'.[35] To unpick the self-serving ideological manipulation embodied in assertions such as these is scarcely difficult – and it is undoubtedly justified (if rather predictable) to indict Chapman for perpetuating the characteristic tropes of colonialist discourse. But it is rather more interesting to perceive the ways in which Chapman himself is conducting a kind of double discourse in the masque, and developing a complex perspective upon the Virginian enterprise. For if Chapman was writing to the King, he was, at least in part, writing in the interests of his immediate patrons, the Inns of Court, and, very probably, in the interests of his major literary patron, Prince Henry.

Henry's death in 1612 had caused the postponement of the marriage festivities, but it is clear that he had been closely involved in the preparation of the planned entertainments, and that therefore it was entirely possible that some at least might reflect his views, rather than those of his father.[36] Elizabeth's marriage was, of course, an event which writers of very different political and religious persuasions attempted to capture. At one extreme, a poet like George Wither exulted that:

> We hope that this will the uniting prove
> Of *Countries* and *Nations* by your love:
> And that from out your blessed loynes, shall come
> Another terror to the *Whore of Rome*.[37]

By contrast, Campion's masque on the wedding night had dramatised James's policies of religious reconciliation through the marriages of his two children, and seems specifically designed to dampen down the more enthusiastic Protestant view of the marriage as the beginning of an anti-Catholic, anti-Spanish league.[38] Chapman's masque, however, might be held to represent a view closer to that of Prince Henry and the anti-Spanish faction.[39]

The relevance of the whole Virginian topic to this marriage lies in the fact that those who most applauded the Protestant alliance as a symbol of a potentially more decisive foreign policy were precisely the same people who were most enthusiastic about pursuing the colonial dream, not simply as a missionary enterprise, but as a part of the anti-Spanish crusade. In lauding the one Chapman is inevitably, if covertly, alluding to the other. He could not, in the presence of the King, make such assertions directly, but, I would argue, his presentation is deliberately inflected in a number of ways to suggest the possibility of a more vigorous expansionist policy than James himself would have favoured. In the text of the masque Chapman does not present in explicit verbal form any 'returns' on the colonisation of Virginia, thus seeming to chime with the more modest ambitions of the Virginia Company at the time. But yet, of course, the visual spectacle is suffused with gold. The masquers processed through the streets of London on their way to Whitehall, and their costumes are thus described:

> Indian habits, all of a resemblance: the groundcloth of silver, richly embroidered with golden suns, and about every sun ran a trail of gold, imitating Indian work; their bases of the same stuff and work, but betwixt every pane of embroidery went a row of white ostrich feathers mingled with sprigs of gold plate. (ll. 47–51)

The masque performance itself was dominated by a mountain, which Chapman describes in these terms:

> First here appeared at the lower end of the hall an artificial rock, whose top was near as high as the hall itself . . . All this rock grew by degrees up into a gold colour, and was run quite through with veins of gold. (ll. 129–34)

And then the masquers themselves are revealed 'in a mine of gold' (1. 495). These golden images can be taken as part of the iconographical programme of the masque, images of alchemical transformation or spiritual aspiration – and so, no doubt, in part at any rate, Chapman meant them. But all this gold has a stubborn materiality, a physical and visual presence which plays across the text's tendency to play down any active desire for riches.

If hopes of gold in Virginia had faded (if not quite disappeared), for one man at least the old economic and political justification for exploration had not died – and that was Sir Walter Raleigh, friend of Chapman, and the man of whom Prince Henry is famously alleged to have said, 'None but my father would keep such a bird in a cage.'[40] Mountains which promised riches haunted him. Keymis, in his relation of the *Second Voyage to Guiana* had claimed to have seen 'far off the mountaine adioyning to this gold mine',[41] and Chapman had, in his prefatory poem to Keymis's volume spoken of:

> Guiana where rich feet are mines of golde,
> Whose forehead knockes against the roofe of Starres.[42]

Raleigh had tried repeatedly to secure his release from prison to go on a further Guyanan expedition. He had raised the possibility in 1607, and in 1609 he had assured Viscount Haddington 'when God shall permit us to arrive, if I bringe them not to a mountain (nere a navigable river) covered with gold and silver oare, let the comander have commissione to cut of my head ther'.[43] But by 1611 there was a new inflection to his pleading; to the Queen he offered riches 'to take all presumption from his [James's] enemies, arising from the want of treasor, by which (after God) all states are defended'.[44] And when he wrote to Salisbury he suggested that his proposal might be the better received 'when I considered wth whatt difficultye such som'es are Raysed in England, as maye serve his Mat^{ies} occasions, and Aunswere the greate Liberallitye, and goodnes of his harte'.[45] And he writes to the King in even more explicit terms: 'I did Lament the refusall made [to the 1607 proposals]; Because yor Matie hath therby reffused a most easye waye of being Inriched, Both dispight of yor Malitious enemyes Abroade; and of yor gruntinge Sub^{ts} att home.'[46]

The context here is the failure of the Great Contract, and the King's consequent poverty. Raleigh was making a shrewd play at this time. It is, therefore, especially interesting that Chapman should not only set his masquers in a golden mine, but choose the figure of Plutus to introduce his masque. Ben Jonson, twelve months before, had himself used the god of riches in his *Love Restored* – a masque which addresses very directly the problematic state of the King's finances to which Raleigh alluded.[47] In that masque, Plutus is represented as blind, an opponent of masquing, and pretends to be Cupid, the god of love. When his imposture is revealed he is expelled from the masque, signifying that the miserliness of city and Parliament should be overturned by the natural 'true' love that ought to subsist between subject and King and supply his wants. Chapman is, it seems, deliberately revising the perspective upon riches that Jonson had offered. Though his character, like Jonson's, begins by commenting on the processes of masque-making itself, his 'sightfulness', and the way he is incorporated within the whole design rather than excluded from it, enable Chapman, through a deliberate process of intertextual revision, to supply a potent reminder to James of a source of wealth that, to Raleigh and others of his ilk, was being needlessly passed up. As Keymis had said in 1596, unlike the Spanish 'we onlie to entertaine idle time, sit listening for Guyana newes, and instentlie forget it, as if it were nought els, but a pleasing dreame of a golden fancie'.[48] Raleigh had returned insistently to this theme in his 1611 letters, arguing that the Spaniards would filch all the gold if a sufficiently well-appointed expedition were not sent. I would argue that Chapman is using the golden dream of this masque to remind the King of the possibilities, and specifically of Raleigh's offer to lead an expedition.

If the visual goldenness of the spectacle brings Raleigh's ambitions to mind, it might also be argued that the presentation of the religion of the Virginians also owes more to him than to any account of Virginia. In Raleigh's account of his Guyana voyage we read:

> The religion of the Epuremei is the same which the Ingas, Emperors of Peru used . . . how they beleeve the immortalitie of the Soule, worship the Sunne.[49]

Chapman's representation of the Virginians as sun-worshippers, and as decked in gold, has usually been construed as sloppy scholarship. But, as Gordon noted,[50] it could be taken as a deliberate attempt to summon the presence of Raleigh into his text.[51]

To invoke Raleigh at all was a risky business, but it is possible that Chapman is even more daring in alluding to his imprisoned friend in the figure of Capriccio. At first blush this seems mere absurdity – for Capriccio, with his bellows on his head and his multinational costume, half French, half Swiss, is a self-evident grotesque. This description is drawn directly from Ripa's *Iconologia*, and D.J. Gordon's characterisation of him as 'false honour' would seem to be just and sufficient. But yet the action of the masque is very much concerned with questions of right perception. The education of the Virginian princes, as we have seen, turns upon their revising their understanding of the true sun, learning that the metaphorical 'sun' which is James transcends the declining deity they worship; and from the very beginning of the masque the audience is invited to question their assumptions about the interpretation of what they see. The masque opens with Plutus making guesses about the next stage of the action, deliberately involving the audience in the processes of reading the masque setting. He contemplates the rocks which make up the setting and anticipates that they might be 'some stony-hearted ladies courted in former masques' or 'flinty-hearted usurers' and the opening of the rocks might represent the 'time of restoring them to their natural shapes'. He is interpreting what he sees by recollection of the rocky scenery of masques such as Jonson's *Oberon*, and also alluding more specifically to Campion's *Lords' Masque*, presented the previous night, where the central device had indeed been of women transformed into stone statues being released from their imprisonment. He sets himself up as the audience, saying: 'See, it is so; and now is the time of restoring them to their natural shapes. It moves, opens. Excellent! This metamorphosis I intend to overhear' (ll. 261–3). But, of course, he is wrong, and it is Capriccio who emerges from the breaking rock. If Plutus is a faulty guide to the interpretation of the scene, it is Capriccio, oddly enough, who actually provides the basic information we need, narrating the conceit of the floating island which brings both Plutus and the Virginian troop to Britain. In his dialogue with Plutus, Capriccio resists the god's reading of him as a Puritan and 'religion-forger' (l. 333), and defends his wit which, properly appreciated, would 'yield the wholesome crop of wisdom and discretion at time o'th'year' (ll. 355–7). It is, after all, his wittiness which has made possible the exposition of the contrivance on which the masque depends. The importance of 'wit' to the masque is perhaps further indicated by the fact that it is Capriccio who drives the four horses pulling the last chariot of the procession which contains the central allegorical figures of the work – Eunomia, Phemis, Honour and Plutus himself. In the procession, then, Capriccio is distant from his troop of baboons, and though he is a fantastic, yet he is entrusted with the delivery of the masque's chief virtues.

This suggests that a double perspective upon Capriccio may be entertained, and once that is allowed, then two particular moments in the antimasque come especially into focus. First, though Capriccio's search for gold can be seen as the inappropriate money-grubbing condemned by the pamphleteers, his remark that 'A poor snatch at some of the golden ore that the feet of Riches have turned up as he trod here my poor hand hath purchased, and hope the remainder of a greater work will be shortly extant' (ll. 310–13) surely sounds an echo to Raleigh's belief that he had indeed found a little gold, and that more could, literally, be picked up in the shale of the mine he saw so vividly in his imagination. It is difficult, certainly, to see what else Chapman could have intended by this reference to a 'greater work' still to be completed.

Equally significant is the exchange between Plutus and Capriccio about reward for service done. Capriccio asks Plutus if his baboons will get fit reward for their antimasque. Plutus promises, but Capriccio continues:

> I know, sir, a man may sooner win your reward for pleasing you, than deserving you. But you great wise persons have a fetch of state – to employ with countenance and encouragement, but reward with austerity and disgrace, save your purses, and lose your honours. (ll. 392–5)

He is, of course, right to suspect. For after the 'antic and delightful' dance, Plutus refuses to give any fee, observing 'the sight of an attendant for reward is abominable in the eyes of a turn-served politician, and I fear will strike me blind again' (ll. 423–5). For all his absurdity, he has a just complaint; and though eventually Plutus does grudgingly find a 'wedge of gold' for him, Capriccio is not well served. These pointed remarks stand out from their surroundings, and could certainly be taken as an allusion to the treatment of Raleigh himself.

What I am arguing is that we need to look at Capriccio with a double vision, to read him simultaneously in two contradictory ways – both as the vain, grasping idler, and yet also as the wrongly abused man of intelligence. The reason for such doubleness is that if Chapman, or Prince Henry behind him, wanted to urge

Raleigh's case upon the King, they would have done well to present it in this displaced fashion in the antimasque. If the point was taken, well and good; if it caused offence, then it would be possible to take refuge in the alternative argument of the masque, or to hide behind the Platonic allegorising. That such a strategy was possible for Chapman is indicated by the poem he was to publish the following year about the marriage of the Earl of Somerset to Frances Howard, his *Andromeda Liberata*. In it he wrote of Andromeda bound to a barren rock in terms which seem quite clearly to allude to the impotence of the Earl of Essex claimed in the notorious annulment hearings. But when this gave offence Chapman ingenuously argued that he didn't mean that at all – readers had taken literally what was intended allegorically. The question of right perception, and the ambivalent ways in which judgements are arrived at is a constant theme in Chapman's work, and memorably expressed in the judgement of Chabot, the central figure in his *Tragedie of Chabot, Admirall of France*. Chapman uses the image of an anamorphic portrait to suggest the different perspectives that may be taken on his hero:

> So men that view him but in vulgar passes,
> Casting but laterall, or partiall glances
> At what he is, suppose him weake, unjust,
> Bloody, and monstrous; but stand free and fast,
> And judge him by no more than what you know
> Ingenuously, and by the right laid line
> Of truth, he truely, will all stiles deserve
> Of wise, just, good, a man both soul and nerve.[52]

It is precisely this double perspective that, I suggest, should be applied to the figure of Capriccio, and that, 'judged ingenuously' he partakes of characteristics of Raleigh, thus enabling the masque to question, even as it apparently endorses, the colonial policies of James.

I would reason, then, that *The Memorable Masque* has a rather more complex political purpose than has sometimes been allowed. Chapman was, I believe, trying to keep alive the anti-Spanish, economic and political arguments for colonisation, even specifically Raleigh's desire for a return to the mines of Guyana, while yet seeming to concur in the newer discourse of the Virginia Company. In so doing he might have taken his inspiration from his friend, who tried in 1607 to persuade Salisbury to allow his expedition to Guyana because it could be undertaken 'under culler of Virginia'.[53]

John Gillies, comparing Chapman's work to Shakespeare's *The Tempest* (performed for the same occasion) argued that its 'gold mine and Indian opulence' would have seemed 'a little anachronistic for 1613 – more Elizabethan than Jacobean'.[54] This, however, is precisely to miss the point, that harking back to an Elizabethan view of the colonial project was a specific and highly contemporary political gesture. Under the guise of courtly play, and within the decorum of the panegyric genre of the masque, Chapman, like other writers before and after him, could do more than simply flatter the monarch and ventriloquise his politics.

Notes

1. Orgel, *Illusion of Power*, p. 38.

2. Bibliographies of masque criticism can be found in David Bergeron (ed.), *Twentieth-Century Criticism of English Masques, Pageants and Entertainments 1558–1642* (San Antonio, 1972); David Lindley (ed.), *The Court Masque* (Manchester, Manchester University Press, 1984); David Lindley (ed.), *Court Masques* (Oxford, Oxford University Press, 1995).

3. Orgel, *Illusion of Power*, p. 51.

4. See, for example, Leah S. Marcus, *The Politics of Mirth: Jonson, Herrick, Milton, Marvell and the Defense of Old Holiday Pastimes* (Chicago, University of Chicago Press, 1986); Sharpe, *Criticism and Compliment*; Martin Butler, 'Reform or Reverence? The Politics of the Caroline Masque', in J.R. Mulryne and M. Shewring (eds), *Theatre and Government Under the Early Stuarts* (Cambridge, Cambridge University Press, 1993), pp. 118–56. David Bevington and Peter Holbrook (eds), *The Politics of the Stuart Court Masque* (Cambridge, Cambridge University Press, 1998).

5. David Lindley (ed.), *Court Masques*, p. 79, ll. 197–8.

6. Jonson specifically attributes the devising of an antimasque for *The Masque of Queens* to Queen Anne who, according to his preface, 'had commanded me to think on some dance or show that might precede hers, and have the place of a foil or false masque'. (Lindley (ed.), *Court Masques*, p. 35.)

7. See Barbara K. Lewalski, *Writing Women in Jacobean England* (Cambridge, Mass., Harvard University Press, 1994); Erica Veevers, *Images of Love and Religion: Queen Henrietta Maria and Court Entertainments* (Cambridge, Cambridge University Press, 1989). Leeds Barroll, 'Inventing the Stuart Masque', in Bevington and Holbrook, pp. 121–43.

8. It is important, too, to remember that many masques were staged away from Court, as private entertainments (as is the case with the *Coleorton Masque*), as welcome masques for visiting royalty (Campion's *Caversham Masque*, or Jonson's late *Love's Welcome at Bolsover* are good examples). Perhaps the most famous of all masques, Milton's *Comus*, was, of course, staged for the Earl of Bridgewater at Ludlow.

9. Helen Cooper, 'Location and Meaning in Masque, Morality and Royal Entertainment', in Lindley (ed.), *Court Masque*, p. 142.

10. Ibid., p. 143.

11. See Sharpe, *Criticism and Compliment*, for the strongest assertion of this case, though his views have been questioned by Martin Butler in his review article, 'Early Stuart Court Culture: Compliment or Criticism', *HJ*, 32 (1989), 425–35.

12. Bulstrode Whitelocke, *Memorials of the English Affairs* (London, 1682), p. 20, quoted in Martin Butler. 'Politics and the Masque: *The Triumph of Peace*', *The Seventeenth Century*, 2 (1987), p. 122.

13. See Martin Butler, 'Politics and the Masque: *Salmacida Spolia*', in Thomas Healy and Jonathan Sawday (eds), *Literature and the English Civil War* (Cambridge, Cambridge University Press, 1990), pp. 59–74.

14. Jonathan Goldberg, 'James I and the Theater of Conscience', *ELH*, 46 (1979), p. 381.

15. Martin Butler, 'Reform or Reverence?', p. 121.

16. Ibid., p. 127.

17. Ian Donaldson (ed.), *The Oxford Authors: Ben Jonson* (Oxford, Oxford University Press, 1985), p. 596.

18. Parry, *Golden Age*, pp. 98–9.

19. D.J. Gordon, 'Chapman's *Memorable Masque*', in Stephen Orgel (ed.), *The Renaissance Imagination* (Berkeley and London, University of California Press, 1975), pp. 194–202 (the essay was written in 1956); Jack E. Reese, 'Unity in Chapman's *Masque of the Middle Temple and Lincoln's Inn*', *Studies in English Literature, 1500–1900*, 4 (1964), pp. 291–305. Gordon does gesture briefly towards the politics of the masque, but leaves his observations undeveloped.

20. Jonson's preface to *Hymenaei* (1606), one of the most important statements of the theoretical justification of the masque, is quoted from Lindley (ed.), *Court Masques*, p. 10.

21. John Parker, 'Religion and the Virginia Colony 1609–10', in K.R. Andrew, N.P. Canny and P.E.H. Hair (eds), *The Westward Enterprise* (Liverpool, Liverpool University Press, 1978), p. 251.

22. William Crashaw, *A Sermon Preached in London before the Right Honourable the Lord Lawarre* (London, 1610), sig. K2.

23. Parker, op. cit., p. 245.

24. Philip L. Barbour (ed.), *The Jamestown Voyages, 1606–1609* (2 vols, Cambridge, Hakluyt Society, 1969), Vol. 1, p. 57.

25. Robert Johnson, *Nova Britannia* (London, 1609), sig. C1^{r}.

26. Crashaw, *A Sermon Preached in London*, sig. C1^{v}–C2^{r}.

27. Johnson, *Nova Britannia*, sig. B4^{v}–C1^{r}. The note of anxiety persists throughout much of the propaganda – Crashaw, for example, seeks to allay the 'conscionable and Christian respects' of those who objected (sig. D3).

28. B.J. Sokol and Mary Sokol, '*The Tempest* and Legal Justification of Plantation in Virginia', *The Shakespeare Yearbook*, 7 (1996), pp. 368–9. The full text is reproduced in S.M. Kingsbury (ed.), *Records of the Virginia Company* (Washington, Library of Congress, 1933), Vol. 3, p. 1.

29. Johnson, *Nova Britannia*, sig. B4^{v}.

30. Robert Johnson, *The New Life of Virginea* (London, 1612), sig. F4^{v}.

31. See H.C. Porter, *The Inconstant Savage: England and the North American Indian, 1500–1660* (London, Duckworth, 1979), pp. 297–9. (It is one of the paradoxes apologists for colonisation frequently ran up against, that though they sought industrious, useful colonists, their defence of the project not infrequently argued that colonisation was necessary because of the expansion of the population at home, and gave a convenient outlet for the undesirables of the nation.)

32. It was not uncommon for masques to incorporate the 'education' of the masquers as part of their fiction, nor for those masquers to be represented as having arrived after a journey in order to honour the King and the occasion of the masque itself. But the closest parallel to this coercive movement is in Jonson's *Irish Masque at Court*, performed earlier the same year for the Carr–Howard marriage, where the Irish are compelled to submit to James before they appear in their full masquing regalia. On this masque, see Philip Edwards, *Threshold of a Nation* (Cambridge, Cambridge University Press, 1979), pp. 1–18, and David Lindley, 'Embarrassing Ben: the Masques for Frances Howard', in

Arthur F. Kinney and Dan S. Collins (eds), *Renaissance Historicism: Selections from English Literary Renaissance* (Amherst, University of Massachusetts Press, 1987), pp. 248–64.

33. Kingsbury (ed.), *Records of the Virginia Company*, Vol. 3, p. 15.

34. Crashaw, *A Sermon Preached in London*, sig. G3[r–v].

35. *True Declaration of the Estate of the Colonie in Virginia* (London, 1610), p. 15.

36. See Strong, *Henry, Prince of Wales*, pp. 175–83.

37. George Wither, *Juvenilia*, Spenser Society, 10 (London, 1871), p. 464.

38. For discussion of the politics of Campion's *The Lords' Masque* and suggestion that it was initially designed specifically to include Prince Henry as a masquer, thus enacting James's marital ambitions for him, see David Lindley, *Thomas Campion* (Leiden, E.J. Brill, 1986), pp. 208–10.

39. David Norbrook has analysed a masque which may have been intended for these celebrations, the so-called *Masque of Truth*, in '"The Masque of Truth": Court Entertainments and International Protestant Politics in the Early Stuart Period', *The Seventeenth Century*, 1 (1986), 81–110. There is considerable doubt whether this apocalyptic piece could ever have been performed, even if Henry had lived, but it is a valuable symptom of the ways in which it might be possible, in imagination at least, to conceive of a masque which very obviously served views different from the royal orthodoxy.

40. Roy Strong, *Henry, Prince of Wales*, p. 51.

41. Lawrence Keymis, *A Relation of the Second Voyage to Guiana* (London, 1596), sig. D1[r].

42. Ibid., sig. A1.

43. V.T. Harlow, *Ralegh's Last Voyage* (London, Argonaut Press, 1932), p. 103.

44. Ibid., p. 107.

45. Ibid., p. 109.

46. Ibid., p. 108.

47. On this masque, see Jeffrey Fischer, '*Love Restored*: A Defense of Masquing', *Renaissance Drama*, New Series, 7 (1977), 231–44, and Leah S. Marcus, *Politics of Mirth*, pp. 29–38.

48. Keymis, *A Relation*, sig. A4[r].

49. Walter Raleigh, *The Discoverie of the Large, Rich and Beautiful Empire of Guiana* (London, 1596), p. 92.

50. Gordon, 'Chapman's *Memorable Masque*', pp. 199–200 (though he makes nothing of the political implications of this recollection).

51. John Gillies notes that 'Chapman may also have gotten the idea for both gold mountains, Guianan and Virginian, from an illustration of the Potosí gold mine on the frontispiece of Theodore De Bry's *America*.' Gillies, 'Shakespeare's Virginian Masque', *ELH*, 53 (1986), 703.

52. G. Blakemore Evans (ed.), *The Tragedy of Chabot*, in *The Plays of George Chapman: The Tragedies*, general editor Allan Holaday (Woodbridge, D.S. Brewer, 1987), l.i., pp. 72–80.

53. Harlow, *Ralegh's Last Voyage*, p. 101.

54. Gillies, 'Shakespeare's Virginian Masque', 675.

4

REINVENTING A MONARCHY: THE CHANGING STRUCTURE AND POLITICAL FUNCTION OF THE STUART COURT, 1603–88

Neil Cuddy

As the British monarchy leaves the twentieth century behind, there is a widely perceived need to 'reinvent' it, and make a late nineteenth-century institution fit for the twenty-first century. Despite some present urgency, however, few would argue that failure to change the House of Windsor would have grave or wide consequences. The British monarchy that entered the seventeenth century was also felt to be in need of reinvention, not least by its chief councillors. Its 'Court' had been established during the last great 'reinvention' of 1471–1540 – and since then, the world had changed around it. But reinventing the Stuart monarchy had consequences which were undeniably grave and wide. Between 1603 and 1688, there were successive attempts to make a late fifteenth-century monarchy fit for the seventeenth. It took much of the seventeenth century, and much spilt blood, for this to be achieved, and the attempts to change Crown and Court – by reform and by force, both the failures, and the successes – had momentous effects. This chapter argues that a survey of the Stuart Court and its functioning can provide a new, and more precise, way of gauging the shape and flow of this turbulent period. The approach adopted here supplements the picture of the Stuart monarchy gained from the study of constitutional abstractions, or indeed from analysis of the theoretical machinery of governmental 'institutions', with a view of what the monarchy was as it was embodied in the Court – an identifiable collection of flesh and blood people, acting in a real setting of bricks and mortar. The history of what the Court was, and how it functioned, how it failed to change, and then did change, in the seventeenth century, offers an important key to understanding the politics, and the leading issues, of a century that can fairly be characterised as a prolonged crisis of the monarchy.[1]

This chapter seeks to clarify what the Stuart Court was, by examining over time its structure and political function – what it consisted of, how it was designed to work, how it did work. We examine in turn its three institutional components – Household, Chamber, and Bedchamber – and consider how they had come to be the way they were in 1603, what they had originally been designed to do, how effectively they were now doing those things, and how far contemporaries perceived a need, not just for reform to increase the Court's functional efficiency, but for deeper change, radically to alter its function.

This is not so simple an undertaking as it sounds, however, because previous work on society, politics, and the Court in this period has created two obstacles. Firstly, it has muddied the definition of the Court, by confounding abstract ideas and attitudes (both contemporary and modern) with its concrete structure. And second, it has discounted contemporary perceptions of what the Court was for. This has meant either concentrating on its 'modern' aspects, more familiar to the social sciences – particularly the Court as a simple 'job market', connecting the local elite to the central power – or making the modern assumption that the Court was merely 'dignified' or ornamental, with little discernible practical function at all. We must take a closer look at these two obstacles – first structure, then function – in order to clear them away.

Structural definitions of the Stuart Court have been as controversial as they have been diverse, and as abstract as they have been elastic. The Court stands at the centre of every major historiographical dispute about early modern England during the past fifty years, and not by accident: for argument about the Court's definition has been a major cause of these disagreements. In the 1950s and '60s, early Stuart historians began to use the terms 'court' and 'country' to describe opposed entities, social or political or moral or religious according to taste, which began to diverge early in the century (or perhaps late in Elizabeth's reign), causing a split in the English polity, governmental breakdown, and civil war.[2] The protagonists in the 'court–country debate' generated a variety of custom-made, and largely abstract, definitions of their 'courts', but nevertheless, by the 1970s the 'court–country' interpretation had become textbook orthodoxy.[3] At that point 'revisionists', above all Professor Conrad Russell, denied there was any such split, and wrote of an ideologically and socially all-embracing 'court' under the early Stuarts. But the 'revisionist' definition of 'the Court' was again purpose-built for elasticity: Russell's 'court' was interchangeable with the abstract term 'government'.[4] In the 1980s, 'post-revisionists' promptly reasserted that there was a court–country split: but their 'court' and 'country' were neither concrete institutional structures, nor even actual groupings of people, but rather subtle complexes of ideas and attitudes, responding to each other within the (largely unexamined) structures of central and local 'government'.[5] And if political historians have dealt in abstractions, it is no surprise to find historians of ideas and culture doing likewise. Professor Peck wrote recently of the 'Mental World' of a 'Jacobean Court' which was 'fluid and polycentric . . . it flowed back and forth from Whitehall Palace through to the West End of London where the nobility had their city palaces to the Inns of Court'; a definition which is perhaps not so much elastic as ectoplastic.[6]

By contrast to the chaos over the Court's structural definition, there has been near-unanimity about how it supposedly functioned (though not about how well). Every participant in the court–country debate applied the same functional test to the early Stuart Court: its efficiency in satisfying the ambitions of the local elite for reward and influence at the centre – in supplying the demands of a job market. However they defined it, their universal conclusion was that the Court was narrow and dangerously isolated.[7] In 1976 Professor Elton briskly dismissed the entire court–country debate, on the grounds that its participants had simply invented their definitions. Yet when Elton proceeded from his own clear structural definition of the Tudor Court, to examine how it functioned politically, he used exactly the same criterion – that of an elite job market. On these terms, Elton saw the Tudor Court as an effective 'point of contact' (along with Parliament and the Privy Council), until the rise of 'corruption' in the 1590s began a process of decline.[8] Early Stuart 'revisionism' used the same functional test. Indeed, it co-opted Elton's structure of Tudor politics, with its institutional 'points of contact' (Parliament, Council, and Court); but it ignored Elton's pessimism about the 1590s, and alleged that the Court of the early Stuarts functioned as effectively as that of the Tudors, to connect centre and locality, and contain ideological division, until the very eve of civil war – a verdict which took full advantage of Russell's highly elastic definition of the Court. 'Post-revisionists', on the whole uninterested in the functioning of concrete political structures, took issue with 'revisionism' rather in the field of ideas and attitudes, and have not dissented from this view of early Stuart centre–locality relations.[9]

Historians have made the second half of the seventeenth century rather less controversial than the first, but the consequence has been that the Court was, at least until recently, largely ignored. Partly this was due to the continuing influence of traditional 'constitutional' history, which dealt in the abstract powers of the Crown, Parliament, and so on. The point of this kind of history was to shuffle the monarchy off the political stage, and make it (and its powers) as abstract as possible; and the restoration of 1660 was traditionally seen as a major milestone in this process. In the late 1970s, John Miller's survey of 'The Later Stuart Monarchy' ignored the Court, covering instead its legal prerogatives, its relationship to local government and the judiciary, and its place in the legislature.[10] But in the last ten years, the influence of early Stuart 'revisionism' has crossed the century's great divide, and the structural 'points of contact' approach has been tried on for size under the later Stuarts.

The results have been mixed. Late Stuart revisionists have adopted the key prescription of early Stuart revisionism – that the Court was the central, continuing point of contact for the political nation, since Parliament was intermittent (an 'event' rather than an 'institution', in Russell's formulation), while the Privy Council, though significant, was a relatively small executive body. So attention has been drawn to the post-1660 Court as the centre of politics, the traditional importance of Parliament has been downgraded (as indeed has the significance of the Restoration itself) – and so generally, the differences between the pre- and post-Civil War monarchies (before 1688–9) have been minimised. Late Stuart revisionists have thus co-opted, at second hand, Elton's sixteenth-century structure of politics. But they have not adopted the rigour of his methods of analysis, with a familiar result: a continuing lack of clear structural definition of a 'court' that was cast in such a central role. Much more attention has been paid to the growth of parliamentary 'parties', one of which was increasingly (and confusingly) labelled a 'court' party after 1660, and to the growth of 'popular' politics, particularly in London. Attention has been drawn to the Court as the motor driving much of this: but how that motor worked, what its components were, and how it differed from and resembled the pre-war Court, have not seriously been addressed.[11]

The previous historiography has thus cast the Stuart Court in a central role, but has failed to draw its character – blocked repeatedly by the obstacles of confusing abstraction regarding the Court's structure, and by insufficient attention to contemporary ideas and assumptions regarding its function. The tools to remove these obstacles are already to hand, however, and have been deployed to great effect in the periods immediately preceding and succeeding 1603–88. Those tools were designed and used to obtain greater clarity about the Tudor Court, by Dr Starkey and Professor Elton; and they were used rigorously in Dr Bucholz's recent book on Queen Anne's Court.[12]

Chief among those tools is greater precision concerning the Court's definition. Bucholz's discussion of the uses of the word 'court' is indeed broadly applicable to the century and a half preceding his period. Contemporaries sometimes used the term 'court' to describe the permanent complex of palaces, government departments, and aristocratic town houses, in Westminster and the West End of London; to refer to a political grouping, primarily in Parliament (especially after 1660); to refer to a complex of attitudes, as post-revisionists have pointed out; or to describe ways of behaving ('court manners'). But when employed like this, the word was being used with the imprecision of general usage, or of the political outsider.[13] There was also a precise contemporary usage, however, employed by insiders, and arising directly from the institutional realities. 'The Court' was where the King was – at a palace, a royal hunting lodge, at one of his greater subjects' country seats, or even lodged at an inn or on board a ship. And by 1603, the 'institutional' structure of the royal Court proper was already long established as consisting of three divisions: the Household, under the Board of Greencloth; the Chamber, under the Lord Chamberlain; and the Bedchamber, under the Groom of the Stool-First Gentleman of the Bedchamber. It was the latter two departments, especially the Bedchamber, which invariably accompanied the King, for the Household operated at full strength only when the King was occupying one of his palaces, or (pre-1642) when formally 'on progress' during the summer months.[14]

It is important to be clear about the uniqueness of the royal Court proper, for at times the delegation of royal power could make the town or country house of a minister (a Salisbury, a Clarendon, a Danby), or of royal 'favourites' and mistresses (a Carr or a Buckingham, the Duchess of Portsmouth), resemble a court. The difference was, however, that the power at the disposal of such figures was always revocable, so that ultimately they themselves had to be courtiers, and constantly tend the root of their power at the Court proper. Queens and princes also inhabited what resembled, in structure though not in size or opulence, satellite 'courts': but even if those members of the royal family had a secure hold on the royal affection (which in fact they often did not), what they could offer independently to suitors was dwarfed by the patronage and power at the direct disposal of the monarch.

So it is with the Court proper – and its three components of Household, Chamber, and Bedchamber – that I deal here. And with this clear structure established, most of what follows is concerned with the Stuart Court's political functioning. How had it come to be the way it was in 1603, how did it change, and how did its political functions adapt, or fail to adapt, to changing circumstances?

THE HOUSEHOLD

The Household continued between 1603 and 1642 – as it had since its last major reorganisations of 1471 and 1526 – to supply traditional 'magnificence', in lavish feasting at about eighty communal 'tables', provided to the King's officers at his expense. The Board of Greencloth, presided over by the Lord Steward (only appointed between 1615–25, 1626–30, 1660–88), the Treasurer and Comptroller (the Steward's deputies during vacancies), the Cofferer, Masters of the Household, and so on, administered this enterprise, overseeing about twenty service departments (Kitchen, Larder, Buttery, Pantry, etc.), which employed directly and indirectly about 500 servants, and which provided and prepared the food. The Greencloth also enforced Purveyance, the royal prerogative to take up supplies at fixed (and, due to inflation, by now beneficially low) prices. This was probably the country's biggest single financial and logistical undertaking. Above all, it was certainly the largest single item of peacetime royal expenditure.[15]

In its origins, the royal Household had been identical to the greater nobility's households, but bigger – 'the house of houses principal of England', as Edward IV's ordinances termed it, 'requisite to be the mirror of others' according to Henry VIII's.[16] Broadly speaking, by the middle of the sixteenth century, this was still the case: king and nobles alike invested heavily in magnificent hospitality as a bond between themselves and their inferiors. But in the Elizabethan decades after 1560 the royal Household stood still, while noble households shrank, to become cheaper and more efficient.[17] England was also out of date compared to the much wealthier monarchy of France, which did not maintain tables, but instead paid courtiers dining expenses, or 'boardwages'.[18] By the 1600s the Household was something of a dinosaur, and its 'magnificence' was widely seen as anachronistic. Sir Thomas Challoner, the Governor of Prince Henry's Household, pointed the contrast in 1607, when the Prince was beginning to press for a more lavish establishment:

> In the Court, who taketh an oath to his Ma[jes]tie, he sweares to discharge his office onlie for the place whereunto he is assigned, whereas in other [noble] houses everie servant is deputed to such service as he is fit [for] or occasion requireth.

In addition to the flexibility which the absence of demarcation now gave the noble household, Challoner also regarded fees there as more realistic, tenure as less secure, and food far better – fixed diet lists did not have to be observed, so that the best and most reasonably priced produce could be bought in. In the first decades of the seventeenth century, Sir John Holles (the future Earl of Clare) reportedly thought that the traditional sort of household of 'magnificence', as run by his grandfather, had been simply an agency for putting money down the privy.[19]

It is against this background that we should set the major initiatives of James I's first years to rationalise the situation. For in this, as in so many other areas, the accession of the new king appeared to present a chance to break the freeze of forty-five years of Elizabethan conservatism. Immediately in 1603 plans were made to replace all but a handful of court tables with boardwages. Boardwages were annual cash sums which each officer would receive in lieu of his court 'table', and could spend as he chose (so, in effect, an augmentation of official salaries). Further proposals to implement boardwages came in 1605 and 1608, and in each case they were linked to, and followed by, an attempt in Parliament – in 1604, 1606, and again in 1610 – to exchange the right of Purveyance for a permanent, annual parliamentary tax. The two proposals were inseparable: since Purveyance was based on the right to take up supplies in kind to feed the Court, for the Court to stop actually serving food at tables would compromise its right; and it made no difference that in practice, since the 1590s most counties had compounded to be free of Purveyors with an annual cash sum, calculated to reflect the benefit to the Crown of its below-market prices. Accordingly, when the Commons refused to bargain for Purveyance in 1606, on the grounds that below-market prices were illegal according to medieval statute, the whole scheme for boardwages stalled.[20] The consistent chief architect of this plan, and of others for 'reinventing' the monarchy in these years, was Robert Cecil, 1st Earl of Salisbury. His most powerful English rivals on the Council, Ellesmere and Northampton, opposed all of his other plans for reinvention. But arch-conservatives as they were, they supported the abolition of the court tables. Northampton's secretary, Sir Robert Cotton, argued that the status quo in the Household was untenable, and that a choice now lay between two paths: either restore the full late medieval panoply of dining publicly in Court (he even proposed reviving the Hall, which had died out by the 1520s); or take a knife to the Household and substitute boardwages 'as France and Spayne doeth'. Ellesmere, otherwise a staunch upholder of the Crown's prerogatives, pointed with approval to the example of France, which under Henri IV had curtailed this antique display with precisely the mechanism of boardwages.[21]

Salisbury's greatest triumph during these negotiations came in July 1610, when he and his parliamentary allies put together a deal attractive enough to persuade the Commons to drop its stance that Purveyance was illegal, and include a bid for it in the draft Great Contract. Indeed, as this was finalised, the most important of Salisbury's Commons allies, Sir Edwin Sandys, explicitly urged the point of the change: it meant that the Household would now have to abolish the tables, to cut itself down to the much more modest expenditure levels of the – very much wealthier – French and Spanish courts, in order to run on what the Commons had offered; and Salisbury enthusiastically agreed with him.[22]

But Salisbury's triumph was brief. Later in 1610, the Great Contract failed; and it failed largely because the king reopened the deal and raised his demands to impossible levels. The explanation for this appears to be that, though James was willing at least to contemplate the radical rethink of the Household that Salisbury was advocating, his underlying attitude to this proposal, as to Salisbury's others, was one of suspicion: suspicion that was strengthened and confirmed by events.[23] When the financial stringency of 1605–6 had forced the suspension of the Household and James's retreat to the country with a skeleton entourage, a petitioner outlined the arch-traditional view which James came to adopt: isolated at Royston, James was now 'subiecte to his councell' and cut off from his poor subjects; while adopting a semi-private retinue, 'giv[ing] over . . . house keapinge' and hospitality, was yet more dishonourable – worsened by the prospect that he would permanently adopt boardwages.[24] Just before the 1610 sessions began, a paper by James to his Council discouraged any measures that might reduce the 'ancient orders and magnificence' of his Household below the levels of his predecessors.[25] Alienated by the attacks on his prerogatives in the 1604–10 and 1614 Parliaments, James made a virtue of the necessity of keeping the court tables, and became a self-conscious protector of English heritage. In 1614 came the first of his proclamations telling the nobility and gentry to do as he did, and keep hospitality in their households at home, instead of following 'a more private and delicate course of life, after the manner of foreine countreys', in London. Half a dozen more proclamations followed.[26] A ruler who had come to the throne amid great expectations of change and reform had settled within a decade into a conservative veneration for an aspect of 'old England' that had lost its function. And since Charles I's views on this were more extreme than those of his father, the missed chance of 1604–10 meant that 'magnificence' would persist until Charles I abandoned London in 1642. Purveyance was newly extended to the north of England. Indeed, as Kevin Sharpe has rightly emphasised, the 1630s saw comprehensive attempts to reimpose medieval standards of display and conspicuous consumption at Court, no longer to compete with other, noble, households, but now rather to exploit its difference from them, in order to make a point about tradition, hierarchy, order, and obedience. And with this assertion of the example at Court, a string of further proclamations in the 1630s told the gentry and nobility to go home, and practise the traditional English virtue of hospitality in the country.[27] The early Stuart kings had taken one of the two paths outlined earlier by Sir Robert Cotton – the road back to the late fifteenth century.

Cotton's other path had to wait until soon after the Restoration, and when it was taken, it marked a large caesura between the pre- and post-Interregnum courts. In 1660, the pre-war court tables, and the Household that supplied them, were fully revived (even though Purveyance was exchanged for a parliamentary revenue). But this revival soon proved as financially insupportable as it was functionally unjustifiable, and in 1663 all but a handful of tables, for above-stairs attendants on duty, were replaced with boardwages. The Greencloth now oversaw a mere staff canteen. The Household proper, its cost cut by two-thirds and its manpower by perhaps half, was no longer the largest item of peacetime expenditure. More than fifty years after James I's English Council had first united in proposing the measure, at last the monarchy had ceased to invest chiefly in magnificent hospitality as a means of confirming its political links with the nation.[28]

The immediate consequence was a tangible change of atmosphere and of function in the royal palaces. New ones, like Winchester and later Kensington, were considerably smaller; old ones like Whitehall used the space vacated by the Household to lodge more people without office. Resort to Court now became less a search for free meals, more a fashionable pastime for those who came.[29] One wider consequence was the removal of the most visible Household that had practised 'traditional' hospitality. As Dr Heal has shown, this in turn part caused and part coincided with a steepening and final decline in the idea that hospitality was a part of gentle behaviour, the rise of commercial houses of pleasure, and in the eighteenth century, of 'assembly rooms'.[30] For the Restoration monarchy itself, the result was a more efficient use of resources. After some arch-conservative doubts about the abandonment of traditional rights in the early years of the Restoration, James II as King cut still further into the Household budget.[31]

THE CHAMBER

The second department of the Stuart Court was the Chamber, under the Lord Chamberlain, Vice-Chamberlain, Gentlemen Ushers (Daily and Quarter Waiters, and of the Privy Chamber), and the Treasurer of the Chamber. The core of the department ran the 'public' Court of ceremony and display, a sequence of state apartments in each royal residence (and always improvised elsewhere), consisting of the Guard Chamber, Presence Chamber, and Privy Chamber. Here they regulated access. In addition, Guard and Presence, open to the gentry and above, each had a security force: the Yeomen of the Guard, under their captain (considerably augmented after 1660); and in the Presence, fifty Gentlemen Pensioners (attending in quarterly shifts), under a captain and a lieutenant.[32]

The chief function of the Chamber under the early Tudors had been to provide a focus for the royal retinue, by attaching substantial gentry to the Court as Gentlemen Pensioners and Gentlemen of the Privy Chamber. The latter had been of particular importance, monopolising as members of a separate department the King's 'private' body service, and sharing their close access only with the Privy Council.[33] But from 1553 to 1603, during the reigns of two women, the largely female Privy Chamber had joined the 'public', outer court, under the Lord Chamberlain, while the body service had gone to Ladies of the Bedchamber.[34]

The Privy Chamber was therefore reinvented in 1603: and the form it took seems to have been a response to circumstance, in particular the need to find somewhere to put the majority of James's Scottish Chamber (which already included some Englishmen), who were too important to discard, but not important enough to join the inner entourage of the Bedchamber which was also now set up as a full department. This new Privy Chamber did retain some of its former, distinctly private character. Access to it was formally restricted to its own staff of 4 Gentlemen Ushers, 48 Gentlemen (cut to 32 between 1610 and 1625), 4 Carvers, Cupbearers and Sewers (added about 1610 to serve at Privy Chamber dinners), and 8 Grooms – a quarter of whom attended at any one time – together with the Privy Council, some legal and administrative officers, and others named in an entrée list.[35] But this distinction declined progressively. In practice, by the early 1620s all peers and bishops also had Privy Chamber access; and Charles I's ordinances officially sanctioned this.[36]

Once again, the royal Chamber and Privy Chamber was a visible anomaly by the period 1603–42. Almost alone, it 'retained' substantial knights in this way. The greater nobility largely ceased to have substantial local gentry serving in their chambers by the 1590s. 'Be not served with kinsmen or friends, or men intreated to stay; for they expect much and do little', Burghley told his son. The nobility, but not the Crown, resorted instead to an emerging class of professional servants, a 'gentlemanly profession of serving men' as one pamphleteer put it. Thus a practice which in the first half of the sixteenth century had possessed a wide political resonance – the King was doing on a greater and more lavish scale what all noble magnates did anyway – had by the early seventeenth century become a curiosity.[37] Along with this decline in the wider meaning of the position went a decline in its value. Since the Gentlemen of the Privy Chamber had lost both their official fees, and their efficient duties – in body service (effectively in 1553, finally to the Bedchamber in 1603), and in serving at dinner (to specialists like the Cupbearers) – the attractions of the place for the locally important declined. There was one qualification to this trend under James I: throughout his reign, the Gentlemen of the Privy Chamber were split equally between Englishmen and Scotsmen, and from the start, the Scots half of the department (but not the English) received £200 pensions on the Exchequer to maintain them. By the 1620s these pensions were treated as belonging to the place. Both in James I's and Charles I's reigns, the Scots Privy Chamber gentlemen were usually more important than the English; a high proportion were kin or closely connected to the Scots nobility. But it is clear that the Scots magnates who invested in these places regarded them as a second best – for the Earl of Mar, it was a way to 'show willing' to the King, and defray the cost of his younger son's attendance until something more valuable and influential came up in the Bedchamber, where he needed a new reliable agent.[38] For the English, in the absence of pensions, by Charles I's reign what attraction lingered about a place that involved simply and literally waiting, not on, but for the King, was probably negative – the immunities it conveyed from taxation, arrest for debt, jury service, and local office, which were increasingly defined and enforced (and in some cases, sold for cash) in the 1630s.[39] By 1641, the Gentlemen proper shared these cheap favours with about 250 'extraordinary' Gentlemen, who did not even have to attend.[40]

The outer Chamber as a whole, under the Lord Chamberlain, remained mainly concerned with the performance of ceremony: processions to chapel, the reception of ambassadors, and so on. But this ceremony was by no means immemorial in its origin. The outer Chamber was very nearly abolished in the reign of Henry VIII as useless, since the Privy Chamber had usurped the body service and royal attendance which had formerly been its raison d'être.[41] It had survived instead by inertia, and was then found something to do under fifty years of female monarchy. Under James I and Charles I those invented traditions continued, and especially after 1625 were refined and elaborated.[42] Under James I, dining in the Privy Chamber became an important event to which spectators might be admitted. But James also revived the pre-Elizabethan practice of dining in state in the Presence on special occasions. Charles I continued and elaborated this. He revived the Elizabethan 'board of state' in the Presence, where an empty chair was served as though the monarch were sitting in it. And from 1630 to 1631 he also began to populate the Great Chamber, and even the Hall, with court tables, in conscious revival of the medieval and Henrician ordinances. The Treasurer of the Household was clearly unimpressed with the order to move his table to the Hall again, after perhaps three generations during which such court officers had eaten in their own lodgings. Since the Household and the tables had survived modernisation, Charles I determined to display them in all their antique magnificence.[43] But in all the 1630s' revival of antique ceremony seems to be a case of artificial respiration. In 1624 the Duchess of Lennox had set up a household on the royal model, with her train borne ceremonially, and whitestaves to regulate her proceeding: John Chamberlain dismissed it as 'apish imitation' taking 'state upon her . . . after the old manner . . . out of date long ago'. Such were the attitudes Charles I had to overcome in seeking to re-establish the social resonance of such practices. Some did follow the royal lead, either through imitation, or emulation: but they were responding to a deliberate royal attempt to make a fashion of what had become ridiculous.[44]

The Lord Chamberlain also controlled several offshoots: the offices of the Revels, Tents, Ceremonies, and Jewels (each under their respective Master), and of Works (under a Surveyor).[45] The masques, balls, dances, tilts, and receptions of ambassadors which they organised have received much attention from cultural historians. But one of the most perceptive of them, Dr Smuts, has put the comparative cost of these activities into perspective:[46] compared to the bill for everyday fine dining (where Shrove Tuesday was observed by simply placing a pancake on top of every meat dish), these activities represented a drop in the ocean, to the extent that they were not even budgeted for by the Household.[47] They did, however, represent a forum for the irregular court attendance of the King's subjects, both noble and gentle, who did not hold court places. This contact extended from great nobles like Shrewsbury or Derby at creation banquets, or processions to open Parliament, to the ability of a law student like Simonds D'Ewes to get a close look at Buckingham at a tilt in honour of a French ambassador in 1621, when they seem to have posed in a room near the tilt yard for what today would be a 'photo opportunity'.[48] The Lord Chamberlain could also appoint court lodgings. And, quite against traditional English practice, in the early seventeenth century this was extended at various times to several nobles without place, either as Councillors (who had no automatic right to lodge or dine at Court), or simply as a royal favour. This widening of the outer Court to include non-officed nobility, though, was always exceptional, and anyway seems to have petered out in the early 1620s. Charles I's insistence on following tradition appears to have ruled it out during the 1630s.[49]

The years 1660–1 saw the restoration of the entire Chamber establishment. All pretence was now abandoned that the Privy Chamber differed in status from the other outer Chambers, since its access was now formally open to 'any gentleman of good ranke and note'. Nevertheless the Privy Chamber's personnel regained their legal and fiscal immunities (which indeed would remain important into the next century).[50] The significance of these places in the Chamber and Privy Chamber remains to be properly assessed for Charles II's reign. Their original rationale, as a means of attaching 'retainers' to the royal dynasty, had long gone by now, but they remained of some use as a cheap source of patronage. The signs from the later courts of Anne and George I suggest that in particular, Privy Chamber immunities could be valuable. But they do not suggest that the significance of Chamber places was as great as simple pensions, and other more remunerative posts, in putting together a 'court' bloc in Parliament. Parliamentary management, in Danby's sense, probably depended more on pensions than Privy Chamber places.[51]

As for the ceremony of the Chamber in general, the restored Court underwent another clear-cut change. The Duke of Newcastle, in his arch-conservative advice to Charles II, had placed great importance on the need to retain ceremony at Court:

> when a nobleman hath so much seremoneye don unto him, whatt doth the people thinke the kinge is when theye see this Nobleman serve as Cupbearer off his knee, or S[ewer], or Carver uppon greate dayes, or uppon any daye to kiss his hande uppon his knee? . . . Sertenlye, S[i]r, this addes much to you, and gives Magistye a greate luster.[52]

But with the exception of the annual Garter feast, the pre-war round of display, including accession-day tilts, which Newcastle had wanted resurrected, was allowed to lapse. Much of the ceremonial of the Chamber had centred around conspicuous consumption at the court tables, which had now been abolished. Instead, the Court became a social focus which became more fully integrated with the London cultural market. 'There is a ball and a comedy every other day', said the French ambassador. There was thus little institutional attraction to the Court: rather, the Court joined the world of fashionable London. In forging a point of contact with the political elite, this may have compensated for the withering of its more traditional 'retaining' and ceremonial functions, but it was dependent on the tastes and force of personality of the monarch. And under James II, the Court seems to have lost this mode of attraction.[53]

THE BEDCHAMBER

The third sector of the Stuart Court, the Bedchamber, formed a 'private' inner sanctum at the end of, and protected by, the sequence of public chambers. Though closely based on Henry VIII's Privy Chamber (which had also been independent of the Lord Chamberlain's control), the Bedchamber was effectively a new department, set up in 1603 by James I's Bedchamber ordinances (which were confirmed, with very minor amendments, by subsequent monarchs up to the Hanoverians).[54] Its territory comprised the Withdrawing Chamber (next in sequence to the Privy Chamber), the Bedchamber itself, and the Privy Galleries and Lodgings, a complex of private apartments (libraries, closets, bathrooms and so on). Its personnel consisted of the Groom of the Stool-First Gentleman of the Bedchamber (head of department); 6, rising to 10, Gentlemen; the Gentleman of the Robes; the Keeper of the Privy Purse (usually one of the existing Gentlemen); 8 Grooms of the Bedchamber; and 6 Pages. The First Gentleman lodged closest to the King's Bedchamber, and the other Gentlemen and Grooms – depending on the palace or lodge – also had quarters in the Privy Lodgings. At night, one of the Gentlemen slept at the foot of the royal bed, while two Grooms slept in the Withdrawing Chamber. By day, the members of the Bedchamber dressed, fed, and constantly attended the King. Only the Bedchamber's staff enjoyed this close access as of right. All others had to ask for an audience, and the Withdrawing Chamber was set aside for this. Councillors and some other officers had a right to wait there, to be called in; audiences were often conducted there.[55]

The functions of this closest entourage, then, were ostensibly domestic; but for centuries, those who performed those duties, so close to the personification of royal power, had themselves been used by monarchs to wield that power. How significant were the political and administrative functions of the Stuart Bedchamber?

Here historiography looms again. The King's Chamber had been the continuing centre of finance and administration from the eleventh century to the sixteenth. It had repeatedly created departments – Exchequer, Chancery – which developed bureaucratic structures and became fixed in London ('went out of court'). Since the entourage remained throughout at the source of direct royal power, however, the medieval chamber had continued to rival and outflank the fixed departments, and in turn to spawn more 'national' offices which took root in London – the Wardrobe, 'the Chamber' as a financial department, the Privy Seal and Signet Offices.[56] But Professor Elton argued that a 'Tudor Revolution in Government' in the 1530s had finally broken the political power of the entourage. Allegedly, this 'revolution' permanently replaced 'government by the King', with 'government under the King', directed by the Secretary of State and Privy Council, running a new 'bureaucratic' machine; and so forever removed the potential for King and entourage to act as the mainspring of government. The Court had become a purely 'domestic' institution.[57] Recent work has overturned Elton's account of what actually happened in the 1530s, and indeed demonstrated that the cycle of going 'out of court' had merely repeated itself, with the Chamber being replaced by the Privy Chamber in administration and politics.[58] But the alleged longer-term consequence of Elton's 'revolution' – that after 1550 the monarch's ability to employ the entourage in politics and administration finally disappeared – has nevertheless survived without challenge.[59]

This has appeared a reasonable conclusion chiefly because of the accident of the late Tudor succession. For in many respects, Elizabeth's reign, with Privy Council and Secretary relegating a female entourage and Privy Chamber to a largely domestic role, does resemble Elton's view of government 'under', rather than directly 'by', the monarch. But on closer examination, it becomes apparent that to sustain his argument for the permanent effect of the 1530s 'revolution', Elton had to take as his yardstick of 'governmental' normality the unprecedented 45-year reign of an unmarried queen regnant, and then use this measure to write off most of the seventeenth century as anomalous.[60]

And, indeed, when Elton's view is tested against the seventeenth-century facts, it becomes clear that the apparent political decline of the late Tudor entourage is better explained as an accident of succession, rather than as the result of any permanent 'revolution in government'. In fact the English monarchy emerged from the sixteenth century with very little formal delegation of its direct power to shape policy and bestow patronage – much less delegation than the French or Spanish monarchies, for example, with their much more extensive formal conciliar structures.[61] Accordingly, under all the Stuart kings, as before during the reigns of adult and politically active male monarchs, the royal entourage – the Bedchamber – regained its central importance as the agency of royal freedom of action, and indeed as the direct instrument of what was arguably the century's central political issue: the royal prerogative.

Under James I, the Bedchamber's constant, private access gave its members a large role in patronage, administration, and politics. And James I exploited this to give himself freedom of action as against the dominance of the Elizabethan Council which he had inherited. A dual-centred politics, of entourage and council, emerged again from its long recess under the last three Tudors. Against unyielding conciliar and parliamentary opposition, James proclaimed Union through his Bedchamber, which until 1615 was, with a single exception, Scottish. The Bedchamber Scots gained massively from Crown patronage, and politically Dunbar was the prime figure among them. He had been James's chief minister in Scotland in the late 1590s and, until his death in 1611, continued to run Scotland for the King. After 1603–4, Dunbar supplied at once the Bedchamber foundation, and the most potent source of instability, for Salisbury's regime as conciliar chief minister in England.[62]

Salisbury countered with another aspect of his efforts to 'reinvent' the monarchy: a series of attempts in 1604–8, by means of administrative 'orders', to put the Council in charge of patronage, and relegate the Bedchamber to a purely 'private' role (indeed, he proposed putting the Bedchamber Scots on what we would call a 'civil list'). When this failed, in 1610 his Great Contract tried to cut off the problem at its source, by abolishing the sources of prerogative finance in which the Bedchamber dealt, and replacing those sources by statute with a regular, public revenue granted by Parliament. The collapse of the Great Contract marked the decisive end to Salisbury's main strategy.[63]

That led to comprehensive reaction by James, as the centre of gravity swung from the Privy Council to the successive Bedchamber favourites, Somerset (1611–15), and Buckingham (1615–28). Somerset was the first of James I's deliberate creations as Bedchamber favourite. His modest gentry roots were quite unlike those of earlier 'favourites' in Scotland. And as a Scotsman and mere gentleman, Somerset's deliberate elevation to an English earldom, one which had previously been bestowed only on members of the royal family, radically demonstrated both James's commitment to his native kingdom, and his view of his prerogative powers. Somerset was married into James's most trusted (and most ancient) English noble dynasty, the Howards; he formed a partnership with his father-in-law (Suffolk) as Lord Treasurer, bridging the power centres of Bedchamber and Council; and he shielded the King from direct management of patronage and politics.[64] Somerset's fall, and George Villiers's rise (to another royal earldom, and later dukedom, of Buckingham), brought into the department Villiers's kin and dependants, so that by 1622 the Bedchamber was split almost equally between English and Scots. And as the Howards also fell, the Villiers connection became by proxy the dynastic root of the House of Stuart among the English elite, as James I insisted that all aspirants to favour first show willing, by marrying into Buckingham's family. Indeed, as Dr Hibbard has discovered, Charles I continued marrying people into the Villiers clan during the 1630s. By then they were the equivalent of Elizabeth Tudor's cousinage, which had been so central to her regime.[65] From the Bedchamber, Buckingham dominated the informal financial and administrative machine, made and helped unmake conciliar ministers such as Bacon and Cranfield, and gave James the freedom of manoeuvre to retain his high-prerogative views, while still angling for what he could get from Parliament.[66]

Buckingham became still more powerful in Charles I's Bedchamber after 1625: he was made First Gentleman, in a department now composed of domestic retainers, and under-age royal kin (like Lennox and Hamilton). Buckingham's monopoly of close access, and the great power over counsel and administration that came with it, accounts for much of his acute unpopularity between 1625 and 1628. But after his assassination, the Bedchamber's active administrative and political role declined, largely because Charles I kept his distance even from his closest attendants. Successive Grooms of the Stool-First Gentlemen, Carlisle (1631–6) and Holland (1636–42), were important figures, but not the great powers that James I's favourites had been. Charles I had an English Privy Council which, at least until 1640, he did not need to bypass. Nevertheless, the Bedchamber was central to the patronage dealing that surrounded the further extension of prerogative finance in the 1630s. The handling of the Scots crisis after 1637 was almost wholly a Bedchamber affair, in the hands of Hamilton, Lennox, and Charles himself: with notoriously disastrous results.[67]

In 1660–1, the pre-war Bedchamber ordinances of James I and Charles I were recovered and re-enacted, and the Bedchamber set up anew. It was larger than before, with 12 (rising by 1682 to 17) Gentlemen, including supernumeraries, and 12 (rising to 18) Grooms.[68] Its political function revived, too, largely due to Charles II's propensity to pursue a 'secret' policy, at variance with that of his formal Privy Council. The phrase 'backstairs intrigue' entered the language. Indeed, Charles at once withdrew further into Bedchamber privacy, and gained greater freedom to act independently of his official ministers. By 1663 he had retreated to a new 'private' withdrawing chamber and bedchamber, some distance from the former Privy Lodgings at Whitehall, near the river (where the Bedchamber's staff continued to serve him). A private 'eating room' was set up here, to replace the now public (and physically distant) Privy Chamber. And with the King himself removed, the old Withdrawing Chamber extended its former function to become the central public audience chamber of the Court; while the old Bedchamber effectively became a 'State Bedchamber', for formal audiences, probably equipped with a balustrade or screen. All this followed the French model, which Charles had experienced first hand in exile.[69]

What did Charles II do with the freedom of action which this private distance gave him? Here the Bedchamber acts as a concrete indicator of the changes to the monarchy which the Restoration of 1660 made on paper, as it confirmed the legislation of 1641. For that legislation, and the changed basis of Crown finance at the Restoration, meant that prerogative finance was no longer the key area of initiative it had been for the early Stuart monarchs, nor the mainstay it had been for their Bedchambers. (Nevertheless, the signs are that Charles II's Bedchamber resumed its role as prime brokers and takers of the patronage which of course remained at the monarch's disposal.)[70]

Instead, it was rather in matters concerning the other extensive prerogatives still intact – religion and foreign policy – where Charles II used his Bedchamber to retain and exploit his freedom of action, in a series of attempts to escape from the Anglican 'stranglehold' on Council and Parliament which had been re-asserted, largely against his wishes, in 1660–2. Clarendon's difficulties, and in 1667 his fall, were partly due to his lack of control of the Bedchamber.[71] Historians have debated whether what replaced him was indeed a 'Cabal' ministry, a contemporary title taken from the initial letters of the ministry's supposed members. The acronym is plainly too neat to be an exact description of the realities of power, but there is an emerging consensus that, after the end of his tutelage to Clarendon, Charles II was in fact exercising personal control during this period of experimentation. And in this context, the Cabal's traditional composition does reflect two underlying realities: divide and rule on the King's part, playing off Catholic and Dissenter extremes against the now absent Anglican mainstream; and the entourage (source of royal favour) making alliances with the Treasury (source of cash). The Dissenters were represented by the 2nd Duke of Buckingham, Gentleman of the Bedchamber; while the Catholics were represented by Secretary Arlington, who (after beginning as

Keeper of the Privy Purse himself in 1661–2) had subordinate Bedchamber agents. Buckingham and Arlington indeed attempted to secure their Bedchamber power by promoting rival royal mistresses – the former, Nell Gwyn, the self-proclaimed 'Protestant whore'; the latter, the Duchess of Portsmouth, who would only admit to being a Catholic. And they each had a contact at the Treasury: Arlington had Clifford; Buckingham, Ashley Cooper.[72] (Lauderdale, the acronym's last element, ran Scotland as Gentleman of the Bedchamber, as had James I's Dunbar.) Having divided, Charles ruled for the Catholic option, the Secret Treaty of Dover, the 1672 Declaration of Indulgence – and the ensuing debacle of the Dutch War.

The result was the rise of the 'Anglican' parliamentary manager Danby in 1673. His rise, however, coincided with revised Bedchamber ordinances, which for the first time explicitly took account of the earlier changes in palace geography, with the introduction of a State Bedchamber, and buttressed Charles's withdrawal. For all his parliamentary efforts, Danby had constantly to deal with the King's propensity to pursue other polices – particularly the alternative of subsidies from Louis XIV – by 'backstairs', or Bedchamber, means.[73] The Popish Plot scare and Exclusion crisis of 1678–81 resulted in both a tightening of Bedchamber security, and a further disjunction of Charles's 'backstairs' policies from those of his formal Council. The real powerlessness of the Council became wholly evident in 1679, when it was revamped with the King's chief anti-Catholic opponent, Shaftesbury, as President.[74] Charles's retreat culminated, in 1682–5, in another move to new lodgings at Whitehall, more restrictions on access, a further tightening of Bedchamber attendance, and the first Stuart years without a parliament since Charles I's reign.[75]

James II confirmed these changes, but made a significant new departure in immediately allowing the Privy Council Foreign Affairs Committee to attend in the State Bedchamber. That eroded the distance between the traditional spheres of 'public' and 'private', both in access and politics – and gave an ominous sign that under James II, Charles II's usually 'hidden agenda', of Catholic and Dissenter toleration, would remain hidden no longer.[76]

CONCLUSIONS

How then are we to assess the political functioning of these successive Stuart courts? In all, three points stand out. The first is the scope of Salisbury's attempt to 'reinvent' the English monarchy in the first Parliament of James I, on a new financial, institutional, and political basis. And in this period of attempted change, it is debatable which is the most remarkable feature. On one hand there is the vision of Salisbury's solutions, which not only sought to address the long-term decline in the Crown's land revenue by putting the finances on a public, parliamentary footing, but also proposed to gut the Household below stairs, abolish the 'ancient orders and magnificence' which there alone had survived the sixteenth century and, in addition, take away the King's means to govern through prerogative finance and the Bedchamber. On the other hand there is James I's eventually successful insistence on retaining the Tudor Court, along with the Tudor fiscal prerogatives, as frozen in the middle of the previous century, with two additions: a curious (and functionally highly questionable) reinvented Privy Chamber, and an exploitation of his Bedchamber for administration, patronage and finance without close parallel since the great 'Age of the Household' in the fourteenth century. Charles I's exploitation of this court structure went hand in hand with his exploitation of these prerogative rights; indeed, this was a king who was asked for advice on etiquette by his own Master of Ceremonies, and whose revival of 'ancient orders' at Court was only one aspect of a broader return to medieval precedent – in finance, in the form of the Council, in his view of the nobility, in the ordering of the Church of England under Laud, and so on.[77]

The second point is the extent to which the Restoration, together with the changes of 1663, broke decisively with the past, and changed the Stuart Court's structure and function. It abolished traditional 'magnificent' hospitality in the Household, drastically curtailed the ceremonial of the Chamber and, in putting the revenues of the monarchy on a wholly parliamentary footing, removed extra-parliamentary prerogative finance as an option – confining the potential for royal initiative through the Bedchamber to the fields of religion and foreign policy. But if the Court of the Restoration monarchy had been reinvented, did that make it once more the key 'point of contact', the main national forum for the successful maintenance of 'social stability', which Professor Elton claimed the Tudor Court had been, and which some late Stuart revisionists have recently argued? The answer suggested by this brief survey is that it did not. Certainly, the court of Charles II and James II, unlike that of James I and Charles I, was no longer essentially the court invented at the turn of the fifteenth century; but neither was it the keystone of politics which the courts of Henry VIII and Elizabeth I had been.

The Restoration was followed by three decades during which Parliament was centrally important, and nearly ever-present. Even during Charles II's period of experimentation, between 1668 and 1673, the real influence of Buckingham or Arlington – Bedchamber favour notwithstanding – hinged on their claims to be able to manage Parliament. In the 1670s and 1680s, the Secret Treaty led on to a more radical strategy, of French subsidies as an alternative to Parliament: and it caused much suspicion. But the domestic impact of this was much shallower than the alternative fiscal prerogatives resorted to by the early Stuarts. James II, of course, attempted to implement his strategies by manipulating Parliament, not by doing without it. Indeed, the actual work produced by late Stuart 'revisionism', as distinct from the polemical stress it has placed on the Court at the expense of

Parliament, emphasises the point: this work centres on Parliament, and the growth of 'court' and 'country', and later 'Whig' and 'Tory' parties there. The remaining prerogatives – over religion and foreign policy – were certainly exercised directly by the late Stuart kings through their courts, and in an important sense, this was a driving force behind the wider politics of the growth of 'party'.[78] But the centre of political gravity had shifted. Parliament was now central, and the option to rule solely through the Court, and the prerogative, had been removed in 1660–3.

A third conclusion follows. There is a close resemblance between what was achieved by the Restoration, and the proposals of the Great Contract fifty years earlier. If the Contract was thus vindicated by the future, does this mean that the intervening decades were an exercise in futility, and that the Court which Salisbury failed to reform was dysfunctional? 'Revisionism' has warned against the use of hindsight, most urgently against allowing the collapse of 1640–2 to colour our view of the preceding regime, and so has argued that doing without Parliament was a viable option for James I and Charles I. But in doing so, it has scarcely considered the Great Contract.[79] This chapter has suggested that as the Stuart century dawned, it was already very clear that the Court and monarchy as it stood had to change. This judgement is not simply based on hindsight, as if to take the Restoration settlement as normative. Nor does it simply accept the Earl of Salisbury's analysis at face value. For during James I's first decade, Salisbury's conciliar opponents also believed that the current situation was untenable. For all its vision, the Great Contract must also be seen as the culmination of Salisbury's campaign to stop a group of conservative Councillors from persuading James I to change the status quo in another direction – to use the fiscal prerogative, through Court and Council, to restore and maintain the finances, independent of Parliament. If 'absolutism' means anything, their strategies added up to 'absolutism'. Fully implemented, and given time to take effect, their exploitation of the fiscal and legal prerogative would have given England – indeed Britain – a polity parallel to that of Bourbon France, with its taxation based on the prerogative, its extensive local bureaucracy which had bought in to and had an interest in exploiting, the franchised legal and fiscal prerogative of the central power, its system of legal and fiscal exemptions for the Court and higher nobility, and the replacement of any formal national consultative body by Court and Council, which could then play off regional and sectional interests.

After the Contract's failure, this alternative strategy was implemented at the Stuart Court more or less consistently for thirty years.[80] But, regardless of how viable a path it may have been, the next chance to block it was seized in 1641. 'Revisionists' have placed great emphasis on the unpredictability of that concatenation of events, in Scotland and England, which in 1637–40 rendered Charles I powerless and allowed this to happen: but however fortuitous the occasion, the way in which it was exploited, and indeed those who exploited it, looked directly back to what Salisbury had stood for in 1610.[81] John Miller concluded that the 'potential for absolutism' under the later Stuart monarchy was in fact negligible and, though his criteria differ from those used here, the judgement is in general terms accurate. The Great Contract had tried to remove that potential in 1610, and it was not accidental that the Restoration of 1660–3, in confirming the legislation of 1641, achieved what the Contract had attempted.[82]

In 1642, the author of *A Deep Sigh Breathed through the Lodgings at Whitehall* painted a vivid outsider's picture of the Court that had existed there, and was now suddenly gone. He described a vanished world of fashion – gallants eyeing women's 'handsome legs' as they took coach at the Court Gate, young men in the Court Yard showing off the latest French 'cringes', perfumed lodgings for lords. He lamented a vanished world of magnificence – creditors queuing for the Greencloth with unpaid bills, the noise of angry cooks in the kitchen, the press at the wine-cellar door, provisions on clandestine sale in the Hall, Beefeaters carrying in the King's dinner. And more seriously, he recalled, outside the Privy Lodgings at the entrance to the Council Chamber, the vanished 'exchange of projectors . . . where the attendants upon the Councell table were wont to coole their toes, and by their whispering consultations digest every trade into the forme of monopolies, and invent arguments of the kingdom's good and his Majestie's benefit to put forward the same'.[83]

After 1660–3, of course, Charles II's Court brought back the handsome legs, the French fashions, and still more perfumed lodgings; but it had dispensed with costly magnificence, and instead of the notorious press of monopolists at the entrance to the Privy Lodgings, there were furtive interviews, via the backstairs, about religious toleration, or French subsidies. This was the world with which later Stuart monarchs and their courts dealt in 1660–88, and in both structure and function it bears little resemblance to the world in which James I and Charles I operated.

Notes

1. Since this essay was written, the new Penguin History of this period has appeared: M. Kishlansky, *A Monarchy Transformed: Britain, 1603–1714* (London, 1996) – which, as its title indicates, takes this as the period's connecting theme.

2. R.H. Tawney, 'The Rise of the Gentry, 1558–1640', *Economic History Review*, XI (1941), 1–38; H.R. Trevor-Roper, 'The Gentry, 1540–1640', *Economic History Review Supplement*, I (1953); and 'The General Crisis of the Seventeenth Century', in T. Aston (ed.), *The General Crisis of the Seventeenth Century* (London, 1965); P. Zagorin, *The Court and the Country: the Beginning of the English Revolution* (New York, 1969).

3. L. Stone, *The Causes of the English Revolution* (London, 1972); R. Ashton, *The English Civil War* (London, 1979).

4. C. Russell, 'Parliamentary History in Perspective, 1604–1629', *History*, 61 (1976); *Parliaments*; D. Hirst, 'Court, Country, and Politics before 1629', K. Sharpe, 'Introduction: Parliamentary History

1603–1629: In or Out of Perspective?', and 'The Earl of Arundel, his Circle, and the Opposition to the Duke of Buckingham, 1618–28', all three in K. Sharpe (ed.), *Faction and Parliament: Essays on Early Stuart History* (Oxford, 1978).

5. R. Cust, *The Forced Loan and English Politics, 1626–28* (Oxford, 1987); A. Hughes, *The Causes of the English Civil War* (London, 1991); R. Cust and A. Hughes (eds), *Conflict in Early Stuart England* (London, 1989).

6. Peck, *Mental World*, p. 3.

7. See the works cited in n. 2 above, esp. Zagorin's definition (*The Court and the Country*, p. 41).

8. G.R. Elton, 'Tudor Government: the Points of Contact', in his *Studies in Tudor and Stuart Politics and Government* (4 vols, Cambridge, 1974–92), Vol. III, pp. 3–57, esp. Part iii, 'The Court', pp. 38–57. Cf. also the same functional criterion used by W. MacCaffery, 'Place and Patronage in Elizabethan Politics', in S. Bindoff, J. Hurstfield, and C. Williams (eds), *Elizabethan Government and Society* (London, 1961), pp. 95–126, and by P. Williams, 'Court and Polity under Elizabeth I', *Bulletin of the John Rylands Library*, 65 (1983), 259–86.

9. Russell, *Parliament*, pp. 10 ff., and n. 3 above; Hughes, *Causes of the English Civil War*, ch. 2, and n. 4 above.

10. J. Miller, 'The Later Stuart Monarchy', in J.R. Jones (ed.), *The Restored Monarchy, 1660–1688* (London, 1979), pp. 30–47.

11. T. Harris, 'From Rage of Party to Age of Oligarchy? Rethinking the Later Stuart and Hanoverian Period', *Journal of Modern History*, 64 (1992), 700–20; *idem*, *Politics under the Later Stuarts: Party Conflict in a Divided Society, 1660–1715* (1993); T. Harris, P. Seaward, and M. Goldie (eds), *The Politics of Religion in Restoration England* (Oxford, 1990); P. Seaward, *The Cavalier Parliament and the Reconstruction of the Old Regime, 1661–1667* (Cambridge, 1989).

12. Elton, 'Tudor Government: the Points of Contact; iii, The Court', drawing largely on D. Starkey, 'The King's Privy Chamber, 1485–1547' (unpublished Cambridge Ph.D. thesis, 1973). See also D. Starkey, 'Representation through Intimacy', in I.M. Lewis (ed.), *Symbols and Sentiments* (1977); and D. Starkey, 'The Age of the Household, *c.* 1350–1550', in S. Medcalf (ed.), *The Later Middle Ages* (London, 1981).

13. Bucholz, *Augustan Court*, esp. pp. 2–3.

14. Elton's definition, employed by Starkey et al., and also by S. Thurley, *The Royal Palaces of Tudor England* (New Haven, 1994). Cf. a dictionary definition of 1617: 'Court with us signifieth diversely, as the house where presently the King remaineth with his ordinarie retinue, and also the place where iustice is iudicially administered.' John Minsheu, *Doctor in Linguas, The Guide into Tongues* (London, 1617; facsimile reprint, New York, 1978), p. 103.

15. Aylmer, *King's Servants*, pp. 26 ff., 472.

16. Starkey, 'Age of the Household', p. 225; Eltham Ordinances, 1526, in *A Collection of Ordinances and Regulations for the Royal Household*, printed for the Society of Antiquaries (London, 1790), p. 146.

17. L. Stone, *The Crisis of the Aristocracy, 1558–1641* (Oxford, 1965), pp. 555 ff. on dining, and 207–17 on reduction in numbers of servants; K. Mertes, *The English Noble Household, 1250–1600* (Oxford, 1988), *passim*, and esp. pp. 187–93.

18. Jean Francois Solnon, *La Cour de France* (Paris, 1987); below, n. 21.

19. PRO, LS13/280, ff. 307r–308r; Gervase Holles, *Memorials of the Holles Family, 1493–1656*, ed. A.C. Wood (Camden Society, 3rd Series, 55, 1937), pp. 41–2. Both Challoner and Holles were close political allies of the Earl of Salisbury: Holles was indeed directly involved in the latter's parliamentary schemes (culminating in the Great Contract of 1610) for abolishing both Purveyance and the court tables, for which see below.

20. P. Croft, 'Parliament, Purveyance, and the City of London, 1589–1608', *Parliamentary History*, 4 (1985), 12–13, 15; E. Lindquist, 'The King, the People and the House of Commons: the Problem of Early Jacobean Purveyance', *HJ*, 31 (1988), 557–9 and n. 56; P.R. Seddon, 'Household Reforms in the Reign of James I', *Bulletin of the Institute of Historical Research*, 53 (1980), 45–6.

21. British Library, Cotton MS Cleopatra FVI, f. 42r, 1612; Huntington Library MS EL 1216, ff. 1r, 2r, c, 1610–15.

22. E.R. Foster, *Proceedings in Parliament, 1610* (2 vols, New Haven, 1966), Vol. 1, pp. 140–3.

23. N. Cuddy, 'The Divided Loyalties of a "Vulger Counselor": the 3rd Earl of Southampton, 1597–1624', in J. Morrill, P. Slack, D. Woolf (eds), *Public Duty and Private Conscience: Essays in Honour of Gerald Aylmer* (Oxford, 1993), pp. 134–9.

24. PRO, SP14/19/47, Anon. to James, *c.* 14 March 1606.

25. P. Croft (ed.), 'A Collection of . . . Treatises . . . of Cecil . . .' (Camden Society, 4th Series, 34, Misc. XXIX, 1987), § V, pp. 296–8, and n. 132, 12 January 1610; § II, pp. 278–80, heads of Salisbury's proposals, perhaps relating to the same meeting.

26. F. Heal, 'The Crown, the Gentry, and London: the Enforcement of Proclamation, 1596–1640', in C. Cross et al. (eds), *Law and Government under the Tudors* (Cambridge, 1988), esp. pp. 213–14. Earlier proclamations of 1603 and 1608 had followed Elizabethan formulae; 'from 1614 onwards, however, new themes and an elaborated rhetoric begin to inform the proclamations', which were penned by James himself.

27. Sharpe, *Personal Rule*, pp. 111, 216–17; Heal, 'Enforcement of Proclamation', pp. 221–5. Following the royal example was indeed the point of the exercise: Charles I's ordinances began with the professed aim 'to establish government and order in our Court, which from thence may spread with more honour through all partes of our kingdomes' (PRO, LC5/180 (and an exact copy of this book in PRO, SP16/375/2), p. 1).

28. J.M. Beattie, *The English Court in the Reign of George I* (Cambridge, 1967), pp. 66–98, esp. p. 85 and n. 4. Bucholz, *Augustan Court*, pp. 12–22, esp. pp. 18–20, appears to miss the significance of this major change, perhaps due to the apparent continuity in the size of the Household budget caused by boardwages (cf. his tables 1.1, 1.2). Household expenditure ostensibly remained high, since the boardwages – in effect the increment which brought a whole range of official salaries back in line with inflation, for the first time since 1539 – were paid by the Greencloth. The significance of the 1663 changes is confirmed below by Andrew Barclay's 'Charles II's failed Restoration', pp. 158–70.

29. Colvin, *King's Works*, Vol. V, pp. 183 ff., 304 ff. (on Kensington, a private house taken over and adapted after 1690, and Winchester). A comparison with the work required to fit up Theobalds as a royal palace after 1607 (op. cit., Vol. IV, pp. 273 ff.), is revealing: almost all the work done there was on additions to accommodate the royal Household below stairs, which the original owner (Salisbury) had of course not needed.

30. F. Heal, *Hospitality in Early Modern England* (Oxford, 1990), esp. ch. 10; J. Rosenheim, 'Landownership, the Aristocracy and the Country Gentry', in L. Glassey (ed.), *The Reigns of Charles II and James VII & II* (London, 1997), pp. 152–70.

31. A. Barclay, 'The Impact of King James II on the Departments of the Royal Household' (unpublished Cambridge Ph.D. thesis, 1993), pp. 59–97.

32. Cuddy and Sharpe in Starkey, *English Court*; Aylmer, *King's Servants*, pp. 26–32, 473.

33. Starkey, 'The Age of the Household', and his 'Intimacy and Innovation', in *The English Court* (together with the piece by David Morgan there) stress the retaining function of royal and noble households, in the fifteenth century and under the early Tudors.

34. P. Wright, 'A Change in Direction: The Ramifications of a Female Household, 1558–1603', in Starkey, *English Court*.

35. Cuddy in Starkey, *English Court*, pp. 174–5, 183–4.

36. PRO, SP14/119/99, Locke to Carleton, 16 February 1621; PRO, LC5/180, p. 22, Charles I's collected Chamber orders, datable post-January 1631 (cf. Chapel orders, pp. 16–21, which amend PRO, SP16/182/31, dated 9 January 1631).

37. Starkey, 'Age of the Household', *passim*, and 'Introduction: Court History in Perspective', in *English Court*, pp. 22–4; Stone, *Crisis of the Aristocracy*, chs 5, 10; Mertes, *English Noble Household*, esp. pp. 183–93; A. Cecil, *A Life of Robert Cecil* (London, 1915), p. 10.

38. N. Cuddy, 'The King's Chambers: The Bedchamber of James I in Administration and Politics, 1603–25' (unpublished Oxford D.Phil. dissertation, 1987), pp. 25–9; PRO, SP15/40/28, November–December 1614, and PRO, SP16/2/118, May 1625 Privy Chamber lists; Historical Manuscripts Commission, *Mar & Kellie Supplement*, pp. 127, 148, 194–5.

39. PRO, LC5/134 shows these immunities being worked out, formalised, and at times sold, after 1636; for example, pp. 97, 146, 172, 199, 301, 431, 448, 452. These schemes were directly following French practice: Solnon, *La Cour de France*, p. 47.

40. PRO, LC 3/1, 1641 Establishment list.

41. Starkey, in *English Court*, pp. 106, 115. Cf. G.R. Elton, *Reform and Reformation* (London, 1977), pp. 219–20.

42. For example, James I's Chapel orders, BL Additional MS 34,324, f. 215, 1 January 1623 (reported in N.E. McLure (ed.), *The Letters of John Chamberlain* (2 vols, Philadelphia, 1939), Vol. II, p. 470); re-enacted and refined by Charles I in January 1631, PRO, SP16/182/31; and further refined when included in Charles I's collected ordinances, PRO, LC5/180.

43. *CSPV*, X (*1603–7*), p. 46, 12 June 1603; *Letters of Chamberlain*, Vol. I, p. 251, 5 January 1608; E.K. Chambers, *The Elizabethan Stage* (4 vols, Oxford, 1923), Vol. I, p. 15; PRO, LS13/169, p. 221, April 1633 on the Board of State; Sharpe, *Personal Rule*, p. 217; PRO, SP16/204/80, 20 December 1631.

44. *Letters of Chamberlain*, Vol. II, p. 594. J. Adamson, 'Chivalry and Political Culture in Caroline England', in K. Sharpe and P. Lake (eds), *Culture and Politics in Early Stuart England* (London, 1994), esp. pp. 165–170, shows clearly the depths to which 'chivalry' had sunk by the late 1620s, and why Charles I needed to revive and refine it.

45. Aylmer, *King's Servants*, p. 473.

46. R.M. Smuts, *Court Culture and the Formation of a Royalist Tradition in Early Stuart England* (Philadelphia, 1987), ch. 5.

47. Kent Archive Office, Maidstone, Cranfield Papers (U269/1) OW 154 (old no. 4808), *c.* 1618, list of items not covered by the official Household ordinances, including lights and fuel at masques, plays, and dancing, St George's feast, installation feasts at Windsor, feasting of visiting princes and ambassadors, special banquets for festivals, for Shrove Tuesday 'everie dish of meat covered with a pancake'.

48. J.O. Halliwell (ed.), *The Autobiography and Correspondence of Sir Simonds D'Ewes* (2 vols, London, 1845), Vol. I, pp. 166–7; cf. p. 92, D'Ewes standing 'very near the Prince's chair' at his creation dinner as Prince, and so getting another close look at Villiers in November 1616.

49. BL Egerton MS 2026, f. 23r, Lodgings at Court 1601–2, shows no anomalies. PRO, LS13/168, ff. 312r, 102r, 124r, 158r, 198v, 227v. Cf. *CSPV*, xi (1607–10), 206, December 1608. PRO, LS13/30, 1627 Household book, and PRO, LS13/279, pp. 180–1, January 1627, show no such anomalies as under James I.

50. Cf. petitions for restoration to office, detailing duties, in *CSPD* 1660–2; for example, PRO, SP29/6/197–8, Gent Ushers Daily Waiters, Yeomen Ushers; BL Stowe MS 561, ff. 3–10, description of Gent Ushers Daily Waiters' duties, put to the Lords Commissioners, 1661; *A Collection of Ordinances and Regulations for the Royal Household*, printed for the Society of Antiquaries (London, 1790), Charles II's collected Ordinances, pp. 352 ff., at p. 361.

51. Beattie, *English Court in the Reign of George I*, pp. 30–5; Bucholz, *Augustan Court*, pp. 188–201 – but cf. p. 196 for an MP 'risking his place in the Privy Chamber' by voting against a government line.

52. 'The Duke of Newcastle on Government', in S.A. Strong (ed.), *A Catalogue of Letters . . . at Welbeck* (London, 1903), p. 213.

53. Bucholz, *Augustan Court*, pp. 12–26.

54. Nottingham University Library MS PwV 92, Charles II's Bedchamber Orders of 30 April 1661: ff. 1v–2v, warrants claiming they were drawn from those of Carlisle (Groom of the Stool to Charles I, 1631–6) and Kelly (Groom of the Stool to James I, 1603–25), which in 1661 were put in the care of Thomas Chiffinch, Keeper of the Closet. By 1683, these 'fundamentall orders of the Bedchamber' had been lost (for example, PRO, SP29/423/68), and remain so to date. The Bedchamber ordinances of James II (Oxfordshire County Record Office, MS Dil. xx/a/2) and of William III (BL Stowe MS 563) are broadly similar to those of 1661. Beattie, *English Court in the Reign of George I*, pp. 11, 54, n. 3.

55. Cuddy in Starkey, *English Court*, pp. 185–91.

56. T.F. Tout, *Chapters in Medieval Administrative History* (6 vols, Manchester, 1920–37).

57. G.R. Elton, *The Tudor Revolution in Government* (Cambridge, 1953); *idem*, 'A Revolution in Tudor History', *Past and Present*, 32 (1965), 106.

58. C. Coleman and D. Starkey (eds), *Revolution Reassessed: Revisions in the History of Tudor Government and Administration* (Oxford, 1986), esp. p. 6, and chs 2, 3; D. Starkey, 'Court, Council and Nobility in Tudor England', in R.G. Asch and A.M. Birke (eds), *Princes, Patronage, and the Nobility: the Court at the Beginning of the Modern Age, c. 1450–1650* (Oxford, 1991).

59. Coleman and Starkey (eds), *Revolution Reassessed*, esp. p. 5, does not deal with the longer-term view examined here. The 'household's' alleged political demise after 1550 was undisputed in the 1960s controversy: P. Williams, 'The Tudor State', *Past and Present*, 25 (1963), 52, 55–6; G.L. Harriss, 'A Revolution in Tudor History?', *Past and Present*, 31 (1965), 92; P. Williams, *The Tudor Regime* (Oxford, 1979), p. 52. For the wider influence of this view, cf. Aylmer, *King's Servants*, pp. 15,

26, 27, and ch. 7, section 1; L. Peck, *Northampton* (London, 1982), p. 215; Beattie, *English Court in the Reign of George I*, pp. 1–2.

60. P. Wright, 'A Change of Direction . . . 1558–1603', in Starkey, *English Court.* Elton simply ignored both 1603–28 and the period after 1660: 'neither Elizabeth in 1558 nor Charles I after Buckingham's death showed the slightest sign of going back to the chamber or other private means of administration': Elton, 'The Tudor Revolution: A Reply', *Past and Present*, 29 (1964), 47, and cf. Elton's *Tudor Revolution in Government*, p. 186.

61. Starkey, 'Introduction; Court History in Perspective', in Starkey, *English Court*, pp. 11–21; R. Stradling, *Philip IV and the Government of Spain, 1621–65* (Cambridge, 1988), esp. pp. 22–32; R. Doucet, *Les Institutions de la France au XVIème Siècle* (2 vols, Paris, 1948).

62. Cuddy in Starkey, *English Court*, pp. 174–7, 195–209; *idem*, 'The Divided Loyalties of a "Vulger Counselor": the 3rd Earl of Southampton, 1597–1624', in Morrill et al. (eds), *Public Duty and Private Conscience* (Oxford, 1993), pp. 125–9.

63. Ibid., pp. 130, 134–8. The contents of these orders (September 1607, January and October 1608, published 'Book of Bounty' January 1611) all closely resemble the Great Contract proposals.

64. GEC, s.v. Somerset; Northampton's comments on the choice of this title, Cambridge University Library MS Dd.3.63, ff. 54r–v, imply Buckingham was also mooted as a possible title for Carr in 1613.

65. GEC, s.v. Buckingham; Caroline Hibbard, 'The Theatre of Dynasty', in Smuts, *Stuart Court*, pp. 170–4.

66. R. Lockyer, *Buckingham*, Part I; Cuddy in Starkey, *English Court*, pp. 214–25.

67. See the essay by Asch on monopolies and patronage in the 1630s, in R.G. Asch and A.M. Birke (eds), *Princes, Patronage, and the Nobility: the Court at the Beginning of the Modern Age,* c. *1450–1650* (Oxford, 1991); P. Donald, *An Uncounselled King: Charles I and the Scottish Troubles, 1637–1641* (Cambridge, 1990).

68. Above, n. 54. According to the warrants at the start of the 1661 ordinances, Lucy, Countess Dowager of Carlisle, had kept Kelly's and Carlisle's books since her husband's death in 1636, and in 1661 delivered them into royal custody. Nottingham University Library MS PwV 93, 1673 Bedchamber orders, has departmental lists at the back for 1660, 1661, 1673, 1678, 1682, from which these numbers are taken.

69. Colvin, *King's Works*, Vol. V, pp. 266–70: in 1667–8 the 1663 Bedchamber in the Turk's Gallery at Whitehall was replaced by new lodgings and a Bedchamber 'by the waterside'. Cf. the plan in R. Latham (ed.), *The Shorter Pepys* (Harmondsworth, 1987), pp. 1036–7, and account and plan in M. Girouard, *Windsor* (London, 1993), pp. 49–54. The Withdrawing Chamber was later enlarged still further, to lend its name to a regular event, the 'Drawing Room', in which Anne and the Hanoverians met their invited subjects.

70. Nancy Klein Maguire, 'The Duchess of Portsmouth: English Royal Consort and French Politician, 1670–85', in Smuts, *Stuart Court*, pp. 247–73; Sonya Wynne, 'The Mistresses of Charles II and Restoration Court Politics', and G.E. Aylmer, 'Patronage at the Court of Charles II' below in this volume, pp. 171–90 and 191–202; Bucholz, *Augustan Court*, pp. 14–15 and nn. on pp. 280–1.

71. R. Hutton, *The Restoration* (Oxford, 1985), Part III, ch. 3, and *idem*, *Charles II, King of England, Scotland and Ireland* (Oxford, 1989), ch. 9, downplays Bedchamber influence: Aylmer, 'Patronage at the Court of Charles II', asserts it below.

72. On the Cabal, cf. Hutton, *Charles II*, ch. 10, rejecting the idea; whereas J. Miller, *Charles II* (London, 1991), ch. 7, partly endorses the concept. L. Glassey, 'Politics, Finance and Government', in *idem* (ed.), *The Reigns of Charles II and James VII & II* (London, 1997) is a useful survey of recent work on these matters; Wynne, 'Mistresses of Charles II', below, pp. 171–90; Maguire, 'Duchess of Portsmouth', on Portsmouth's self-image as Charles's wife.

73. Cf. above, n. 58; Nottingham University Library MS PwV 93, reissue of the 1661 orders dated 18 December 1673. The only substantial change is in the definition of the Bedchamber's territory (§ 1), now including 'our old and new Bedchamber, the great Withdrawing Room next to the . . . Vane Room, the lesser Withdrawing Room on the other side of our said Bedchamber, formerly called the Horn Room, our Cabinets or Closets, our new Withdrawing Room to our New Bedchamber, and all other rooms belonging to our old and new Private lodgings . . . at our Pallace of Whitehall'.

74. Nottingham University Library MS PwV 93, towards the back of the book, further Bedchamber orders dated 10 November 1678, tightening Bedchamber attendance and access, and confirming the 1661 and 1673 orders; E. Turner, 'The Privy Council of 1679', *English Historical Review*, 30 (1915).

75. Colvin, *King's Works*, Vol. V, pp. 276–7 on the 1682 new Whitehall lodgings by the river, and pls 34B, 37. In January–June 1683 this occasioned a major dispute about access to the Bedchamber: cf. E.M. Thompson (ed.), *Hatton Correspondence, Vol. II* (Camden Society, New Series 23, 1878), p. 21; PRO, LC5/201, pp. 9–47, 71–5, 456; PRO, SP29/423/69, /41, /42, /68, /40, PRO, SP29/424/70, /69, /71. BL Egerton MS 3350, ff. 7r, 8r, dated Windsor, 17 May 1684, tightening Bedchamber attendance.

76. Oxfordshire County Record Office, MS Dil. xx/a/2, James II's Bedchamber ordinances, 14 April 1685, at p. 20.

77. Starkey, 'Introduction: Court History in Perspective', in *English Court*, pp. 22–4, suggested the lack of realism of Charles I's attempt to maintain and revive the form of the early Tudor 'bastard-feudal' court, without any solid functional underpinning.

78. See for example, M. Knights, *Politics and Opinion in Crisis, 1678–81* (Cambridge, 1994), for stress on the Court's power, but practical concentration on the effects in Parliament; and works cited in n. 11 above.

79. For example, C. Russell, 'Parliamentary History in Perspective, 1604–1629', *History*, 61 (1976), 5; *idem*, *The Causes of the English Civil War* (Oxford, 1990), pp. 161, 168–74, 181.

80. N. Henshall, *The Myth of Absolutism: Change and Continuity in Early Modern European Monarchy* (London, 1992), esp. ch. 9, though a useful corrective, throws out the baby with the bathwater in attacking the term; it has become a modern shorthand for one real contemporary English view of the French monarchy as 'arbitrary', and a danger to be avoided, current from the fifteenth century into the late eighteenth century. Cf. Sir Thomas Overbury, *Observations in his Travels . . . 1609* (London, 1626), in *Harleian Miscellany*, VII. Above, n. 39.

81. Sharpe, *Personal Rule*; C. Russell, *The Fall of the British Monarchies, 1637–42* (Oxford, 1991). The roots of the Pym–Bedford–Essex–Pembroke faction of 1640–1, in the circle around Salisbury in

1604–10, are worked out in N. Cuddy, *Bedchamber, Parliaments and Politics in the Reign of James I* (forthcoming). Anon., *A Record of Some Worthie Proceedings in the Honorable, Wise and Faithful House of Commons Holden in the Yeare 1611* (London, 1641), reprinted in *Somers Tracts*, Vol. II, pp. 151–4.

82. J. Miller, 'The Potential for 'Absolutism' in late Stuart England', *History*, 69 (1984), 187–207. P. Seaward, *The Cavalier Parliament and the Reconstruction of the Old Regime, 1661–1667* (Cambridge, 1989), *passim*, ch. 2, outlines Clarendon's determination to avoid prerogative finance in shaping the Restoration settlement; cf. esp. p. 23 on the 'ultras' around James, Duke of York, who called for full restoration of all pre-war legal and fiscal prerogatives.

83. Anon., *A Deep Sigh Breathd Through the Lodgings at Whithehall Deploring the Absence of the Court and the Miseries of the Palace* (London, 1642).

5

THE HOUSEHOLD OUT OF DOORS: THE STUART COURT AND THE ANIMAL KINGDOM

Arthur MacGregor

How theatrical, and yet how apposite, that news of King James VI's accession to the English throne should have been transmitted from the dead Queen Elizabeth's bedside at Richmond to the King's Court at Holyrood with an epic horse ride. The task was entrusted to Sir Robert Carey:

> This noble Gentleman's care was such, that . . . notwithstanding his sundry shift of horses and some falls that bruised him very sore . . . having ridden neare 300 miles in less than three days . . . [he] came to Edenburgh on Saturday night, where being admitted to the King, bebloodied with great falles and bruses, brought his Highnesse the first newes of Queen Elizabeth's death.[1]

The subsequent progress of the Court in the reverse direction further presaged the shape of things to come: at Widdrington Castle in Northumberland the King 'suddenly beheld a number of deere . . . [and] according to his wonted manner forth he went and slew two of them';[2] at Worksop the company dallied while further deer were annihilated;[3] at the approach to Burleigh, 'live haires in baskets [were] carried to the heath, that made excellent sport for his Majestie';[4] and on the last leg of the journey from Stamford Hill to London itself, while the royal party kept sedately to the road, they were entertained by hunters following a 'traine' or trail, laid alongside the route but '. . . with such twinings and doubles, that the hounds could not take it faster than his Majestie proceeded'.[5]

Tableaux such as these were to characterise the entire reign of James VI and I, and indeed became so vital a feature of it that as often as not the King was to be found in the field or at one of his hunting lodges rather than at the Palace of Whitehall. The following survey concerns itself with the activities that carried James and his successors beyond the protective confines of the Chamber, with the officers who supervised and facilitated these purusits, and with those representatives of the animal kingdom who sweated and toiled, who ran their hearts out, or who fought and died for the entertainment of the Crown.

EQUESTRIANISM AT THE STUART COURT

All the Stuarts were horsemen to be reckoned with. James I was never happier than when in the saddle and the importance he attached to good horsemanship is underlined in the advice he gave to his young son Prince Henry:

> . . . the honorablest and most commendable games that yee can use, are games on Horse-backe; for it becometh a Prince beste of any man to bee a fair & good horse-man. Use therefore to ride and daunton greate and coragious horses . . . & use specially such games on horse-back as may teach you to handle your armes thereon, such as the Tilte, the Ring, and lowe ryding for handling of your sword.[6]

In the year of James's accession to the English throne, Henri IV of France sent him for the instruction of Prince Henry 'ung escuier choisy de ma main', namely Pierre Antoine Bourdin, Seigneur de St Antoine, who brought with him a present of six horses 'des mieux dressez, fort richement enharnachez' for the Prince's use.[7] Prince Henry duly responded by throwing himself into the practice with all the natural enthusiasm of his father, but neither one of them ever had to prove himself in battle. Apart from the chase, their horsemanship was tested not on the field of war but on the tilt yard, where medieval ideals of chivalric prowess were preserved in a self-consciously archaic and formalised manner, for the skills with the lance demanded of participants had lost all relevance to contemporary combat.

Throughout the reign of James I (who, it must be said, displayed a marked reluctance to enter the lists on his own account), almost every tilt recorded took place on the 'King's Day', 24 March, marking the anniversary of his accession. Others on record (numbering no more than nine or ten) were arranged to mark royal weddings, visits by foreign princes, and other celebratory occasions. Some twelve to sixteen participants are usually listed, never including the King but embracing the royal princes as they came of age. The practising that went on beforehand[8] seems to emphasise the infrequency of these events and the need of the courtiers for annual refreshment of their martial skills. The arrangement of a particularly splendid tilt at Whitehall to mark the creation of Henry as Prince of Wales in 1610 serves only to underline the resonances of ancient princely virtue that such an occasion evoked, contributing to the iconographical programme with which the Stuarts consciously sought to consolidate perceptions of their inherited birthright to the English throne:

> Uppon Wednesday in the Afternoone, in the Tilt-yeard, there were divers Earles, Barons, and others, being in rich and glorious armoure, and having costly caparisons, wondrous curiously imbroydered with pearls, gould, and

> silver, the like rich habiliaments for horses were never seen before. They presented their severall ingenious devices and trophies before the King and Prince, and then ran at Tilt, where there was a world of people to behold them.[9]

It was indeed around Henry rather than his notably uncombative father that the tradition – which had flourished under Elizabeth, with the Virgin Queen acting as a potent focus for the sentiments of chivalry that it evoked – seemed set to crystallise, for the tournament field provided a peculiarly appropriate forum for development of the image of the Warrior Prince on whom the kingdom's hopes came to rest. In the years following Henry's early death, Prince Charles, while acquitting himself with distinction, notably in the Accession Day tournaments of 1620 and 1621 when he drew the admiration of the Venetian ambassador,[10] never managed to attract the same measure of adulation. Charles's failure to capture the public imagination in this way may be counted among the contributory factors[11] that led to the extinction of the tournament in favour of more introverted and exclusive forms of courtly entertainment, for following the jousts arranged to celebrate Charles's marriage in 1625 to Henrietta Maria and the royal couple's ceremonial entry into the capital in the following year, no further royal tournament was ever held.

Less physically demanding than the tilts but requiring just as steady an eye was the sport of running at the ring, in which the horseman aimed his lance point at a suspended hoop. The King himself might safely participate in such an event: it provided welcome respite from an incessant programme of hunting for Christian IV during his visit in 1606, when both kings and Prince Henry participated in a contest,[12] and in March 1609, 'to please the prince', James accepted a challenge to tilt at the ring with five gentlemen on either side.[13]

Tilting and running at the ring were frequently combined in chivalric contests; in 1610 it was recorded that 'The King's Day passed over with the ordinary solemnity of running and ringing' and on the same anniversary in 1620 Prince Charles 'got all the praise' by running twelve courses at the ring.[14]

By 1628 there is evidence that more attention at Court was being directed to the demands of contemporary battlefield tactics[15] and before long the remnants of courtly nostalgia for the chivalric virtues of medieval England were ridden into the dust by low-born troopers of the Parliamentary cavalry, consolidated by military discipline and backed by firearms that took no account of gentle breeding.

Charles had had to overcome severe childhood weakness in order to become an adept horseman. He inherited the services of M. de St Antoine as riding master and equerry from his elder brother (pl. I) and in time became highly competent.[16] For the instruction of his own son Charles engaged as governor William Cavendish, Duke of Newcastle, a brilliant horseman who had himself been a pupil of M. de St Antoine[17] and who was later to become the acknowledged authority in Europe on horse breeding and the manège. The young Prince Charles proved an exceptionally talented pupil, attracting the approbation not only of Newcastle himself but also of the King.[18] At the age of twelve, however, Prince Charles found himself propelled from the riding school[19] into the field of battle where he held nominal command of the Royalist forces in the west. Following the Restoration we find him not only sponsoring horse racing at Newmarket but on more than one occasion competing his own account and successfully carrying off the trophy himself.

James II's dedication to the hunt is well known (see pp. 101, 103) and he too was esteemed a first-rate horseman and a hard rider who could still outpace the field in rough territory well into his middle age.

The importance of the horse in the public image which the Stuarts sought to invent for themselves, given physical form in the pageants of James I's reign already mentioned, received a new impetus with the advent of Van Dyck as court painter. For the first time the monarch had access to an iconographer capable of transmuting horseflesh into the stuff of heroism, and in what might be judged the definitive canvases of his oeuvre it is the majestic chargers represented by Van Dyck that quite literally carry the image of the King beyond the realms of representation and into hagiography (fig. 1, overleaf).[20] Such was the symbolic force of this imagery that Cromwell evidently could not resist plagiarising it to his own ends in engraved form (fig. 2, p. 91).[21]

When Newcastle came to publish his manual of horsemanship in 1658, profusely illustrated with images of the most elegant accomplishments of equestrian art, he included also a heroic portrait of Charles II; although the King was then still in exile, the image hardly admits of any possibility other than his ultimate resumption of his birthright.

Yet there is much more than imagery to the role of the horse at Court in Stuart England. The very real preoccupations of the Household with the everyday problems of maintaining and administering the stables commands equal attention.

THE ROYAL STABLES AND THE MASTER OF THE HORSE

Within the Household, formal responsibility for equestrian matters lay with one department, the Stables, under the command of the Master of the Horse, esteemed then as now '. . . the third Great Officer of the Court, giving place only to the Lord Steward and the Lord Chamberlain of the Household'.[22] His duties were summarised in 1742 as follows:

> . . . to him is committed the charge of ordering and disposing all matters relating to the King's stables, races [studs], breed of horses, as he had

1. Sir Anthony Van Dyck, *Charles I on Horseback, with M. de St Antoine*. (The Royal Collection © 2000 Her Majesty Queen Elizabeth II)

2. *Oliver Cromwell on Horseback*, Sutherland Collection, Ashmolean Museum. (Ashmolean Museum, Oxford)

> anciently of all the Posts in England. He hath the power of commanding all the equerries, and all other tradesmen employed in the King's stables. . . . He has the charge of the revenues appointed for the service and maintenance of the King's horses, for the expenses of the stables, for coaches, litters, sumpter horses, etc.[23]

A century earlier, the prestige attached to the office was even greater, accurately reflecting the importance of the Stables at a time when the Court retained some vestiges of its former mobility. Inevitably, favouritism proved as important a factor as talent in the choice of officers, and the office of Master of the Horse was occupied by men of widely varying abilities.

Edward Somerset, 4th Earl of Worcester had been appointed by Elizabeth in 1601 and kept his office under James until 1616 when he was succeeded by George Villiers, 1st Duke of Buckingham. Whatever the King's motives in appointing Buckingham, the Stables benefited considerably from the reflected prestige of their controller, and Buckingham is credited with bringing about long-term improvements to the royal bloodstock. He continued in the post until his assassination in 1628 when it was granted to another confidant, the 22-year-old James, 3rd Marquis (later 1st Duke) of Hamilton, who occupied it without significant impact until his execution in 1649.

Under the later Stuarts, Prince Rupert first held the office under Charles II in exile, but although he cut a dashing figure on horseback, Rupert never found himself in a position to exercise influence in the Stables. He was followed at the Restoration by the more weighty figure of George Monck, 1st Duke of Albemarle and then in turn by the more frivolous George Villiers, 2nd Duke of Buckingham. One of Charles's illegitimate sons, James Scott, Duke of Monmouth, proved a less than fortunate successor to Villiers and was dismissed for his intriguing. A second was then appointed, Charles Lennox, 1st Duke of Richmond, aged only ten at the time; two commissioners were charged with the running of the Stables during the Duke's minority, but on the death of Charles II the still-youthful Richmond was removed from office.[24] James II's only appointee, George Legge, 1st Baron Dartmouth, ended his days in the Tower, imprisoned on suspicion of conspiracy against King William.

In numerical terms, the establishment of the Stables was modest while its constituent posts have been characterised as mostly honorific or menial. Four consecutive surveys of the Stables, one each from the reigns of Charles I,[25] Charles II (1668),[26] James II (1685),[27] and from the opening year of the reign of William III,[28] combine to provide a picture of its changing fortunes. Although the personnel fluctuate to some degree, variations in nomenclature and administrative practice make it hard to reach firm conclusions concerning its development or decline. There are, however, common factors which combine to characterise the composition of the Stables.

Everyday control was delegated by the Master of the Horse to the Avenor who, with the aid of his Clerks of Avery, administered and directed the personnel.[29] A number of Equerries and Pages of Honour were attached to the Stables, the former reaching a maximum number of twelve under Charles II.[30] One or more Surveyors of the Stables and a further clerk ran the daily business of the stable premises, with their fluctuating complements of Grooms and Riders, various of whom were assigned to specific categories of animals. A number of Saddlers and Farriers saw to the shoeing and harnessing of the horses as well as to their physical well-being.[31] In addition to the working stables a stud or 'race' was maintained for the replenishment and improvement of stock among the King's horses, under the control of the Master of the Stud and Surveyor of the Race. The Serjeant, Yeomen and Grooms of the Carriages were at times augmented by a Coach-maker;[32] on occasion personnel are designated specifically as Coachmen or, in one instance, as Chariot-Driver. Others involved in transportation include Littermen, Packmen, Sumptermen and Chairmen, while posts were in the hands of the Yeoman of the Mail; the Surveyor of the Highways[33] was responsible for repairs to the King's 'private Wayes'. Provisioning of the Stables fell to the Purveyors and Granators, whose number rose to eleven under Charles II, some of them specifically designated Riding Purveyors. A number of Footmen, Porters, Pages and Messengers completed the establishment. The Queen's Household had its own, more modest staff for the Stables under a separate Master of the Horse.

The numbers of horses assigned to the King's own service (and that of the Master of the Horse who had the privilege of their use) are listed variously between about sixty-five and a hundred or more.[34] They included hunting horses, coursers or racing horses, pads or pacing horses, coach horses, chariot horses, sumpters, pack horses and bottle horses; a 'stoole horse' and a 'male horse' are each mentioned once and two are designated 'chyrurgeon horses'.[35]

Maintenance of appropriate numbers of mounts for the Household was a principal responsibility of the Master of the Horse and most of his appearances in the State Papers are concerned with their purchase. To mention only a few such payments, sums of £400 were dispensed to the Earl of Worcester in 1605, 1609, 1610 and 1611, and similar sums were paid on a number of occasions to the Duke of Buckingham.[36] In 1632 Hamilton suggested that 'if £7,000 were yearly paid to him, he would furnish the King and Queen with all provisions for their stables, including those of the Prince and Princess Mary';[37] nothing came of it, however, for in the following year we find £500 paid to him for the provision of horses for the Queen and in 1636 a further £400 for the Queen and Prince.[38] Sums of £400 and £500 are mentioned almost on an annual basis thereafter.

While the regular needs of the Household were met in the market place,[39] the demand for high-quality bloodstock for the King's use required more specialised attention. The seventeenth century proved a crucial period in the development of English bloodstock and the royal Stables were at the forefront of improvements wrought by the introduction of oriental strains to which so much significance attaches. Arab horses, imported directly from the Middle East or captured from the Turkish armies which suffered a series of defeats on central European soil in the late sixteenth and early seventeenth centuries, were to remain highly prized though very scarce throughout the Stuart period.[40] More accessible and much sought after were Barbary horses and Andalusian jennets from Spain[41] and coursers (also designated Barbary horses) bred in Italy, notably at the courts of Naples, Florence and Mantua, all of which already had flowing in their veins the precious Barbary blood that had first enriched the English royal stud during the reign of Henry VIII.

By the time of James I's succession the principal royal stud lay at Tutbury in Staffordshire; a second one survived at Malmesbury, Wiltshire, despite a recommendation to Elizabeth from Prospero d'Osma, the renowned Neapolitan authority on stud management, that it was fundamentally unsuitable for its purpose and should close.[42] Smaller studs operated at Hampton Court and Eltham, and the first major gift of horses that we hear of during James I's reign was sent to Greenwich, indicating the presence of a further stud within easy reach of Whitehall.[43] On the latter occasion Archduke Albert presented the King with twelve mares, all in foal, four horses and eleven stallions, all of them prized Neapolitan coursers.[44] Other Italian acquisitions arrived in 1616, when Sir Thomas Edmonds, Treasurer of the Household, returned thence with six Barbary horses, and George Digby purchased a further four in Naples and Genoa at the behest of the Duke of Buckingham.[45]

Spanish horses reached the royal studs in some numbers throughout the mastership of the Duke of Buckingham, but the major influx was to arrive in 1623 in the wake of the visit to the Spanish Court by Buckingham and Prince Charles: on that occasion the Prince acquired a total of fifty-nine horses and mares from the Spanish royal stud at Cordova and Buckingham a further thirty.[46] Stud records from Hampton Court in that year show that all the stallions were then of Spanish blood and many of the mares too,[47] indicating a highly purposeful breeding programme.[48] A survey of Tutbury in 1624 lists forty-seven mares covered in that year by six stallions, one designated 'The Arabian Colt', one 'the Darke gray Barbary' and one 'The Spanish Ginnet'; of the remainder one is referred to as 'the white frensh horse' and the others simply as coursers.[49] Only one further survey of Tutbury exists (from 1628 when there were 44 brood mares) before that undertaken in 1649, on the eve of its dispersal under the Commonwealth, when there were 25 mares among a total stock of 140 horses, valued overall at £1,982.[50]

Following the Restoration the centrifugal forces that had led to the dispersal of the stock were thrown into reverse as Charles II sought to retrieve his property.

The small stud at Hampton Court, which Cromwell had maintained throughout the Commonwealth, received such stock as the King was able to recover. One of the most fruitful sources was the 1st Duke of Buckingham's former estate at Helmsley in Yorkshire, which in 1651 had been given to General Fairfax. When in 1657 his daughter had married George Villiers, son of the 1st Duke, Fairfax gave them Helmsley as a wedding present, and with the appointment of the younger Villiers (now 2nd Duke) as Master of the Horse in 1668, the benefits of the bloodline returned to the King. Other horses had gone to the D'arcy family at Sedbury, also in Yorkshire, one of whom, James D'arcy, was at the Restoration appointed Master of the Stud and Surveyor of the Race at Tutbury. A visit to Tutbury by its new Surveyor revealed the place so despoiled as to be useless; accordingly, he proposed to the King that rather than incurring the expense of re-establishing the royal stud, which he calculated had cost the Crown £1,200–£1,500 a year and yielded but five to seven colts, he, D'arcy, would undertake to supply the King with twelve colts a year for a fee of £1,000, which suggestion was accepted. In this way the King regained the benefits of the old royal breeding stock while the D'arcys contrived to keep the bloodstock they should rightly have surrendered.

Charles II also acquired animals from overseas, though mostly in ones and twos apart from a larger number that came as part of the dowry of Catherine of Braganza.[51] For his own stables Charles received a gift of six Barbary horses from the Moroccan Ambassador, Mohammed Ohadu (fig. 3, overleaf), in 1681, which horses he later raced at Newmarket.[52] Charles II is acknowledged as the principal patron of racing and under his reign Newmarket became firmly established as the sporting capital of England. He even rode there himself and twice won the Newmarket Town Plate, a race he had established in 1665.[53]

In addition to the cost of the horses themselves, fodder and tack made regular inroads into the privy purse. A series of warrants[54] issued in 1626–30 includes provision for twenty of the King's hunting horses maintained on the establishment of the Master of the Horse; ten saddles a year are mentioned as appropriate for the King, all of them richly ornamented.[55] Ample evidence for the undoubted splendour of seventeenth-century equippage is provided by the saddle and other accoutrements made for the Duke of Monmouth while Master of the Horse (fig. 4, p. 97), which survive today in the Duke of Buccleuch's residence at Bowhill in the Scottish Borders.[56]

The sums expended annually on feed for the horses rose to some £7,500 a year under Charles II. The following 'yearly charges' were recorded in a review dated 1668:[57]

Hay for 298 horse & Naggs Liveries at one botle a night is by y^e^ yeare 1010 loades at xxxvi*d.* load	1818

3. Sir Godfrey Kneller, *Mohammed Ohadu, the Moroccan Ambassador*, 1682, Chiswick House, London. (English Heritage Photo Library)

4. Accoutrements of the Duke of Monmouth, preserved at Bowhill. (Alex Starkey/ Country Life Picture Library)

oates for 272 horses & 26 Naggs at iip^{es} for a horse & 1p^{e} for a Nagg per Noctem is by ye yeare 6501q^{rs} 4b^{s} 2p^{es} at 16^{d} per quarter		5201 5
Straw by Estimate 570 Truses at vi*d*. a trus		741
Bread & Beanes by Estimat		500
Forrage for 298 horses and Naggs at i*d*. a p^{e} a day		433 4 2
Total	[£]	8173 9 2

An extensive Bill Book covering the period 1680–2[58] details the precise costs of all the equipment and liveries consumed by the Stables during those years. By

1689 the annual expense of each horse was computed at £52 10*s* and the overall cost of King William's Stables was put at £16,400 19*s* 3½*d*, including £708 3*s* 8*d* for 'Annual stipends or Pentions, to be allow'd to Servants of the Stables to his Late Matie King Charles the Second who are not Employed in y^r Mat.^ies Service'.[59]

The periodic removes of the Household made particularly heavy demands on men and equipment. Under Charles II, by which time the Court had become largely sedentary, a survey was ordered in 1663 of 'the proportions of carriages and other furniture in the royal stables yearly required for the King and Queen and allowed to the officers and servants of the stables'. A few years later, in 1668, fifty-five officers and departments are assigned carts and carriages for removes on the King's side and forty-nine on the Queen's side, several of them requiring more than one carriage.[60]

HUNTING, HAWKING AND SOME OTHER PURSUITS

James I had been an addict of the hunt since his youth. One observer said of him in 1584 that:

> He loves the chase above all the pleasures of this world, staying in the saddle for six hours on end . . . [He is] too much addicted to his pleasure, principally that of the chase, leaving the conduct of business to [others]. I know very well that this is pardonable in one of his youth but it is to be feared that it will become a habit.[61]

Just how prophetic this observation was to prove emerged within two years of James's accession to the English throne, when it was further reported that:

> The King . . . finds such felicity in that hunting life, that he hath written to the Councill that it is the only means to maintain his health, which being the health and welfare of us all, he desired them to take the charge and burden of affairs, and foresee that he be not interrupted or *troubled with too much business*.[62]

The very real difficulties raised by this predilection in the running of state affairs was remarked upon by a number of foreign ambassadors. Among the reports of successive Venetian envoys we find, for example, on 4 September 1603 a note that '. . . for the next twenty days he [the King] will be without his council, away upon a hunting party, and everything is at a standstill';[63] 'This perpetual occupation with country pursuits', observes another diplomat, 'though possibly not distasteful to those who hold the reins of government, is extremely annoying to those who don't';[64] on 22 February 1607 the ambassador reports to the Doge his inability to communicate with the monarch for the present, since he knows that '. . . the King is very much put out if his own Ministers, and much more foreign Envoys, dare to mention business to him at such a time. He desires to enjoy the chase in the company of very few and with a most private freedom';[65] and a later ambassador in 1618 reports that he has had to contact James through the Secretary (Sir Thomas Lake), for the King '. . . does not like to be disturbed in his usual pleasures of the chase, and desires such matters to be negotiated with ministers, who communicate them to him by means of couriers, whom they dispatch daily'.[66] A contemporary woodcut (fig. 5, overleaf) shows the King in his element.

The practice followed in the course of the hunt was recorded by another Venetian in 1618:[67]

> [The King] gives orders over night for one of the largest and fattest and strongest stags to be selected. On the following morning the hounds rouse him from his lair, pursuing him from natural instinct and never losing the scent, even should he hide himself in a thousand woods or among as many other deer. The king accompanied by a number of cavaliers riding the quickest horses, follows the game over the country and often for the space of eight whole days, until it is quite exhausted and dead, and to effect this without killing the horses, relays are posted in various places. Being thus freshly mounted, the sportsmen are enabled to continue the hunt with greater spirit. On his Majesty coming up with the dead game, he dismounts, cuts its throat and opens it, sating the dogs with its blood, as the reward for their exertions. With his own imbrued hands, moreover, he is wont to regale some of his nobility by touching their faces. This blood it is unlawful to wash off, until it fall of its own accord, and the favoured individual thus bedaubed is considered to be dubbed a keen sportsman and chief of the hunt and to have a certificate of his sovereign's cordial good-will.

Such was the single-mindedness with which the hunt was prosecuted that on occasion the careful arrangements outlined above proved inadequate: on 16 May 1609, for example, the chase was so prolonged that a number of horses died in the headlong pursuit, one under Prince Henry himself, and the party found itself benighted at such a distance from the Court that they were forced to sleep in a cottage, their absence causing much anxiety to the Queen and courtiers.[68] Some years later, in 1616, the King injured his leg in a fall while hunting, '. . . but in spite of all, he will not lose an hour of his hunting, and as he cannot ride on horseback he either goes in a carriage or has himself carried'.[69]

In facilitating the royal chase several Household departments each played their distinct roles. Principal among these were the Privy Buckhounds which, immediately on James I's accession enjoyed a striking change of fortune, having endured something of a lean time under Elizabeth. At the close of her reign the Master of the Privy Buckhounds disposed of a staff comprising one Serjeant,

The Booke of Hunting. 133

that the Prince or chiefe (if ſo pleaſe them) do alight and take aſſaye of the Deare with a ſharpe knife, the which is done

I 3 in

5. James I 'taking the assaye' of a newly slaughtered deer, from Turberville's *Noble Art of Venerie*, 1611, 4°P 69 Jur (2). (Bodleian Library, University of Oxford)

three Yeomen Prickers (who rode with the pack) and five Grooms (who did not), but under James the establishment was immediately enlarged and within a year had gained an extra Serjeant, eight 'newly erected' Yeomen Prickers and one Groom; the pack had in addition a Waggoner or 'keeper of the hound van'.[70] Besides the Privy pack maintained by the Household, a second pack of Buckhounds had existed since 1528 under the control of a hereditary Master, the incumbent in James's day being Sir Pexall Brocas. The hereditary branch evidently failed to satisfy the needs of such a demanding huntsman as James I and within the first year of his reign he initiated attempts to annexe the hereditary kennel to the Privy pack, so as to gain direct access to its hounds. It was only in 1613, however, that he succeeded in reforming part of the hereditary pack (together with a portion of the Privy pack) into a separate kennel for Charles, Duke of York. At this time the establishment of the hereditary pack stood at a Serjeant, eight Yeomen Prickers, six Grooms and a Waggoner, with Timothy Tyrrell as acting Master. At the amalgamation several staff of the old pack were pensioned off, but Tyrrell was retained as Master. On Charles's accession this pack was merged with the Privy pack, although attempts to extinguish the privileges of the hereditary mastership were less easily achieved and it survived in nominal form up to the eighteenth century.[71]

Under Charles II the salary of the Master of the Buckhounds was increased and the budget of the pack rose in 1662 to £2,378, although much of it remained unpaid; in common with other royal servants the officers found themselves *in extremis* over the next few years, lamenting that they were 'utterly undone' for want of payment. Later attempts to discontinue some liveries and allowances were abandoned in the face of renewed protests from the servants, but extracting payment from the Crown proved no easier.[72]

Charles I inherited his father's love for the hounds and even took them with him on military expeditions.[73] Charles II occasionally distinguished himself in the field[74] but he was perhaps more at home on the turf at Newmarket. James II got little opportunity to enjoy the Buckhounds although as Duke of York he had been a passionate huntsman, having a separate pack of Buckhounds costing £1,341 5*s* a year.

The hounds themselves had traditionally been augmented by animals which reverted to the King on the deaths of certain bishops or abbots who ran packs of their own. A number of sheriffdoms and serjeanties also carried obligations to contribute towards them. The King further exercised rights of seizure over other citizens' hounds: in 1616, for example, the Master of the Otterhounds was granted a licence '. . . to take hounds, beagles, spaniels, and mongrels for His Majesty's disport. Also to seize such hounds &c as may be offensive to the King's game.'[75] Control of the export of hounds was placed in the hands of the Master of the Buckhounds, in an attempt to regulate the supply.[76] Each pack would additionally have bred its own pups, and manuals giving advice on such matters were already being published.[77] Under James I and Charles I the number of hounds in the pack seems to have been stabilised at sixteen couples.[78]

Royal warrants empowered the Masters and Purveyors to provide for the needs of the hunt at the expense of the community in which they found themselves. In 1614 Sir Thomas Tyringham was given authority to take up sixteen beds, together with provision for thirty horses and for the King's hounds, in all places adjacent to the Court, 'at reasonable prices'.[79] In April 1621 a similar warrant authorized him to take up beds, stables, rooms, etc. on his own terms, which must have been a questionable blessing to those who had such places to let.[80]

It should not be thought that the deer (principally red deer) which were the quarry of the Buckhounds were regarded as a passive resource, for it is clear that they were managed on a considerable scale.[81] Not only were they protected from the public at large by stringent laws and by extensively emparked reserves[82] but hundreds of animals were bodily transported over hundreds of miles in efforts to improve the game in one royal park or another. Neither were these efforts limited to native deer: under James I and Charles I animals were introduced to royal parks from Denmark, Germany, France and Ireland,[83] while others were exported as gifts to the royal houses of Austria and France. The stocks inherited by Charles II had been decimated during the years of conflict; to encourage indigenous regeneration he declared a closed period of from three to five years to be observed in all royal forests, during which time no fallow deer or red deer were to be killed. Other landowners helped build up the royal stocks, to judge by a sum of £75 'paid to several keepers for their fees at 5*s* a head for 300 deer, presented to his Majesty by several noblemen and others, and delivered into Windsor Forest, Waltham Forest and Enfield chase'. Replenishing with foreign deer began in the first winter following his coronation, when £148 1*s* was paid out '. . . for taking 33 Jermayne Deere out of a shipp at Tower Hill and Conveying them in five waggons to Waltham fforest'; the master of the ship *Angel Gabriel* received £44 for 'freight of the stags that came from the Duke of Oldenburgh'; Sir Richard Ford was paid £176 8*s* 8*d* for freight and other disbursements in Hamburg 'for a parcel of deer that were sent to H[is] M[ajesty] by the Duke of Brandenburgh' in 1661.[84] During James II's reign further large-scale movements of deer are recorded, including one consignment of 108 animals from Germany, for which a detailed costing survives.[85]

Responsibility for these onerous arrangements fell to the Master of the Toils, with his staff of serjeants and yeomen. It was arduous and demanding work, with much of the movement of stock taking place during the worst weather in the winter months. Waggons transported both the deer and the heavy 'toiles' of canvas and netting with which the animals were caught and which gave their name to the office. Something of the pattern of life in this department emerges from a warrant of 1 October 1686 for £152 7*s* 2*d*, to be paid:

> To Thomas Howard, yeoman of the tents and toyles, for his charge in removing the toyles and waggons from Whaddon Chace in Buckinghamshire to Haddam Hall Park in Hertfordshire, and taking and removing the redd deere there to Epping Forest and to Bagshot Parke, and for removing the said waggons and toyles from Bagshott Parke to Lord Ailesbury's parke in Wilts, called Tottenham Parke, and taking and removing 192 fallow deer to the forrest of Alice Holt in Hampshire.[86]

The Tents and Pavilions are sometimes referred to in association with the Toils, at times sharing the same master and at others not.[87] The former department provided shelter for the Court while in the field and during its progresses. Henry Seckford received a commission on 18 August 1603 'to procure timber, iron &c' for making tents:[88] clearly they were heavy and cumbersome items. In 1610 the respective Masters of the Tents and Toils received 100 marks between them 'for keeping and airing the same'.[89] In 1633 the Master of the Tents and Pavilions received a warrant 'to deliver one tent fitted and furnished for the use of the gentleman-waiters this summer progress'.[90]

Before quitting the field, mention should be made of some further personnel maintained for sporting purposes and of the animals for which they had responsibility. In addition to the packs of buckhounds we find occasional mention of leash-hounds, presumably bloodhounds and the like. James I's son Prince Henry had in his establishment in 1610 a 'Bowe Bearer and Master of the Lime Hounds', an office which appears again in Henrietta Maria's Household as Master of the Bows and String Hounds.[91] John Cary, Master of the Buckhounds under Charles II, also occupied the office of Master of the Harthounds for a time, before relinquishing his appointment to a Mr Pott, who had been Master of the Beagles to James, Duke of York.[92]

A pack of royal otter-hounds is first recorded in the reign of Henry VII; James II maintained a pack, though their history is otherwise obscure.[93] James also kept a pack of foxhounds, a royal revival of the Plantagenet era, which cost £700 a year, and a pack of harriers costing £1,000. His enthusiasm for the chase is revealed in a request made while he was in exile at Brussels, when he asked for his hounds and huntsman to be sent over: 'I now begin to have plenty of stag-hunting', he says, 'and the country looks as if the fox-hunting would be very good.'[94]

Hawking provided further diversion for the monarch and was supported by further posts in the Household establishment. On the evidence of an account submitted by one of the falconers in 1624 the King then maintained as many as twenty-four falconers and thirty cast of hawks.[95] There were also hereditary offices associated with the hawks: under James II the Earl of Carnarvon unsuccessfully advanced a claim to be Marshal, Surveyor and Conservator of the King's Hawks in England, and three years later the 1st Duke of St Albans successfully gained the reversion of the office of hereditary Master Falconer.[96]

The hawks themselves were of several varieties and came from various sources: gerfalcons, jerkins and merlins are mentioned from Ireland, Barbary falcons from Morocco and white hawks from Muscovy; sixteen cast of hawks arrived together with horses and 'setting dogs' from Louis XIII in 1624 while others sent periodically by Christian IV originated as far away as Iceland.[97] In addition to numerous and specific requests from James I and Charles I to the Lord Deputy and others in Ireland for the supply of as many hawks as could be spared, are several references to 'rent hawks',[98] implying, perhaps, a duty on certain landholders to supply hawks to the Crown.

James I seems to have been responsible for the introduction of a novel sport involving the use of cormorants for fishing. The technique had been developed in China and seems likely to have been transmitted to western Europe by the Dutch East India Company.[99] We first hear of them in 1611 when John Wood was paid the sum of £30 'in respect he hath been at extraordinary charge in bringing up and training of certain fowls called cormorants, and making of them fit for the use of fishing'. Although the first birds to be used for this purpose may have been imported from the Far East it is clear that a local training programme was soon instituted. A year later the same John Wood, now designated Keeper of His Majesty's Cormorants, was paid an additional £30 'to travel into some of the furthest parts of his realm for young cormorants' and others arrived in 1619 as gifts from the French king. Further species evidently were drafted into service in this way, for in 1618 Robert Wood, designated Keeper of His Majesty's Cormorants, Ospreys and Otters, was assigned £286 for building various fish ponds, sluices and houses for his charges within the vineyards at Westminster.[100] An account of these curious birds was transmitted to Venice in 1618:[101]

> Then there is another most extravagant hunt or rather fishery, effected by a large bird called a cormorant, the site of whose exploits belongs to the king. His Majesty constantly has a pair of them hooded at this Court. This very day he was to fish with them in the Thames from a boat. They have a very wide craw, and being well trained, dive in the ponds or streams, and after remaining some while under water, come to the surface with the prey in their mouth, or even in their craw, as they are unable to swallow because their throat is bound with a lacet.

Interest in this sport might be thought to have died with James I, for in 1626 a Royal Commission appointed to consider 'retrenchment of His Majesty's charges' recommended that the office of Keeper of the Cormorants be abolished, with an annual saving to the Household of £84.[102] That it lived on for some further decades is shown by a list of yearly charges to be paid by the Treasurer of the Chamber, dated 1665, which includes a cormorant keeper at £84 per annum, payments to whom were two years behind at the time.[103]

Even more arcane diversions occasionally took the King's fancy but required no provision with the Household. In 1605, for example, James I is said to have 'fallen into a great humour of catching larks', taking 'as much delight in it or more than hunting deer'.[104]

Captive birds were sometimes pressed into the royal sport, notably in cock-fights. A Cockmaster was appointed to take charge of the arrangements and under James I the permanent and substantially built cockpits at Whitehall and Greenwich were augmented by a new 30-ft diameter structure erected at Royston where the King might while away the hours not spent in the chase.[105] In these contests single birds were normally pitted against each other, but occasionally the proceedings were enlivened by putting large numbers of cocks into the pit together. James I was made 'very merry' by such an event at Lincoln in 1617.[106]

The baiting of bulls and bears with savage dogs also provided regular sport for the Court. The tilt yard at Whitehall was adapted to this purpose, with the erection in 1604 of posts and rails 'to keepe the people from the bearestake' and with iron staples added later 'for the tying of doggs'. Greenwich, too, had a stake at which bears and bulls might be tethered and worried to death.[107] A description of these activities in Italian, dated 10 July 1618, seems to refer to Whitehall and to the adjacent St James's Park:

> Then there is a certain theatre, a place belonging to the king, where he keeps a quantity of bears and other wild beasts, such as lynxes and tigers. In another part of it there are a number of bulls. In separate kennels they have got over a hundred trained mastiffs. Every week they bait both bull and bear with dogs belonging to private individuals such as butchers and others curious in these matters, as those of the kennel are only used on rare occasions in the presence of his Majesty or other grandees. We went one day by invitation to see this sight and the result of our observations after various assaults was that the bull and the bear overpower the courage of the dog, who although he occasionally makes some good hits, yet in the end is frequently killed on the spot, either from being tossed by the one or hugged, torn or bitten by the other. . . . The bull can hardly get at anybody, as he wears a collar round his neck with only fifteen feet of rope which is fastened to a stake deeply planted in the middle of the theatre . . . the tips of [his horns] are covered with thick leather to prevent them from disembowelling the dogs.[108]

In 1636 Thomas Caldwell, the King's barber, was appointed 'chief master of his Majesty's games and pastimes, that is to say, of his bears, bulls and mastiffs', with powers '. . . to take up for the King's service any bear or bull upon such price as he can agree with the owner'; if no agreement could be reached, then: '. . . it shall be lawfull for two justices of the Peace near the place to set an indifferent price upon the same, whom his Majesty requires to be assisting Caldwell, and that the owner of such a bear or bull shall not refuse the price so imposed'.[109]

THE KING'S MENAGERIE

Finally, mention should be made of the animals that constituted the royal menagerie. Several sites housed exotic animals. Outside London, Theobalds was most important, with mention there of 'Herons, French fowls, Elks, silk worms, partridges & pheasants' while at Kenilworth Castle instructions had been issued in 1605 for the preparation of 'a dry place in the old park to bee rayled in to keep Elks, reindeer and other strang[e] beasts'. All of these references are from the reign of James I and the later history of these establishments is uncertain.

In London itself exotic animals were concentrated at St James's Park and the Paris Garden, with the exception of the lions kept in more secure accommodation at the Tower. St James's emerges as a preserve for exotica within a few years of James I's accession[110] and a rare pictorial record survives of some of the creatures to be seen there (fig. 6). A series of payments made in March 1611 to William Walker, Keeper of his Majesty's Fowls at St James's, mentions parrots and a cassowary as well as 'a Beast called a possom, presented to his Matie from Virgenia'; Walker also claimed coals for stoves with which an attempt was being made to incubate ostrich eggs.[111] A series of accounts drawn up in the same year by Viscount Rochester for 'Charges for keeping the fowle and Beastes att St James Parke and Garden' for the period April to June 1611 totals £23 4*s* 7*d*[112] and embraces an astonishing variety of creatures, among others Guinea goats and Arabian sheep, African crane, Muscovy sables, pelicans from Astrakhan given by the Russian ambassador, a leopard from the King of Savoy, crocodiles and a wild boar from Hispaniola, Canada geese, flying squirrels from Virginia,

6. Animals from the royal menagerie (together with another rarity – a Virginian Indian) at St James's Park. (Edinburgh University Library, Michael van Meer's Album amicorum, La.III.283, fol. 254v)

a beaver, deer of several sorts including an elk, camels, and an elephant. Later additions to the park included twenty-four ostriches presented by the Moroccan ambassador in 1682.[113] It is clear from the accounts that exceptional care was taken with the diet provided for each of these creatures: there is mention of wheat for the Guinea hens and turtle doves, oats and barley for the ducks, peas for the pigeons, bread for the crane and bustards, 'eeles, livers and frogges' for the heron and stork, and fruit and carrots for the beaver. One payment is to 'Laborers ymployed in gatheringe of Antes for the yonge Fesantes'!

The impact of these living curiosities on the populace at large was considerable. The arrival of the elephant and the camels caused minor sensations, fuelled in the case of the elephant by the secrecy in which it was at first kept, for the King decreed on 6 July 1623 that it should be 'well dressed and fed, but not led out to water, nor allowed to be seen by any', on pain of the 'uttermost peril'.[114] Thomas Peacham drew public attention to the Guinea hens, the cassowary and the beaver in his preface to *Coryat's Crudities* (1611), the beaver going about his business 'downe-shearing willowes with teeth as sharp as a hand-saw'.

In the lives these creatures led, however, there was always an element of precariousness: we hear, for example, that in 1623, after the Spanish ambassador had been treated in the Paris Garden to a spot of bull and bear baiting, the King's servants '. . . turned a white bear into the Thames, where the dogs bated him swimming; which was the best sport of all'.[115]

Lions had been kept at the Tower before the advent of James I but he developed the facilities there (fig. 7, overleaf) in order to make them more accessible for viewing, especially during the periodic baiting by hounds to which they were subjected. So it was that in the spring of 1605:

> . . . the Kinge builded a wall, and filled up with earth all that part of the mote or ditch about the West sid[e] of the Lions' den, and appoynted a drawing partition to be made towards the South part thereof, the one part thereof to serve for the breeding Lionesse [which had produced two cubs on 27 July] when she shall have whelps, and the other part thereof for a walke for other Lions. The Kinge caused also three trap doores to bee made in the wall of the Lyon's den, for the Lyons to goe into their walke at the pleasure of the keeper, which walke shall bee maintayned and kept for especiall place to baight the Lyons with dogges, beares, bulles, bores, &c.[116]

When on 3 June of that year the King visited the 'Lyon's Tower' with a company of nobles and gentlemen, a temporary viewing platform was erected 'because, as yet the two galleries were not yet builded, the one of them for the King and great Lords, and the other for special personages'.[117]

The accounts that survive of encounters between the lions and other savage beasts are, perhaps, too graphic to bear contemplation in detail: they include a

7. Drawing of the 'Lyon-den' at the Tower of London, 1779. (© The Board of Trustees of the Armouries, I.216 5)

combat with 'a great fierce Beare' which had killed a child, enlivened by the introduction of six mastiffs and a horse, inconclusive in outcome and not redeemed by a report that later '. . . according to the King's commandment, this Beare was bayted to death upon a stage; and unto the mother of the murthered child was given twenty pounds out of part of that money which the people gave to see the Beare kild'.[118] A later account, of 20 April 1610, records an incident during the visit of Prince Frederic Ulric of Brunswick, who was brought to the Tower by Prince Henry, when several mastiffs were destroyed by one of the lions before the lion fell into danger of being overpowered by additional dogs; at this point a 'young lusty Lyon and Lyonesse were both put out together, to see if they would rescue the third, but they would not, but fearfully gazed upon the Doggs . . . . '[119] With the exception of the mastiffs, the various beasts showed what might be interpreted today as a commendable reluctance to fight with each other and from our perspective it may be easier to take pleasure from reports of encounters which would have been deemed abysmal failures by those present. On one such occasion, having already sacrificed two cocks and two mastiffs to the lions, a lamb was introduced at the King's command, '. . . and being come to the grounde, the lambe lay upon his knees, and both the Lyons stoode in their former places, and only beheld the lambe, but presently the lambe rose up and went unto the Lyons, who very gently looked uppon him and smelled on him without signe of any further hurt', before it was again 'softly drawne up againe in as good plight as hee was let down'.[120] Later, a spaniel was similarly spared, the lion and he, according to contemporary report, becoming friends and living together for several years thereafter.[121]

No doubt such sentiment would have been deemed hopelessly mawkish in Stuart England, although Keith Thomas detects the emergence of a more humane attitude to animals during the seventeenth century.[122] Such principles tended to be held by the Puritan faction, however: the Stuarts, in their dealings with the animal kingdom, would have been the last people to detect so much as a whiff of the suggestion that their attitudes to animals were on a course that was doomed to becoming increasingly unacceptable to the public at large, much as their own dynasty was to fall from public favour. The end of their line was brought about in abrupt fashion with the arrival of William of Orange, but the Stuarts had no prerogative on the exploitation of the animal kingdom and that has taken somewhat longer to extinguish.

Notes

1. 'The True Narration of the Entertainment of his Royal Majestie, from the time of his Departure from Edenborough, till his Receiving at London . . .' (London, 1603), reprinted in John Nichols, *The Progresses, Processions, and Magnificent Festivities of King James the First* (London, 1828), Vol. I, pp. 53–4. A. Fitzgerald, *Royal Thoroughbreds. A History of the Royal Studs* (London, 1990), p. 6, states that Carey left Richmond Palace at 6.00 a.m. on 24 March, within minutes of the Queen's death, and arrived in Holyrood on the evening of 26 March.

2. Nichols, op. cit. (n. 1), Vol. I, p. 44.

3. The King '. . . was somewhat stayed, for there appeared a number of huntsmen all in green, the chiefe of which with a Woodman's Speech did welcome him, offering his Majestie to shew him some game, which he gladly condiscended to see; and, with a traine set, he hunted a good space, very much delighted': Nichols, op. cit. (n. 1), Vol. I, pp. 85–6.

4. Nichols, op. cit. (n. 1), Vol. I, p. 94.

5. John Savile, 'King James his Entertainment at Theobalds, with his Welcome to London', in Nichols, op. cit. (n. 1), Vol. I, p. 139.

6. James I (as James VI of Scotland), *Βασιλικὸν δῶρον, devided into Three Bookes* (Edinburgh, 1599), p. 144.

7. That is to say, 'a rider chosen by my own hand', bringing with him six of the best-trained horses, very richly caparisoned. See Oliver Millar, *The Tudor, Stuart and Early Georgian Pictures in the Collection of Her Majesty The Queen* (London, 1963), p. 94, discussing Van Dyck's equestrian portrait of *Charles I on Horseback with M. de St Antoine* (see pl. I).

8. On 10 March 1605 Sir Dudley Carleton, writing from Court, mentions to his correspondent that 'The tilting this year will be at this place, here is much practising . . .'; these rehearsals evidently proved less than adequate, for on 28 March Samuel Calvert records that 'The tilting on Sunday last

(Coronation-day [*sic*]) was not performed with the accustomed solemnity . . .' (Nichols, op. cit. (n. 1), Vol. I, pp. 499–500).

9. Nichols, op. cit. (n. 1), Vol. II, p. 361.

10. *CSPV, 1619–21*, pp. 190, 225, 227; on the first of these occasions (6 March 1620) the real dangers involved in the participation of the heir apparent are alluded to: '[The Prince] is practising in order to take part in a tilting match in a few days. The public and solemn combat will take place first, although many of the Lords of the Council are humbly trying to dissuade him, owing to the risks run and a reasonable regard for the preservation of his life.' See also *CSPV, 1621–3*, pp. 4 (where reference is made to 'jousts and horsemanship . . . in which are his chief delights'), 13.

11. These factors are reviewed in an excellent survey by A. Young: *Tudor and Jacobean Tournaments* (London, 1987), esp. pp. 38–42, 177, 184, 205–8. They included James I's distaste for public spectacles in general, the decline in participants sufficiently skilled in the handling of arms on horseback and their reluctance to invest in costly new caparisons, so that the spectacle became increasingly amateur and tawdry. Most interestingly, according to Young's thesis, the rise of the courtly masque, with specially designed scenery and costume and with subtle employment of lighting, music and dialogue by the best talents of the day, gradually displaced the ritualistic and propagandist roles of the tournament; the consequent removal of the spectacle to an exclusive, indoor setting also contributed to the alienation of the Court from the populace at large.

12. *CSPV, 1603–7*, p. 391.

13. *CSPV, 1607–10*, p. 243. On this occasion the Prince won, 'though it cost him dear, for he lost a diamond of value out of his hat'.

14. Nichols, op. cit. (n. 1), Vol. II, pp. 287, 592.

15. A meeting of the Council of War in that year resolved to put into operation '. . . the four advices of Mons. La Broue, how to make horses acquainted with war – vizt. that the groom dressing him should be in armour, that provender should be given him on a drum-head, that while he is eating a piece should be discharged, and that he should be ridden against a suit of armour, which he may overthrow and trample under his feet' (M.M. Reese, *The Royal Office of the Master of the Horse* (London, 1976), pp. 175–6).

16. Of Charles the Venetian ambassador reported that 'He excels at tilting and indulges in every other kind of horsemanship, and even if he were not prince one would have to confess that he surpassed others' (*CSPV, 1621–3*, p. 452). A more qualified reminiscence was later provided by one of Charles's secretaries, who recalled that '. . . he rid the great horse very well; and on the little saddle he was not only adroit, but a laborious hunter or field-man; and they were wont to say of him, that he fail'd not to do any of his exercises artificially, but not very gracefully; like some well-proportion'd faces, which yet want a pleasant air of countenance' (Sir Philip Warwick, *Memoires of the reigne of King Charles I* (London, 1701), p. 66).

17. Margaret, Duchess of Newcastle, *The Life of the Thrice Noble, High and Puissant Prince William Cavendishe, Duke . . . of Newcastle* (London, 1667), p. 142, mentions that the Duke's father, Sir Charles Cavendish, had himself tutored the Duke '. . . and kept him also several Masters in the Art of Horsemanship, and sent him to the *Mewse* to *Mons. Antoine*, who was then accounted the best Master in that Art'.

18. Newcastle mentions as much in the dedication to the then exiled Charles II of his hugely influential work, the *Methode et Invention Nouvelle de Dresser les Cheveaux* (Antwerp, 1658): after recording

his own admiration of his former pupil's prowess, Newcastle recalls that: 'Le Roy, Vôtre Pere, de glorieuse Memoire, disoit, qu'il n'avait jamais veu aucun de Vôtre âge qui Vous approchât de bien loin à monter à cheval. (Sa majesté étoit tres-capable d'en juger) il disoit qu'il cherchoit quelque faute, mais qu'il n'en pouvoit treuver.' For further accounts of Charles II's prowess on horseback (and in handling coach horses) see B. Vesey-Fitzgerald (ed.), *The Book of the Horse* (London, 1946), pp. 56–7.

19. The principal school of the Court was to be found in the 'riding house' that had been built at St James's Palace in 1607–9: see Arthur MacGregor, 'The King's Goods and the Commonwealth Sale: materials and context', in A. MacGregor (ed.), *The Late King's Goods. Collections, Possessions and Patronage of Charles I in the Light of the Commonwealth Sale Inventories* (London and Oxford, 1989), p. 23, with references.

20. A comparably majestic equestrian portrait of the King by Van Dyck is that in the National Gallery, London (reproduced in MacGregor, op. cit. (n. 19), pl. 69).

21. For an analysis of the several states of this engraving see G.S. Layard, *The Headless Horseman. Pierre Lambart's Engraving: Charles or Cromwell?* (London, 1922). The importance attached to the imagery of the horse in the King's iconography is underlined in the commission issued by Lord Treasurer Weston to Hubert Le Sueur in 1630, for production of the equestrian statue of the King that now stands at the top of Whitehall, '. . . in the making wereof he shall take advice of his Maj: Ridders of greate Horses, as well for the shaepe and action of his Maj: figure one the same' (Charles Avery, 'Hubert Le Sueur, the "unworthy Praxiteles" of King Charles I', *Walpole Society*, 48 (1982), 146–7).

22. W.J. Thoms, *The Book of the Court* (London, 1838), p. 385; Reese, op. cit. (n. 15), p. 13.

23. Quoted in Reese, op. cit. (n. 15), pp. 13–14.

24. The commissioners were Major Theophilus Oglethorpe and George Fielding; on the removal of Richmond, Oglethorpe was made principal equerry to James II. For Richmond's appointment see *Loyal Protestant and True Domestick Intelligence*, 109 (28 January 1681/2).

25. Aylmer, *King's Servants*, p. 474. The same survey indicates that the Master of the Queen's Horse had an additional establishment of seventy-seven persons.

26. 'The Booke of the Establishment of His Ma's Household 1668': Royal Archives, Windsor Castle, RA EB 10; the section dealing with the Stables is reproduced in A. MacGregor, 'The Royal Stables: a Seventeenth-Century Perspective', *Antiquaries Journal*, 76 (1996), 185–92. References to this source are made by the gracious permission of Her Majesty the Queen.

27. 'Stable Establishment Book, 1685': Royal Archives, Windsor Castle, RA EB 12, reproduced in MacGregor, op. cit. (n. 26), pp. 192–200. References to this source are made by the gracious permission of Her Majesty the Queen. I am grateful to Lady de Bellaigue, Registrar of the Royal Archives, for drawing this and the previously cited document to my attention and for facilitating access to them.

28. 'Sallaries of the Master of the Horse, and Officers and Servants of Our Stables': BL, Harley MS 5010, f. 35.

29. One occupant of this post, Robert Vernon, was rewarded with a knighthood in 1615 by James I (Nichols, op. cit. (n. 1), Vol. III, pp. 78–9.

30. Royal Archives, Windsor Castle, RA EB 10, p. 33; see MacGregor, op. cit. (n. 26), p. 185.

31. For example, in 1640 Henry Woodcock, yeoman farrier for His Majesty's hunting horses, was reimbursed for 'divers drenches, oyntments and other medicines by him employed', the sum of £26 4*s* 2*d* (J.P. Hore, *The History of the Royal Buckhounds* (London, 1893), p. 143).

32. PRO, SP14, 51/13: 'The charges of a caroche with the furniture to it belonging, made under the Earl of Worcester's direction and oversight.'

33. See MacGregor, op. cit. (n. 26).

34. The Household as a whole would, of course, have required a far greater number.

35. Royal Archives, Windsor Castle, RA EB 10, p. 36; see MacGregor, op. cit. (n. 26), pp. 187, 193. Hore (op. cit. (n. 31), p. 144) finds references to two Bonesetters in Ordinary to the Buckhounds and, from the reign of James II, mention of one Dr Frazer, 'hunting chirurgeon'.

36. *CSPD, 1619–23*, pp. 102, 305, 390; *CSPD, 1623–5*, p. 344.

37. *CSPD, 1631–3*, pp. 483–4.

38. *CSPD, 1633–4*, p. 214; *CSPD, 1635–6*, p. 151. Also in 1636, £500 was paid 'for horses from His Majesty and the Queen to the French King and His Majesty's sister the Lady Elizabeth, Princess Palatine (ibid., p. 253).

39. For a general survey covering this period see Peter Edwards, *The Horse Trade in Tudor and Stuart England* (Cambridge, 1988). Although specific references are lacking, Ireland may have played an important part in supplying the royal needs: a review of exports from Ireland during the twelve months ending 25 December 1665 mentions 3,961 horses sent to England during that period, and 41 to other parts (*CSP Ireland 1663–5*, pp. 694–5).

40. Sylvia Loch, in *The Royal Horse of Europe* (London, 1986), pp. 189–90, observes that apart from one renowned beast, the Markham Arabian, purchased by James I in 1616, only one Arabian stallion is mentioned in the royal stud books from the reign of Elizabeth to that of Charles II. Cromwell, too, had tried to secure Arab horses, but despite the best efforts of his ambassadors he received only one, in 1657.

41. C.M. Prior, *The Royal Studs of the Sixteenth and Seventeenth Centuries* (London, 1935), p. 41, explains that jennets (or genets) are specifically Andalusian horses, while the term Barbary horses covers blood animals from elsewhere in Spain and from Morocco.

42. D'Osma had been commissioned by Elizabeth's Master of the Horse, Robert Dudley, Earl of Leicester, to survey the royal studs. In his report, dated 1576, he concludes that since Malmesbury is situated in a damp, clayey valley, producing fodder unsuitable for mares in foal, the entire stock should be transferred to Tutbury. The report is reproduced by Prior (op. cit. (n. 41), pp. 11–38).

43. Elizabeth had earlier maintained a stud at Greenwich Palace (Fitzgerald, op. cit. (n. 1), p. 7). James had received a gift of a single horse in the course of his initial progress from Edinburgh to London when, at Apethorpe in Northamptonshire, he was presented by Sir Anthony Mildmay with 'a gallant Barbary horse, and a very rich saddle, with furniture suitable therunto' (Nichols, op. cit. (n. 1), Vol. I, pp. 97–8). The Eltham stud survived until the Civil War, but when John Evelyn visited on 13 April 1656 he found 'both Palace & Chapell in miserable ruines, the noble woods & park destroyed by Rich the Rebell' (Evelyn, *Diary*, Vol. III, p. 170).

44. Fitzgerald, op. cit. (n. 1), p. 7. An alternative source gives two stallions rather than eleven: John Packer to Mr Winwood, 2 April 1605, reproduced in Nichols, op. cit. (n. 1), Vol. I, p. 505. Another significant gift followed a decade later when the Queen's brother, Christian IV of Denmark, sent her twelve mares, all in foal (Fitzgerald, op. cit. (n. 1), p. 8).

45. Fitzgerald, op. cit. (n. 1), pp. 7–8.

46. Prince Charles received '. . . eighteen Spanish genets, sixe Barberies, sixe breeding mares, and twenty foles, all covered with cloths of crymson velvet, garnisht and garded with gold lace, and scutcheons of his

arms; and one of them had a saddle of fine lambe-skinnes, the other furniture set and embroydered with most riche pearle . . . and two stallions, with their mares', while the Duke of Buckingham was presented with 'twelve Spanish genets, four Moriscos or Barbarie horses, four mares, and ten foales, covered with mantles of crimson velvet garnisht with gold' ('A relation of the departure of the most illustrious Prince of Wales from Madrid', reproduced in Nichols, op. cit. (n. 1), Vol. III, pp. 909–10).

47. 'A Noat of the Daie of the Month that my Lord [Buckingham] his Mares were Covered, and with what Horses, in Anno 1623', reproduced in Prior, op. cit. (n. 41), pp. 40–1.

48. In 1620 a survey of Malmsbury Race found a total of thirty-nine mares of which only eight had foals, suggesting that the remainder were recent acquisitions; all were covered with stallions of foreign blood (Prior, op. cit. (n. 41), pp. 66–8). See most recently, Arthur MacGregor, 'Strategies for Improving English Horses in the Sixteenth and Seventeenth Centuries', *Anthropozoologica*, 29 (1999), 65–74.

49. 'An Accompt of all his Ma[ts] Mares and Colts, within the race of Tutbury in Staffordshire, and with what Horses the Breeding Mares were Covered in this Yeare, 1624', reproduced in Prior, op. cit. (n. 41), pp. 48–9.

50. 'A True Inventory of all the Horses Belonging to Titbury Race being part of the late Kings personall estate taken July 24, 1649', reproduced in Prior, op. cit. (n. 41), pp. 56–61. The dismantling of the royal stud at this time had the beneficial effect of dispersing prime breeding stock among private studs up and down the country. Six horses were reserved for Cromwell's own use and others were acquired by two Parliamentary military commanders, Lieutenant-General Michael Jones and Colonel Sir Arthur Hazelrigg (Fitzgerald, op. cit. (n. 1), p. 14; Reese, op. cit. (n. 15), p. 182); the remainder were sold off. Cromwell appointed his own Master of the Horse in the person of his son-in-law, John Claypole. The latter made no significant impact on the stud, but Cromwell maintained the establishment at Hampton Court, the only royal stud to survive the Commonwealth.

51. As a further part of that settlement the Crown received the port of Tangier, where large numbers of Portuguese cavalry horses were stationed: these henceforth became the property of the British garrison and saw active service as the Tangier Horse until 1684, when the regiment returned to England to form the King's Own Regiment of Dragoons (the Royals).

52. See *True Protestant Mercury*, 107 (14 January 1681/2). The ambassador himself became something of a celebrity in equestrian circles: Evelyn records that Ohadu was 'entertained by most of the nobility in Towne; and went often to *Hide-Park* on *horse-back*, where he and his retinue shewed their extraordinary activity in Horsemanship, and the flinging & Catching their launces at full speede. They rid very short, & could stand up right in full speede, managing their speares with incredible agility' (*Diary*, op. cit. (n. 43), Vol. IV, pp. 268–9 (24 January 1682)). See further *True Protestant Mercury*, 111 (25–8 January 1681/2; *Loyal Protestant and True Domestick Intelligence*, 103 (14 January 1681/2); 119 (21 February 1681/2); and *Monthly Recorder*, 3 (1 February–1 March 1681/2).

53. Fitzgerald, op. cit. (n. 1), p. 18.

54. From a collection of stable warrants dated 1626–30 (PRO, LC5/78, reproduced and analysed in Arthur MacGregor, 'Horsegear, Vehicles and Stable Equipment at the Stuart Court: a Documentary Archaeology', *Archaeological Journal*, 153 (1996), 148–200), it seems that there were at this time twenty of the King's hunting horses maintained on the establishment of the Master of the Horse. The King was furnished through this department with hunting saddles covered with red velvet

and garnished with gold and silver lace. Provisions for a number of office-holders at Court are similarly listed.

55. 'A Furniture for a Horse of Crimson Velvett being Studed wth Silver Enamelled' and three velvet-covered saddles, one sewn with pearls, were among items disposed of in the Commonwealth sale: see Arthur MacGregor, 'The King's Disport; Sports and Pastimes of the Early Stuarts', in MacGregor, op. cit. (n. 19), p. 403.

56. I am grateful to Dr David Howarth, who drew my attention to the survival of these items, and to His Grace the Duke of Buccleuch and Queensberry, who kindly supplied me with details of them.

57. Reproduced in full in MacGregor, op. cit. (n. 26).

58. PRO, LC9/263.

59. BL, Harley MS 5010, ff. 35v–6r.

60. Royal Archives, Windsor Castle, RA EB 10, p. 42; MacGregor, op. cit. (n. 26), pp. 191–2.

61. M. de Fontenay to Mary Stuart's secretary, 15 August 1584: Historical Manuscripts Commission, *Calendar of the Manuscripts of . . . the Marquis of Salisbury, Preserved at Hatfield House*, Part III (London, 1899), pp. 60–1.

62. Mr Chamberlaine to Mr Winwood, 26 January 1605, reproduced in Nichols, op. cit. (n. 1), Vol. I, p. 491.

63. *CSPV, 1603–7*, p. 90.

64. *CSPV, 1603–7*, p. 353, dated 31 May 1606. The ambassador, Zorzi Giustiniani, continues: 'The people, too, desire to see their sovereign. The discontent has reached such a pitch that the other day there was affixed to the door of the Privy Chamber a general complaint of the King . . .' Needless to say, it had no effect.

65. *CSPV, 1603–7*, p. 469.

66. *CSPV, 1617–19*, pp. 116–17.

67. *CSPV, 1617–19*, pp. 259–60.

68. *CSPV, 1607–10*, p. 276.

69. *CSPV, 1615–17*, p. 309.

70. See Hore, op. cit. (n. 31), p. 98. Horses were also required for the deer van and for the canvas-covered 'hound van', although these may at times have been interchangeable in their functions: three new 'dog waggons' were bought in 1660 to remove the deer from place to place (ibid., p. 174). Under James I, Richard Little was Waggoner for the Buckhounds in the summer and for the Harriers in the winter (ibid., p. 104). One waggon mentioned in the accounts of the Great Wardrobe for 1630 cost £236; repairs on an old one cost £94 14*s* 4*d*. From another source we learn that all mayors, sheriffs, justices, etc. were to see that due provision was made, when required, for a sufficient team of horses or oxen with harness to draw the waggons to such places as the King might appoint (Thomas James, Master of Toyles, for taking deer from Windsor Forest to Richmond 18 April 1640) (ibid., p. 134).

71. Hore, op. cit. (n. 31), pp. 89–110. The extinction of Brocas's hereditary rights proved less than straightforward. At first he was paid a per capita fee for the use of his hounds but later his hereditary fees had to be restored. When the Brocas's hereditary manor at Little Weldon was sold in 1633, the rights passed to purchaser Sir Lewis Watson, 1st Baron Rockingham, and they remained with the Rockingham family until a final amalgamation in 1707 (Reese, op. cit. (n. 15), p. 175).

72. Reese, op. cit. (n. 15), pp. 190–1.

73. John Cary to the Earl of Rutland, 31 May 1640: 'Some days the war goes on, some days not. However I believe the King does not, for yesterday he began to hunt and has ordered more hunting horses for his own saddle.' HMC, *The Manuscripts of His Grace the Duke of Rutland, Preserved at Belvoir Castle*, Vol. I (London, 1888), p. 520.

74. Pepys, *Diary*, Vol. II, p. 152, tells of 'a great match of hunting of a Stagg the King had yesterday [10 August 1661], and how the King tired all their horses and came home with not above two or three able to keep pace with him'.

75. *CSPD, 1611–13*, p. 382.

76. Hore, op. cit. (n. 31), p. 134, for example, mentions that Sir Timothy Tyrell, together with Sir Thomas Badger and Thomas Potts enjoyed a royal licence to transport beyond the seas 'all manner of hounds, beagles, and sporting dogs', and issued an express command to officers of ports not to allow any person to transport such dogs without their permission.

77. George Turbervile's *Noble Arte of Venerie or Hunting* (London, 1575), pp. 1–28, for example, contains hints on the varieties of hounds and how to manage them.

78. The number of hounds in the pack is referred to in 1635 when Anthony Dodsworth, Serjeant of the Buckhounds, received payment of 'the several allowances of £50 and £50, as well as £100 per annum more, for keeping sixteen couple of buckhounds for his Majesty's service': *CSPD, 1634–5*, p. 505.

79. Hore, op. cit. (n. 31), p. 116.

80. Witness the countrymen of Royston, who on one occasion abducted one of James I's favourite hounds, named Jowler, later returning him with the following note tied round his neck: 'Good Mr. Jowler, we pray you speake to the King (for he hears you every day, and so doth he not us) that it will please his Majestie to go back to London, for els the country whilbe undoon; all our provition is spent already, and we are not able to intertayne him longer.' The plea fell on deaf ears, however, for 'it was taken for a jeast, and so pas'd over, for his Majestie entends to ly thear yet a fortnet' (Sir Edmund Lascelles to the Earl of Shrewsbury, 7 November 1604, reproduced in Nichols, op. cit. (n. 1), Vol. I, p. 465.

81. Summarised in Arthur MacGregor, 'Deer on the Move: Relocation of Stock between Game Parks in the Sixteenth and Seventeenth Centuries', *Anthropozoologica*, 16 (1992), 167–79.

82. Some 2,000 acres were emparked at Richmond alone by Charles I during the 1630s: see further, Arthur MacGregor, 'Animals and the Early Stuarts: Hunting and Hawking at the Courts of James I and Charles I', *Archives of Natural History*, 16 (1989), 305–6 and n. 1.

83. MacGregor, op. cit. (n. 82), pp. 307–8; see also MacGregor, op. cit. (n. 81), pp. 171–3, appendices 4, 5, 7. Mention is made in 1623 of 'His Majesty's park, which is to be enclosed, near Dublin, for the breeding of deer and maintenance of game (*CSPD, 1615–21*, p. 429).

84. Hore, op. cit. (n. 31), pp. 173–4.

85. Ibid., p. 179.

86. J.Y. Akerman (ed.), *Moneys Received and Paid for Secret Services of Charles II and James II* (Camden Society, 52, London, 1851), p. 135.

87. The title and extent of responsibility seems to have varied over the years: a grant to Sir Henry Seckford and Thomas Bedingfield of 15 August 1603 is for the mastership of the Tents, Hales and Pavilions (*CSPD, 1603–10*, p. 32), while on 17 May 1609 Thomas Jones was appointed Master of the Toils and Pale of Canvas for Hunting (ibid., p. 513); at other times these offices evidently formed separate areas of responsibility.

88. *CSPD, 1603–10*, p. 32.

89. Ibid., p. 583.

90. *CSPD, 1633–4*, p. 154.

91. J.H. Round, *The King's Serjeants and Officers of State* (London, 1911), p. 279n. A lime (or liam) hound is a leash-hound.

92. Hore, op. cit. (n. 31), p. 158.

93. MacGregor, op. cit. (n. 82), p. 311.

94. Reese, op. cit. (n. 15), p. 199.

95. *CSPD, 1623–5*, pp. 204, 293.

96. Round, op. cit. (n. 91), p. 309.

97. MacGregor, op. cit. (n. 82), p. 312.

98. General requests can be found in *CSPI, 1622*, pp. 353, 409; *1633–47*, p. 7; rent-hawks are mentioned in *CSPI, 1625–32*, p. 540; *1633–47*, p. 7.

99. For a general account of this sport, published after the present chapter was submitted for publication, see C.E. Jackson, 'Fishing with Cormorants', *Archives of Natural History*, 24 (1997), 189–211.

100. MacGregor, op. cit. (n. 82), pp. 313–14.

101. *CSPV, 1617–19*, p. 258, dated 10 July 1618.

102. Prior, op. cit. (n. 40), p. 51.

103. Akerman, op. cit. (n. 86), p. vi. Other officers included in this list who are of interest in the present context are falconers (12), huntsmen, otter-hound keepers, officers of the leash (6), officers of the bears (3) and a bird keeper.

104. Keith Thomas, *Man and the Natural World. Changing Attitudes in England 1500–1800* (London, 1983), p. 275.

105. MacGregor, op. cit. (n. 55), p. 403.

106. Thomas, op. cit. (n. 104), p. 144, with references.

107. Colvin, *King's Works IV 1485–1660 (Part II)* (London, 1982), p. 102.

108. *CSPV, 1617–19*, p. 258.

109. *CSPD, 1635–6*, p. 218. At the same time Caldwell was appointed 'chief keeper of his Majesty's bandogs and mastiffs' at a fee of 10*d* a day (ibid., p. 220).

110. A description of the park by a German nobleman in 1598 (H. Walpole (ed.), *A Journey into England by Paul Hentzner in the Year MDXCVIII* (Strawberry Hill, 1757), p. 34) mentions only deer there.

111. PRO, SP14/62, 167. Sir Thomas Browne later possessed a 'fine green channelled egge' laid by a 'cassaware or emeu' during Charles I's reign (S. Wilkin (ed.), *The Works of Sir Thomas Browne* (London, 1852), Vol. III, pp. 469–70).

112. Museum of London, reg. no. Z6312; reproduced with useful discussion by Rosemary Weinstein, 'Some Menagerie Accounts of James I', *Transactions of the London and Middlesex Archaeological Society*, 31 (1980), 133–41.

113. *CSPD, 1682*, p. 39; *Domestick Intelligence*, 70 (19–22 January 1681/2).

114. *CSPD, 1623–5*, p. 9.

115. Nichols, op. cit. (n. 1), Vol. IV, p. 879.

116. Ibid., Vol. I, p. 515.

117. Ibid., Vol. I, pp. 515–16.
118. Ibid., Vol. II, p. 259.
119. Ibid., Vol II, pp. 307–8.
120. Ibid., Vol. I, p. 516.
121. J. Bayley, *The History and Antiquities of the Tower of London*, Part 1 (London, 1821), p. 271.
122. Thomas, op. cit. (n. 104), p. 101.

6

TASTE AND CONNOISSEURSHIP AT THE COURT OF CHARLES I: INIGO JONES AND THE WORK OF GIULIO ROMANO

Jeremy Wood

'His M[ajest]^{tie} knowes best what he hath *gusto* in'. This concise verdict on Charles I as a connoisseur was made by Thomas Howard, Earl of Arundel, in 1636.[1] But, despite the King's lasting reputation as a collector, royal taste depended on the advice of specialists and was moulded by astute courtiers, both at home and abroad. Indeed, works of art could be used in the hope of influencing and even manipulating the King. A series of vivid eyewitness accounts from the 1630s record how several diplomatic gifts were received by Charles and his consort, Henrietta Maria. For example, in January 1636 Cardinal Francesco Barberini (nephew of the reigning Pope, Urban VIII) sent a group of works by sixteenth-century Italian masters to the Queen, of which more later.[2] The papal agent in England, Gregorio Panzani, had written to Cardinal Francesco that the King and Queen 'do not care whether the pictures are old or modern, so long as they are good'. Soon after, he added that though the King had a 'good nose' (*buon naso*) for pictures, old ones might please him more because of their rarity.[3] In March 1636, the States General of the Netherlands tried to emulate the success of Barberini with the gift of a small group of pictures, seven horses and a clock,[4] but the Dutch, unlike the shrewd papal agent, did not understand the royal taste in art. The presentation of some works by early Netherlandish masters aroused far less enthusiasm than seven white coach horses with trimmings of red velvet and bridles and harnesses wrought with gold.

London had become a competitive centre of the art trade even before the accession of Charles I, despite the fact that it had no dealers with large stocks of pictures like those found in Venice, Rome, Amsterdam and Antwerp. Although some of the London dealers were *marchands amateurs* of sorts, others acted as agents who bought works both on commission and as a speculation, acquiring pictures individually and in large consignments. The market itself was entirely focused on the Court and dealers catered for a much smaller circle of aristocratic clients than was the case in Italy or the Netherlands. Since the trade was largely concentrated on the import of Italian pictures, it was essential for a dealer to have good contacts abroad, or the opportunity to travel. While the role of ambassadors, such as Sir Henry Wotton and Sir Dudley Carleton, is well known, much less attention has been given to the activities of a small number of men who did not simply sell works of art but provided the expertise with which to appraise them. This group, which had strong ties to the community of artists in London, included Jan van Belcamp, Diego Duarte, Nathaniel Garrit, George Geldorp, Edward Norgate, Nicasius Russell, and Symon Stone.[5] Two experts, however, were pre-eminent at Court, indeed they seem to have acted as the eyes and ears of Charles I in matters to do with his collection: Nicholas Lanier, Master of the King's Musick, and Inigo Jones, Surveyor of the King's Works.

Lanier's expertise in this field was recognised when he was given authority to negotiate the purchase of the Mantuan collection on behalf of the King.[6] In addition, the status of both Lanier and Jones as art experts is shown by a warrant issued in August 1628 that required them 'to cause a p[re]sent Inventory to be made of all his M[ajestie]s Pictures Statues and Meddalls of mettall and Stone'.[7] The reason for this warrant was surely the arrival of the first portion of the Mantuan pictures in London, which had been dispatched from Malamocco on 15 April of that year.[8] This lost inventory of the royal collection (which must have been used by van der Doort when he compiled his celebrated inventory a decade later),[9] was clearly drawn up by the two most prominent experts on art then at Court.

Inigo Jones's importance as an arbiter of taste emerges vividly from Panzani's account of the reception of the Barberini gift of 1636, already mentioned. He described how the King hastily summoned Jones – as well as other courtiers – to the Queen's bedchamber where the pictures were displayed. Jones threw off his riding cloak, put on his spectacles, and examined the works minutely. He was the most-travelled expert on art at the Court – as well as its leading architect and designer of masques – so his opinion was important, but Panzani described him as 'vain and boastful' because he did nothing to hide his self-satisfaction at identifying the names of the artists in question, repeating one of his attributions often 'to show his great expertise in painting'. Panzani had placed 'the note of the painters' on each picture, but the King removed these, and it is clear that this was done to test Jones's powers as a connoisseur and to put him on his mettle.[10]

The author of the most substantial account of the art market in Britain from 1680 to the mid-eighteenth century has claimed that in the earlier Stuart period there were few collectors; that it was illegal to import paintings for sale; and that the Civil War had a catastrophic impact on art dealing.[11] Nonetheless, it could be argued that the importance of what was collected far outweighed the number of collectors; that there appears to have been a brisk trade in works of art to and from the Continent throughout the period; and that the dispersal of Charles I's collection had a stimulating effect on the developing British art market. This chapter, however, looks at the topic from a different angle and examines the emergence of early seventeenth-century connoisseurship and expertise in art. It considers what was known about the kind of sixteenth-century Italian painting that had such high status at Court, and, in particular, it reflects on the appreciation of one of the first Italian artists to be celebrated in England: Giulio Romano. Indeed, Giulio was the only Renaissance artist to be named by Shakespeare who, in *The Winter's Tale*, mentions 'that rare Italian Master, *Iulio Romano*, who (had he himselfe Eternitie, and could put Breath into his Worke) would beguile Nature of her Custome, so perfectly he is her ape'.[12] In some notes on Italian art that Jones provided for Thomas Marshall of Lincoln College, Oxford, he discussed Michelangelo, Raphael, Giulio Romano, Polidoro and Giovanni da Udine, in what was probably intended as a survey of the most important sixteenth-century artists.[13]

There are several neglected sources that throw light on Jones as an art expert and connoisseur. One is provided by the notes that he wrote in his copy of the 1568 edition of Vasari's *Vite*, of which one volume survives at Worcester College Library, Oxford.[14] Another can be found in his annotated copy of Lomazzo's *Trattato* of 1584, now in the National Art Library at the Victoria and Albert Museum.[15] Jones annotated the Life of Giulio Romano in his copy of Vasari heavily (see Appendix towards the end of this chapter), and his comments on Giulio's life and work have a particular resonance in the context of Stuart collecting, given the large numbers of his transportable works (as opposed to immovable frescoes) that were to arrive in London in the late 1620s among the pictures obtained from Mantua. Jones's notes indicate something of what was known at Court about the artist's life and work, and they fit into a sequence of visits made to Mantua that began before the acquisition of the Gonzaga collection had even been contemplated, and that culminated in the negotiations for its purchase. Jones and Arundel were in the city either in 1613 or 1614; the Countess of Arundel visited Mantua in 1623, and Lanier was there on a number of occasions in 1625–6 and 1627–8, at which time he appears to have obtained a significant group of drawings by Giulio from what remained of the artist's studio. Lanier was even to buy several paintings by him during the dispersal of the King's goods in the 1650s.[16] For a small – but influential – group of English connoisseurs, the Mantuan collection was not a random assembly of pictures and sculptures, but part of a late Renaissance court which had been fashioned by one of the greatest sixteenth-century artists who was both a painter and an architect.

Jones began his annotations to the Life of Giulio by endorsing Vasari's view that the artist 'expressed his conceyt better in desine than in collors' (see Appendix, no. 1).[17] His subsequent notes are focused on Giulio's work in Mantua, not Rome; indeed, Jones treated the *Vita* as if it were a guidebook to Palazzo Te although, in addition, there are a few comments on Giulio's interest in antiquity at the end of the biography (Appendix, nos 22–3), as well as on the prints made after his work which Jones knew (Appendix, nos 9, 11, 20). Jones paraphrased Vasari's observation that the idea of a new palace emerged out of Giulio's remodelling of Duke Federigo's stables (fig. 1, overleaf; Appendix, no. 2); that he made use of the old walls; and that he built in brick because of the lack of local stone (Appendix, no. 3).

Jones's reference to rustication (Appendix, no. 6) is a reminder that Giulio's work has long been recognised as a source for the Banqueting House in Whitehall.[18] Although Palladio's palaces in Vicenza are rightly understood as a crucial model for Jones, it is known he believed that Palladio's Palazzo Thiene was derived from designs by Giulio. This is a building with a high rusticated base which contrasts, by means of channelled ashlar in the upper storey, with a more crisp suggestion of rustication on this level. The attribution is found in a note that Jones made in his copy of the *Quattro Libri*: 'Scamozo and Palmo saith thes designes wear of Gulio Romano and executed by Palladio', adding at a later date (as if after visiting the building), '& so yt seemes'.[19] Scholars have previously transcribed 'Palmo' as 'Palermo', along with other inaccuracies,[20] but, in fact, this note suggests that (in addition to meeting Vincenzo Scamozzi while in Venice) Jones also talked to the eminent painter Palma Giovane (b. 1548) and discussed Giulio's work with him.

Jones's note that the courtyard at Palazzo Te has four entrances (Appendix, no. 6) may appear a mistake since in reality there are only three that lead directly from the exterior into the courtyard. However, Vasari's account was obviously written as if standing in the main *cortile* where there are indeed four imposing doorways.[21] It is probable that Vasari worked from a plan showing how the building was meant to be completed, provided not by Giulio himself at the time of their meeting late in 1541,[22] as has been widely assumed, but by Jacopo Strada.[23] On the other hand, Vasari's description evokes a visit that passes through a sequence of rooms and also reflects first-hand experience.[24] Nevertheless, although Vasari visited Mantua for a second time in May 1566, he did not correct those details that are clearly wrong in the first edition of the *Vite*, and which concerned the actual location of frescoed decorations rather than the ideal conception of the building.[25] Jones appears unconcerned with any such niceties and at this point he simply endorsed Vasari's correct account of two of the main rooms, adding in the margin: 'The haall painted in fresco wth horses' (Appendix, no. 7). This is the celebrated Sala dei Cavalli, painted with Duke Federigo's horses which stand in front of fictive windows opening onto views of the surrounding countryside. 'From this', Jones wrote, 'on[e] passes in to a corrner chamber the volt with stucco & ye marrage of Cupid and Psiches paynted' (Appendix, no. 8); and 'other stories of Psiches in ye same roome in the *fattziati* [=*facciati*] below' (Appendix, no. 9).

Although Jones's visit to Mantua appears not to have been observed in the literature before now,[26] his next note makes it certain that he did indeed see the

dendo, che non haueua caualcatura,
chiamato Luggieri glie lo donò,& montato,che G
darono fuor della porta di S. Baſtiano,lontano vn t
Eccel. haueua vn luogo,& certe ſtalle chiamato il T
ria,doue teneua la razza de'ſuoi caualli,& caualle.
Marcheſe,che harebbe voluto,ſenza guaſtare la mu
dare vn poco di luogo da poterui andare,& riduru
cena per iſpaſſo. Giulio vdita la volontà del March
nata la pianta di quel ſito,miſe mano all'opera; &
chie fece in vna parte maggiore la prima sala, che
col seguito delle camere,che la mettono in mezzo.
pietre viue,ne commodi di caue da potere far conci
ſi vſa nelle muraglie da chi puo farlo; ſi serui di m
uorandole poi di ſtucco.Et di queſta materia fece c
nici,porte,fineſtre,& altri lauori,con belliſsime p
& ſtrauagante maniera gl'ornamenti delle volte,c
liſsimi,e con ricetti riccamente ornati: Il che fu ca
cipio,ſi riſolueſſe il Marcheſe di far poi tutto quell
palazzo : perche Giulio fatto vn belliſsimo modell
cortile d'opera ruſtica,piacque tãto a quel Signore
uiſione di danari, & da Giulio condotti molti ma
con breuità al suo fine. La forma del quale palazzo
difizio quadro,& ha nel mezzo vn cortile scopto a
za,nella quale sboccano in croce quattro entrate:
prima viſta trafora,ouero paſſa in vna grãdiſsima l
altra nel giardino;e due altre vanno a diuerſi appa
ornate di ſtucchi,& di pitture. E nella sala,alla qu
dipinta infreſco la volta fatta in varij spartimenti:
tratti di naturale tutti i caualli piu belli,& piu fau
cheſe,& inſieme con eſsi i cani di quello ſteſſo ma
no i caualli,co'nomi loro: che tutti furono diſegn
pra la calcina a fresco da Benedetto Pagni,& da Ri
ri,e suoi creati,& nel vero coſi bene,che paiono vi
in vna ſtanza,che è in sul canto del palazzo,laqual
timento belliſsimo di ſtucchi,&con variate cornic
d'oro. E queſte fanno vn partimento con quattro
piu alto della uolta con quadro,nel quale è cupido
ue(che è abbagliato nel piu alto da una luce celeſte
tutti gli Dei Pſiche. Della quale ſtoria non è poſsib
grazia,& diſegno; hauendo Giulio fatto scortare

1. Inigo Jones's annotations concerning the plan of Palazzo Te and the decoration of the Sala di Psiche from the *Vita* of Giulio Romano in G. Vasari, *Le vite de più eccellenti pittori, scultori et architettori*, 1568, p. 330. (The Provost and Fellows of Worcester College, Oxford)

2. Giovanni Battista Franco after Giulio Romano, *Feast of Cupid and Psyche*, left-hand section. (Engraving)

Sala di Psiche: 'an errour in Batti[sta] franco to make mars in the Bath for thear is an armour and a helmet hanging[.] this commes for waant of history' (Appendix, no. 9). Jones evidently owned the most celebrated early engraving of the fresco (figs 2–3, above and overleaf),[27] which rearranges and reverses some of the scenes on the walls of the Sala di Psiche depicting *The Feast of Cupid and Psyche*. Jones was sharp-eyed in noting that in the group of Mars and Venus from the north wall, the helmet, shown lying on the ground and which Mars has sensibly taken off before getting into the bath, has been moved to the branch of a nearby tree in Battista Franco's engraving. Jones can only have made this observation when standing in the room itself, but why did he think that this discrepancy between engraving and fresco showed the printmaker's 'want of history'? The helmet is included in both, albeit differently. In what way is it either anachronistic or a misunderstanding of the story? Indeed, if the subject is depicted wrongly, it is surely Giulio rather than the engraver who is at fault. Vasari puzzlingly identified the woman in the bath as Psyche, rather than Venus, but Jones did not correct this, probably because he was confused – as were many later commentators – by Giulio's inclusion of this scene (and the adjacent one of

3. Giovanni Battista Franco after Giulio Romano, *Feast of Cupid and Psyche*, right-hand section. (Engraving)

Mars expelling Adonis), in what is otherwise a straightforward series of subjects taken from Apuleius. Jones also did not notice that Vasari provided a probable reason for Battista Franco's omission, since he observed that the engraving was made from Giulio's preparatory cartoon. It would have been standard practice for this to omit a detail such as the helmet because a specialist assistant would have been delegated to paint it. Jones's interest in *The Feast of Cupid and Psyche* is also shown by his reuse of the elephant and camel in the proscenium that he designed in 1634 for the Queen's masque, *The Temple of Love*, staged one year later.[28] There is no doubt that he adapted these animals from one of the available prints (as the differences between the fresco and the engravings reveal), and this was typical of his practice as a masque designer.

Following in Vasari's footsteps, as if touring the building with him, Jones surprisingly endorsed several more of his mistakes. Jones, reiterating Vasari, wrote that a room decorated in imitation of Trajan's column is next to the Sala di Psiche (Appendix, no. 12) when in fact it is further along in the sequence of rooms. He also noted a 'Suffitto [=*soffitto*, ceiling] of an anticamero of Icearos' (fig. 4, opposite; Appendix, no. 13) in the Camera delle Aquile, when the subject

4. Inigo Jones's annotations concerning the Camera delle Aquile, Camera dei Venti and construction of the Sala dei Giganti at Palazzo Te from the *Vita* of Giulio Romano in G. Vasari, *Le vite de più eccellenti pittori, scultori et architettori*, 1568, p. 332. (The Provost and Fellows of Worcester College, Oxford)

is actually the *Fall of Phaeton*;[29] and he placed a 'history of ye 12 monoth in ye saa[m] room' (Appendix, no. 14),[30] when it is in fact in the Camera dei Venti.[31] The explanation may be that Jones made some of his notes *before* visiting Palazzo Te, or that he only gained access to the Sala dei Cavalli and the Sala di Psiche; the other rooms being more private. Indeed, the Camera delle Aquile was one of the smallest in the palace and had originally been used as a bedroom.

On reaching the celebrated Sala dei Giganti, Jones's comments again follow the sequence of Vasari's account, noting how the fabric was constructed (on strengthened foundations because it was on marshy ground), before turning to the room's decoration: 'Jove kylling ye giants painted in yt' (Appendix, no. 16). Jones particularly noted the size of the room and the way in which the patterning of the stones on the floor (unfortunately heavily restored during the eighteenth century), seemed to merge with the lower part of the walls (Appendix, no. 18),[32] so that the space appeared fluid, and it was difficult to see where the painting ended and the floor began. Jones did not make any particular comment on the spectacular drama of the room where a building seems to collapse on top of the spectator, crushing the painted giants to death, and threatening the living viewer; although one would think that as an architect he would enjoy the joke and as a designer of court masques he might admire the illusion. His annotations suggest that he approached the palace as a coherent architectural whole that contained painted decoration, and the phrase that Vasari used to suggest Giulio's style: 'new and fantastic' (*nuova e stravagante*; Appendix, no. 5) is repeated by Jones (Appendix, no. 15) as if telegraphing the character of Giulio's work.

When making some of these annotations Jones underlined key phrases in the text and then translated them in the margin.[33] But, in a number of other cases, translation and underlining do not correspond exactly, and the translation relates to a comment or a series of comments that have been framed by underlinings. These underlinings are clearly intended as pointers to particularly interesting passages, while the marginal notes give a succinct guide to their contents. In one case, as observed above, Jones transposed a word from another part of the text as a comment on a particular passage (Appendix, no. 15). Some of his observations reveal how he used engravings to amplify Vasari's text (Appendix, nos 9, 11, 20) and, towards the end of the passage on Palazzo Te, Jones added a laconic comment that 'Vasari is weary of ye discription of this Pallas' (Appendix, no. 19). Only in a few cases is there evidence of the order in which the notes were made, but it is clear they did not simply follow the sequence of the text. For example, the note beginning 'Discription of the Palasso dell T' (fig. 1; Appendix, no. 6) was written before the preceding ones beginning 'Julio safes ye ould waales' (Appendix, no. 3) since the section 'Manor of ye vots new and stravagant ornamente' (Appendix, no. 5), which follows on from it, had to be squeezed into the available space. It could certainly be argued, however, that some of the annotations were made in preparation for a visit to the palace, rather than as a critical commentary on a building that was already familiar to Jones.

Jones is likely to have visited Mantua with Lord Arundel either in July 1613 on the way from Milan to Padua via Parma,[34] or on the return journey from Rome in July of the following year.[35] The fruits of this visit can be seen in the one paid for by Lady Arundel to Mantua some time later in 1623.[36] In July of that year she wrote to Count Alessandro Striggio, on behalf of Lord Arundel, requesting a scale model of Palazzo Te to be made by a skilled craftsman: 'to show every detail, together with a clear description of the principal things to be seen inside by way of sculpture and painting, that is, what is in each room and how it is arranged. And if it were possible to have the original model that was used for the same building, he would be even more grateful.'[37]

Vasari refers to the 'very beautiful model' that Giulio had made for the building, but the Countess had presumably seen it for herself when she visited the palace.[38] The interpretation of her letter has recently become very confused and has been said to refer to Palazzo Ducale in Mantua,[39] despite the fact that Lady Arundel explicitly asks for a model of 'the palace of his Serene Highness the duke of Mantua known as the Te'. The letter cannot refer to the ducal palace which housed the bulk of the Gonzaga pictures, including Titian's *Emperors* (since destroyed) and Mantegna's *Triumphs*, now at Hampton Court.[40] Indeed, between 1592 and 1608 Vincenzo I Gonzaga had constructed a vast room in Palazzo Ducale, the Galleria della Mostra, to house both paintings and antique sculptures.[41] As a consequence, the letter to Striggio cannot have anything to do with the projected sale of the Gonzaga pictures.[42] Lady Arundel's request for 'a clear description of the principal things to be seen inside by way of sculpture and painting' should be understood as meaning a written text explaining Giulio's decorations, which not only included frescoes but stuccoes in high relief.

The notes that Jones made in his books occasionally refer to specific pictures, although he did pass in silence over topics which one might expect to have been of interest. In his copy of Lomazzo's *Trattato*, Jones ignored some comments at the opening of a chapter on ideal proportion, which criticise Parmigianino's inappropriate use of elongation in his figures. Despite Jones's known enthusiasm for the artist's work,[43] he wrote nothing here, nor surprisingly did he annotate the Life of Parmigianino in his copy of Vasari. However, when Lomazzo goes on to say that some great masters – whom he will not name – have made their figures all look alike, Jones adds 'Michelangelo' in the margin.[44] Lomazzo then claims that Raphael excelled in depicting slender and agile figures, with good proportions, as in his *Saint George and the Dragon* now in the National Gallery of Art, Washington,[45] originally painted for the Duke of Urbino, and Jones adds: 'The Saint Giorg that my lo[rd] Cha[mber]lain hath. [T]he proportion of slender young [bo]dy of 9 hedes.'[46] This picture was engraved by Lucas Vorsterman in 1627 (fig. 5, overleaf) as in the possession of William Herbert,

5. Lucas Vorsterman after Raphael, *St George and the Dragon*, 1627. (Counterproof engraving; © Copyright The British Museum)

3rd Earl of Pembroke, then Lord Chamberlain,[47] but it is known from Van der Doort that not long afterwards Charles I obtained it by exchange for Holbein's famous book of portrait drawings.[48] (The idea that the *Saint George* was a ducal gift to Henry VII is now largely discredited, and nothing certain is known about how it came to England.)[49] Part of the picture's attraction for the King was no doubt that St George wears the Order of the Garter. Jones's appreciation of it was certainly informed by what Lomazzo had to say about proportion, and the chapters on numerical ratio and the human body are the most heavily annotated in Jones's copy of the *Trattato*.

In at least one case it is possible to see how Jones used his copy of Vasari as a connoisseur's handbook. As already noted, a gift of pictures arrived at the Court from Cardinal Francesco Barberini on 30 January 1636[50] which, incidentally, included some cartoons by Giulio of *putti* climbing trees, picking fruit and fighting.[51] These have recently been confused with two allegories of *Diligence* and *Fame*, now at Hampton Court,[52] which were included in the same gift, but there can be no doubt that the works attributed to Giulio – and which pleased the King greatly – were from a series of designs for Gonzaga tapestries, which must surely have been sent because of the King's known interest in the tapestry factory at Mortlake.

Among the other works was a so-called Leonardo, now at Chatsworth (fig. 6, overleaf),[53] which, according to the papal agent, Gregorio Panzani, was 'especially pleasing to the Queen',[54] to whom the gift was ostensibly directed. Cardinal Francesco had commissioned the sculptor Bernini to find something suitable and it had been purchased in July 1635.[55] The Cardinal hesitated over the picture; he thought the skull painted on the reverse might frighten the Queen, and endanger her current pregnancy.[56] However, the work was dispatched, and Panzani recorded that: 'Jones, the king's architect, believes that the picture by [Leonardo] da Vinci is the portrait of a certain Ginevra Benci of Venice, and he concludes this from the G. and B. inscribed on her breast.'[57] Panzani did not know that the authority for Jones's identification came from his copy of Vasari. At the point in the Life of Leonardo where the famous portrait is mentioned, Jones wrote: 'la Ginevra di Amerigo Benci' in the margin.[58] That work, though, is the well-known picture now in the National Gallery of Art, Washington.[59] It was unfortunate for Jones's modern reputation as a connoisseur that there should be a Leonardesque portrait which fits Vasari's description, and that this work, now at Chatsworth and attributed to Boltraffio, should have come to England in 1636. However, although modern connoisseurship can distinguish between Leonardo and the Leonardesque, Jones was sufficiently expert to identify the style of this work, and he knew his copy of Vasari well enough to make a plausible connection with Ginevra de'Benci. How many other English courtiers could have done this in 1636?

It is far from clear how Jones became an art expert and connoisseur, but these skills were a logical development of his other interests, and it has long been known

6. Giovanni Antonio Boltraffio, *Portrait of a Young Man*. (Devonshire Collection, Chatsworth. Reproduced by permission of The Duke of Devonshire and the Chatsworth Settlement Trustees; photograph: Photographic Survey Courtauld Institute of Art)

that he began his career as a painter on the basis of a payment in the Earl of Rutland's accounts in 1603.[60] The frenzy of collecting at the Stuart Court created a need for men who could appraise and authenticate works of art. Since Jones and Lanier were among the few royal servants who had actually visited Mantua, their knowledge of the Gonzaga collection – the single greatest acquisition made by the King – gave them a special status.

Van der Doort's inventory of the royal collections, compiled in the late 1630s, shows that paintings by Giulio from Mantua were scattered throughout the Palaces of Whitehall, St James's and Greenwich. Although Giulio had produced several coherent series of pictures for particular rooms in the Palazzo Ducale, only one of these remained intact in the Gallery at St James's. It depicted horsemen who were mistakenly thought to represent Roman emperors, and was displayed alongside Titian's *Emperors* which had originally been hung with Giulio's series in the Gabinetto dei Cesari at Mantua.[61] Elsewhere, any decorative coherence that Giulio had intended was lost and, throughout the royal houses, secular and religious paintings by Giulio were placed side by side. His great altarpiece of the *Nativity with Saints Longinus and John the Evangelist*, now in the Louvre,[62] dominated the Second and Middle Privy Lodging Room at Whitehall, flanked – in a manner that was clearly not thought inappropriate at the time – by two of his mythologies that depicted the nativities of the gods: the *Birth of Diana and Apollo*, now at Hampton Court,[63] and the *Birth of Jupiter*, now in the National Gallery, London.[64] Although Everhard Jabach bought a few of the best works by Giulio from Charles I's collection when it was dispersed, many remained in Britain, and a surprising number were returned to the Crown in 1660.

The sale of Charles I's collection in 1649–51 is often seen as an act of cultural barbarism, but an alternative view is possible. Although the very finest works soon left the country, few if any were destroyed. Richard Symonds's notes record that a glut of pictures could be found at this time in the homes of former royal servants and that these were mostly for sale.[65] The profusion of paintings on the market made Italian art more accessible to a wider public than it had ever been before in London; it stimulated native artists in a way that the King had never thought necessary; and it created an art market that was no longer restricted to the Court.

APPENDIX

The following are Inigo Jones's annotations to the Life of Giulio Romano in his copy of the third part of Vasari's *Lives: Delli vite de'piu eccellenti pittori scultori et architettori scritte da M. Giorgio Vasari pittore et architetto Aretino, Primo Volume della Terza Parte*, Florence, 1568. Worcester College Library, Oxford, LR.A.3.13.

1. [*p. 327*]

'Julio expressed his conceyt better in desine than in collors' [*in margin*].

Jones here summarises Vasari's opinion that Giulio's ideas were expressed more strongly in his drawings than in painterly execution, and Jones underlines the phrase 'che Giulio esprimesse' in the text: 'Benche si puo affermare, che Giulio esprimesse sempre meglio i suoi concetti ne' disegni, che nell' operare, o nelle pitture: redendosi in quelli piu vivacita, fierezza, & affetto'.

2. [*p. 330*]

'The T a place of Stabols [*underlined*] first' [*in margin*].

Jones's note in the margin endorses Vasari's observation that Palazzo Te was constructed on the nucleus of some buildings previously used as stables by Federigo Gonzaga.

3. 'Julio safes ye ould waales[.] The haalle and seguito of chabard first maad' [*in margin*].

Jones underlines the words '& servedosi delle mura vecchie fece in una parte maggiore la prima sala' in Vasari's account of how Giulio reused the existing walls for the entrance hall and, because there were no local quarries, built with brick ('mattoni') and terracotta ('pietre cotte').[66] At this point Jones underlines the words 'si servi di mattoni'.

4. 'Bozi and colloms Bases and capitols of bricke' [*in margin*].

Jones's note endorses Vasari's comment that columns, bases and capitals were made of stuccoed brick.

5. 'Manor of ye vots new and stravagant ornamente' [*in margin*].

Jones's note endorses Vasari's comment that the decoration of the vaults at Palazzo Te was carried out in a new and fantastic style.

6. 'Discription of the Palasso dell T neear Mantoa: Rustica: Square[.] a court. 4 enterances. the first enterance lookes through a loggia into a garden. ye 2 other go to logings adorned' [*in margin*].

Jones here follows Vasari's account of the planning of Palazzo Te, and underlines the opening phrase 'La forma del quale palazzo è cosi fatta'. Jones's next reference to rustication relates back to a slightly earlier statement that the model was 'tutto fuori, e detro nel cortile d'opera rustica'. At the point where Vasari describes the building as quadrangular, Jones underlines the word 'quadro', and where Vasari states that it has an open courtyard like a piazza Jones underlines the word 'cortile' in the text. Vasari next (incorrectly) states that the building has four entrances and Jones underlines the word 'entrate'. The comment that one of these entrances faces a loggia that leads into a garden is summarised in Jones's note and, at the statement that two of the other entrances lead to rooms that are decorated in stucco and fresco, Jones underlines the words '& di pitture' at the close of this sentence.

7. 'The haall painted in fresco wth horses' [*in margin*].

Jones's note relates to Vasari's description of the chamber decorated with frescoes of Federigo Gonzaga's favourite horses (the Sala dei Cavalli) and, at this point, Jones underlines the phrase 'E nella Sala' at the opening of the passage as well as the slightly later reference to 'i cavalli'.

8. 'From this on[e] passes in to a corrner chamber the volt with stucco & ye marrage of Cupid and Psiches paynted' [*in margin*].

Jones's note follows Vasari's description of the room placed at a corner of the palace with a ceiling decorated in stucco and frescoes of the story of Cupid and Psyche (the Sala di Psiche). Jones underlines 'Da questa' at the opening of this sentence, as well as the words 'canto del palazzo' and 'stucchi'. At the close, where Vasari refers to the scene showing the 'marriage' of Cupid and Psyche, Jones underlines the phrase 'sposa alla presenza di tutti gli Dei' (who witness the event).

9. [*p. 331*]

'other stories of Psiches in ye same roome in the fattziati [*underlined*] below. an errour in Bati: franco to make mars in the Bath for thear is an armour and a helmet hanging[.] this commes for waant of history' [*in margin*].

Jones annotates Vasari's comment that the largest scenes from the story of Psyche are painted on the walls of this room, and Jones underlines the words 'restante' and 'di Psiche sono nelle faccie' in the text. Jones's remaining comments reveal his knowledge of an engraving by Battista Franco of Giulio's fresco.[67]

10. 'in the same quadro more of ye samm story' [*in margin*].

Jones's note relates to Vasari's inaccurate comment that nearby can be seen Psyche, attended by women, who catches sight of Apollo in the chariot of the Sun.[68] Jones underlines 'Poco lontano' at the opening of this sentence.

11. 'this History draune and Printed by B franco: the wch Print I haue' [*in margin*].

At Vasari's comment that Battista Franco engraved these episodes from the story of Cupid and Psyche from Giulio's cartoons for the frescoes, Jones adds that he owns the print,[69] and underlines 'Battista Franco Viniziano' in the text.

12. 'from this chambar of Psiches you go in to an other roome wth dubble fresses of stucco doo[n] by Primattitio imitating the Collona Traiano' [*in margin*].

Jones underlines the words 'si passa da q[uesta]' at Vasari's remark that the Sala di Psiche leads into a room (the Camera degli Stucchi) decorated by Francesco Primaticcio to Giulio's designs,[70] with stucco friezes imitating the scenes and costumes on Trajan's Column in Rome.

13. [*p. 332*]
'Suffitto of an anticamero of Icearos' [*in margin*].
Jones underlines 'E in un palco' at the opening of this passage, where Vasari describes the subject of Icarus and Daedalus, said to have been painted in oils on the ceiling of one of the antechambers, but probably confused with the *Fall of Phaeton* in the Camera delli Aquile.[71]

14. 'History of ye 12 monoth in ye saa[m] roome' [*in margin*] .
Jones underlines the words 'medesimo luogo' in Vasari's account of the stories ['storie'] of the Twelve Months, although these were in the Camera dei Venti, next to the Camera delli Aquile.[72]

15. 'Pas the grreat loggia you enter in to a Corner roome Stravagantly donn' [*in margin*].
Jones underlines the phrase 'Passata qlla loggia grande lavorata di stucci' at the opening of this sentence, describing how this loggia leads to the Sala dei Giganti. Jones here uses the word 'extravagant' which is not found at this point in Vasari's text, but is taken from an earlier passage in the Life of Giulio where Vasari refers to a 'nuova & stravagante maniera' of decoration.

16. 'because this corner was on mars[h] yt [was *deleted*] had dubble foundations[.] this is a round roome wth thyck waales to sustaine a dubble volte and round[.] in the corrners were ye chymney and dors and wyndowes. rusticke ruining[.] Jove kylling ye Giants painted in yt' [*in margin*].
Jones underlines the phrase 'Fatto dunque fondare quel catone, che era in luogo paduloso [*sic*]' at the opening of Vasari's account of how Giulio had to sink double foundations for this room because of the marshiness of the ground. Jones also underlines the words 'una gran stanza tonda' describing the shape of the room, which had thick walls to support a double vault like an oven, and Jones underlines the phrase 'tondo a uso di forno'. Vasari incorrectly describes the doors, windows and fireplace as rusticated.[73] He also states that they are shown in a state of collapse, and that the walls are painted with Jupiter overthrowing the Giants.

17. [*p. 333*]
'this round roome longe 15 yoards' [*in margin*].
Jones underlines the words 'e lunga piu di quindi braccia', describing the size of the Sala dei Giganti.

18. 'Stones of ye Pafement imytated in ye stones of ye Painting make ye roome see[m] greate th [than?] yt is by much' [*in margin*].

Jones underlines the phrase '& il cominciare delle mura, che vanno per diretto dipinte de'[medesimi falsi]' from the description of how Giulio extended the pattern of the floor into the illusionistic painting of the walls.

19. 'Vasari is weary of ye discription of this Pallas:' [*in margin*].

Jones underlines the phrase 'Oltre a questo palazzo' at the opening of this sentence, and his comment probably arises from Vasari's statement that to avoid prolixity he will pass over many other projects by Giulio.

20. [*p. 336*]

'Sebastia. da Regio Cutt ye natviti of St Jo: bab: that I have' [*in margin*].

Jones underlines 'Sebastiano da Reggio' at this reference to his engraving of the *Birth of St John the Baptist* after Giulio.[74]

21. 'Julio dissines infint' [*in margin*].

Jones underlines 'disegnare' and 'fatto piu di lui' in the text where Vasari comments that Giulio was so facile a draughtsman that no artist was more productive.

22. 'Julio a good discousr[.] he loved medales' [*in margin*].

Jones underlines 'medaglie' and 'spese assai danari' in the text where Vasari writes that Giulio could discourse on any subject, but particularly liked to talk about medals, on which he spent large sums of money. At the close of the next sentence Jones underlines 'degl' amici' where Vasari writes that although Giulio was extremely busy he would find time to oblige his friends.

23. [*p. 337*]

'Julio shoawith to gior[g]io Vassari all the pianti of ye antiche buildings of Rome Napels and Poziolo and Campania:' [*in margin*].

Jones underlines 'particolarmente tutte le piante degli edifizij antichi di Roma, di Napoli, di Pozzuolo, di Campagna' in Vasari's account of the plans of ancient buildings that Giulio showed to him when they met late in 1541.[75] Jones also underlines the words 'Di poi, aperto un grandissimo Armario' where Vasari begins his description of how Giulio opened a cupboard to show him the plans for buildings that he had designed himself.[76]

AUTHOR'S NOTE: My warm thanks to Paul Davies, Clare Tilbury, and John Peacock, who read early drafts of this chapter and suggested many improvements. I am grateful to the Provost and Fellows of Worcester College, Oxford, for their kind permission to quote from Jones's annotations to his copy of Vasari.

Notes

1. Arundel to William Petty, 21/31 November 1636; Mary F.S. Hervey, *The Life, Correspondence and Collections of Thomas Howard, Earl of Arundel: 'Father of Vertu in England'* (Cambridge, 1921), p. 393.

2. See Gordon Albion, *Charles I and the Court of Rome: A Study in Seventeenth-Century Diplomacy* (London, 1935), pp. 394–6; Rudolf Wittkower, 'Inigo Jones – "Puritanissimo fiero"', *Burlington Magazine*, XC (1948) 50–1; and Michael Levey, *The Later Italian Pictures in the Collection of Her Majesty the Queen* (Cambridge, 1991, second edition), pp. xxiiii–xxv.

3. London, PRO, 31/9/17B. Panzani to Francesco Barberini, 11 July 1635. See Wittkower, op. cit. (n. 2), p. 50 nn. 7–8. The second of two reports of this date establishes that Panzani had discreetly approached Orazio Gentileschi for his advice on the King's knowledge and interest in art.

4. Josua Bruyn and Oliver Millar, 'Notes on the Royal Collection – III: The "Dutch Gift" to Charles I', *Burlington Magazine*, CIV (1962), 92.

5. Little has been written on the careers of these men, but for biographical details of the Russell family, see Mary Edmond, 'Limners and Picturemakers: New Light on the Lives of Miniaturists and Large-Scale Portrait Painters working in London in the Sixteenth and Seventeenth Centuries', *Walpole Society*, XLVII (1978–80), 84–8. For Stone, see Jeremy Wood, 'Van Dyck and the Earl of Northumberland: Taste and Collecting in Stuart England,' in Susan J. Barnes and Arthur K. Wheelock, Jr. (eds), *Van Dyck 350*, Studies in the History of Art, 46 (Washington, 1994), pp. 289–90, 295–6, 302.

6. See Ian Spink, 'Lanier in Italy', *Music and Letters*, XL (1959), 242–52; and Michael I. Wilson, *Nicholas Lanier: Master of the King's Musick* (Aldershot and Brookfield, Vermont, 1994), pp. 83–90, 111–22.

7. PRO, SO (Signet Office), 3/9 (August 1628).

8. See Sir Isaac Wake to Secretary Lord Conway, 18–28 April 1628, in W. Noël Sainsbury, *Original Unpublished Papers Illustrative of the Life of Sir Peter Paul Rubens, as an Artist and a Diplomatist . . .* (London, 1859), pp. 326–7.

9. For this inventory, see Oliver Millar (ed.), 'Abraham van der Doort's Catalogue of the Collections of Charles I', *Walpole Society*, XXXVII (1958–60).

10. PRO, 31/9/17B. Panzani to Francesco Barberini, 6 February 1636 (New Series). See Wittkower, op. cit. (n. 2), pp. 50–1.

11. Iain Pears, *The Discovery of Painting: the Growth of Interest in the Arts in England, 1680–1768* (New Haven and London, 1988), p. 1.

12. See Ernst H. Gombrich, '"That rare Italian Master . . ." Giulio Romano, Court Architect, Painter and Impresario', in David Chambers and Jane Martineau (eds), *Splendours of the Gonzaga* (exhibition catalogue, Victoria and Albert Museum, London, 1981), pp. 83–4, reprinted in *New Light on Old Masters, Studies in the Art of the Renaissance, IV* (Oxford, 1986), pp. 159–60.

13. See Jeremy Wood, 'Inigo Jones, Italian Art, and the Practice of Drawing', *Art Bulletin*, LXXIV (1992), 269. Jones emphasises that some of these artists were both painters and architects, or were painters who worked as decorative specialists on buildings.

14. Giorgio Vasari, *Le vite de'più eccellenti pittori, scultori, et architettori* (3 vols, Florence, 1568). The third volume with Jones's annotations, now at Worcester College Library, has the pressmark LR.A.3.13. For Jones's annotations to the Proemio to the third part of the *Vite* and the Life of Raphael, see Wood, op. cit. (n. 13), 247–70.

15. Giovanni Paolo Lomazzo, *Trattato dell'arte della pittura, scoltura, et architettura*, National Art Library, Victoria and Albert Museum, London, Safe 2.B.8 (Milan, 1585).

16. See Oliver Millar (ed.), 'The Inventories and Valuations of the King's Goods, 1649–1651', *Walpole Society*, XLIII (1970–2), 64–6.

17. Jones refers to Giulio's 'g[rea]t disegne' in the notes on Italian art that he provided for Thomas Marshall; these also reveal that Jones considered that Giulio's principal works were to be found in Mantua and that he had embellished the entire city; see Wood, op. cit. (n. 13), 269.

18. See John Summerson, *Inigo Jones* (Harmondsworth, 1966), p. 56.

19. See B. Allsopp (ed.), *Inigo Jones on Palladio being the Notes by Inigo Jones in the Copy of 'I Quattro libri dell' architettura di Andrea Palladio', 1601, in the Library of Worcester College, Oxford* (2 vols, Newcastle upon Tyne, 1970), Vol. II, Book II, p. 14.

20. See James S. Ackerman, *Palladio* (Harmondsworth, 1977, second edition), p. 94, and Lionello Puppi, *Andrea Palladio* (London, 1975), p. 253, both of whom also incorrectly give 'executed' as 'adjusted'.

21. For convenient plans of the ground floor of Palazzo Te, see Egon Verheyen, *The Palazzo del Te in Mantua: Images of Love and Politics* (Baltimore and London, 1977), p. 9 (Plan 2); and Ernst H. Gombrich, Manfredo Tafuri, and Sylvia Ferino Pagden, et al., *Giulio Romano*, (exhibition catalogue, Palazzo Te and Palazzo Ducale, Mantua, 1989), p. 318 (names for the rooms in the palace vary widely in the literature; the terminology adopted in this chapter follow those given here).

22. For the meeting, see Frederick Hartt, *Giulio Romano* (2 vols, New Haven, 1958), Vol. I, pp. 80, 257, where the date is wrongly given as both 1544 and 1542. For this meeting and Vasari's later visit to Mantua in May 1566, see Patricia Lee Rubin, *Giorgio Vasari: Art and History* (New Haven and London, 1995), pp. 129–31, 209–10.

23. See Verheyen, op. cit. (n. 21), pp. 56–7, n. 5, with further references.

24. Rubin, op. cit. (n. 22), p. 130, argues that Vasari did not rely on ground plans but had a confused memory of his visit to Palazzo Te.

25. *Idem*, p. 131. For the two versions of the Life of Giulio, see Giorgio Vasari, *Le vite de'più eccellenti pittori, scultori e architettori nelle redazoni del 1550 e 1568*, eds Rosanna Bettarini and Paola Barocchi (6 vols, Florence, 1966–87), Vol. V, pp. 55–82.

26. See J.A. Gotch, 'Inigo Jones's Principal Visit to Italy in 1614: the Itinerary of his Journeys', *Journal of the Royal Institute of British Architects*, XLVI (21 November 1938), 85–6; and Gordon Higgott, 'The Making of an Architect: Inigo Jones's Second Tour of Italy, 1613–14', in John Harris and Gordon Higgott, *Inigo Jones: Complete Architectural Drawings*, (exhibition catalogue, The Drawing Center, New York; London, 1989), pp. 52–7. However, brief mention of Jones's admiration for Palazzo Te can be found in Edward Chaney, 'Pilgrims to Pictures', *Country Life*, CLXXXIV, 40, (4 October 1990), 148, and *idem*, *The Evolution of the Grand Tour: Anglo-Italian Cultural Relations since the Renaissance* (London and Portland, Oregon, 1998), p. 211.

27. Adam Bartsch, *Le Peintre-graveur* (21 vols, Leipzig, 1803–21, Vol. XVI, p. 135, no. 47; see Henri Zerner (ed.), *The Illustrated Bartsch*, 32, *Formerly Volume 16 (part 1): Italian Artists of the Sixteenth Century School of Fontainebleau* (New York, 1979), pp. 202–3.

28. See John Peacock, *The Stage Designs of Inigo Jones: the European Context* (Cambridge, 1995), pp. 252, 258, but citing Diana Ghisi's version of this engraving, dated 1575 (Bartsch, op. cit. [n. 27], Vol. XV, p. 449, no. 40), rather than Battista Franco's earlier print which is actually mentioned by Jones. Peacock silently corrects Stephen Orgel and Roy Strong (*Inigo Jones: the Theatre of the Stuart Court*

(2 vols, London, Berkeley and Los Angeles, 1973), Vol. II, p. 604, no. 292), where an engraving after *The Battle of the Romans and Persians* is proposed as Jones's source.

29. For Vasari's error and its repetition in the later literature, see Hartt, op. cit. (n. 22), Vol. I, p. 124, n. 23. For Vasari's possible use of a drawing by Giulio for the *Fall of Icarus* related to a ceiling in Palazzo Ducale, see Gombrich, Tafuri, and Ferino Pagden, op. cit. (n. 21), p. 394, with further references.

30. Although both Vasari and Giacomo Strada believed these subjects to depict the occupations of the months, they have more recently been identified by Ernst H. Gombrich ('The Sala dei Venti in the Palazzo del Te', *Journal of the Warburg and Courtauld Institutes*, XIII (1950), 189–201) as illustrations of passages in *Matheseos Libri VIII* by Firmicus Maternus; see Hartt, op. cit. (n. 22), Vol. I, pp. 117–19 and n. 19; and Verheyen, op. cit. (n. 21), p. 119.

31. For Vasari's error, see Hartt, op. cit. (n. 22), Vol. I, p. 124, n. 23; and Verheyen, op. cit. (n. 21), p. 119.

32. See Verheyen, op. cit. (n. 20), p. 128.

33. For Jones's annotations, the practice of making marginalia in the period, and mnemonic systems, see Christy Anderson, 'Learning to Read Architecture in the English Renaissance', in Lucy Gent (ed.), *Albion's Classicism: the Visual Arts in Britain, 1550–1660* (New Haven and London, 1995), pp. 242–50.

34. For the date of Arundel's arrival in Padua, see Hervey, op. cit. (n. 1), p. 76.

35. For the movements of Arundel's party, see Edward Chaney, 'Inigo Jones in Naples', in John Bold and Edward Chaney (eds), *English Architecture, Public and Private: Essays for Kerry Downes* (London and Rio Grande, 1993), pp. 35–40.

36. See Hervey, op. cit. (n. 1), pp. 227, 230.

37. In a letter of 18/22 July 1623, written to Striggio from Milan. See Alessandro Luzio, *La Galleria dei Gonzaga venduta all'Inghilterra nel 1627–28* (Milan, 1913), p. 68. The relevant passage reads in full: 'L'Ecco S. Co. d'Arrondel Gran Mariscial d'Inghilterra desideraria poter haver il modello del Palazzo del S.^{mo} S. Duca di Mantova detto del Tei, ma vorre' che fusse fatto con ogni puntualità e per mano di persona inteligente e che mostrasse ogni particolarità con una distinta naratione delle cose principale vi son dentro, in materia di scultura e pittura, cioè in camera e sala tale vi è la tale e tal cosa, e quando si potesse havere il modello istesso originale sopra il quale fu fatto l'edificio sara molto più grato'. The Countess was also interested in obtaining a second model, this one of the courtyard (called the *Rustica* or Cortile del Mostra) at Palazzo Ducale, because a separate excerpt also published by Luzio reads: 'Desidera parimente S.E. il modello di un cortile del palazzo di Mantova di ordine rustico fabricato non è molto tempo con la medema puntualità'. David Howarth, 'The Patronage and Collecting of Aletheia, Countess of Arundel, 1606–54', *Journal of the History of Collections*, X (1998), p. 130, inserted this passage into the middle of the request for a model of Palazzo Te, but it is not linked to any demand for information about pictures in the ducal collection.

38. For the reliability of Vasari's account, see Hartt, op. cit. (n. 22), Vol. I, p. 92.

39. David Howarth, *Lord Arundel and his Circle* (New Haven and London, 1985), p. 159, referring to Daniel Nys rather than Striggio. However, a more accurate account was provided earlier by the same author, '"Mantua Peeces": Charles I and the Gonzaga Collections', in Chambers and Martineau, op. cit. (n. 12), p. 95. In both cases it is wrongly said that the letter dates from after Lady Arundel's return to London. See also Howarth, op. cit. (n. 37).

40. The *Triumphs* were installed in the Sala Grande of the palace at San Sebastiano, known as the Palazzo della Pusterla, by 1512, and returned to the Palazzo Ducale before 1626 when they are

recorded in the Galleria della Mostra; see Ronald Lightbown, *Mantegna: With a Complete Catalogue of the Paintings, Drawings and Prints* (Oxford, 1986), p. 430.

41. See David Chambers in Chambers and Martineau, op. cit. (n. 12), p. 229, under no. 245, with further references.

42. Christopher Brown, *Van Dyck* (Oxford, 1982), p. 62, suggested – without evidence – that Striggio approached Lady Arundel with an offer to sell the Mantuan collection to Prince Charles. Wilson, op. cit. (n. 6), p. 88, elaborated this to suggest that the model was intended to assist the purchase, without noting that the pictures were largely kept at Palazzo Ducale, not Palazzo Te. Francis Haskell, 'Charles I's Collection of Pictures', in Arthur MacGregor (ed.), *The Late King's Goods: Collections, Possessions and Patronage of Charles I in the Light of the Commonwealth Sale Inventories* (London and Oxford, 1989), p. 212, was more doubtful about any possible connection between the model and the purchase of the Mantuan collection.

43. See P. de Chennevières and A. de Montaiglon (eds), 'Abecedario de P.J. Mariette et autre notes inédites de cet amateur sur les arts et les artistes', *Archives de l'art français*, III (1854–6), 314–16. In addition, see Wood, op. cit. (n. 13), pp. 249, 253, n. 36.

44. Lomazzo, op. cit. (n. 15), p. 48.

45. See David Alan Brown, *Raphael and America* (exhibition catalogue, National Gallery of Art, Washington, 1983), pp. 135–57.

46. Lomazzo, op. cit. (n. 15), p. 48.

47. Antony Griffiths, *The Print in Stuart Britain, 1603–1689* (exhibition catalogue, British Museum, London, 1998), pp. 79–80, no. 34.

48. Millar, op. cit. (n.9), p. 79. See also Jane Roberts, 'The Limnings, Drawings and Prints in Charles I's Collection', in MacGregor, op. cit. (n. 42), p. 121.

49. See Brown, op. cit. (n. 45), p. 138.

50. See n. 2 above.

51. See the list of 'Quadri diversi donati da sua Em.za mandati in Inchilterra', in Marilyn Aronberg Lavin, *Seventeenth-Century Barberini Documents and Inventories of Art* (New York, 1975), pp. 22–3.

52. Now attributed to a North Italian artist, working *c.* 1530; see John Shearman, *The Early Italian Pictures in the Collection of Her Majesty the Queen* (Cambridge, 1983), pp. 164–7, nos 162–3. The confusion with works by Giulio is made by Christopher Lloyd (*The Queen's Pictures: Royal Collectors through the Centuries*, exhibition catalogue, National Gallery, London, 1991, p. 31), and is based on a more cautious (but still over-elaborate speculation) in Shearman, op. cit. (n. 52), p. 165, who considers that the attribution of the two allegories (then given to Garofalo) might have been confused with the tapestry cartoons in the same gift.

53. The identification was first made by Shearman, op. cit. (n. 52), p. xii, n. 4. It is also found, at more length, in Helen Ettlinger, 'A Postscript to Inigo Jones – "Puritanissimo fiero"', *Burlington Magazine*, CXXXIII (1991), p. 776.

54. 'Piaquero straordinariamente alla Regina quello del Vinci . . .', Wittkower, op. cit. (n. 2), p. 51, n. 9.

55. See Lavin, op. cit. (n. 51), p. 6, document 40 (dated 25 July 1635).

56. Susan Madocks, '"Trop de beautez découverts" – New Light on Guido Reni's late "Bacchus and Ariadne"', *Burlington Magazine*, CXXVI (1984), 546.

57. PRO, 31/9/17B. Panzani to Francesco Barberini, 6 February 1636 (New Series). 'Il Gions

Architetto del Rè crede, che il Quadro del Vinci sia il ritratto d'una tal Ginevra Benzi Venetiana, e lo raccoglie da G. e B. che hà nel petto', Wittkower, op. cit. (n. 2), p. 51 n. 10. Translation modified from Lloyd, op. cit. (n. 52), p. 31. On the back of the Boltraffio at Chatsworth is an old painted inscription ('INSIGNIE SVM IERONYMI CASII') which has led to an identification of the sitter with the poet Girolamo Casio.

58. Vasari, op. cit. (n. 14), p. 8. Jones also underlines the words 'Ritrasse la Ginevra d'Amerigo Benci' at this point in the text.

59. For the circumstances of this commission, see Jennifer Fletcher, 'Bernardo Bembo and Leonardo's Portrait of Ginevra de'Benci', *Burlington Magazine*, CXXXI (1989), 811–16. For recent discussions with further references, see Martin Kemp in *Circa 1492: Art in the Age of Exploration*, ed. Jay A. Levenson (exhibition catalogue, National Gallery of Art, Washington, 1991), pp. 270–1, no. 169, and David Alan Brown, *Leonardo da Vinci: Origins of a Genius* (New Haven and London, 1998), pp. 101–21.

60. See Harris and Higgott, op. cit. (n. 26), p. 13.

61. Millar, op. cit. (n. 9), pp. 226–8; Shearman, op. cit. (n. 52), pp. 123–5, under nos 120–1.

62. Painted for Sant'Andrea in Mantua; see Hartt, op. cit. (n. 22), pp. 208–11.

63. See Shearman, op. cit. (n. 52), p. 128, no. 124.

64. See Cecil Gould, *National Gallery Catalogues: the Sixteenth-Century Italian Schools* (London, 1975), pp. 118–20.

65. See Mary Beal, *A Study of Richard Symonds: His Italian Notebooks and their Relevance to Seventeenth-Century Painting Techniques* (New York and London, 1984), pp. 298–313.

66. See Hartt, op. cit. (n. 22), Vol. I, p. 88, citing a document of 26 February 1526 that confirms Vasari's account.

67. Bartsch, op. cit. (n. 27), Vol. XVI, p. 135, no. 47.

68. For Vasari's confusion with the ceiling of the Camera del Sole e della Luna, see Hartt, op. cit. (n. 22), Vol. I, p. 109.

69. For an account of the engravings after the frescoes in the Sala dei Psiche, see Verheyen, op. cit. (n. 21), pp. 118–19; and Suzanne Boorsch, Michal Lewis, and R.E. Lewis, *The Engravings of Giorgio Ghisi* (exhibition catalogue, The Metropolitan Museum of Art, New York, 1985), p. 168, n. 2.

70. For the reliability of Vasari's attribution to Primaticcio, and the dating of this room to 1529–30, see Hartt, op. cit. (n. 22), Vol. I, p. 148.

71. For Vasari's error, see Hartt, op. cit. (n. 22), Vol. I, p. 124, n. 23.

72. For a different interpretation of the subjects, and Vasari's mistake over the location of these frescoes, see nn. 30 and 31 above.

73. For Vasari's confusions of detail in his account of the Sala dei Giganti, see Hartt, op. cit. (n. 22), Vol. I, pp. 153–4.

74. For a copy, inscribed *Sebastianes a Regibus Clodiensis incideb*, of an engraving by Diana Scultori, see Stefania Massari, *Incisori Mantovani del '500: Giovan Battista, Adamo, Diana Scultori e Giorgio Ghisi dalle collezioni del Gabinetto Nazionale delle Stampe e della Calcografia Nazionale* (exhibition catalogue, Istituto Nazionale per la Grafica, Rome, 1980), p. 93, under no. 148.

75. See n. 22 above.

76. For this passage, see Hartt, op. cit. (n. 22), Vol. I, pp. 193–4, 257. For Vasari's access at this time to Raphael's drawings after antique buildings, see Rubin, op. cit. (n. 22), pp. 130, 364, n. 45.

7

'THE MOST CONSPICUOUS SOLEMNITY': THE CORONATION OF CHARLES II

Lorraine Madway

The splendour of Charles II's coronation in 1661 left those who witnessed it all but speechless. Regardless of who they were or where they were sitting, they were overcome by the spectacle of what they were watching. Sir Edward Walker, Garter Principal King of Arms and one of the event's organisers, wrote:

> And upon Tewsday the 23th of Aprill, being St. George's day, [King Charles II] was with . . . state & Solemnity Crowned in the Abby Church in Westm^{er} . . . the like whereof had not beene in that place since the Coronation of Queen Elizabeth 102 yeares past.[1]

The Venetian Resident in England, Francesco Giavarina, informed his superiors:

> [H]is Majesty's coronation has been accomplished this week, so desired by his subjects, with all possible splendour and decorum, no one sparing his money to make it exceptional and memorable for ages to come, and it was certainly the most conspicuous solemnity that has ever been seen in this realm.[2]

The ever curious Samuel Pepys recorded in his diary:

> And then in the Quire at the high altar [the King] passed all the ceremonies of the Coronacion – which, to my very great grief, I and most in the Abbey could not see.
>
> . . . I can say that besides the pleasure of the sight of these glorious things, I may now shut my eyes against any other objects, or for the future trouble myself to see things of state and shewe, as being sure never to see the like again in this world.[3]

As the preceding statements show, the impressions of eyewitnesses rarely went beyond the sumptousness of the display. Even if they were close enough to see what was actually happening – and most of them, like Pepys, were not – they could not tell us what they saw. It is the task, then, of the historian to reconstruct what was going on at the coronation and to illuminate why it is important. The coronation is one of the defining moments of Charles's reign. It demonstrates three things: the dominant position of the Church of England in fashioning the Restoration settlement; the ambiguity of that settlement; and the early efforts of the monarchy to develop a language of kingship that would help it to assert its power among the competing political forces of the Restoration.

PREPARATIONS

The extant records dealing with the preparations for the coronation are noteworthy as much for what they omit as what they reveal. All of them refer to the planning committee of twenty-one members and to the involvement of Sir Edward Walker, but none of them refers to the participation of key churchmen like William Juxon, Archbishop of Canterbury, or Gilbert Sheldon, Bishop of London, in arranging what was essentially a religious ceremony. Nor are there surviving Church records to indicate what sort of discussions took place. This means that either the records were lost or the arrangements were made orally. What is significant is that Charles did not deem it necessary or expedient to appoint a single Church leader to the planning committee, including Sheldon who was the effective head of the Church.

Nor do the records indicate why the original date of 7 February was chosen. This date was five days after Candlemas which commemorated the purification of the Virgin and was the date of Charles I's coronation in 1626. None of the accounts mentions this fact but it is impossible to believe that Charles and his advisers did not know the significance of this date or have it in mind when they chose a date close to it. Yet the day itself was neither a Sunday nor a holy day as tradition demanded.[4] This deviation from established practice is all the more noteworthy in light of Charles's expressed wish to Sir Edward Hyde, soon to be the Earl of Clarendon, to follow ancient precedents:

> that the Novelties and new Inventions, with which the Kingdom had been so much intoxicated for so many years altogether, might be discountenanced and discredited in the Eyes of the People . . . his Majesty had directed the Records and old Formularies should be examined . . . and all Forms accustomed to be used, that might add Lustre and Splendour to the Solemnity.[5]

That Charles and the committee saw the 'Forms accustomed' as guides rather than binding precedents is shown by the subsequent change of date. In late December or early January the coronation was postponed until 23 April 'being St. George's day'.[6] Walker merely stated that the changes were due to 'many weighty reasons', but Giavarina got right to the point: 'The King being in deep mourning for the princess of Orange and it being impossible to have everything ready for the coronation by the 16th February, they have decided to have it on the 23rd April, old style.'[7] So in the end the organisers accommodated their need for time and satisfied tradition by paradoxically choosing a date never used before for a coronation.

The choice of St George's Day was deliberate and an immensely successful political manoeuvre. This day to honour England's patron saint was not an official holiday authorised by the Church of England, but popular observance had long invested it with secular and patriotic significance.[8] There were communal festivities throughout the country to commemorate the saint's heroic deeds against the dragon. It mattered little to the celebrants whether St George had ever performed them or was even a historical figure. At Court there were tilts and challenges and the Knights of the Garter traditionally convened on that day in St George's Chapel at Windsor. Many of the ceremonies associated with the Order had declined since the time of the Tudor kings. Puritan critics denigrated the saint and discouraged celebrations for him as frivolous and vain. Charles I showed a renewed interest in the feast of St George and the Order of the Garter. In 1629 he revived the custom of the sovereign's procession to Windsor on the eve of the holiday in order to exemplify 'the courtly culture of chivalry and piety, orderliness and chastity'.[9]

The revival of this holiday after the Restoration represents one of the more successful efforts of the later Stuart monarchy to use popular customs to serve its own interests. As David Cressy notes, 'court and country saw the promotion of the calendar of "merry England" as well as a calendar of deliverances'.[10] Charles II was not interested in reinstituting a courtly culture, but in celebrating his slaying the dragon of rebellion and rescuing his people from chaos. The monarchy's linkage of popular associations and elite politics was calculated, clever and arguably vain, but certainly not frivolous.

The sources available draw an official curtain around the proceedings. From the extant minutes of two meetings, it is evident that Charles himself decided the most important aspects, such as choosing to have a royal entry on the day before the coronation and the content and language of the oath.[11] He was present during the discussion and approved all the arrangements, however minute, that Walker and the committee members made. The records refer to Walker as the one 'by whom the whole Ceremonie and proceedings were principally drawn and Ordered up'.[12] How did he achieve a key role in the preparations for the coronation? He was thoroughly unpopular with members who were close to the King, notably Clarendon and Sir Edward Nicholas, who felt nothing but contempt for him. Nicholas had previously told Clarendon that Walker 'is a very importunate, ambitious, and foolish man, that studies nothing but his own ends'.[13] Clarendon had responded to Nicholas: 'Why should you wonder that a herald who is naturally made up of embroidery, should adorn his own services? – he has written letters heretofore which would make a stranger guess he had merited as much as any general could do.'[14]

Did Walker's influence come about because he made himself indispensable and did work that others lacked the inclination or time to do? Perhaps there is a more fundamental reason: that he had an intuitive understanding of the importance of ritual to legitimate and empower, an understanding which eluded more practical men like Clarendon and Nicholas.

As for the involvement of Charles himself, there can be little doubt of his insistence on shaping as well as approving the details of the ceremony. After all, he had waited more than twelve years for this momentous event. Literally it was the crowning achievement of his years of exile and struggle, even though ironically he had little to do with its final fruition. Nor could he forget the humiliation he was forced to endure at his coronation in Scotland ten years earlier. The Presbyterian ministers refused to anoint him and harangued him rather than preached to him. That ceremony was a 'fresh farce . . . and his Majesty had a principal part to play in it'.[15] This time Charles was determined that the coronation would be high drama and he would be the central player. But could he ensure that the Church of England would not try to overshadow him?

THE CEREMONY

The tone and texture of Charles II's coronation can be appreciated only if the ceremony is put into its historical context. Several important developments occurred in the eight months preceding the King's coronation which reduced the government's ability to manoeuvre between rival interests and weakened the case of those who advocated reconciliation. First and foremost, Charles failed in his efforts to establish an episcopate not dominated by any single group. It soon became clear that the militants were in control. As J.R. Jones points out,

> Charles underestimated the energy, determination and political courage and skill of Sheldon, who became the architect of the 1661–62 religious settlement. . . . Indeed Sheldon proved to be the only politician whom Charles never got the better of, his only superior as a tactician, who consistently defied him and defeated his toleration policies.[16]

The actions of some of the Dissenters who still controlled livery companies of the City, also helped to defeat the cause of toleration. When they returned four strongly anti-court members to the new Parliament, this move made the Dissenters, including the Presbyterians, look like the principal obstacle to a conciliatory religious settlement and gave the Anglican hardliners the upper hand.

The Anglicans pressed their advantage when the government commissioned a conference of leading Anglican and Presbyterian clergy to try to effect a comprehension. The conference mapped out an aggressively Anglican religious settlement. The general parliamentary elections in March and April gave a clear indication of where the country was moving: most members supported both monarchy and episcopacy. If the forces of monarchy were triumphant, so were the forces of Anglicanism. Theirs was arguably the greater victory since they now had a base of governmental influence outside the Court.

It is against this background of a resurgent and militant Anglicanism that the coronation took place. Whatever Charles's private religious views, he had to use the ceremony to advance his position as head of Church and State. He wanted to make religion serve the needs of the monarchy, whereas for the Church establishment the monarchy existed to serve the cause of organised religion. The coronation was one more place for the two forces to do battle. The struggle was elegant, dignified and subtle, but the conflict was evident to those relative few who understood its terms. Both forces engaged in a delicate balancing act. The question which must be investigated is whether the shaping of the ceremony enabled Charles to conciliate the Anglican establishment and simultaneously to assert his own royal independence, or whether it resulted in yet further acquiescence to the Church. The records available suggest that both sides could claim victory. Charles's victory was certainly the more visible, but it also came at a greater political cost to his future programme.

The three most significant features of the ceremony are the King's choice of George Morley to preach, the almost total reliance on the order and content of Charles I's coronation, including the retention of his controversial oath, and the addition of public festivities, namely the procession from the Tower and the banquet, both of which his father had cancelled.

Morley, then Bishop of Worcester, had given the King many demonstrations of his loyalty and support during the long years of exile. Although he was part of Sheldon's circle, he had long been on close terms with Clarendon and even served as his agent in negotiations for Charles's return in March 1660. He based his sermon on the theme of benevolent kingship expressed in Proverbs 28:2: 'For the transgressions of a land, many are the princes thereof; but by a man of understanding and knowledge shall the state be prolonged.'[17]

The tone of the sermon is surprisingly moderate. In a text that runs to more than sixty pages Morley made relatively few criticisms of Puritans' religious practices. For most of his talk he resisted the temptation to harangue and relied on the more effective pedagogical tools of praise and exhortation. He emphasised the merits of a monarch guided by constitutional and Christian values and Charles's attributes of kingliness. Since Charles was not well known even to many of the people sitting in the abbey, Morley had the advantage of drawing a portrait which selectively embellished reality. The features which he called attention to included '[Charles's] courteous and fair language, that he stole away the hearts of the people . . . Affability of Speech and behaviour together with gravity, and yet Serenity, and Benigness of Aspect.'[18]

Most importantly, Morley applied biblical imagery to Charles, comparing him especially to King David, who drew strength from his years of suffering and exile which helped him to be a more prudent, patient and charitable ruler. This iconography transformed Charles's adversity and struggles into political advantages. It even imparted to his wanderings an air of messianic redemption which the reality of debauchery and despondency would certainly have contradicted had they been better known. Morley's typology helped not only Charles but the Anglicans as well because, as Paul Hammond observes, it wrested 'from the radicals the language of divine guidance which had been as characteristic an idiom of the 1650s'.[19]

Amid his praise and advice, the Bishop interpolated oblique criticisms of the King's behaviour. These were couched in a coded language that only the King and those close to the royal circle would have understood. For example, in his discussion of Charles as a man and a prince, Morley reminded him that 'the best way for a Sovereigne Prince . . . to exercise his kingly authority' is 'by curbing, Restraining, and Regulating the inordinateness and immoderateness of his own passions'.[20] Elsewhere he admonished Charles that 'Princes ought, for their Peoples' sake as well as their own, to be very careful how they behave themselves, especially in publick, where all mens eyes are upon them.'[21] These two comments reveal that Charles's laziness and sexual indiscretions were already arousing the disapproval of many people in and close to the Court within the first year of his restoration.[22] Morley knew the measure of the man he was dealing with when he urged him first to read the whole Bible, then suggested he read those portions written for the instruction of kings (i.e., the Books of Kings, Chronicles, Psalms and Proverbs), and finally – 'if this still be too much' – to read Psalm 101 once a week, which 'though it be but a very short one'[23] yet conveyed the essence of kingship.

Morley concluded his sermon with thanksgiving to God for a day of national deliverance which he likened to 'the Resurrection from the Dead'.[24] His parallel between Charles's efforts to rebuild England and Christ's efforts to rebuild God's kingdom must have delighted the King as much as it moved his listeners:

> And when he hath setled . . . the Church and the State, and seen them both flourish . . . and when God hath no more work for him to do here; then, and not till then, may he exchange the Crown of cares he is to put on now, for a Crown of glory which he shall wear forever.[25]

So in the end Charles heard the sort of sermon he wanted, although he probably would have preferred a much shorter version of it.

The imitation of Charles I's coronation service is the most important aspect of the ceremony inside Westminster Abbey. Indeed, a comparison of the form and content of both services shows they are 'almost identical'.[26] The resemblance includes the retention of not only his father's coronation oath but also minor stylistic details as well, such as omitting the traditional exorcism of the ring and not wearing the outer shirt of red silk during the anointing.[27] The coronation oath has long been 'regarded as the compact or covenant made between [the monarch] and his people, sealing as it were his election to the throne'.[28] That many men in the seventeenth century saw the oath as the central feature of the service is clear from the attention it received during the constitutional debates of the 1640s and the revisions it later underwent in 1689.

Charles's decision to retain his father's version of the oath underscores the ambiguity of the Restoration settlement and the extent to which it left fundamental constitutional issues unresolved. The controversial clause refers to the addition of the royal prerogative as a check on the laws granted to the people and the clergy.[29] The change in the oath was among the charges levelled against Archbishop Laud in his trial in 1644 and against the King in his trial in 1649.[30] Royalists argued that Charles had not changed the oath even if they were vague about when the offending clause was incorporated into the oath. Walker, for example, stated that the oath was 'agreeable to the forme used at the Coronation of the late King Charles & former Kings'.[31]

Should the decision of Charles II to retain the oath be seen as filial devotion or at least loyalty to the Stuart dynasty, or should it be viewed as evidence of the same political calculation which prompted him to shape other aspects of the coronation? Jones would argue for the latter interpretation: '[Charles] frequently referred to the malice of those who had destroyed his father . . . but (unlike the anglican clergy) he maintained a revealing silence about his father's reign and failures.'[32]

But if Charles wished to disavow his father's legacy, then why did he choose to imitate almost every detail of his coronation? He had other models of coronation services to follow, but he chose his father's. Perhaps he felt motivated by the same pressures that had provoked Charles I to change the oath in the first place and, like him, was determined to define his powers as broadly as possible. But why risk arousing the passions of the 1640s by retaining the offending words? The answer must focus on Charles II's *politique* approach to kingship. Dynastic loyalty and political calculation were not mutually exclusive concerns. Quite the contrary. It was politically pragmatic for him to inaugurate his rule with a show of support for the basic conception of kingship for which his father had fought and died.

Even more significant than Charles's decision to retain the offending clause was the fact that its retention elicited so little comment at the time. One explanation is that Walker's successful censorship of other coronation accounts ensured that only a limited number of people knew about the retention of the royal prerogative.[34] But the imperfect censorship of the Restoration could not repress discussion of a topic that people wanted to talk about, such as the King's promiscuity. Popular silence about the oath went deeper; it was a form of acquiescence. As Hammond notes, 'the strength of the conservative reaction' that brought back the monarchy 'should not be underestimated'.[34] People had come to realise after twenty years of unrest that the prerogative powers of Parliament and the army could pose as great a danger to their liberties and welfare as those of the King.

Popular silence about the oath might even have been a form of assent. Far from rejecting the idea of a powerful king, most people endorsed it as long as the monarch's policies did not go against the popular will.[35] The problem, then, was not Charles I's declaration of his prerogative but the way that he used it. Similarly, people accepted Charles II's assertion of broad royal power until he pursued religious and foreign policies which were antagonistic to the views of the majority. They were prepared to acknowledge that he was in charge as long as he led them in a direction they were willing to go.

Charles's decision to stage an elaborate royal entry on the day before his coronation and to hold a banquet after the service are the two most important aspects of the ceremony outside the abbey. His father had cancelled both ceremonies and thereby caused disappointment and resentment among the people who felt they had been cheated of the opportunity to look at, and celebrate with, their king.[36] Charles II made sure he did not repeat his father's mistakes. He was also astute enough to understand that these aspects of the coronation, particularly the procession, gave him the opportunity to display himself directly to his subjects without any interference from the Church regarding the form and content of his presentation.

The pageantry which John Ogilby organised for the procession has received a great deal of attention.[37] He planned the entertainment around four triumphal arches depicting monarchy, naval power, concord and plenty.[38] Previous discussions of the pageantry have not considered how the iconography relates to the coronation service. Did the procession through each of the four arches and the multimedia performances beside them harmonise or contrast with the depiction of kingship in the cathedral?

The first arch demands particular attention because of its subject matter and elaborate design. It showed Monarchy triumphing over Rebellion and portrayed three representations of Charles on the front and one on the back (for which no engraving exists). Charles is shown landing at Dover (lower left of arch), putting Usurpation, resembling Cromwell, to flight (lower centre), and standing amid a tableau of oak leaves (upper centre). According to Ogilby's description, the fourth representation depicted Charles receiving the keys of the City.[39] Hammond argues that the symbolism of the arch was secular, notwithstanding the designation '*DIVUS*' accorded to representations of James I, Charles I and

1. The first triumphal arch, depicting monarchy, erected in Leadenhall Street, near Lime Street, for Charles's entry on 22 April 1661. (Ashmolean Museum, Oxford)

2. The second arch, depicting naval power, was erected near the Exchange in Cornhill. (Ashmolean Museum, Oxford)

3. The third arch, depicting concord, was erected near the end of Wood Street. (Ashmolean Museum, Oxford)

4. The fourth arch, representing plenty, was erected in Fleet Street near Whitefriars. (Ashmolean Museum, Oxford)

Charles II on the arch. He cites Ogilby's explanation for the designation on the basis of classical precedent: 'The title of "*DIVUS*" was constantly attributed by the *Romans* to their *Emperours* after their consecration.'[40] Yet a diary entry from the Puritan preacher Ralph Josselin reveals that not all the viewers understood it that way. For 3 May he wrote:

> Rid into London and saw the triumphal arches, stately variety; no rich cost; in ye front of one, besides Heathnisme, y^{r} [there] is y^{s} [this] troubled mee.

A statue of K. James	In ye midle above promin^{t} a death statue of Charles[41]	of K. Charles
Divo Jacobo	Imperium sine fine dedi[42]	Divo Carolo[43]

Another observer, William Smith, wrote that the second arch, which was designed to represent naval power, 'holds forth Presbytery, and with it the decay of Trade' and the third arch, which was designed to represent the Temple of Concord, depicted 'the honours due to the Hierarchy, and showeth the restoration of Episcopacy'.[44] It is evident that at least two observers did not interpret the arches in secular terms. It is reasonable to assume that others with strongly Puritan or Anglican leanings shared their sentiments and imputed religious meanings which the organisers did not intend.

What about other viewers, men like Pepys and Evelyn? As mentioned earlier, they were impressed and dazzled by the pageantry but they did not record any other reactions to the arches or the dramatic entertainments offered to the King as he made his progress through the city. If we assume that Hammond is correct and most observers experienced the procession in secular terms, then why is this significant? What Charles was offering his subjects was a startling way of looking at themselves and their history: a national epic devoid of a religious perspective. Not only was the procession different in tone from the religious service in the abbey and previous coronation entries, but it was at odds with the religiously charged atmosphere which shaped the way people lived and made sense of their world. To the extent that the procession succeeded, it did so not because it convinced all people of an alternative system of values but because it dazzled and overwhelmed them and stopped them from thinking at all.

KINGSHIP

The coronation enabled Charles to demonstrate two important attributes of kingship: majesty and accessibility. He gave his subjects a spectacular display of rank and grandeur and reinforced the aura of legitimacy surrounding his restoration. His majesty is evident in Wenceslaus Hollar's well-known engraving of the coronation service (see p. 153) which emphasises the regal dignity of the newly crowned monarch.[45] But something was missing amid all the pomp and pageantry. The royal charisma that he projected during the procession lacked the vital element of sacrality for which all the august solemnity of the service could not compensate.

The early modern English monarch was supposed to embody a confluence of religious, civic and national values. As R. Malcolm Smuts points out, the royal entry enabled the ruler 'to demonstrate his sense of membership in a civic and national community' and 'to assert publicly his commitment to the religious and secular values which should have united the realm'.[46] He became for his subjects 'the visible symbol of the religious and patriotic values uniting England'.[47] Charles II did not fulfil this role in his procession. His entry is significant not because, as most historians have argued, it was the last coronation entry but because it was the first (and only) one to present an image of kingship largely devoid of religious content.

Was the sacredness of the King's person, arrayed in all its majesty, enough to compensate for the lack of religiosity? The enthusiastic acclaim of the crowds indicates that they were satisfied with what they saw and heard. The appearance of souvenir coronation mugs (see p. 154) – the first ever known – underscores popular support for the newly crowned monarch.[48] But what was the basis for

The coronation of Charles II in Westminster Abbey, 23 April 1661 (engraving by English School, seventeenth century). (British Museum, London, UK/Bridgeman Art Library)

people's support and for how long would they give it uncritically? The fact that none of the observers' accounts talks about the content of what they experienced during the royal entry suggests that something was missing in the presentation. It was impressive and entertaining but hardly edifying. The imagery of restoration and stability in the pageantry transmitted a message that was immediate rather than transcendent. Immediate and yet ahistorical since the concept of government being acted out for the viewers divorced itself from the religious concerns which dominated the thoughts and actions of the people in the crowd.

In the short run, the King's publicly avowed commitment to Anglicanism was an effective strategy of legitimation and re-presentation of the Stuart monarchy. Charles showed that he was an astute *politique* king and truly the heir of his grandfather Henry IV. If 'Paris was worth a mass', as historical mythology has asserted, then London and all of England were worth an Anglican ceremony in

Commemorative mugs celebrating Charles II's coronation, 1661; these were the first mugs produced to commemorate a royal coronation. (Courtesy of the Museum of London)

which he not only acknowledged the power of the Church of England but fairly seemed to glory in it. But his appropriation had its price and the Church and its supporters demanded payment all too quickly. At this point the iconography of the service became more of a liability than an asset. In the abbey Charles encouraged and played on the nation's traditional expectations of kingship only to undermine them afterwards by his tolerationist policies and notorious sexual behaviour. Too often he gave his subjects occasions to feel that his presentation of kingship was not a show of majesty but a spectacle of mockery.

There is a very telling moment at the beginning of the service. The opening anthem is several verses from Psalm 122. The fifth verse refers to the 'thrones of judgment' that were set up in the abbey: 'For there are set thrones of judgment, the thrones of the house of David.' Charles no doubt thought the verse applied to him; after all, he sat in six different chairs during the course of the ceremony. But there was another chair near the altar, a chair of purple velvet for Bishop Sheldon. He, too, sat in one of the thrones of judgement. If Charles overlooked this at the coronation, then subsequent events soon reminded him that the Church was not about to relinquish its seat to anybody, not even the King.

Notes

1. Sir Edward Walker, *A Circumstantial Account of the Preparations for the Coronation of His Majesty King Charles the Second and A Minute Detail of That Splendid Ceremony . . .* (London, 1820), pp. 130–1.

2. *CSPV, 1659–61*, p. 286.

3. Pepys, *Diary*, Vol. II, pp. 84, 88.

4. The *Liber Regalis*, a coronation service book used since the reign of Edward II (1307–27) and translated into English for James I's coronation, prescribed that the coronation should be on a Sunday or a holy day. The *Liber Regalis* is reprinted and translated in Leopold G. Wickham Legg (ed.), *English Coronation Records* (London, 1901), pp. 81–130, esp. p. 113.

5. *The Continuation of the Life of Edward Earl of Clarendon . . .* (3 vols, Oxford, 1759), Vol. II, p. 186, f. 99.

6. Walker, op. cit. (n. 1), p. 29.

7. *CSPV, 1659–61*, p. 244. Princess Mary died on 24 December. In this entry, as in those on pp. 220 and 223, Giavarina referred to 6/16 February as the date set for the coronation.

8. See David Cressy, *Bonfires and Bells: National Memory and the Protestant Calendar in Elizabethan and Stuart England* (London, 1989), pp. 20–1.

9. Sharpe, *Personal Rule*, pp. 219–20. See also Roy Strong, *Van Dyck: Charles I on Horseback* (1972), pp. 261–2.

10. Cressy, op. cit. (n. 8), p. 171.

11. BL, Stowe, MS 580.1. Proceedings of the Committee appointed to arrange the Coronation of Charles II, 26 September and 22 October 1660, ff. 17a–b.

12. PRO, SP44/48, f. 20 (a pencilled margin note dates this reference as '1661 May'); PRO, SP44/7, f. 24 (25 April 1662).

13. G.F. Warner (ed.), *The Nicholas Papers*, II, p. 11 (Camden Society, New Series, 50, 1892).

14. *Calendar of the Clarendon State Papers*, II (Oxford, 1869), p. 346.

15. William Harris, *An Historical and Critical Account of the Life of Charles II* (2 vols, London, 1747), Vol. I, p. 93. For an account of his coronation in Scotland, see *Coronation of Charles the Second, King of Scotland, England, France, and Ireland, done at Scone, the First Day of January, 1651*, reprinted in Somers, *Collection of Scarce and Valuable Tracts* (second edition, London, 1811), Vol. VI, pp. 118–43.

16. J.R. Jones, *Charles II: Royal Politician* (1987), pp. 50–1.

17. George Morley, *A Sermon Preached at the Magnificent Coronation of the Most High and Mighty King Charles the II^{d}* (London, 1661).

18. Ibid., pp. 38–9.

19. Paul Hammond, 'The King's Two Bodies: Representations of Charles II', in Jeremy Black and Jeremy Gregory (eds.), *Culture, Politics and Society in Britain, 1660–1800* (Manchester, 1991), p.18.

20. Morley, op. cit., p. 47.

21. Ibid., p. 49.

22. A few weeks after the coronation Giavarina observed: 'The king listens to all and promises to all, but performs nothing whatsoever, his sole delight being in play and recreations with pleasure in certain trifles which cause remark and general amusement (*con diletto in certe bagatelle che causano l'osservatione e riso di tutti generalmente*), and he possesses little firmness or stability in himself, like the climate of the country' (*CSPV, 1659–61*, p. 297).

23. Morley, op. cit. (n. 17), p. 55.

24. Ibid., p. 60.

25. Ibid., pp. 61–2.

26. Reginald Maxwell Woolley, *Coronation Rites* (Cambridge, 1915), p. 73.

27. See *English Coronation Records*, pp. 245, 262, n. 2.

28. Woolley, op. cit. (n. 27), p. 79.

29. The disputed sections of the oath are italicised or marked with an asterisk: '[Bishop.] S^r^. Will you grant & keepe, & by yor. Oath confirme to the People of England and the Lawes & Customes to them granted by the Kings of England yor. lawful & religious Predecessor, & namely the lawes, Customes & ffranchises granted to the Clergie* by the glorious King St Edward yor. Predecessor, *according to the lawes of God, the true profession of the Gospel established in this Kingdome, and agreeing to the prerogative of the Kings thereof & to the antient Customes of this Realme.*

'[The King.] I Grant & Promise to keepe them.

'*['and to the people' omitted].'

Reprinted from Walker, op. cit. (n. 1), pp. 95–6.

30. The extant accounts of Charles I's coronation are presented and analysed in Charles Wordsworth (ed.), *The Manner of the Coronation of Charles the First of England* (London, 1892). They support the parliamentary claim that Charles did amend the oath. For an opposing view, see Percy Ernst Schramm, *A History of the English Coronation*, trans. Leopold G. Wickham Legg (Oxford, 1937), pp. 218–19.

31. Walker, op. cit. (n. 1), p. 95.

32. Jones, op. cit. (n. 16), p. 2.

33. For Walker's censorship of Elias Ashmole's account, see C.H. Josten (ed.), *Elias Ashmole (1617–1692): His Autobiographical and Historical Notes, his Correspondence, and Other Contemporary Sources Relating to his Life and Work* (5 vols, Oxford, 1966), Vol. III, pp. 823–5.

34. Hammond, op. cit. (n. 19), p. 42.

35. For a good discussion of popular support for a strong monarchy, see J.R. Western, *Monarchy and Revolution: the English State in the 1680s* (London, 1972), pp. 1–77; and Carolyn Edie, 'The Popular Idea of Monarchy on the Eve of the Stuart Restoration', *Huntington Library Quarterly*, 39 (1976), 343–73.

36. See R. Malcolm Smuts, 'Public Ceremony and Royal Charisma: the English Royal Entry in London, 1485–1642', in A.L. Beier, David Cannadine and James Rosenheim (eds.), *The First Modern Society: Essays in English History in Honour of Lawrence Stone* (Cambridge, 1989), p. 83; and Judith Richards, '"His Nowe Majestie" and the English Monarchy: The Kingship of Charles I before 1640', *Past and Present*, 113 (1986), 82–3.

37. See, for example, Hammond, op. cit. (n. 19), pp. 19–20; Katherine van Eerde, *John Ogilby and the Taste of His Times* (Folkestone, Kent, 1976), pp. 48–62; and Ronald Knowles, Introduction to a facsimile edition of Ogilby, *Entertainment of His Most Excellent Majestie Charles II* (London, 1662, reprinted Binghampton, NY, 1988), pp. 9–49.

38. David Loggan's engravings of the arches in the Ashmolean Museum, Oxford, are reproduced above, pp. 149–51. They are found in Ogilby, op. cit., facing pp. 13, 43, 111, 139. The arches were designed by Peter Mills, Surveyor to the City, and paid for by the City. The paintings on them were done by two City painters, Andrew Dacres and William Lightfoot. They received £1,130 for their work which was one of the most substantial expenditures of the pageantry. See Guildhall Library

MSS 289 and 290 and the appendix to Eric Halfpenny, 'The Citie's Loyalty Display'd' (A literary and documentary causerie of Charles II's Coronation 'Entertainment'), Guildhall Miscellany, 1 (1952–9), 28–35. The artist Balthazar Gerbier may have drawn the plans (based on a Hapsburg entry in 1635), but the evidence is insufficient to draw any conclusions.

39. Knowles, op. cit. (n. 37), pp. 19–20; Ogilby, op. cit. (n. 37), p. 38.

40. Hammond, op. cit. (n. 19), p. 19; Ogilby, op. cit. (n. 38), p. 32.

41. This is a curious usage of the word 'death'. Neither the *Oxford English Dictionary* nor the glossary in the Latham and Matthews edition of Pepys's *Diary* clarifies the meaning. The context suggests that the depiction of Charles II reminded Josselin of the waxen effigies displayed at an important person's death.

42. Josselin took an inscription from the back of the arch and mistakenly included it in his diagram of the front of the arch. For the correct inscription, see Knowles, op. cit. (n. 37), p. 31; Ogilby, op. cit. (n. 37), p. 28.

43. E. Hockliffe (ed.), *The Diary of the Rev. Ralph Josselin, 1616–1683* (Camden Society, 3rd Series, 15, 1908), p. 138.

44. William Smith to John Langley in HMC, *Appendix to the 5th Report* (1876), Part 1 (Duke of Sutherland), p. 175, f. 101. I am grateful to Dr Mark Knight for pointing out this reference to me.

45. The engraving is misleading in that it combines two different moments of the ceremony, the crowning and the enthronement. See Richard Pennington, *A Descriptive Catalogue of the Etched Work of Wenceslaus Hollar 1607–1677* (Cambridge, 1982), p. 92.

46. Smuts, op. cit. (n. 36), p. 93.

47. Ibid., p. 91.

48. Impressive examples of coronation mugs are on display at the Museum of London and the Victoria and Albert Museum. I am most grateful to the staffs of both institutions for kindly permitting me to view them closely. Several photographs of mugs are found in Frank Britton's *London Delftware* (London, 1987), pp. 86, 123.

8

CHARLES II'S FAILED RESTORATION: ADMINISTRATIVE REFORM BELOW STAIRS, 1660–4

Andrew Barclay

To any informed observer, looking back from the reign of James II to that of James I, there was one difference in the character of the royal Household which would have been especially striking. Under James I and Charles I, the King had still been required, in accordance with the conventional notions of hospitality, to feed (as well as house and clothe) the members of his entourage. Twice daily under the early Stuart kings meals were still being served to the royal servants in the Great Hall and, although it was not quite what it had once been, the tradition of communal dining remained a central part in the life of the Court.[1] By the late 1680s, however, that tradition was no more than a token gesture, represented in the survival of a handful of tables. As I have shown in my doctoral thesis, the reforms of the early 1660s, which had brought about the virtual demise of this practice, were a memory which disorientated the Household departments throughout the rest of the century and were, I would suggest, the defining event in the history of the royal Household in this period.[2] How had that change come about?

To many in 1660, it seemed obvious that Charles II should seek to reconstruct the Court so that it resembled as closely as possible that of his father. Quite apart from the symbolic continuity, there was the understandable assumption that the royal Household as it had existed before the Civil War had been the only way in which a monarch could properly organise his domestic affairs.[3] The Household departments, therefore, resumed their old functions as soon as was practical. The Exchequer would later deem that the accounts of the Cofferer, William Ashburnham, had commenced from as early as 19 June 1660.[4] By about that time detailed proposals existed for staffing levels to be adopted below stairs, with the number of positions envisaged being 307, a figure almost exactly matching the size that department had been under Charles I.[5] Appointments made on the basis of this plan allowed progress to be made towards the reintroduction of the old forms of commensality. From 3 August selected diets were being prepared daily in the Side Kitchen.[6] The crucial development came on 16 October when the King ordered that a new establishment based on that from the sixth year of Charles I's reign be prepared and that, from 1 November, the full diets be accordingly revived.[7] The diet book for December 1660 shows the Great Hall was by then back in use and that 194 meat dishes were being served at dinner.[8]

Most of the diets had been resumed by the time Parliament confirmed that it would legislate against Purveyance. It is true that the decision to abolish Purveyance had never really been in doubt and the need to compensate the King for its loss was probably already implicit in the recommendation by the Commons' committee on the King's revenue on 4 September that the total revenue grant should come to £1,200,000. It was not, however, until 21 November that the Solicitor-General, Sir Heneage Finch, told the Commons that the King's preference was for a half excise grant in return for the inclusion of Purveyance among the traditional revenues to be abolished. The alternative was the proposal the Commons had been working on until then, which was for a £100,000 assessment to compensate for the abolition only of the Court of Wards and the feudal tenures.[9] The Treasury was calculating that a full excise grant would bring in £300,000, indicating that Purveyance was thought to be worth £50,000.[10] Had the Commons gone ahead with the original assessment proposal, it is likely that they would still have provided compensation for Purveyance by using other means to reach the agreed total of £1,200,000. The assumption that the Crown now deserved some sort of grant to replace Purveyance would appear to have gone unquestioned by the Commons.

The compensation deal approved, the arrangements below stairs could fall into place. By May 1661 the number of meat dishes at dinner had risen to 224 and this was to remain the basic provision over the next eighteen months. Four extra dishes were served whenever Parliament was in session so that MPs could be invited to share the Lord Steward's hospitality.[11] Admittedly, the comparable figure for the total meat dishes in the one surviving Charles I establishment had been 307.[12] The main difference to account for this fall was that the more minor servants were now on boardwages (the money payments which were the usual way of compensating those who had had their diets removed) but it may well be that this discrepancy reflected later unrecorded reforms under Charles I.[13] What can be said is that all the senior- and most of the middle-ranking officials were now being provided with diets and that these diets, apart from a few minor modifications, were at their old levels.

However grateful most of the courtiers would have been, it must be pointed out that some had their doubts. There were already a few who appreciated the difficulties this revival would bring. One of the Clerks of the Greencloth, Sir Henry Wood, made himself unpopular with his colleagues by arguing against the whole idea of diets.[14] Lord Treasurer Southampton also disapproved because of the expenditure involved and, in this, he was supported by Sir Edward Hyde, soon to become Earl of Clarendon. According to Clarendon's own version of what happened, the revival of the diets was nothing less than the spineless betrayal by the King of what he had agreed when in exile. Clarendon would claim that on taking up office, the new Lord Steward, the Duke of Ormonde, and the Master of the Horse, the Duke of Albemarle,

> had both their tables erected according to the old models, and all those excesses, which the irregular precedents of former times had introduced, and which the king had so solemnly resolved to reform, before it could be said to trench upon the rights of particular persons. But the good humour the king was in, and the plenty which generally appeared how much soever without a fund to support it, and especially the natural desire his majesty had to see every body pleased, banished all thoughts of such providence; instead whereof, he resolved forthwith to settle his house according to former rules, or rather without any rule, and to appoint the officers, who impatiently expected their promotion. He directed his own table to be more magnificently furnished than it had ever been in any time of his predecessors; which example was easily followed in all offices.[15]

It did not take the King long to realise his mistake.

The Board of Greencloth, in fact, failed to produce the establishment the King had requested and, until one was finally put together in late 1662, the thirty-year-old version seems to have been the only authoritative statement of how the Court should operate. The delay did not mean that all was well. When the Exchequer called on the Board of Greencloth early in 1663 to account for the period up to October 1662, they explained their failure to produce their accounts before then by confessing that, until the establishment had been completed, the Household was 'in some disorder'.[16] In April 1661, Southampton had had to write to the customs commissioners to demand an emergency payment to cover the Cofferer's bills for the Garter and Bath feasts and for the coronation banquet, 'the credit of the officers of the Household being at a stand by reason of their present arreares . . . .'[17]

At that point the Household arrears were indeed vast. Worse, they were also growing. In the fifteen or so months to the end of September 1661, £165,060 had been paid out on ordinary and extraordinary expenditure below stairs.[18] With little of this money having been spent before Michaelmas 1660, this represented serious trouble, for the aim had probably been to keep expenditure to £100,000 per annum. That limit would not have been picked at random. It compared with the figure of £70,000 Charles I had set himself and that had included £20,000 for Henrietta Maria's Household. Actual expenditure had been £87,928 (in its time a notably large sum) during the last year of peace.[19] The Purveyance compensation meant that an increase to £100,000 made sense. An increase to the sorts of levels that were actually being spent did not. Although some of this increase may have been the result of inefficiency, it is clear that the cost of hospitality without Purveyance had been massively underestimated. The blame for this must rest with the royal officials, for Parliament had simply accepted their calculations on the levels of expenditure which would be necessary. It made this mistake all the calamitous that the Exchequer was now struggling to find the money to cover even the expenditure which had been foreseen. All the ordinary revenues were in difficulty and, in the case of the excise (from which it was hoped the bulk of the Household's costs could be paid), the yield from the full grant had probably fallen to less than £190,000.[20] As a consequence, Ashburnham had received only £89,935 from the Exchequer and even some of that had been expedited by borrowing money using tallies anticipating the excise revenues. Once other sources of income available to the Household were taken into account, the deficit by Michaelmas 1661 was well over £50,000.[21]

During the following twelve months the crisis deepened. Total annual expenditure was pushed up to £168,784, with there probably having been little alteration in the underlying rate of ordinary expenditure.[22] As a further complication, the arrival in England of the new queen in May 1662 carried the threat of additional essential spending. Over and above the meals laid on for her personally, some diets were (at least initially) provided to those servants Queen Catherine had brought with her from Portugal and to the handful of English servants already appointed.[23] Despite the easing of the government's overall financial predicament through the emergency grants allowed by Parliament to make up the revenue and by the windfall of the Queen's dowry, this expenditure increase was combined with a squeeze on the money provided to the Cofferer. Much of the £81,500 Ashburnham nominally received from the Exchequer was in fact raised by borrowing money (probably £58,000) from the trio of City goldsmiths and bankers, Edward Backwell, Francis Meynell and Robert Vyner.[24] This allowed Ashburnham to get his hands on some money earlier than he would otherwise have done but the arithmetic remained against him. The gap between what he was spending and what he could pay for had by the end of September 1662 risen to over £70,000. The substantial guaranteed increase in excise revenues promised by the farming of their collection commencing from Michaelmas 1662 could only partially circumvent the other sources of difficulties below stairs: unpredicted expenditure and the accumulating arrears.[25] Shortly after Michaelmas 1662, Ashburnham still had to borrow £36,000 from Backwell, Meynell and Sir Thomas Vyner on the promise of repayment from the money raised by the sale of Dunkirk, and he probably borrowed a further £34,000 using tallies struck on the Queen's dowry.[26] The need for a fundamental rethink was urgent.

Implemented at last on 1 December 1662, the first Household establishment of the reign was aimed principally at eliminating the diets of all but the most senior servants.[27] The honoured few who retained this privilege were Prince Rupert, the members of the Board of Greencloth, the Lord Chamberlain, the Master of the

Horse, the senior Secretary of State, the Groom of the Stole, the Clerk of the Kitchen, the Dean of the Chapel Royal, the Chaplain on duty and, an anomalous exception, the Countess of Chesterfield (who had been Groom of the Stole to the Princess Royal). As these were the persons with the largest allocations, this still left the number of meat dishes being served at dinner to the King's servants at 180.[28] On the other hand, the elimination of entitlements fell disproportionately on the numerous servants whose diets had consisted of smaller numbers of dishes. Boardwages were extended to these individuals. Even the Duke of York now received them in the form of an annual payment of £10,400.

The opportunity this provided to restructure the Household's organisation was not neglected. The text of the establishment itself recognised that

> for as much as wee have by this Booke of Establish[men]t converted all the inferior diete of our Offic[e]rs and servants (heretofore served in kind) into Boardwages whereby some of the Clerke of our Kitchen, Cooke and many others of our household servants heretofore imployed about those diets, are become unnecessary and useless.[29]

The 125 servants below stairs to which this applied were demoted to supernumeraries, reducing the ordinary complement of the Household to about 220. Prominent among the casualties was the Master of the Household, Sir Herbert Price.[30] Given the financial difficulties of the government, these servants should perhaps have counted themselves lucky that most of them continued to receive the same wages as their colleagues in ordinary, with the only instant savings arising from the lower boardwages granted to them. Above stairs, the seven Grooms of the Privy Chamber and thirty-four members of the Stables staff who had lost their places were given pensions.[31] If these individuals, who were to be paid sums on which it was almost possible to live for doing nothing, were to be a burden on the diminished royal income into the medium term, at least there was the hope of eventual savings.

Accompanying these reductions was an entirely new set of ordinances which strengthened the powers of the Board of Greencloth to ensure that the gains made were not undone. Extraordinary expenditure was in future to be closely supervised with only the Lord Steward, together with the Lord Treasurer, to have authority to prepare the warrants for privy seals for such expenditure, and with the King undertaking to consult the great officers of the Greencloth before approving any alterations to the establishment. The sale of lesser offices was banned so that the Board would know exactly who they were employing. More mundane economy measures, such as the recyling of candle stubs, were also ordered.[32]

The reform was incomplete in one respect only, because plans for the Queen's Household remained in limbo. The establishment's silence on the subject hides the fact that, as the diets to the King's servants were being limited, the Queen's Lord Chamberlain, her Groom of the Stole and the Maids of Honour were receiving them for the first time. At dinner each day this amounted to another thirty dishes. In effect, large numbers of servants in the royal Household had had their diets removed to allow the senior members of the Queen's Household to be fed. It would not be until the following June that it became possible to bring into being a full Household for Queen Catherine. Its approved expenditure was then in line with that of Henrietta Maria in the previous reign. Shortly after, many of her Chamber servants may have been granted diets.[33] The hope in December 1662 had probably been that the salaries, boardwages and pensions of the Household, which came to just over £42,000, taken together with £10,400 for the Duke of York and the cost of the remaining diets, would amount to around £100,000. Adding in the cost of the Queen's Household brought this up to £120,000.[34]

Dramatic though these changes were, even more drastic plans had been prepared. A draft made in mid-1662 had proposed that the number of dishes to be served at dinner be reduced to only sixty-four, by including the Lord Steward, the Lord Chamberlain, the Master of the Horse, the Treasurer, the Comptroller, the principal Secretary of State and the Groom of the Stole among those to be paid boardwages.[35] Had the full reduction in the diets gone forward there would have been scope for further cuts in manpower and this was reflected in the rest of the draft's contents. Twenty-two posts below stairs which, in the event, survived were here earmarked for demotion to supernumerary status. The Lord Chamberlain and the Master of the Horse were, moreover, to be encouraged to look for potential redundancies within their departments. The adjustments in salaries and boardwages would have cost over £7,000 but against this would have been the saving resulting from the suppression of the diets which, it was hoped, would have reduced total expenditure on both Households to £110,000. The most likely reason why the changes were revised downwards is opposition from the great officers, the major interest group who would have been affected. As it was, the Board of Greencloth only agreed to the revised scheme after Clarendon took the unprecedented step of forcing his way into one of their meetings to make sure that they approved the essential changes.[36]

The target of £110,000, in fact, would still have been too high. The new establishment did push total Household expenditure between Michaelmas 1662 and Michaelmas 1663 down to £121,330, so it clearly had the intended effect.[37] This allowed a substantial part of the £229,302 received by Ashburnham from the Exchequer or from his borrowings to be devoted to paying off most of his debt. Apart from the balance of this debt remaining on his own account (which fell comfortably below £20,000), repayment was now more of a problem between the Exchequer and those to whom he had sold his tallies.[38] On the face of it, the Household had gone most of the way to rectifying its immediate financial problems. The fundamental problems, however, remained. The emergency parliamentary grants which had been provided to tide the government over initial deficiencies in the yield from the permanent ordinary revenue, together with casual receipts such as the Queen's dowry and the Dunkirk money, were now declining in value at a rate at which the increases in the still disappointing ordinary revenues could not replace.[39] The Secretary of State, Sir Henry Bennet, for one, came to realise that, as he put it to Ormonde, 'unlesse hee [the King] cutt off their expenses we mind of this, the Gov[er]n[men]t will not bee able to stande longe soe farre does the Expence excede the income and little likelihood there is of an addition or improvement of it' and Sir Henry therefore backed Southampton's efforts to persuade the King to introduce further economies.[40]

It was no longer possible to cushion any impact. On 20 August 1663 Charles II agreed that from Michaelmas that year all diets, boardwages and pensions would be halted. Of the diets, only those for Prince Rupert and, in the Queen's Household, those for the Maids of Honour were exempted, while the King's own allocation was cut to only ten large and four small meat dishes for himself and the Queen each day. This reduced expenditure on meals to £23,000 and saved £27,000. Combined with the £20,000 no longer paid in boardwages and the £5,000 in suspended pensions, plus more minor savings on smaller items of expenditure, this was expected to reduce the cost of the Household by £58,000 to only £62,000 and, inclusive of extraordinary expenditure, the figure over the next year turned out to be £62,647. Expenditure had been almost halved but only by depriving many royal servants of more than two-thirds of their official incomes.[41]

The Earl of Anglesey voiced concern to Ormonde that 'on a sudden above three hundred below stairs, most of which have families, are deprived of a livelihood, the splendour and dignity of the Court is taken away, and general discontent and murmuring occasioned hereby', while the following March Pepys was told that 'the poor wretches' were 'ready to starve'.[42] Suspecting correctly that Ormonde, whose absence in Dublin had prevented him from being consulted, would be deeply uneasy about the shabbiness of the plan, Bennet offered reassurance that it was a temporary measure until the King 'findes himselfe a little more at ease in his Exchequer' and even held out the possibility that, even with only five weeks to the Michaelmas deadline, money might be forthcoming to prevent it.[43] A deliberate breaking with the past recalled to Ormonde too many former traumas but, with considerable misgivings, he acquiesced in the plans, bowing to his king's commands rather than to their inevitability.[44] Temporary though the retrenchment did turn out to be, in retrospect it can be seen to have brought about the end of the tables of the great officers. Whether this was realised at the time is debatable. If it was, it was a fateful lost opportunity.

Commitment to this reform was sufficiently impermanent for plans for the partial restoration of the diets to be advanced to the stage of having an official vellum version of an establishment almost ready for the King's signature which, had it not been abandoned at the last minute, would have led to the resumption of selected diets on the first anniversary of their suspension.[45] Preparations for the ending of the emergency arrangements can be seen in a memorandum prepared, on his orders, for Ormonde by the Board of Greencloth in August 1664 in which they sketched out proposals to achieve what had become their immediate objective: to return the Household to as much normality as was possible on £100,000 per annum.[46] In both this memorandum and in the abortive establishment which was developed from it, the proposals regarding diet were admittedly limited because none of them would have been returned to their former levels. The Board's initial hope was that those diets which had survived the 1662 reform could be revived, with those formerly of ten dishes reduced to eight and those of seven or less reduced by one. Their fall-back position outlined in the establishment was more restricted still. With the abandonment of this establishment as it neared completion, the Board was forced to rethink yet again. Another establishment was produced and this replacement was implemented on time on 1 October 1664.[47] As a result, the payment of boardwages and pensions resumed, but not the diets, which continued at their minimal levels. (It was however, recognised that the waiters had a theoretical right to a table of sixteen dishes and this would be granted to them seven months later.)[48] The great officers, who remained dietless, now, for the first time, received their boardwages entitlements in lieu of them.

The Board of Greencloth had advised in their August memorandum that 'the number of servants in each office to be reduced to a competent number, according to the number of diets continued'.[49] There was, though, nothing in the first version of the establishment which had foreshadowed the extensive reduction in staff introduced by the final version, with accompanying shifts in salaries and boardwages from their pre-1663 levels. Reductions within departments were accompanied by mergers of departments and the rationalisation of staffing.[50] Altered arrangements for the Queen's servants also made possible a reorganisation of the kitchens. Instead of a few minor modifications as envisaged in the abortive establishment, the system was changed completely. Her kitchen staff were amalgamated with those of the King's Household Kitchen, which was itself reorganised along with the King's Privy Kitchen. The result of this was that, whereas the royal kitchens had hitherto had a combined total of sixty employees, they now needed only twenty-one.[51]

The net effect of abandoning the first establishment for a more drastic reorganisation was that the number of Household staff was reduced from 225 to 147. This, however, was offset by an increase in salaries and particularly boardwages. The staff cuts enabled the total salary bill for the Household to be brought down from £1,669 to £1,346 while increasing the average individual salary. These savings were swallowed up by the marked increases in boardwages which, when the payment of them resumed, went up from the pre-suspension figure of £7,285 to £8,436 (rather than down to £7,072 as had first been proposed). This meant that more money was being spent on salaries and boardwages for fewer people.[52] Added to this was the fact that almost all those dismissed became supernumeraries, the number of which therefore increased from 127 to 197. As few of the salaries of those being demoted to supernumerary status were significantly reduced, with most being frozen at their existing levels, there was a corresponding increase in the total salaries and boardwages of the supernumeraries.[53] Far from contributing to the reduction in expenditure, this reorganisation placed additional burdens on the Household. Any pay-off would only come when vacancies and death reduced the number of supernumeraries. The savings, in the meantime, had to be found elsewhere.

It was in the Stables – which had, thanks to Albemarle's influence, survived the 1663 changes entirely intact – that the vital economies were undertaken which helped make the relaxation of the suspension possible. In August 1664 the Board of Greencloth had highlighted the Stables as a possible source of savings. This approach would have borne fruit in the unfinished establishment with a sweeping cut in manpower being envisaged to bring its costs down from just under £19,300 to only £4,315. Further alterations in the final version (of which the granting of £1,460 in boardwages to the Master of the Horse was the most important) pushed the figure for salaries and boardwages to £6,263. This still represented a saving of over £10,000.[54] Together with the confirmation of the abolition of the diets, this enabled the Board of Greencloth to meet what it had set from the previous August as its main objective and this was re-emphasised by Charles II when, on being presented with the completed establishment, he annotated it with the instruction (or promise): 'For the defraying the whole charge in this booke, there shall be one hundred thousand pounds p.Ann allowed and no more CR.'[55]

Yet the outcome of the complex genesis of this establishment was a defeat for the Board of Greencloth. At the beginning, they had assumed that the diets suspended in 1663 could be resurrected, although they had recognised that any such resurrection would only be incomplete, and something of this hope survived into the unfinished establishment. It was, indeed, almost certainly these parts of it which ensured that it did remain unfinished. Someone had compelled the Board to abandon it in favour of the revised version which not only kept the diets to the absolute minimum but also restructured the Household in the light of the decision not to revive the old diets. Seemingly, there were those at Court who regarded the diets as being not just suspended but abolished permanently. What is more, they now had this interpretation enshrined on the vellum folios of a Household establishment. Or, rather, partly enshrined. Given that it would have been the Board of Greencloth who would have overseen the detailed preparation of the final document, it is possible to read significance into the apparent distinction made between those (like the Lord Chamberlain to the Queen or the Master of the Horse) who were now only listed as being entitled to boardwages, and those in receipt of boardwages who continued to be listed at the very beginning of the establishment among those entitled to a specified number of dishes, even though it was in lieu of these that they were receiving the boardwages. Over the latter cases, which included most of those whose diets had survived until 1663, there seemed a reluctance to give up the notion that these courtiers *were* entitled to diet in kind. It was probably this anomaly which caused Charles II to add an annotation against this list of dishes to clarify that 'all diets except Prince Rupert and the maides of honour to be at usuall boardwages'.[56] It would seem that Charles had grasped the point of this latest round of reform. There is thus a strong temptation to identify the key player in the decision to abandon the unfinished establishment in the autumn of 1664 as having been the King himself. With his support, the makeshift 1664 scheme (combined with occasional retrenchments) remained the basis for the Household finances for the rest of the reign.[57] The bitter reality Charles II was coming round to appreciate was that, for the foreseeable future and for reasons which he probably did not himself fully understand, a court on the scale his predecessors had thought appropriate would not be an affordable option.

Notes

1. For the traditional system of serving meals, see G.E. Aylmer, *The King's Servants* (London, 1961), pp. 168–9; Thurley, *Royal Palaces*, pp. 145–61. See also F. Heal, *Hospitality in Early Modern England* (Oxford, 1990). Although the abuse of consuming the food elsewhere had long been practised, the meals were still served in the Great Hall. (M. Exwood and H.L. Lehmann (eds), *The Journal of William Schellinks' Travels in England 1661–1663* (Camden Society, 5th Series, I, 1993), p. 91).

2. A.P. Barclay, 'The Impact of James II on the Departments of the Royal Household', (unpublished Ph.D. thesis, Cambridge 1993), esp. pp. 59–97, 222–5.

3. It was overlooked that, in this respect, as in most others, the legacy of Charles I was ambiguous (G.E. Aylmer, 'Attempts at Administrative Reform, 1625–40', *EHR*, LXXII (1957), 229–59; Sharpe, *Personal Rule*, pp. 235–40).

4. PRO, E351/1836, Pipe Office declared accounts: Cofferer of the Household, 1638–40, 1660–8, rots 6–8.

5. HMC, *Ormonde*, New Series, III, pp. 2–5; Aylmer, *King's Servants*, p. 472.

6. Bodleian Library, MS Carte 60, f. 51: [?Board of Greencloth] to Ormonde, *c.* August 1660; PRO, LS1/2, f. 6v: Greencloth minute, 3 August 1660; PRO, LS9/1, unfol.: October 1660 diet book. See also *LJ*, XI, 148.

7. BL Add. MS 51319, f. 7: Ormonde to Greencloth, 16 October 1660. Cf. Bodl. Lib., MS Rawl. B35, ff. 22–3: Charles II to Ormonde [16 Oct. 1660]; W.L. Sachse (ed.), *The Diurnal of Thomas Rugg* (Camden Society, 3rd Series, XCI, 1961), 120–2. Investigation revealed that they would have to make do with a copy of the establishment of 6 Charles I as the original had been lost, along with the bulk of the Household archive, during the Civil War. (Bodl. Lib., MS Carte 60, ff. 40–3: Greencloth to

Ormonde, n.d.). The original of one of the Charles I establishments survives in the PRO as LS13/30 but, despite the date of 1 October 1630 later added to the cover, when it was compiled has been uncertain. Dr Aylmer judges that it was put together between 1627 and 1630, with him suggesting 1629. ('Attempts at administrative reform', p. 251 and n.). It can now be shown that there were two separate establishments compiled during the early years of the previous reign, for the 1662 establishment speaks of 'the Bookes Signed by our Deare father of Blessed memory in the third and sixt[h] yeares of his Reigne'. (PRO, LS13/31, f. 21, clause 8). PRO, LS13/30 itself, in the first clause of its ordinances, states that it was 'grounded upon former like books signed by our Anncestors', implying that it was the first issued by Charles I. Taken together with the reported loss of the establishment of 6 Charles I, this points to PRO, LS13/30 being that from 3 Charles I.

8. PRO, LS9/2, unfol.

9. *CJ*, VIII, 11, 40, 45, 107, 111, 150, 178–9, 186, 187; *LJ*, XI, 216, 225; *The Parliamentary or Constitutional History of England* (1762–3), XXIII, pp. 17–18, 21–2, 24–5; G.E. Aylmer, 'The Last Years of Purveyance, 1610–1660', *Economic History Review*, 2nd Series, X (1957–8), 90–1; Chandaman, *Public Revenue*, pp. 38–9, 200–2.

10. *CJ*, VIII, 274; Bodl. Lib., MS Tanner 49, ff. 55–6: estimates of the revenue, 1660; Chandaman, *Public Revenue*, p. 38. This is one reason for thinking that historians of the previous reign have underestimated the value of Purveyance. (Barclay, 'Impact', 75 n.).

11. PRO, LS9/1–4.

12. PRO, LS13/30, unfol.

13. See n. 6 above. The summary of the diets served during the previous reign published by Chamberlayne in 1669 may represent an intermediate stage. These figures (which do not add up to the totals stated) perhaps show that very minor savings were later made by deducting one dish from most of the diets of four dishes (E. Chamberlayne, *Angliae Notitia* (1669, 2nd edn), pp. 292–3).

14. *Calendar of the Clarendon State Papers* (5 vols, Oxford, 1872–1970), Vol. V, p. 216; G. Younghusband, *The Jewel House* (London, 1921), p. 238; *HC 1660–1690*, III, p. 755.

15. E. Hyde, 1st Earl of Clarendon, *The Life of Edward Earl of Clarendon* (3 vols, Oxford, 1827), Vol. I, p. 367 – cf. Vol. I, p. 365; Vol. III, pp. 237–8. Although tantalisingly ambiguous and undated, one of Clarendon's notes appears to confirm that, at about this time, he and Southampton were attempting to limit increases in Household expenditure (W.D. Macray (ed.), *Notes Passed at Meetings of the Privy Council between Charles II and the Earl of Clarendon* (1896), p. 9).

16. PRO, LS13/104, p. 10: Greencloth to Southampton, 26 February 1663.

17. *Calendar of Treasury Books, 1660–7*, p. 234.

18. PRO, E351/1836, rots 6–8. The totals from this account are printed in *CTB, 1667–8*, pp. xxix–xxx.

19. PRO, LS13/30; Aylmer, 'Attempts at Administrative Reform', pp. 229–59.

20. Chandaman, *Public Revenue*, pp. 310, 332, 348.

21. Chandaman, *Public Revenue*, pp. 350; PRO, E351/1836, rots 6–8; *CTB, 1660–7*, p. 284; *CSPV, 1661–4*, p. 20.

22. PRO, E351/1836, rots 9–11. One analysis of the 1660 settlement, now to be found among Clarendon's own papers, gives £150,000 as its estimate for Household expenditure. This document

was probably prepared for Southampton in the summer of 1662 and the £150,000 should be interpreted as a rough total of current expenditure, rather than as the estimate used when calculating the revenue settlement in 1660 (T.H. Lister, *Life and Administration of Edward, First Earl of Clarendon* (1837–8), Vol. III, p. 507; *Calendar of the Clarendon State Papers* (Oxford, 1872–1970), Vol. V, p. 53).

23. From 17 June 1662 ten dishes for dinner were granted to the Queen. Her servants were then allocated fifty-three dishes (PRO, LS1/4, unfol.: liveries to be served to Portuguese servants, 1 June [1662]).

24. *CTB, 1660–7*, pp. 296, 309, 359, 360, 398. Vyner was the royal goldsmith.

25. Chandaman, *Public Revenue*, p. 312.

26. *CTB, 1660–7*, pp. 440, 459, 460–1, 491, 526–7; D.K. Clark, 'Edward Backwell as a Royal Agent', *Economic History Review*, IX (1938–9), 45–8.

27. PRO, LS13/31 (1662 establishment).

28. The table of diets at the beginning of the establishment appears to indicate that the great officers had lost their second course of six meat dishes. Further on, however, the details of what was to be served to those entitled to receive ten dishes at dinner and supper makes it evident that this second course was still to be included. The diet books confirm this (PRO, LS13/31, ff. 1, 4; PRO, LS9/3, unfol.; PRO, LS9/4, unfol.).

29. PRO, LS13/31, f. 21, clause 9.

30. Bodl. Lib., MS Carte 60, f. 9: memorial of Master of the Household, [1662]. Full powers were restored to Price in 1666 (PRO, LS13/253, pp. 3–4: Charles II to Greencloth, 21 November 1666).

31. PRO, LS13/31, ff. 16–18.

32. PRO, LS13/31, ff. 20–1.

33. HMC, *Ormonde*, New Series, III, pp. 174–5; PRO, LS9/3, unfol.; PRO, LS9/4, unfol.; PRO, LS13/32 (establishment of the Queen's Household, [1663]); *CSPD, 1663–4*, pp. 159, 404. The date of the establishment referred to in HMC, *Ormonde*, which is given as 'the 2nd of December, 1663', obviously should be December 1662. Ambiguities in the text of PRO, LS13/32 mean that its exact date and full significance remain unclear. The warrants of appointment and swearing certificates for the Queen's servants from July 1663 were entered towards the end of the volume containing the accounts of the Comptroller of the Household (PRO, LS1/5, unfol.).

34. Unlike the later establishments, PRO, LS13/31 does not conclude with a complete summary of projected expenditure. The figure of £120,000 derives from a note attached to f. 18. (cf. *CTB, 1660–7*, pp. 526–7). That it includes the Queen's domestic expenditure is conjecture. Comparison with PRO, E101/541/9A and LS 13/32 suggests that it does.

35. PRO, E101/541/9A. This draft must pre-date Nicholas's removal from the principal Secretaryship of State in October 1662 and was probably compiled after (or conceivably in anticipation of) the Queen's arrival the previous May.

36. Younghusband, *Jewel House*, pp. 238–9.

37. Chandaman's claim that in 1662 and 1663 the increase in court extravagance was 'particularly marked' (*Public Revenue*, p. 204), may be true for 1662 but is unfounded for 1663 when Household expenditure fell. Chamber expenditure was also in decline (*CTB, 1667–8*, p. xxviii; Chandaman, *Public Revenue*, p. 350). Debt repayment distorted the Exchequer issues on which he based his assertion.

38. PRO, E351/1836, rots 12–15; Chandaman, *Public Revenue*, p. 350.

39. Chandaman, *Public Revenue*, pp. 332–3.

40. Bodl. Lib., MS Carte 221, f. 77: Bennet to Ormonde, 22 August 1663.

41. HMC, *Ormonde*, New Series, III, pp. 78–9, 88, 91, 92, 174–5; Bodl. Lib., MS Carte 221, ff. 77–8: Bennet to Ormonde, 22 August 1663; Bodl. Lib., MS Clarendon 80, f. 189: [Ormonde] to Charles II; PRO, LS9/5, unfol.; PRO, E351/1836, rots 16–17; *CSPV 1661–4*, pp. 261, 263; Evelyn, *Diary*, Vol. III, pp. 360–1; Alnwick Castle, Northumberland MS 18, f. 261: Warner to Seymour, 15 October 1663; f. 265: H.M. to Seymour, 24 October [1663]; f. 287, letter to Seymour, [August 1663]. I am grateful to His Grace the Duke of Northumberland for granting permission to me to consult the Northumberland MSS.

42. HMC, *Ormonde*, New Series, III, p. 78; Pepys, *Diary*, Vol. V, p. 73. In glossing Pepys's entry, his editors misconstrued Anglesey's comments to mean that the 300 servants had been dismissed.

43. Bodl. Lib., MS Carte 221, f. 77, Bennet to Ormonde, 22 August 1663.

44. Bodl. Lib., MS Carte 143, pp. 175–6: Ormonde to Charles II, 9 September 1663. Cf. Bodl. Lib., MS Clarendon 80, f. 189. The first of these references was kindly supplied to me by Dr Aylmer.

45. PRO, LS13/33 (1664 establishment [incomplete]).

46. HMC, *Ormonde*, New Series III, pp. 177–8.

47. PRO, LS13/34 (1664 establishment).

48. PRO, LS13/253, p. 7: Charles II to Greencloth, 11 January 1667.

49. HMC, *Ormonde*, New Series III, p. 178.

50. PRO, LS13/31; PRO, LS13/33, ff. 11–14; PRO, LS13/34, pp. 11–12.

51. PRO, LS13/32, f. 8; PRO, LS13/33, ff. 13, 17; PRO, LS13/34, p. 12.

52. PRO, LS13/33, ff. 11–15; PRO, LS13/34, pp. 11–13.

53. PRO, LS13/33, ff. 18–19; PRO, LS13/34, pp. 24–8.

54. HMC, *Ormonde*, New Series III, pp. 78, 174–5, 178; PRO, LS13/31, f. 15; PRO, LS13/33, ff. 20–1; PRO, LS13/34, pp. 16–17. The King also personally directed that, apart from those for himself, the Queen, the Master of the Horse and the Equerries, horse liveries were to be commuted into money (PRO, LS13/34, f. 35: annotation in hand of Charles II).

55. PRO, LS13/34, p. 59.

56. PRO, LS13/34, p. 3.

57. R.O. Bucholz, 'Introduction', in J.C. Sainty and R.O. Bucholz, *Officials of the Royal Household 1660–1837* (Office-Holders in Modern Britain, XI–XII, 1997–8), Vol. I, esp. pp. lvi–lviii.

9

THE MISTRESSES OF CHARLES II AND RESTORATION COURT POLITICS

Sonya Wynne

Seventeenth-century strictures on the participation of women in public life decreed that women were not part of the political world but the dynamics of the early modern court meant that in practice they could have a significant political role. The Court contained a complex mixture of government, administration and the royal Households, with no clear separation between the public and private sphere. This situation was reinforced by the courtiers' aims (which were often scarcely distinguishable) to influence both the King's domestic and foreign policies and his distribution of Crown patronage. The merging of public and private interests at Court could, in turn, confuse the prohibitions on women having a recognised role or authority in politics. In so far as court politics was still a personal business, a business which had as much to do with family as State interests, female participation was permissible. The King, of course, was central to the Court, and in exercising his considerable power he could take advice from many quarters and, indeed, favour particular individuals. This gave considerable scope for informal or 'extra-institutional' politics, which had obvious implications for female courtiers who were excluded from such formal political institutions as the Privy Council. These structural elements were always affected by the important variable of the King's personality. The extent to which a woman might have direct influence with the King depended upon his individual inclinations. Thus the merging of public and private, the informal channels of power at Court and the character of the King, were all significant factors in the role of women in court politics.[1]

Charles II's mistresses devoted much energy to making public demonstrations of their hold on the King's favour. This attempted manipulation of the opinion of the Court, if successful, resulted in an enhanced reputation for influence and participation in the patronage networks of the Court as clients, brokers and patronesses. In turn, this led to the development of relationships with male officials which became part of the court factions that formed as courtiers tried to advise and influence the King over the promotion and demotion of ministers and political policies. In an atmosphere of 'open secrecy', a system whereby much was guessed at but little known for certain, the inside information held by women close to the King was valuable. Women also provided informal access to the King, acted as intermediaries, conducted 'invisible' negotiations, and accepted the gifts which cemented political relationships and signalled successful negotiations; activities conducted the more easily due to the informal nature of female participation. Women were not officially recognised as having any part in decisions at this high level, but the potential of this official blindness for concealed political activity was eagerly exploited by both men and women. In some respects, therefore, the operation of the political process at the Restoration Court actually relied on the subordinate status of women.

Only a few of Charles's mistresses were particularly prominent or long-lasting and this chapter is concerned mainly with the two who held most importance at Court: Barbara Palmer, Countess of Castlemaine and Duchess of Cleveland, and Louise de Kéroualle, Duchess of Portsmouth. Barbara Palmer, a member of the Villiers family and married to a lawyer, Roger Palmer, was Charles's principal mistress from 1660 to 1670. Their affair was already largely finished when Louise de Kéroualle arrived from France in 1670. Louise had been a Maid of Honour to Henriette Anne, Charles's sister, and after her death in 1670 was offered the same position with Charles's wife, Catherine of Braganza. Louise soon attracted the King's attention and from 1671 until Charles's death in 1685 she was his most important mistress.

THE POLITICS OF DISPLAY

The mistresses proved adept at demonstrating the King's favour to the Court. After a very public disagreement between Charles and Catherine, in which many courtiers took sides, Barbara Palmer was made a Lady of the Bedchamber.[2] The victory of Barbara in the Queen's Household affected the Queen's position for the rest of the reign. Catherine did not put up the same struggle against any of Charles's other mistresses, although it is very likely that she refused to sign the warrant of 1673 making Louise de Kéroualle a Lady of the Bedchamber.[3] The mistresses' prominence at court balls and other formal occasions,[4] their attendance at routine events such as riding in the park and going to the theatre,[5] the entertainments they put on for the Court,[6] and their show of wealth in such items as jewels[7] and coaches,[8] were all carefully watched by the courtiers as possible signs of the King's favour.

Much of court life was lived in public and many court events had a significance beyond their ostensible social purpose. They were often opportunities for displaying and establishing oneself in the hierarchies of the Court and at any event something might happen which would alter the perception of a courtier's position. In October 1662 Barbara insisted on being the first Lady of the Bedchamber in precedence after the Countess of Bath, although in theory her Irish title conferred a lesser status than the other Ladies and she should have been last.[9] When a Lady of the Bechamber, Jane, Lady Gerrard attempted to influence the Queen to assert her position against Barbara, she was publicly humiliated by

Charles to the point where she was forced to leave the Court. In late January 1663, Lady Gerrard invited Charles and Catherine to dinner. Charles left the gathering just as all was prepared and the guests assembled, and went to Barbara's where he stayed the whole evening.[10] At a ball arranged by the Queen in February 1663, Charles again humiliated Lady Gerrard by disdainfully refusing to dance with her when asked.[11] In July 1663 Samuel Pepys was able to observe, after an argument between Barbara and the King over his attention to Frances Stuart, that when the courtiers went out riding, Charles rode hand in hand with the Queen and Barbara appeared 'very melancholy; nor did anybody speak to her or she so much as smile or speak to anybody'; such was the sensitivity of the Court to changes in the King's favour.[12]

The mistresses were only too well aware of this close scrutiny and encouraged belief in the King's favour. In February 1664 Barbara called attention to herself by leaning past the other ladies in her box at the theatre to talk with Charles and then left it to sit between the King and the Duke of York. It was thought 'she did it only to show the world that she is not out of favour yet – as was believed'.[13] Some people spent as much time watching the courtiers at the theatre as the play itself. In January 1668 Elizabeth Pepys and her servant were able to report that Barbara had been at a play at Whitehall, but so was

> Mis Davis, who is the most impertinent slut . . . in the world, and the more now the king doth show her countenance and is reckoned his mistress . . . the king gazing on her, and My Lady Castlemayne being melancholy and out of humour all the play, not smiling once. The king it seems hath given her a ring of £700, which she shows to everybody, and owns that the king did give it her. And he hath furnished a house for her in Suffolk-street most richly for her.[14]

When challenged by courtiers, the mistresses' best answer was to draw attention to Charles's esteem for them. In August 1674 Louise, now Duchess of Portsmouth, decided to make a visit to Tunbridge Wells from Windsor. Louise's servants went ahead to arrange accommodation for her stay there and picked out a desirable residence but, while they were waiting for Louise's arrival and her approval, a maid of the Marchioness of Worcester rented the house. This greatly offended Louise who made her feelings known to the Marchioness. A loud and very public scene ensued. Louise reminded the Marchioness of her duty to her, being of higher rank, and Lady Worcester replied that titles gained by prostitution had never impressed persons of good sense. Louise's response was that it was true that she had been thought worthy to enter the King's bed. Lady Worcester, not to be outdone, replied yes, and the *comte* de Sault's bed and that of the Duke of Hamilton, because they were the first. Such attacks on mistresses' sexual morality were a common form of insult. Louise's answer was an effective demonstration of the King's favour: having sent a message to Charles saying that she feared for her life, she obtained his guards to provide her with an escort back to Windsor.[15]

On Charles's death, the absence of his favour was immediately apparent and the mistresses' illegitimate position once more emerged. Louise could not 'with propriety' be at Charles's bedside, the Queen taking her position there.[16] Moreover, the mistresses were prevented from using the special mourning 'nails' reserved for the royal family's coaches, and from putting their houses in mourning.[17]

The lodgings of the King's mistresses were a source of continual speculation for courtiers. Their location, size and decoration were part of the interpretative framework by which the King's relationship with a mistress was judged. Equally important was how often a mistress was visited by the King. According to the Earl of Clarendon, Catherine's condition for accepting Barbara was that 'shee should never live in court'.[18] Thus the importance of keeping Barbara out of Whitehall was clear in the Queen's mind, but contrary to Catherine's wishes, Barbara was given lodgings there. To begin with these may have been some of the King's own rooms but she soon moved to the apartments previously occupied by the Duke of Ormonde, situated in Holbein Gatehouse.[19] Barbara's apartments and the dinners she gave there quickly came to be taken for granted by the King. Pepys heard in April 1663 that the Queen grieved at Charles's neglect, 'he having not supped once with her this Quarter of a year, and almost every night with my Lady Castlmayne'.[20] In May 1664 Pepys noted that it was with Barbara that Charles celebrated his birthday, 'dancing with fiddlers all night almost and all the world coming by taking notice of it – which I am sorry to hear'.[21] In August it was reported that Charles still dined every night with Barbara and in September she gave a magnificent dinner for the French ambassador's wife, where it was remarked that Charles behaved more as a host than a guest.[22] Barbara's move out of Whitehall to Berkshire House, opposite St James's Palace, in 1668 appeared to herald a loss of favour but for some time Charles continued to make frequent visits to Barbara. These contradictory signals caused much speculation. As one newsletter writer wrote: 'the Countess of Castlemain is removed to Barkshire house with all her family, tis reported she is in disfavour but I beleeve tis only her remove occasions it. For she hath newly made her a most stately pleasure boat, and somebody supt with her aboard it this weeke.'[23] The most accurate assessment would seem to be that of the French ambassador who thought that Barbara was no longer the King's favourite but that she would undoubtedly continue to retain some credit with him.[24]

On her arrival in 1670 Louise de Kéroualle would have taken up residence in Whitehall in the apartments reserved for the Maids of Honour. At some point, (certainly before June 1672 when her son Charles was born), she was given lodgings at the end of the Matted Gallery, which she occupied for the rest of the reign. Louise greatly enlarged the original apartments until they came to include about 60–70 ft of the gallery. When they burnt down in 1691 they consisted of some twenty-four rooms and sixteen garrets.[25] Louise had the apartments redecorated and rebuilt several times. Their opulence fascinated John Evelyn who first saw them in 1675, 'luxuriously furnished & with ten times the richness & glory beyond the Queenes'.[26] Their appearance and superiority to the Queen's apartments was again noticed by Evelyn in 1683. Louise's rooms contained:

> the new fabrique of French Tapissry . . . Japon Cabinets, Skreenes, Pendule Clocks, huge Vasas of wrought plate, Tables, Stands, Chimny furniture, Sconces, branches, Braseras &c., they were all of massive silver and without number, besides of his Majesties best paintings . . . Lord what contentment can ther be in the riches & splendour of this world, purchased with vice & dishonour.[27]

These apartments became a focal point for Louise's entertainment of the King and the Court and it is significant that Louise never acquired a house and always remained in her apartments at Whitehall, close to the King.

Access to the mistresses' apartments meant access to the King, either directly because he was so often there, or indirectly with the mistresses as intermediaries. Charles's visits to Barbara were not always private.[28] In 1663 the Earl of Sandwich was pleased to be invited to Barbara's lodgings by Charles and was happy to lose £50 at cards there for the honour of the invitation, the point being that such invitations were a mark of favour.[29] Lord Conway and the Earl of Ossory were another two courtiers welcome at Barbara's apartments. Conway frequently went to play cards with the King and Barbara, and in October 1666 he commented favourably on the arrangements. Barbara had invited him to come every night 'which I shall frequently embrace as an opportunity of the king's conversation which is very desirable'. Lord Ossory, the Duke of Ormonde's son, and Conway had 'agreed to goe halfes there this winter' and Conway claimed that it might give him an opportunity of serving Ormonde.[30] In the 1670s attention switched to Louise's apartments. The Earl of Arran wrote that he often met and played cards with the Earls of Danby and Ranelagh at Louise's.[31] An alternative to Louise's was Nell Gwyn's house in Pall Mall, where men such as the Duke of Buckingham and the Duke of Monmouth preferred to meet the King.[32] The King's ministers were not slow to realise the value of meeting the King informally at the homes of his mistresses, as Charles was often prepared to discuss business there.

The mistresses were able to provide an alternative to meeting the King in the Queen's apartments; an alternative which seemed more congenial and more useful to many. The mistresses were also able to give such a display of the King's favour in the magnificence of his gifts to them and the entertainments they put on for the Court at which Charles was present, that courtiers looked to them rather than Catherine for influence with the King.

MISTRESSES AND COURT PATRONAGE

The intense competition shown by courtiers in asserting their status with the King was motivated in part by the desire to influence his distribution of Crown patronage. The King was the central source of patronage in the form of grants of land, annuities, presents and offices. However, obtaining grants and then collecting payments on them involved not just the King's favour but that of many other important officials, and a great deal of perseverance was required by the recipient of the grant in conducting her business. The King's mistresses were particularly well placed to gain a share in the King's wealth, and they energetically pursued this goal. Moreover, as brokers of Crown patronage they had considerable success in attracting clients who would give loyalty and service, or money, in return for benefits. Thus, the mistresses became deeply and necessarily involved in patronage networks at court.

Barbara, Nell and Louise all assisted many people who had business with the King. They supported petitions to him for help from those who were in trouble, either with the law,[33] or for more dramatic reasons, such as the man whose son had been kidnapped by Algerians.[34] Many clients wanted a court appointment,[35] or assistance with business affairs which involved the King or his ministers in some way.[36] Clerics who wanted promotion might apply to the mistresses. Barbara helped Dr Thomas Wood become Bishop of Litchfield because her dispute with some members of the Wood family over control of Sir Henry Wood's estates meant that she was only too pleased to have at least one member of the family obliged to her.[37]

Courtiers who aided the mistresses in their own pursuit of the King's patronage were rewarded for their services. For example, several people became involved in helping to further Barbara Palmer's claims to Irish lands. In March 1672 Sir John Trevor, who was evidently employed by Barbara as her lawyer, wrote a paper detailing the two sorts of remainders and reversions in Ireland belonging to the Crown: 'the ancient and those expectant on estates for life or tail decreed by the Court of Claims'. Barbara had a sweeping general grant of the latter and Trevor advised her on how to claim these lands.[38] In return, in 1672 Trevor's long career in politics was launched when Barbara used her influence with Henry Howard to have Trevor nominated for election as a Member of Parliament.[39] In 1676 Henry Savile was protecting Barbara's rights to lands in Ireland. He entered caveats in January and August that no grants would pass of any remainder on estates tail in Ireland, as the King had granted them to Barbara.[40] Two years later, Savile wanted Barbara's help in getting the King's permission to sell his Bedchamber post and grant him some extra money.[41]

It is clear that women's activities both as recipients and brokers in the exercise of royal patronage were widespread, and although Charles does not appear to have allowed any one person, male or female, to dominate the patronage process, the ability of Barbara Palmer and then Louise de Kéroualle to influence the King favourably seems to have been almost taken for granted. The number and variety of people and affairs the mistresses advanced suggest that they shared the contemporary attitude to the patronage system: having successfully advanced themselves to a position of power, they were obliged to advance others in order to stay there, thereby entrenching themselves in a network of obligation and consequently reinforcing their own position.

At a higher level, the state of the mistresses' relationships with important officials was very much related to their contacts within the patronage process. It was the refusal of the Earls of Clarendon and Southampton to countenance any grants to Barbara that led her to add her weight to the ministers who opposed these two men, and to concentrate on promoting her own friends to the post of Keeper of the Privy Purse from whence she was paid in the 1660s.[42] Some ministers of the 1670s, such as the Earl of Danby, were far more ready to help the mistresses achieve their financial ambitions and they consequently supported these ministers in their posts.[43]

Another means by which patronage ties were developed was marriage. For example, as part of an attempt to interest Louise in supporting his bid to regain the Lord Lieutenancy of Ireland, John, Lord Berkeley arranged a marriage between Louise's sister Henriette and Philip Herbert, Earl of Pembroke, in 1674.[44]

The King's great interest in and affection for his children by the mistresses led many courtiers to show an interest in arranging marriages with them. Henry Howard told John Evelyn that he was 'going to marry his Eldest sonn to one of the King's natural daughters, by the Dutchess of Cleveland; by which he reckon'd he shall come into might[y] favour'.[45] The daughter he preferred was Charlotte but in May 1674 she was contracted to marry Edward Henry Lee, Earl of Litchfield.[46] Edward was the son of Elizabeth, Countess of Lindsey, by her first marriage. At the time of the contract between Edward and Charlotte, Elizabeth was married to Robert Bertie, Earl of Lindsey. The Lindseys provided a connection for Barbara with the Lord Treasurer Danby through the Earl of Lindsey's sister Bridget who was Danby's wife. Lindsey was keen to promote this connection for the sake of the marriage and emphasised to Danby that, although he was not sure how useful Barbara would be to Danby, 'I can scarce think her interest so inconsiderable (shee having such a numerous issue by his Majesty), butt that sometime or other shee may be serviceable to your Lordship.'[47] Lindsey wrote to his sister Bridget on 1 August 1674 to thank her for the 'great favour' she and Danby had done him in making a visit to Barbara.[48] He soon heard that Barbara had in fact not been in and wrote again on 2 August to apologise on Barbara's behalf and assure Bridget that no insult was intended. Clearly, what he wanted was Bridget's influence with Barbara for the promotion of the marriage. The prosperity of his family, he declared, 'depends now very much uppon the suckses of this Mach of my sones'. He was confident Barbara had 'made a very firm resilution with her selfe, if she may but be reseved now, in to my Lord Trisiors frindship, for to remane from hence forth, very true to him and all his Intrists'.[49]

For her part, Barbara obviously expected the Lindseys to pursue her interests with Danby. Barbara, the Earl of Lindsey wrote, was pleased with the interest shown by Danby and Bridget in the marriage, and had written to his wife Elizabeth of her appreciation for Danby's moving of her pension onto a more reliable fund. She hoped that the Treasury would now assign her some money for her sons; one to go to Oxford and another overseas. Otherwise, Barbara was afraid, they would fall into the Earl of Arlington's care. Arlington was not a friend and Barbara associated him with her rival the Duchess of Portsmouth and believed that the marriage of her son Henry and Arlington's daughter, Isabella, was Arlington's main support with Charles, and if she left her sons to his care 'it will but be the occasion of his growing more powerful, when he shall be possessed of those considerable pledges of the King's affection'. Barbara wanted to prevent this by putting them into Danby's hands, which would be 'more agreeable to hers and your owne interest then into the hands of my Lady Portsmouth['s] creature, her mortall and irreconcilable enemy'. Barbara also requested that Danby interest himself in promoting a marriage between her son George and the heiress Lady Elizabeth Percy, again to prevent Arlington having a hand in it, as he would 'highly value himself on it if it be committed to his care'. If Danby agreed, Barbara would get Charles to engage him in the project.[50]

The marriage between Edward and Charlotte was a success and the Countess of Lindsey was able to report with satisfaction to her sister-in-law Bridget that Charles was very affectionate towards Charlotte, being

> infinitely fonder of my Lady Litchfield thin ever I saw him in all my life, and bouth my Lady Portchmouth and Mrs. Guine telles me that he dos confes he loves her better and better, and lickwis that he saes littel sharp things of late of my Lady Susix, and thay bouth advised me by whot they observed in him for to cepe her as neare to him as I could.[51]

Louise and Nell evidently felt no threat from Charlotte to their own children's interests, and Elizabeth's connection with Danby was probably their motivation for passing on such useful information as this.

Elizabeth was also able to inform Bridget that Arlington had tried to tempt Nell to come to his house at Euston when Charles would be visiting Newmarket. He had promised 'that if she will come thether to him the quene of England shall not be nobler entertained thin she shall', and if Nell did come he would 'ingage for to use his intrist with the King for to bestow a titil uppon that butifull cretur her sone'. On the face of it an innocent offer, but Nell understood this to be an invitation to give up Danby's friendship and 'she says she will not goe, nor forsack my Lord Trisior . . . becous she is convinced that he is not only the best man in the world, but becous she is shure he loves the King bettor thin any other body dos that is about him'.[52] Despite such good information Danby does not appear to have been careful of Nell's friendship. A year later she had turned against him and was reported to encourage the ridiculing of him and his wife at gatherings at her house in Charles's presence.[53]

MISTRESSES, MINISTERS AND COURT POLITICS

Mistresses were more successful in court politics than other women because of their unique intimacy with the King. This intimacy caused high anxiety and one response was to attempt to make the woman involved 'safe' and to profit from the relationship by being her manager. Barbara Palmer's success as a mistress led to many attempts to promote others, such as Frances Stuart, Nell Gwyn and Hortense, Duchess Mazarin, and to ruin those already in place. For example, in June 1671, it was hoped that Alice, Lady Clanbrassil, would attract Charles away from Nell Gwyn. Lord Conway wrote to Sir George Rawdon that 'you cannot imagine how my Lord Arran and many others do value themselves upon the account of managing Lady Clanbrassil on this affair'.[54] However, most of the plans to establish new mistresses and ruin others failed. The most successful was the promotion of Louise de Kéroualle by the Earl and Countess of Arlington and the French ambassador, Colbert de Croissy.

Arlington's conversation with de Croissy in October 1671 is a unique record of a would-be manager's hopes of a potential mistress.[55] Arlington said he was very glad to see Charles's attraction to Louise and although it was not the King's nature to communicate his affairs to ladies, as they could on occasion destroy those they disliked and consequently ruin much business, nonetheless, it was much better for all the good servants of the King that he was attracted to a woman who was not of an ill nature and was a lady, rather than to actresses or other 'little' creatures with whom an honest man could make no arrangements. The sort of woman, complained Arlington, promoted by the Duke of Buckingham, who was always dragging the King off to see them, thereby removing him from the eyes of the Court and possessing him alone. On the other hand, Louise's apartments were in Whitehall and everyone could expect to see Charles there and to go in and pay court to him. Arlington was going to advise Louise to manage the King's favour well, not speak to him of any business and show no aversion for those around the King and, finally, never to allow him to find anything but pleasure and enjoyment at her lodgings.

Arlington's speech reveals much wishful thinking about the King and his mistresses. He was evidently concerned to minimise the influence a mistress could have in politics, envisaging her role as that of decorative hostess only and encouraging others to believe that this was the case. He also objected to

Buckingham carrying Charles off to see other mistresses to the exclusion of courtiers such as himself. Based on the fact that Louise was living in the palace and the easy access he expected all to have to her lodgings, Arlington hoped to thwart this monopolisation of the King. He also expected (unrealistically as it turned out), to control Louise's actions. Arlington did not stop at offering his own advice; Lady Arlington was going to advise Louise to consent to all the King desired and that her only other course of action was to enter a convent in France. Arlington asked for de Croissy's help and he agreed to give Louise a sign of approval, and to inform her of her obligations to Arlington.

It is clear that Louise's early relationships with the King's ministers, and the French ambassadors, were based on attempts to 'manage' her. Unfortunately for Arlington's plans, by July 1673 he and Louise were on bad terms and, his hopes dashed, he could be heard complaining bitterly of her ungratefulness.[56] Mistresses, once established, tended to escape from their managers' control and behave in a distressingly independent manner.

Factions, then, formed around the mistresses with the idea of promoting them or supplanting them. It can also be shown that mistresses and other women were much involved in the factions which formed with the same object around male courtiers.

To take one example, the end of 1668 and the beginning of 1669 saw increasing friction between Barbara and Ralph Montagu's sister, Elizabeth, Lady Harvey. This was closely related to Barbara's bad relations with the Duke of Buckingham and the Earl of Arlington and her new friendship with the Duke and Duchess of York.

According to the French ambassador, Buckingham and Arlington had agreed to try and remove the Earl of Clarendon's son Henry, Lord Cornbury, from his post of Lord Chamberlain to the Queen in order to get the place for the Earl of Sunderland. However, they were blocked by Barbara who, having been reconciled with the Duchess of York (Cornbury's sister), agreed to use her credit with Charles in Cornbury's favour. It appeared certain that Charles would not dismiss Cornbury and that he would continue to keep his post. This failure and (surely unfounded) suspicions that Barbara was working with the Duchess of York for the re-establishment of the disgraced Clarendon were the cause of Arlington's and Buckingham's decision to use all means to destroy Barbara's credit with the King.[57]

To accomplish this they had thought of Elizabeth, Lady Harvey. In December 1668 it was reported around the Court that during a dinner arranged by Buckingham to reconcile Arlington and a minor courtier George Porter, Elizabeth had made a toast to the prosperity of Lord Arlington and all his friends, and to the confusion of all the rogues with whom Porter had formerly been allied. This, it was claimed, was meant to include Barbara and her friends and even the Duke of York. Porter apparently joined in the toast enthusiastically and promised Elizabeth that he would not fail to tell his former friends of it.[58] Moreover, Elizabeth, an acknowledged wit, conducted a campaign of criticism against Barbara's conduct in front of the King and Queen. Barbara retaliated in kind, eventually denouncing Elizabeth as a hermaphrodite and claiming that Elizabeth's anger against her was because she had refused Elizabeth's advances. Elizabeth replied that she was amazed that Barbara, who did not refuse anyone, should say such a thing.[59]

This tension erupted into the glare of the stage in January 1669. The actress Mrs Corey had caricatured Lady Harvey on stage to loud applause from the audience. It seems likely that Barbara had arranged for this caricature to take place.[60] Elizabeth used her connection with the Lord Chamberlain, her second cousin, to have the actress imprisoned but Charles released her, probably influenced by Barbara, who urgently requested it.[61] The play, including the caricature, was acted again, encouraged by the presence this time of Barbara and the King. The third time the actress performed, Elizabeth was ready and had provided people to hiss and fling oranges at the actress.[62] Thus, although the incident was over Lord Cornbury's post, in one area at least the conflict took the form of sexual insults traded by Barbara and Elizabeth in order to discredit one another, eventually resulting in the public ridicule of Elizabeth.

Buckingham tried to obtain from Charles a command that the actress would make amends to Elizabeth but was told that if this were done then the whole Howard family and many other Lords, who had wisely ignored similar caricatures, would require satisfaction.[63] The episode culminated in a victory for Barbara. Buckingham, who had not visited Barbara for some time, swiftly presented himself at her house and a reconciliation was effected (there were of course doubts as to its sincerity), while Lady Harvey retired to her house and received only close friends.[64] Barbara's friendship with the Duke and Duchess of York continued. She was seen enjoying herself at a party arranged by James and Anne in March 1669, and in August de Croissy reported that everyone attributed James's apparent closeness with Charles to Barbara 'who for a long time has not ceased to work to disabuse the king of the bad impressions that some wanted to give him of his brother'.[65]

The involvement of the mistresses in alliances and enmities with the King's ministers extended to participation in domestic and foreign policy where, in a variety of ways, the unofficial nature of female participation proved useful.

When the Spanish and French ambassadors realised the advantages of being on friendly terms with the mistresses, they too began to cultivate them and to try and gain entry to their lodgings. In the 1660s Barbara favoured the Spanish. They were said to spend money lavishly in order to get news from Barbara's table and to promote their point of view there.[66] The French ambassador, Courtin, although he had a promise from the Earl of Falmouth to take him to eat at Barbara's in 1665, did not gain access until 1669.[67] The French were more successful with Louise. The ambassadors' reports and the instructions to new ambassadors often mention the advantages to be drawn from remaining on good terms with Louise.[68] Charles was found playing cards at Louise's on many occasions by the French ambassadors and when they wanted to talk business they could easily withdraw to an alcove or another room. These private talks often included Louise.[69]

An incident in October 1682 demonstrates the significance placed on admittance to Louise's apartments at this time. The Dutch ambassador, Van Beuning, complained during an interview with the Earl of Conway and Edward Seymour of the French ambassador, Barrillon's, easy access to Louise's lodgings. He saw this as something which gave cause for the suspicion that the interests of France were managed by those who were most intimate with Charles. He added that such access at all hours signified a confidence and an alliance which must provoke the King's allies and it was useless to have ambassadors in England who could only see Charles in public places while the French ambassador could see him at any hour in the most private places. Van Beuning added that Charles must be told and asked to consider the consequences of this. Seymour and Conway reported the conversation to Louise, who was annoyed and complained of it to Charles, representing it as lack of respect for him for which he should demand reparation. James and Lawrence Hyde were also of the opinion that a public reprimand should be administered but Charles would not engage himself to do this, possibly because Conway and Seymour drew back when they saw how far the matter had gone and softened their report of Van Beuning's outburst, saying he had not asked them to speak of it to Charles (although this is what they had told Louise). Van Beuning nevertheless regretted his speech and, via the Earl of Sunderland, offered to apologise and explain himself. It was arranged that Van Beuning would come to Newmarket (where Louise and the Court were) and make his excuses himself to Louise.[70] Many ambassadors and courtiers must have felt as Van Beuning did, but visiting at the mistresses' apartments was unofficial and therefore could not be successfully challenged.

The French had no hesitation in including women in the political landscape. First the King's sister, Henriette Anne, and then Louise were particularly important to the French as women who were favoured by the King and whose ties to France made them acceptable intermediaries. Henriette Anne, who helped to negotiate the Treaty of Dover between Charles and Louis XIV, is a good example of a woman conducting 'invisible' negotiations. Throughout the 1660s Charles had written to Henriette Anne for her help with Louis XIV over particular points of conflict between himself and the French, and about the possibility of a treaty. The existence of the Treaty of Dover was secret, known only to a trusted few, and the protection offered by Henriette Anne's sex was indispensable to this secrecy. It would not be expected that Henriette Anne, a woman, would be negotiating a treaty, and her trip to Dover in 1670 for its signing could be convincingly presented as simply a social visit to see her brother.[71]

Louise only gradually took over the role of female intermediary left vacant by Henriette Anne's death. In the early 1670s Louise greatly annoyed the French with her interference in the Duke of York's marriage, while her attachment to the Earl of Danby caused some reservations and her support for Exclusion meant that she played little part in Anglo-French relations from 1680–2. However, like any clever go-between, Louise was always keen to stress her zeal for the side to which she was communicating unpleasant news, or from which she was attempting to extract favourable terms. Thus she constantly emphasised her keenness for France's interests to the French ambassadors and the French usually, on balance, felt able to trust Louise.[72] They were able to point to the concrete evidence of her own considerable interests in France and felt that the French king's acknowledgement of her services was sure to keep her loyal.[73]

When relations between France and England became strained towards the end of 1677 and it looked as if England might declare war on France, it was at Louise's apartments that the behind-the-scenes meetings between the French ambassador, Barrillon, and Charles took place.[74] Louise suggested herself as an intermediary and put forward plans for a resolution of the difficulties.[75] Barrillon was evidently comfortable negotiating with Louise and felt able, on at least one occasion, to express himself more freely to her on the subject of English conduct than to the King's ministers.[76] When the prospects of war faded the possibility of a subsidy from France to enable Charles to do without Parliament seemed more likely and from August 1679 it was Louise and her ally the Earl of Sunderland who were employed to negotiate over specific amounts.[77]

Louise ceased acting as an intermediary between the French and Charles when she decided to support the exclusion of the Duke of York from the succession. When the third Exclusion Bill failed in 1681, Louise gradually returned to helping the French and directed a constant flow of information to Barrillon about the sentiments of Charles and his ministers towards France. Louise wrote to Louis XIV in 1682 to guarantee the Earl of Sunderland's future good conduct[78] and assured him of Charles's good intentions.[79] In the 1680s Louise consistently pressed Charles to accept French aggression in the Netherlands.[80]

The mistresses also fulfilled another delicate role. Thanks to the great favour bestowed upon them by the King, some thought that unpleasant or difficult matters might be best communicated through them. In 1678 Barrillon wrote that he did not doubt that Danby used Louise to succeed in things that he did not want to propose himself.[81] In January 1682 Louise reported that Lawrence Hyde and Edward Seymour had asked her to find out confidentially from Charles whether he intended to remain firmly neutral in his policy on the Netherlands. They wanted Louise to give the King a message that if he did then they would always support him, but they asked him not to expose them to a sure ruin if he decided to change his mind. Louise said that Charles had replied that he did not blame his ministers if they took some precaution for their own security but they had nothing to fear and he would stay firm.[82] Louise also performed this role for Charles who often delegated her to express his displeasure at French conduct, as in 1679–80 when she informed Barrillon of the King's wrath at Barrillon's revelations to the French ambassador in Holland about Charles's interest in preventing a Franco-Dutch alliance.[83]

Another result of the officially unacknowledged participation of women in politics was that they might publicly accept gifts, in return for political co-operation. These gifts were often aimed more at the husbands of the women who accepted them, or in the case of the mistresses, they were a compliment not only to themselves but to Charles, as well as something which might encourage them to act in the giver's interests. Women could accept gifts on their own behalf and on behalf of a man, without the true nature of the gift, which everyone knew, becoming a successful point of attack for their enemies. Given the important but increasingly problematic status of the gift in politics this was an important function.[84] Thus in 1669 Barbara was given a gift worth about £1,000 from the French when they wanted to reward and encourage her recent cooperation with them.[85] To make the giving of such a gift even less open to attack it could be given 'woman to woman'. Madame Colbert de Croissy negotiated the giving of a substantial present to Lady Arlington after the successful completion of the Treaty of Dover. It was a present which the cautious Lord Arlington, one of the main negotiators of the treaty had refused to receive but which was finally accepted by his wife with great satisfaction all round in 1672.[86] In 1676 the Duke of York passed on a present to himself from Louis XIV to his wife the Duchess of York, in order that 'it might appear less'. He also told the French ambassador that Lord Danby was so attached to the Prince of Orange that he had allowed his wife's sister to receive a present worth £2,000, which in all likelihood was really for Danby.[87] Charles was as delighted with the many presents from Louis XIV to Barbara and Louise as they were themselves.[88] The point was that women were not officially involved in politics at this level and therefore they could show the gifts around the Court, to be admired by all, with impunity whereas a man could have been open to charges of bribery, even treason.

The mistresses' unofficial political actions were undoubtedly useful to the King, his ministers and the French ambassadors, but the mistresses were not simply passive handmaidens for men in the political process. Barbara surprised some courtiers by speaking out strongly in September 1662 for the nonconformist ministers who were about to be ejected from their livings.[89] Louise appears to have come close to succeeding in persuading the Duke of York to marry one of the Mademoiselles d'Elboeuf in 1673, against the wishes of the Earl of Arlington and the French.[90] In 1680 when Louise and the Earl of Sunderland came out in favour of Exclusion they both apparently believed that Charles would agree to it and we may suppose that they influenced each other on the truth of this belief. The details of Louise's actions during the Exclusion crisis remain obscure but she appears to have kept her options open in the sense that she maintained contact both with the Earl of Sunderland and the supporters of William and Mary, and the Earl of Shaftesbury and the Duke of Monmouth's supporters.[91] She also acted as an intermediary between Charles and the opposition Members of Parliament, as it emerged at the trial of Edward Fitzharris for treason in 1681 that Louise had arranged the secret meetings of Lord Howard of Escrik, who advocated Exclusion, with Charles in October 1680.[92]

One of the questions most often asked about the mistresses was whether or not they were able to influence policy decisions. This raises the question of to what extent the possibility of influence for any courtier, male or female, was determined by the inclinations of the King. The structure of the political system which included a powerful sovereign makes this a difficult question to answer. Courtiers had to be wary of appearing 'over mighty'; proclaiming their own influence might incur the King's displeasure. The inferior status of women meant it was even more unlikely that female influence would be admitted by the King. Moreover, Charles was a particularly secretive king whose ministers sometimes had to confess they did not know what he would do.

With regard to the mistresses, the simple answer is that it cannot be claimed that any of the mistresses convinced Charles to do something he did not wish to do (indeed, they had some spectacular failures), and there is not enough evidence to tell us whether they influenced him on matters where he did not already have a strong opinion. However, the few clues left to the historian suggest that female influence should not be discounted. In 1669 the French were hesitating over giving Barbara a present, afraid that if it was too large it would imply she had too much power and Charles would take offence. Charles was obviously aware of the French dilemma, making it known to the French ambassador through an intermediary that the only woman who influenced him was his sister and anyone who thought otherwise was mistaken. Charles, then, was concerned with public appearances but he did not rule out female influence completely and it should be noted that the comment was made before the arrival of Louise.[93] Prominent men such as the Duke of York, Lawrence Hyde, the Earl of Sunderland and the Marquis of Halifax certainly thought that Louise had significant influence with Charles.[94] We may add that the mistresses fulfilled the necessary preconditions of influence; they had the requisite access to the King and knew many of his secrets.[95] The mistresses themselves made few surviving comments on this subject. They were not shy of expressing their opinions on policy, which may suggest the expectation of being listened to seriously. Barbara reported to the French ambassador conversations she had had with the King in which she forcefully expressed her opinion on the relative merits of Buckingham and Arlington and their likely duplicity over a French treaty. She said that as a loyal subject she had given her views and always would.[96] In one instance, Louise did openly claim that she had influenced Charles on policy: this was to remain neutral on the French siege of Luxembourg in 1682 and not come to the aid of the Spanish.[97]

The full extent of female influence on Charles II needs further exploration, and to some degree may always remain an unknown quantity. However, a close look at the political activities of the King's mistresses does reveal that the informal part of politics, which was still significant in the Restoration period, was open to female participation under Charles's rule and the mistresses took advantage of this. Women had always been active in advancing family interests in the wider society and continued to be accepted in this role in court politics. On the other hand, seventeenth-century belief in female inferiority meant that women's presence in high politics was duly overlooked. The consequent theoretical non-participation of women combined with an involvement in practice, which enabled the mistresses to play a significant part in the conduct of court politics.

Notes

Sources: As the French diplomatic correspondence has been foliated several times, folio numbers have been omitted to avoid confusion and, as the correspondence is arranged in chronological order, writer, addressee and the date have been given instead.

1. Starkey, *English Court*, pp. 6–16; R. Shephard, *Royal Favourites in the Political Discourse of Tudor and Stuart England* (unpublished Ph.D, Claremont Graduate School, 1985), pp. 33–49; B. Harris, 'Women and Politics in Early Tudor England', *HJ*, 33:2 (1990), 259–81; A. Muhlstein, *La femme soleil: les femmes et le pouvoir. Une relecture de Saint-Simon* (Paris, 1976), pp. 33, 38–41, 171–4.

2. E. Hyde, Earl of Clarendon, *The Life of Edward, Earl of Clarendon, Lord High Chancellor of England . . .* (3 vols, new edn Oxford, 1827), pp. 164–95; Public Record Office (PRO), London, French Diplomatic Correspondence, Baschet Transcripts, PRO 31/3/110, Batailler to Lionne, 3, 10 July 1662, 10 August 1662; Pepys, *Diary*, Vol. III, p. 147; Bodl. Lib., Carte MSS 31, f. 602, O'Neill to Ormonde, 28 August 1662; PRO, State Papers, Domestic, SP 29/75, p. 33, warrants, 1 June 1663.

3. W.D. Christie (ed.), *Letters Addressed from London to Sir Joseph Williamson . . . 1673 and 1674* (2 vols, 1874), Vol. I, p. 169.

4. Pepys, *Diary*, Vol. III, pp. 300–1.

5. Pepys, *Diary*, Vol. IV, p. 95.

6. *Williamson Letters*, Vol. I, p. 130; Evelyn, *Diary*, Vol. IV, pp. 267–8; M.A.E. Green, F.H.B. Daniell and F. Bickley (eds), *Calendar of State Papers, Domestic (CSPD)* (28 vols, 1860–1938), *1682*, pp. 43–4.

7. Pepys, *Diary*, Vol. VI, p. 29, Vol. VII, p. 372; BL, Add. MSS, 36 916, ff. 62, 119; Evelyn, *Diary*, Vol. III, p. 505.

8. *CSPD, 1671*, p. 271; *Williamson Letters*, Vol. I, p. 74; E.M. Thompson (ed.), *Letters of Humphrey Prideaux . . . to John Ellis . . . 1674–1722* (1875), p. 121.

9. Bodl. Lib., Carte MS, 214, f. 379v.

10. PRO, PRO 31/3/110, London, Baschet Transcripts, Comminges to Louis XIV, 25 January 1663.

11. Pepys, *Diary*, Vol. IV, p. 68; Archives des Affaires Étrangères, (AAE), Paris, Correspondance Politique Angleterre, (CPA), 79, Comminge's court news, [15] February 1663, Comminges court news, [27] February 1663. That Lady Gerrard was intended to be a Lady of the Bedchamber appears from the draft list of the Queen's servants of early 1662: PRO, SP29/47, f. 209. Pepys's *Diary*, Vol. IV, p. 68, indicates she was in waiting on the Queen, but she was not sworn in with the other Ladies on 1 June 1663, nor was she with Catherine at Oxford in 1665. However, she must have been admitted at some point as she was one of the Ladies to attend the Queen at Dover in 1670: *CSPD, 1670*, p. 190.

12. Pepys, *Diary*, Vol. IV, p. 230.

13. Ibid., Vol. V, p. 33.

14. Ibid., Vol. IX, p. 24.

15. AAE, CPA, 114, Ruvigny to Pomponne, 16 August 1674.

16. PRO, PRO 31/3/160, Barrillon to Louis XIV, 18 February 1685.

17. HMC, *Ormonde MSS*, New Series, (8 vols, 1902–20), Vol. VII, p. 323.

18. Bodl. Lib., Carte MS, 47, f. 5v.

19. Colvin, *King's Works*, Vol. 5, 1660–1782 (London, 1976), pp. 267–8; Bodl. Lib., Carte MSS, 32, ff. 9, 598v, Carte MS, 47 f. 5v.

20. Pepys, *Diary*, Vol. IV, p. 95.

21. Ibid., Vol. V, p. 164.

22. PRO, PRO 31/3/113, Comminges to Lionne, 15 September 1664.

23. BL, Add. MS, 36 916, f. 101; see also, Pepys, *Diary*, Vol. IX, p. 190.

24. PRO, PRO 31/3/118, Ruvigny to Pomponne, 20 February, 5 April 1668.

25. Colvin, *King's Works*, pp. 277–9.

26. Evelyn, *Diary*, Vol. IV, p. 74.

27. Ibid., p. 343–4.

28. Pepys, *Diary*, Vol. III, p. 215; PRO, PRO 31/3/110, Comminges to Louis XIV, 25 January 1663.

29. Pepys, *Diary*, Vol. IV, p. 134.

30. Bodl. Lib., Carte MS, 34, ff. 459–459v.

31. HMC, *Ormonde MSS*, New Series, Vol. IV, p. 95.

32. Ibid., pp. 199, 376; E.M. Thompson (ed.), *Correspondence of the Family of Hatton . . . 1601–1704* (2 vols, 1878), Vol. I, p. 156; Henry Sidney, *Diary of the Times of Charles II, Including his Correspondence with the Countess of Sunderland . . .*, ed. R.W. Blencowe (2 vols, 1843), Vol. I, p. 20.

33. *CSPD, 1668–9*, p. 255.

34. *CSPD, 1673–5*, p. 80.

35. A. Browning (ed.), *The Memoirs, of Sir John Reresby. The Complete Text and a Selection of his Letters*, (Glasgow, 1936), pp. 331–2.

36. For Barbara and Nell, BL, Add. MS, 27 447, ff. 310, 447; for Louise, *CSPD, 1673*, p. 420; *CTB, 1676–9*, p. 1394; Bodl. Lib., Carte MS, 216, ff. 415v, 486.

37. *CSPD, 1671*, p. 329; HMC, *Twelfth Report, appendix, pt. vi, The manuscripts of the House of Lords, 1689–1690*, (1889), pp. 383–4; HMC, *Fourteenth Report, appendix, The manuscripts of the House of Lords, 1692–1693*, (1894), pp. 112–4; BL, Harleian MS, 5277, ff. 22–3. For Louise's support of Mr Hawkin's desire for preferment see *CSPD, 1675–1676*, p. 469.

38. *CSPD, 1671–2*, p. 250.

39. S. Pepys, *Diary and Correspondence of Samuel Pepys, F.R.S., Secretary to the Admiralty in the Reigns of Charles II and James II*, ed. Richard Braybrooke, Lord Braybrooke, Vol. 4 (6th edn, 1858), p. 204. For Trevor's career see *HC 1660–1690*, Vol. 3, pp. 604–7.

40. *CSPD, 1675–6*, p. 523; *CSPD, 1676–7*, pp. 270, 433.

41. A. Browning, *Thomas Osborne, Earl of Danby and Duke of Leeds*, (3 vols, 1951), Vol. II, p. 344.

42. G. Burnet, *History of his own times* (6 vols, Edinburgh, 1753), Vol. I, p. 239; E. Hyde, Earl of Clarendon, *The Life of Edward, Earl of Clarendon, Lord High Chancellor of England . . .* (2 vols, Oxford, 1857), Vol. I, p. 637, Vol. II, p. 262; AAE, CPA, 86, Courtin to Lionne, 16 July 1665; Henriette Anne to Charles II, 22 June 1665, printed in C.H. Hartmann, *The King my Brother*, (London, 1954), p. 173; Pepys, *Diary*, Vol. VIII, pp. 324–5.

43. *Essex Papers*, Vol. 1, 1672–1679, ed. O. Airy (1890), pp. 199–200; Vol. 2, 1675–1677, ed. C.E. Pike (1913), p. 50; HMC, *Report 9, pt. 2, appendix* (1884), p. 456; BL, Add. MS, 28094, f. 54.

44. AAE, CPA, 113, Ruvigny to Pomponne, 8 November 1674; Bodl. Lib., Carte MS, 243, f. 161v; see also, *Essex Papers*, i, p. 242.

45. Evelyn, *Diary*, Vol. III, p. 592.

46. PRO, PRO 31/3/131, Ruvigny to Pomponne, 28 May 1674.

47. *Catalogue of the collection of autograph letters and historical documents formed between 1865 and 1882 by Alfred Morrison*, ed. A.W. Thibaudau, 1st Series (6 vols, 1883–1892), Vol. III, p. 170.

48. BL, Egerton MS, 3338, f. 51.

49. BL, Egerton MS, 3338, ff. 52–3.

50. *Morrison Letters*, Vol. III, p. 170.

51. Ibid., p. 173. 'Lady Susix' was Anne, Countess of Sussex, Charlotte's elder sister.

52. Ibid., p. 173.

53. A. Browning, *Danby*, Vol. II, p. 40; HMC, *Ormonde MSS*, New Series, IV, pp. 106, 376. The reason for Nell's enmity was said to be a refusal by Danby to promote her desire for a title for herself.

54. *The Rawdon Papers, Consisting of Letters . . . To and From Dr. John Bramhall*, ed. E. Berwick (1819), p. 251; HMC, *Rutland MSS* (1889), II, p. 17.

55. AAE, CPA, 101, De Croissy to Louvois, 8 October 1671.

56. AAE, CPA, 107, De Croissy to Pomponne, 27 July 1673; *Essex papers*, ii, p. 3.

57. PRO, PRO 31/3/121, De Croissy to Lionne, 31 January 1669.

58. PRO, PRO 31/3/120, De Croissy to Lionne, 24 December 1668.

59. PRO, PRO 31/3/121, De Croissy to Lionne, 31 January 1669.

60. PRO, PRO 31/3/121, De Croissy to Lionne, 14 January 1669.

61. PRO, PRO 31/3/121, De Croissy to Lionne, 21 January 1669.

62. Pepys, *Diary*, Vol. IX, p. 415.

63. PRO, PRO 31/3/121, De Croissy to Lionne, 31 January 1669; Charles's mention of the Howard family referred to Sir Robert Howard being ridiculed as Sir Positive Att All in 'The Impertinents' in May 1668, see Pepys, *Diary*, Vol. IX, pp. 186, 190–1.

64. PRO, PRO 31/3/121, De Croissy to Lionne, 14 February 1669.

65. Pepys, *Diary*, Vol. IX, pp. 417, 468; PRO, PRO 31/3/122, De Croissy to Louis XIV, 19 August 1669.

66. PRO, PRO 31/3/114, Lionne to the ambassadors, 13 May, the ambassadors to Lionne, 21 May 1665; AAE, CPA, 86, Courtin to Lionne, 9 July 1665.

67. AAE, CPA, 85, Courtin to Lionne, 27 April 1665; PRO, PRO 31/3/121, De Groissy to Lionne, 31 January 1669. This dispatch contains the first indication that the French ambassador had gained entry to Barbara's house.

68. PRO, PRO 31/3/132, instructions to Courtin, 15 April 1676, 133, Courtin to Louis XIV, 1 April 1677, 136, instructions to Barrillon, 16 August 1677.

69. PRO, PRO 31/3/134, Courtin to Louis XIV, 5 November 1676, 139, Barrillon to Louis XIV, 12 May 1678.

70. AAE, CPA, 148, Barrillon to Louis XIV, 18 October 1682; PRO, PRO 31/3/153, Barrillon to Louis XIV, 28 October 1682.

71. C.H. Hartmann, *Charles II and Madame* (London, 1934), passim, for Charles's and Henriette Anne's correspondence and the Treaty of Dover.

72. For example, PRO, PRO 31/3/130, De Croissy to Pomponne, 11 January 1674, Ruvigny to Louis XIV, 14 March 1674, 142, Barrillon to Louis XIV, 27 March 1679, 153, Barrillon to Louis XIV, 20 August 1682.

73. PRO, PRO 31/3/132, instructions to Courtin, 15 April 1676, 139, Barrillon to Louis XIV, 12 May 1678, 152, Barrillon to Louis XIV, 27 July 1682.

74. PRO, PRO 31/3/137, Barrillon to Louis XIV, 25 November, 13, 16 December 1677, 138, Barrillon to Louis XIV, 10 January 1678.

75. PRO, PRO 31/3/138, Barrillon to Louis XIV, 31 January 1678.

76. PRO, PRO 31/3/138, Barrillon to Louis XIV, 3 February 1678; Barrillon also found Louise was more frank with him than Sunderland, PRO, 31/3/144, Barrillon to Louis XIV, 22 February 1680.

77. PRO, PRO 31/3/143, Barrillon to Louis XIV, 3, 31 August, 21 September, 2 October, 30 November 1679.

78. West Sussex Record Office, Goodwood MS 4, ff. 9/11–9/12, Duchess of Portsmouth to Louis XIV, August 1682, f. 9/5, Louis XIV to Duchess of Portsmouth, 8/18 February 1683.

79. AAE, CPA, 148, Barrillon to Louis XIV, 10, 24 December 1682.

80. PRO, PRO 31/3/150, Barrillon to Louis XIV, 20, 24 November 1681, 151, Barrillon to Louis XIV, 1, 8, 12–13, 15 January, 9, 12, 16 February, 13 April 1682.

81. AAE, CPA, 130, Barrillon to Pomponne, 25 July 1678.

82. PRO, PRO 31/3/151, Barrillon to Louis XIV, 9 February 1682.

83. PRO, PRO 31/3/144, Barrillon to Louis XIV, 15 January 1680. For other examples see PRO, 31/3/142, Barrillon to Louis XIV, 18 May 1679, 155, Barrillon to Louis XIV, 17 June 1683.

84. Linda Levy Peck, *Court Patraonge and Corruption in Early Stuart England* (Boston, 1990), pp. 18–20.

85. PRO, PRO 31/3/122, de Croissy to de Croissy, 20 May 1669, de Croissy to Louis XIV, 23 May 1669; HMC, *Buccleuch MSS* (1899), I, p. 422.

86. PRO, PRO 31/3/125, de Croissy to Louis XIV, 10 June 1670, 126, de Croissy to Louis XIV, 9 November 1671, 127, de Croissy to Louis XIV, 11 April 1672.

87. PRO, PRO 31/3/133, de Croissy to Pomponne, 11 August 1676.

88. PRO, PRO 31/3/122, de Croissy to Louis XIV, 23 May 1669, 130, de Croissy to Pomponne, 11 January 1674, 157, Barrillon to Louis XIV, 21 February 1684.

89. Bodl. Lib., Carte MSS, 32, ff. 3–3v.

90. PRO, PRO 31/3/129, de Croissy to Pomponne, 17 April, 17, 24 July, 29 August, 15 September 1673; AAE, CPA, 107, de Croissy to Pomponne, 1 June, 24, 27 July 1673.

91. PRO, PRO 31/3/146, Barrillon to Louis XIV, 24, 31 October 1680, 147, Barrillon to Louis XIV, 18, 21, 25 November 1680, 148, Barrillon to Louis XIV, 9, 13 16 January 1681; HMC, *Ormonde MSS*, New Series, V, pp. 445–6, 454, 458, 560–3; J.S. Clarke, *The Life of James, the Second, King of England* . . . (2 vols, 1816), Vol. I, pp. 591–2; Burnet, *History*, Vol. II, pp. 289–90.

92. Anon., *The Tryal and Condemnation of Edward Fitzharris* (1681), pp. 31–5.

93. PRO, PRO 31/3/121, de Croissy to Lionne, 14 January, 7 February 1669.

94. PRO, PRO 31/3/150, Barrillon to Louis XIV, 20 November 1681, 154, Barrillon to Louis XIV, 1 April 1683, 155, Barrillon to Louis XIV, 17 June, 5 July 1683, 157, Barrillon to Louis XIV, 13 January, 21 February 1684; Sidney, *Diary*, Vol. I, pp. 13–14; George Savile, Marquis of Halifax, *Complete Works*, ed. J.P. Kenyon (London, 1969), p. 254.

95. For evidence of Louise's inside information see PRO, PRO 31/3/154, Barrillon to Louis XIV, 28 January 1683, 158, Barrillon to Louis XIV, 27 April 1684, 159, Barrillon to Louis XIV, 16 October 1684; AAE, CPA 149, Barrillon to Louis XIV, 4 February 1683.

96. PRO, PRO 31/3/121, de Croissy to Lionne, 21 March 1669.

97. PRO, PRO 31/3/151, Barrillon to Louis XIV, 1, 8, 12–13, 15 January 1682.

10

Patronage at the Court of Charles II

Gerald Aylmer

Patronage is a very general concept which is used by historians in many different ways. Even when applied to the court of a single monarch over a period approximately equivalent to a generation (or twenty-five years), its elasticity invites, perhaps indeed requires, some definition, however imprecise.

In this chapter, which is no more than a provisional report on work in progress, I shall be concerned with patronage as the exercise of influence and the doing of favours, mainly but not exclusively of a political and financial nature. Defined in this way, the principal objectives involved were offices under the Crown and rewards, both material and titular. Patronage could, of course, also involve sex, religion, literature and the arts, as is shown in other chapters presented in this book.

Those who exercised patronage could do so either directly or indirectly. Some historians prefer to reserve the term patron for the former, employing the designation 'broker' for the latter. This is certainly less inelegant than the possible alternative 'middleperson' (since a broker could be of either gender). My own preferred choice of 'intermediary' may seem a little colourless and drab but may also be more accurate. The methods and procedures involved in the exercise of patronage could vary widely: they might take the form of outright gifts of offices, money, land, privileges and exemptions, or titles of honour; they might be mere acts of friendship or favour; but payment could also be involved, whether in the form of a capital sum for the grant in question, or a fee, gratuity or present (which might shade off into a bribe), made to the grantor himself, the intermediary, or both. Equally there might be no such transaction, but only an understanding – whether spoken or unspoken – of future loyalty and support on the part of the client or suppliant. Such an understanding, or alternatively a relatively small gift in money or in kind, would most often occur where the intermediary's role was simply to effect an introduction of the candidate for office, or the petitioner for favour, to whoever had the actual gift of the position, or the power to make the grant in question; again the would-be grantee might be a servant of the grantor, an on-going client, a relative, friend or equal, even a merely casual acquaintance. Where the intermediary had political ambitions, or was already the recognised leader of a faction or grouping, then the exercise of influence in return for the expectation of support was the commonest type of relationship.

Under any kind of personal monarchy one of the historian's principal problems lies in trying to assess how much had to be decided by the King or Queen in person, which is not the same thing as how much had to be referred to them for formal authorisation. For example, within the royal Household the Lord Steward and the Board of Greencloth were empowered to dispose of many minor offices, especially menial and petty clerical posts. By contrast, above stairs in the Chamber – in part just because there were proportionately fewer clerical and menial places – the Lord Chamberlain and the Groom of the Stole had the outright gift of rather few offices; but the opportunities open to those serving in the Privy and Bed Chambers, to act as intermediaries between aspirants and suppliants and the monarch was proportionately much greater. When Clarendon referred disapprovingly to 'the Bedchamber' in the *Continuation of his Life*, we may assume that he had in mind not so much the First and other Gentlemen as the Grooms and even the Pages there. The Grooms of the Bedchamber were indeed superbly well placed to act as brokers. But we should not leap to the conclusion that, either individually or collectively, they exercised a decisive influence in the making of senior appointments, let alone on the formation of major policy decisions. Among the original Grooms at the Restoration, only Daniel O'Neal was a potentially serious political figure in his own right, and he died in 1664. The others (Chiffinch, May, Progers, Seymour and the rest) did, I would judge, help to create a climate of opinion immediately around the King which contributed to the Chancellor's downfall, given the public events culminating in the disasters of 1667. Even in respect of this, a careful reading shows that Clarendon regarded William Coventry (ironically his own son-in-law's secretary) and Henry Bennet (who was intruded as Secretary of State in place of the Chancellor's old friend Edward Nicholas back in 1662) as his most consistent and dangerous enemies. He may have been wrong about this; the *Continuation* is not exactly a detached, objective historical analysis. But, if Clarendon exaggerated the enmity of Bennett and Coventry as a factor in his own overthrow, it does not follow from this that he underrated that of the Bedchamber.

The historian of patronage should not overlook the obvious fact that May 1660 was no ordinary accession. Legally the King's reign dated from 30 January 1649, so that the first year of his actual reign was its twelfth regnal year. More to the point, at the highest political level only Hyde and Nicholas were already occupying the posts in which they were to be continued. In one sense all the remaining great and secondary offices of state were to be bid for; in reality of course, as many historians have shown (most recently Ronald Hutton, John Miller and Paul Seaward), the King had many obligations which combined to reduce his freedom of manoeuvre, and thus also correspondingly lessened the scope for intermediaries to exercise their influence. Of those who were rewarded with high office and other comparable rewards for their parts in bringing about the Restoration, or for their loyal services during the years of adversity, some seem to have been content to exercise patronage limited to their own immediate areas of responsibility, and not to engage in the construction of wider networks to strengthen and extend their political followings. Although some may dissent from this, I would place George Monck, Duke of Albemarle, in that category; and among ex-Cavaliers the Earl of Southampton (who was very soon appointed Lord Treasurer), John Grenville, Earl of Bath (who succeeded as Groom of the Stole when the Duke of Somerset died after only a few months) and William Lord, then Earl of Craven (second in command of the armed forces).

Unfortunately, there is all too little documentation in either archival or private sources to show how the multitude of middling and lesser positions were filled. The records of the Household below stairs (the Lord Steward's series in the Public Record Office), taken in conjunction with Ormonde's own papers (in the Bodleian Library's collection of the Carte Manuscripts and the Historical Manuscripts Commission's *Calendars* of the residual collection at Kilkenny Castle, now largely at the National Library in Dublin), reveal that a systematic investigation was conducted into those whose past disloyalty might render them unfit to enter or remain in office.[1] Many more were exempted from having to pay for their positions, either because of their past services to the royal cause or because of individual recommendations made by the King and others.[2] And there are, of course, innumerable petitions in the *Calendars of State Papers, Domestic Series* (see in particular *1660–1* and *1661–2*), relating not only to the Household but also across the whole range of central and local government, from claimants often detailing their own loyal services and sacrifices in the royal cause, the disloyal past activities of rival candidates or the existing holders of the posts concerned, and sometimes both. It is seldom possible even to guess, let alone to establish, the importance of patronage, including intervention by intermediaries in deciding the outcome of such instances where there were disputes between rival claimants, or in other cases where there was a genuine vacancy and only one candidate, although common sense would suggest that there must have been more scope for the exercise of influence in contested cases. Among the best documented instances is the long, drawn-out campaign by Samuel Pepys to secure his position as Clerk of the Acts against the pretensions and residual claims of Thomas Turner, chief clerk in the Navy Office before the Restoration. Pepys's own patron, Edward Montagu (shortly to become Earl of Sandwich), presumably lacked the authority to dismiss Turner outright, even if he had wished to do so; the principal officers and other Commissioners of the Navy probably lacked the common purpose (and ideological uniformity) to do so, while it may have been considered unwise or inappropriate to involve the Duke of York in his capacity as Lord Admiral, especially if – as Pepys himself came to believe – Turner had secured Monck's backing by bribing Sir William Penn.[3]

By 1662–3 the disputes arising from such contested cases and conflicting claims had almost all been resolved. Naturally this was not achieved to the satisfaction of everyone concerned; nonetheless something that we can reasonably consider as political and administrative normality was once more in operation.

At different stages during his reign Charles II had principal ministers, just as he had principal mistresses, though perhaps with rather less freedom of choice with the former than with the latter. Among successive first or chief ministers, Clarendon, then the leading figures of the mis-called Cabal, notably Arlington, then Danby, and finally the successive triumvirs and duumvirs of the King's latter years (Sunderland, Halifax, Rochester, Godolphin and co.) undoubtedly exercised great, sometimes predominant influence as patrons and intermediaries. So, in rather different ways, did those middle-women or female intermediaries, Cleveland, alias Castlemaine and then Portsmouth, though never on so politically extensive a scale.

Did Charles have male favourites? Obviously he had servants in his entourage whom he found congenial as companions, in some cases one might say as cronies. As to those for whom the term favourite seems appropriate, only Buckingham was also a major political figure in his own right, and one of a most unusual kind in the various dramatic changes which marked his relations with the King. It might be argued that Monmouth should be included in this category, depending on whether or not a first and favourite illegitimate son is to be so reckoned; here too, relations were, to say the least, uneven. Among more conventional figures, some contemporaries thought that Charles Berkeley the younger, created Earl of Falmouth, was in the process of becoming a truly influential royal favourite, but his premature death in battle (1665) must leave this in the realm of speculation. A little later in the reign, Richard Jones, Earl of Ranelagh might equally well be described as a high-grade confidence trickster or as a royal favourite of the second rank. From the King's and the Lord Treasurer's points of view his foremost asset was an ability to funnel alleged but actually non-existent revenue surpluses from Ireland to the royal privy purse, and secondarily to provide good company at the King's late-night supper and card-playing parties. Glancing back to chief ministers, political patronage could, of course, operate negatively as well as positively. When in 1676 the King told Sir John Duncombe that he must surrender his office as Chancellor of the Exchequer because he was obstructing royal business and policies, this was tantamount to saying that Lord Treasurer Danby wanted him removed; unfortunately it is less clear whether this was done in order to bring in his successor, Sir John Ernle, or whether the latter's appointment was simply a consequence of Duncombe's removal, though there do seem to have been familial as well as political reasons for Ernle's advancement.[4]

Family networks and connections were in general no less important under Charles II than at other times. It is only necessary to list some of the greater 'political' families, several of whose individual members have already been mentioned: Berkeleys, Butlers, Finches, Hydes, Norths, Osborne-Berties,

Seymours, Villierses. Others could well be added. In such a society, imbued with aristocratic as well as with courtly values, it is always a difficult matter of definition to decide where patronage ends and patrimony begins. Many individual recipients of favours, including grants of office, owed their success in varying measure to family connections, either by blood or marriage. It may be helpful to draw a distinction between families already at the apex of the social hierarchy, whose senior male representatives could expect high office almost as of right, unless they were guilty of some gross disloyalty (or suffered from a very severe physical or mental disability): the Arundel Howards, the Ormonde Butlers and the Somerset Seymours might be placed in this category. Other networks only came into existence through the successful career of one outstanding individual, such as Edward Hyde or Thomas Osborne. Members of such relatively new families, whose own rise was in part consequential upon that of, so to speak, a founding father, might be more or less deserving in their own right. As with the Cecils at the end of the previous century, so Clarendon's younger son, Laurence, later Earl of Rochester, outshone his elder brother and possessed the capacity for high office on his merits.

By contrast we may consider the situation of those who rose from relatively humble or lowly origins without such family advantages, where patronage by itself could only take them a limited way up the ladder of preferment. In addition to hard work, ability, good luck and some of the right connections, we need to invoke a characteristic or feature of personality which is not quite the same as being congenial, convivial or 'clubbable': I suggest the term 'obligingness'. To name but a few of the most obvious, Stephen Fox, Sidney Godolphin and Samuel Pepys were obliging, over and above their other assets and attributes. Weighed in the same balance, William Coventry and William Petty conspicuously were not. While Coventry had more of the advantages of being an insider, and thus got correspondingly further, both are instances of individuals where defects of personality outweighed their altogether exceptional talents. William's brother, Henry Coventry, by comparison had ability well above the mediocre, but he rose higher and stayed near the top for longer because he was obliging and not awkward.

As the reign went on, we can remark both generational and structural changes which affected the exercise of patronage, notably in its political and administrative dimensions. I have already touched upon the former, involving what might be called 'ageism' together with mortality, and will return to this shortly. By 'structural' I include obviously the political (and religious) realignments of the 1670s and early 1680s, but also the more substantive developments in central government. The Treasury, together with its associated revenue departments, above all the Customs and the Excise, and up to a point also the armed forces, came to be further removed from the Court; these institutions were by no means totally exempt from influence exercised in and through the royal entourage, but they came to enjoy relatively greater autonomy.

On the other hand, appointments and promotions in Ireland, in the diplomatic service, and in the upper ranks in the Church and the law, as at the very top in the army and navy, remained wide open to direct royal intervention, besides the influence of patrons and intermediaries. The pathology, one might almost say the psycho-pathology, of political interference can be seen at its most acute in the extraordinary succession of Chief Justices of King's Bench between 1676 and 1683.

In this connection it is revealing to look across the board, at the Court and the central administration, to see how many of Charles's original servants stayed in office throughout the reign (if not necessarily in the same post). At the very top, among the great officers of state, only Ormonde as Lord Steward appears so to qualify. At the next level down, John Granville, Earl of Bath lasted the course as Groom of the Stole, at least from later in 1660. Henry Bennet, Lord and later Earl of Arlington, was in one office or another throughout the reign, though there is evidence of serious loss of favour and influence by the time of the King's death.[5] At the upper-middle level, we may cite Fox and Godolphin – if we count the latter's entry as a Page Boy and overlook one brief hiccup in each case. In the Bedchamber the odious 'Bab' May and two or at most three others survived all the way; at an only slightly further remove from the monarch, the Master of the Jewel House, Sir Gilbert Talbot, was another such survivor. In the Wardrobe of Robes, the Yeoman Tobias Rustat, having outlived his royal master by nine years, became a major benefactor of Jesus College, Cambridge and other charitable causes. Outside the royal Household and its various offshoots, it is likewise necessary to look hard for comparably long careers. One archetypal Cavalier courtier, the dramatist Sir Robert Howard, who began as Sergeant Painter, ended his days as Auditor of the Receipt of Exchequer, outliving one and outlasting another king in his tenure of that office; since he became a quasi-exclusionist (and finally a Williamite Whig), this is a reminder that removals from office were selective, sometimes even haphazard. In the Excise we may remark two doughty old warriors, different in so much save their toughness and longevity: Elias Ashmole, the Comptroller and John Birch, the Auditor. No similar survivors are known to me in the Customs administration. On the military side, Sir Thomas Clarges (originally 'in' as Monck's brother-in-law) is the nearest that we can get; in the maritime sphere there is Pepys himself, moving from the Navy Office to the Admiralty in 1673 and suffering a forced withdrawal during and after the Popish Plot. As for judges, Crown law officers and holders of administrative posts in the law courts, we are hard pressed to identify any who showed similar staying power, though Sir Harbottle Grimston (Master of the Rolls, 1661–84) qualifies as a near miss. Apart from him and one Master in Chancery, there must be a few others whom I have overlooked. Overall it seems fair to emphasise the small number in all branches of the King's service. This is not to imply that the longest-lived and the least controversial (or, to be more positive, the most indispensable) were the most significant as clients, intermediaries or patrons; rather, it should remind us of contingency as a factor in history. Nor, thinking of the relatively rapid turnover in many offices, does this prove that the King's favour was notably fickle or capricious, or that large-scale purges were by any means the general rule. Relatively few individuals went out with Clarendon, with the so-called Cabal, or with Danby. The First Test Act (of 1673) indeed eliminated several, from York and Clifford at one extreme to Benjamin Worsley at the other. The Court or Tory reaction of Charles's last years (1681–4) did see something nearer to a purge, though by then age and infirmity had taken a heavy toll of the King's original servants from the early 1660s.

Charles II was basically easy-going and (whatever some historians may say) in some sense even lazy, but this does not mean that he ever delegated the exercise of royal patronage to one individual or to a single clique or coterie. The path to royal favour and reward was never systematically channelled through a single monopolistic conduit. It is worth noting that, whereas the names of successive Secretaries of State feature on a very large number of Signet Office docquets, authorising grants and appointments, only two holders of that office (Arlington from the late 1660s to 1672 or 3, and Sunderland near the end of the reign) ever approached to the first place in government or, it seems, even aspired to sustained political leadership.[6]

The diary kept by Arthur Annesley, 1st Earl of Anglesey, illustrates some of the cross-currents, not to say double-crossings, involved in these matters. His original and principal claim on the King's generosity lay in the fact of his having been (in his capacity as an MP in the Long Parliament) the President of the Council of State from the time of General Monck's readmission of the members secluded since Pride's Purge in late February 1660, until the decision to restore the monarchy and invite the King back early in the following May. His part in effecting a peaceful and substantially unconditional Restoration was less decisive and dramatic than that of Monck or Edward Montague (as Commander of the Fleet), but at a formal, constitutional level it was nonetheless considerable. This, together with his father's part in securing support for the royal cause in Ireland, must account for the rewards which Annesley received and – presumably – for the prolonged tacit toleration of his opposition to many aspects of the King's regime and its policies in Church and State. By the time that the diary began, its author had not only succeeded to his father's title as an Irish viscount but had been created an earl in the peerage of England. More relevant to our present concerns, he had, since the beginning of the decade, been effectively in charge of the Irish revenue system, as Vice-Treasurer and Treasurer-at-Wars, in spite of the 2nd Earl of Cork's position as Lord Treasurer there and his own absence in England for long stretches at a time.

In June 1667, on whose initiative remains unclear, Anglesey was allowed to exchange this office for the Treasurership of the Navy, hitherto held by

Sir George Carteret, an old Cavalier who was also Vice-Chamberlain of the Household above stairs – evidently a sinecure, since he continued to hold this post while absent in Ireland. Each of them apparently planned in this way to reduce, if they can scarcely have hoped altogether to avoid, unwelcome scrutiny of their official conduct in their respective previous positions. This gambit did not work out very successfully, especially for Anglesey, who was suspended from his new office after only a year and four months (at the end of October 1668). As with Carteret, when he in turn lost his Irish office not long after this (but retaining that in the Chamber), the Earl was a Privy Councillor and so kept the privilege of access to the King, at least short of entry to the Bedchamber. Near the beginning of the diary we find him suspended from the Treasurership of the Navy, indeed superseded in it by Osborne and Lyttleton, and concerned to secure the £3,000 per annum compensation which he believed that he had been promised and to which he felt more than entitled. Some of his private surmises about his own prospects were not simply unrealistic but quite wild: such as the possibility of his becoming Lord Keeper of the Great Seal through the Duke of York's influence, though his hopes of the Privy Seal did eventually prove more realistic. He also believed that he had secured the appointment of Ormonde's bugbear, Sir James Shaen as Secretary to the commission on Irish lands. Shortly after this, Henry Jermyn, Lord St Albans, who had previously promised to back Anglesey's claim to the £3,000 pension, told him that the King intended to have him become Master of the Rolls: unless it related to a reversion, this was another unlikely canard. His relations with the King were far from subservient, and indeed could verge on the abrasive. On being told that the pension grant was being allowed to go through, the Earl thanked the monarch for a mere act of justice, but added that he deserved to receive additional royal favours. On the same day as this, at least in the privacy of his diary, he charged Ormonde with accepting bribes when he had himself foregone such opportunities. Once, if not twice, he felt that he was being deceived by Arlington; once, if not twice, he made it up with the man who was currently the nearest to a chief minister in a deeply divided government.[7]

Carteret seems to have done less badly out of the 1667 exchange. When he was in turn eased out of the Irish Vice-Treasurership, he may well have received compensation for this. His immediate successor was Ormonde's client and later ally, Lord Aungier, subsequently Earl of Longford; since this appointment was made in the latter days of Lord Robartes's tenure as Lord Lieutenant at a time when Ormonde was himself in semi-disgrace, or at least on the defensive with his own conduct as viceroy under investigation, this is another reminder of the pluralist nature of influence and patronage.[8]

Anglesey was eventually made Lord Privy Seal in April 1673. This in turn, if quite incidentally, discountenanced another diarist, Sir Edward Dering who had been one of the commissioners in charge of that seal and so had been sharing in its profits.[9] The Earl now disagreed with the King as to whether or not it was reasonable for him to keep the £3,000 a year compensation for the loss of his Navy office several years before, as well as to receive the earnings from his new post; this was to be a source of continuing vexation to him.[10] When, more than nine years later, he eventually surrendered the Privy Seal in August 1682, Anglesey professed to be glad that he was 'now delivered from Court snares'.[11] In fact he was compelled to resign following his final, tremendous row with Ormonde over Lord Castlehaven's *Memoirs* and his own counter-allegations about Royalist dealings with the Irish Confederates back in the 1640s. At the same time the King must have been pleased to have another major office at his disposal in the prolonged and complex ministerial reshuffles of the early 1680s.

Evidence from the diary in fact suggests an added reason for Anglesey's disgrace and loss of office: while there is no suggestion that he ever involved himself in treasonable activities, he was on close terms socially with the Earls of Essex and Shaftesbury, while among his most frequent dinner guests was the Duke of Monmouth himself. All this while the Earl continued to importune the King and even James, Duke of York, on his own behalf and that of his relatives and in-laws. He did obtain an Irish barony for his second son and the deanery of Exeter for his third, although the peerage which he sought for his son-in-law over years if not decades continued to elude him (and was not to be granted until well into the reign of William III, more than ten years after his own death). Financially the Earl might be said to have fought the Crown, in the persons of the Treasury Commissioners, to a draw. His £4 a day as Lord Privy Seal, received in place of diet, plus another £1 a day, assigned on the Customs, was paid up to the date of his dismissal; the £3,000 annual pension does not appear to have been bestowed; as against this, while he was still reckoned to owe the Crown no less than £20,000 from his time as Irish Vice-Treasurer back in the 1660s, no extreme steps were taken to exact this sum from him, or even to pressure him into compounding by paying off some part of it.[12] All in all Charles may be thought to have shown considerable forbearance in his dealings with Anglesey, both as suitor and as councillor.

It is hard to tell how much political influence the Earl ever exerted. We have both the advantage and disadvantage of his diary, surviving from 1667 (or substantially from 1671) until after the end of his active career. The impression it conveys is that of an assiduous, conscientious administrator with a less than attractive personality; yet we must not forget that its author built up what was by consent one of the finest private libraries of his time, although perhaps symptomatically least strong in holdings of Shakespeare and some of the other poets and dramatists.[13] More to the point is the lack of comparably intimate journals written by other leading political figures. Many Anglicans and other Royalists, from Clarendon down, wrote histories or memoirs; while allowing for Evelyn and to a lesser extent for Reresby as exceptions to this, there seems little doubt that Puritans and ex-Puritans were more prone to keep introspective diaries or journals, in part at least as exercises in self-examination. The historian's ideal requirement, in order to be sure of having a full and balanced explanation for any act of patronage or decision of policy, is corroboratory evidence from two or more independent primary sources. How seldom this is possible! Very occasionally we find the same individuals or episodes described by Ashmole (whose '*Notes*' do not really comprise a diary), by Evelyn and by Pepys; a little more often by two out of the three. But superb as these texts are for our purposes, none of the three men was actually a member of the inner circle around the King. It may be argued that this is precisely where resort should be had to more formal 'official' sources, such as the Signet Office docquet books; but, as already indicated, this in turn runs into the question of whether the person who formally procured the King's signature was decisive as patron or intermediary for a particular grant or other matter at issue.

In case this has not already been made sufficiently clear, in terms of patronage Ireland and the Crown colonies, also known as the royal plantations, should be seen as extensions of the English domestic scene. An office, a land grant or some other favour in Connaught, Leinster, Munster or Ulster, in Jamaica, Barbados or Virginia, would be sought after, brokered where this arose, and be granted in the same way as was operative for England and Wales; these territories were appendages of the English State, and thus not surprisingly subject to favour and influence at the royal Court. Scotland by contrast formed a distinct polity, albeit one in an unusual special relationship to the Crown, due to its monarch being a permanent absentee; but it was categorically not an extension or subordinate part of the English State. The chartered and proprietary colonies, too, were outside the scope of the system, but their autonomy was more vulnerable than that of the northern kingdom. The calling in of the Massachusetts Bay Company's charter was logically of a part with the campaign, by threat or use of *Quo Warranto*, against the City of London and numerous other chartered corporations; and all these cases carried implications about broadening the scope of royal patronage. Yet the Crown did not possess, or at least did not pursue, a consistent policy aimed at reducing all the overseas plantations to Crown colony status. Even if some of those in the King's service would have liked to see such a policy in operation, this would have involved disobliging too many other groups and individuals for whom the King felt no positive ill-will, and to some of whom he was in various ways beholden for their services and support. So, to put it a little solemnly, the imperial-colonial sphere reveals the limits on the consistency and uniformity of royal policy and the internal contradictions, the 'checks and balances', which operated within the system.

Except occasionally in passing, nothing has been said so far about venality, the traffic in offices and privileges, which formed the third strand along with patronage networks and ties of kinship. This might involve intermediaries taking their cuts as part of the process, or sometimes simply taking soundings as to whether such an approach would be acceptable. The nearest parallel which comes to mind is that of the early modern marriage market among the propertied classes; however, the intermediaries who helped to arrange matches more often acted out of friendship or as part of doing mutual favours than for direct pecuniary considerations. There was no concerted drive against administrative venality under Charles II; nor, on the other hand, was there any deliberate resort to it by the Crown as under his grandfather. The scope and conditions for the purchase of offices were more affected by the intermittent campaign against the granting of reversions, and by the more sustained drive to reduce the tenure of all offices from life and 'good behaviour' to pleasure.[14]

In conclusion we might ask ourselves how much of all this should be seen merely as a function of the political and social system of the time, in its administrative and courtly aspects, and how much it reflected the particular monarch and his characteristics. Ideally, some comparison should be attempted with France, Spain, Austria and perhaps Sweden in the same era. Less ambitiously I would suggest looking backward and forward in time, to Charles I, James II and perhaps William III. Many criticisms can be, and have been, brought against the Restoration regime as a whole and against Charles II as a personal ruler (whether an absolute or constitutional one may be left for others to debate). While he was capable of harshness and severity, even on occasion of punitive vindictiveness, the King was more often criticised in restrospect – notably by his own servants, men who had known him well – for having been excessively good-natured and easy-going, and thus too often imposed upon. I would argue that the plural nature of patronage at his Court may well be seen as a consequence of this, but further to that as one important reason for Charles's relative success as king and ruler, most certainly by contrast with his father and his brother.

Notes

1. See esp. Bodl. Lib., Carte MS 59, f. 108. Out of 298 individuals, two were investigated but cleared, two were found to have been disloyal in the past, but only one of them was dismissed, 5 December 1661.

2. Ibid., ff. 121–124v, various lists dating from 1662 to 1663, complementing other lists of places which were sold for the Lord Steward's benefit.

3. For Turner, see G.E. Aylmer, *The State's Servants: the Civil Service of the English Republic 1649–1660* (London, 1973), pp. 93–4, 267, 414, n. 84; and Pepys, *Diary*, entries for 30 January 1666 and 21 May 1667. It seems in character that it was from Mrs Turner that Pepys got the story about her husband, Penn and Monck.

4. See *HC 1660–1690*, Vol. II, pp. 247, 272.

5. *Hatton Correspondence*, Vol. II (Camden, New Series, XXIII, 1878), p. 21, cited by O. Airy in his edition of Gilbert Burnet, *History of My Own Time the Reign of Charles II* (2 vols, Oxford, 1897–1900), Vol. II, p. 342, n. 1.

6. See F.M.G. Evans (Mrs C.S. Higham), *The Principal Secretary of State: A Survey of the Office from 1558 to 1680* (Manchester and London, 1923), ch. VII and Appendix XII; M.A. Thomson, *The Secretaries of State 1681–1782* (Oxford, 1932; reprinted London, 1968), Introductory Survey and Appendix XII; J.C. Sainty, *Office-Holders in Modern Britain*, II: *Officials of the Secretaries of State 1660–1782* (London, 1973), pp. 22–3, 63–119. The docquets are in PRO, SO 3/13 et seq.

7. BL, Add. MS 40, 860. There is a full, almost verbatim transcript of this volume, the diary for 1671–5, in HMC, 32 (*13th Report*, Part VI), *Fitzherbert and other Collections*, pp. 261–78, Papers of General Lyttelton-Annesley. So far as I am aware the second volume (BL, Add. MS 18, 730) remains unpublished.

8. *CSPI, 1669–70* and *Addenda 1625–1670*, p. 60.

9. M.F. Bond (ed.), *Diaries and Papers of Sir Edward Dering 2nd Bart, 1644–1684* (London, 1976), pp. 55, 112.

10. BL, Add. MS 40, 860, f. 46.

11. BL, Add., MS 18,730, f. 98.

12. For the unpaid pension, see Bodl. Lib., MS Eng. Hist., b. 79, f. 140. The whole story can be traced through numerous entries in *CTB*, VII: *1681–5*, ed. W.A. Shaw (in 3 parts, London, 1916).

13. *Bibliotheca Angleseiana, sive catalogus . . .* (London, 1686), Wing, *Short-title Catalogue*, no. A 3166.

14. See the two seminal articles by J.C. Sainty in *English Historical Review*, LXXX (1965) and *Bull. Inst. Hist. Res.*, XLI (1968).

11

Access and Petitioning during the Reign of Charles II[1]

Brian Weiser

In this chapter I would like to move away from the physical constraints of the Court and investigate how an ordinary subject could gain access to the King, how he or she could be present at the Court through his or her representation on paper, a petition.

Charles II and his subjects conducted their relationship on a number of levels and communicated through a variety of media. But petitions, perhaps the most formal of these media, had a special resonance. The facts that the right to petition the King was, in theory, universal, and that in petitions subjects could explicitly inform the King of their requests, imply that petitioning presented a direct avenue of access to the monarch. A statistical analysis of the petitions preserved in the State Papers during the first ten years of Charles's reign (1661–70) gives some clues as to petitioners's expectations of their sovereign. It will also reveal much about the restored King's priorities and his views on his obligations to his subjects.

Petitions of the 1660s differed markedly from the famous monster petitions of the Exclusion crisis.[2] The Act Against Tumults and Disorders (1661)[3] prevented subjects from amassing signatures on a petition in order to demonstrate in a menacingly quantitative way the popular support behind a particular issue. Instead of brazen demands followed by long lists of names, the constructions of the 1660s were humbly phrased pleas which came mostly from single individuals[4] touching national issues only peripherally. Most entreaties asked for mundane things like jobs or grants. These documents were legalistic in form and followed a standard pattern.

They commenced with the address, 'To the King's Most Excellent Majesty' in letters which dwarfed everything else on the page.[5] Next, the words 'the humble petition of' introduced the identity of the petitioner. Below this heading came the main body of the petition divided into two parts. The first section explained the situation which caused the concerned party to seek the King's favour and highlighted any reasons why the King should grant the request. The shorter second section, instituted perhaps by bureaucrats weary of reading long explanations, succinctly set out the exact nature of the petition. The plea always concluded with the assurance of the subject's devotion, 'and we shall always pray etc.'.[6]

Composing a petition that would receive the attention of the administration took some effort. A petitioner had to hire a scribe, often obtain evidence and testimony to the legitimacy of his request and then convey it to the King. The most efficient way to draw the monarch's attention to a particular plea was to hand it to him. The most efficient way to draw the monarch's attention to a particular plea was to hand it to him, and well-connected petitioners personally presented their request to the King or had a well-placed court contact deliver their written suits. Those with less influence presented petitions to the Privy Council in a ritualistic manner. The petitioner entered, knelt at the upper end of the board, presented his petition and 'withdrew without talking or troubling the council until called again'.[7] The Clerk of the Privy Council would then record the petition, but seldom would the petitions served that day be discussed unless they were 'brought in by some particular hand or for a matter needing dispatch'.[8]

Those lacking the resources to approach the King or the Council, could employ a third institutional avenue for petitions, the Masters of Request. Each of the Four Masters of Request served three months out of the year. Their function was to receive petitions from those who could not present them directly to the King and to shepherd those petitions through the administration. The effort and cost of composing and delivering the petitions probably deterred all from importuning the King except for those with realistic hopes of having their petitions answered and the truly desperate.

Unfortunately, comprehensive data exists only for those petitions which reached the Secretaries of State.[9] The original petitions submitted to the Masters of Requests do not survive. The only information about such petitions comes from a curious pair of notebooks kept by Gervase Holles, one of the four Masters of Requests (1660–1674), which record and summarise those petitions that received favourable replies. This recording exclusively successful petitions suggests that Holles used the notebook as a record to ensure that petitions which received the King's approval were acted upon by the royal officers. Or considering that he indexed the work, Holles may have wanted a list of people who owed him favours. This absence of unsuccessful petitions, along with the fact that the four Masters may not have divided the work equally, complicates any attempt to use this data to see how trends changed over time.[10]

Unlike Holles's notebooks, the petitions preserved in the State Papers present few problems of an evidential nature. In fact, Mary Everitt Greene, the editor of the *Calendar of State Papers, Domestic Series*, catalogued the petitions in a way that makes it possible to determine whether the government paid attention to or ignored a given petition. The *CSPD* records all the marginalia which the administration wrote on petitions. Since the compositor rarely dated the petition[11] the marginalia which are almost always dated serve as the date for the Calendar. Furthermore, in the rare cases when officials recorded on a separate piece of paper an action taken on a particular petition the editor placed that petition next to this often dated account. Hence, we can be sure that all petitions which are dated in the *CSPD* had received some attention from the government; conversely those petitions which Greene categorised as undated were largely ignored by the administration. The only real caveat to remember when using this collection is that it represents only those petitioners who had sufficient political or financial resources, or social connections to deliver their petition to the King or high officials.

The monarch had a number of options when dealing with a petition that managed to reach him. He could immediately grant it, refer it to the government official under whose purvey the matter lay, or reject it outright. Referred petitions proceeded to a government official who investigated the matter and then reported his recommendations to the King. Those lucky enough to receive approval went to the Chancery office where they were affixed with seals. Throughout this process the petition itself acted as a bureaucratic form recording its own progress. Endorsements, referrals, and logs of reading at Court cram the margins and reverse of many a petition. Theophilius Hart's petition for a residue of a land lease presents an extreme example. The margins of this petition overflow with a reference to the Lord Treasurer, his reference to the Surveyor General, the report of the Surveyor General on the demesne lands in Kirton (county of Lincoln) and the final report of the Lord Treasurer which stated that 'Mr Hart refused to serve against Sir George Booth, was active against the committee of safety, joined in the Restoration, and is one of the ten officers recommended by the Lord General [Albemarle], he therefore thinks the petition must be granted and Mr Sanderson, the former tenant who suffered so much for the late king, must be gratified in some other way.'[12] Because of the existence of such information, the historian can glean not only the nature of requests but also their reception.

The personal nature of the petitions renders them particularly valuable for ascertaining how the English wanted the King to act towards individual subjects. One expectation of the monarch not explicit in the documents, but implicit in the entire process of petitioning was that the King would receive petitions from all. Judith Richards has made clear the subjects's inclination to petition the King in person and the damage done to Charles I's image when he frustrated this urge.[13]

An accessible king undoubtedly seemed more human to his subjects, more in touch with the people. While such a notion went against conventional wisdom, which accentuated the neccessity for the King to put distance between himself and his subjects,[14] literary sources indicated the desire that the King should not separate himself from his people. The popularity of accounts of Charles's escape from the Battle of Worcester, which detail how he disguised himself as a servant, attests to this aspiration. Indeed, Charles II was not the only king praised for mingling with commoners. Broadside ballads relate Henry VIII's drinking with a cobbler and James V of Scotland roaming around the countryside.[15] Shakespeare's Henry V, who donned a common soldier's garb to converse with his troops, provides a particularly famous example. While no one expected to meet the King in this fashion, the idea that Charles II had an inkling of the common life must have reassured his subjects.

Whether because of an informal personality, acquired from being stripped of his regality during his formative years, or because of his resolution not to duplicate his father's mistakes, Charles II actively cultivated accessibility throughout his reign. The Duke of Tuscany reported that the King 'returned the salutes of all whom he encountered, whatever their rank'. Indeed, Charles II often took walks where virtually anyone could meet, talk and deliver petitions to him. The Popish Plot started in this manner when a chemist by the name of Christopher Kirby accosted the King to tell him about a regicide plot. Charles, after hearing this, agreed to meet the two informants, Titus Oates and Israel Tongue, and then proceeded on his solitary walk.[16]

Beyond this relaxed attitude towards access to the royal person, Charles took concrete action to ensure that his subject's pleas could reach him. At the beginning of the reign, when departments were establishing the borders of their authority, a number of turf battles broke out. The Masters of Requests and the Secretaries of State had one such scuffle over who had the right 'to procure answers from his Majesty to all petitions whatsoever'. A committee, headed by Lord Chamberlain Manchester, sat to decide the question. At the hearings, the Masters of Requests claimed that they, along with the Secretaries of State, had that right. They supported their claims by calling on precedent and by emphasising that 'any innovation or practice to the contrary will prove a disservice to his majesty and a prejudice to his people'. The Secretaries of State relied on the testimony of George Digby, Earl of Bristol who had held that office until his conversion to Catholicism disqualified him. Bristol also cited precedent, though only from Charles I's reign, as proof that the Secretaries of State should be the only ones who brought petitions to the King's attention. He also indicated that he had originated the practice:

> Before becoming Secretary of State I wished to reform some abuses, first the presumption that almost all persons of any near access to his Majesty did take to present to him warrants of all kinds and to procure his hand unto them and next the royal signatures going about without any attestation. Whereupon after some days of consideration and debate his Majesty was pleased . . . to declare by word of mouth to all about him that none should presume to offer any paper to his signature save only the two principal Secretaries of State . . .[17]

Charles I clearly picked order over accessibility, making sure that only a select few came into contact with his person. Charles II came down on the other side, disregarding formality[18] (for which he did not have such a high regard), the conventional wisdom (shown by his rival Louis XIV) of how a monarch should behave, and, most importantly, his father's practice, and decided in favour of the Masters of Requests.

The English seem to have noticed the difference in accessibility between father and son. Of the 48 petitions preserved in the State Papers for October and

November 1635, 9 were addressed to the King, 15 to the Council and 24 to other officers of the State. In October and November 1663, of the 39 petitions recorded, 34 were addressed to the King, 3 to other officers of the State and 1 to the King and Council. Such disparity suggests that in the 1660s the English were more confident that the King would pay attention to their needs than they had been in the 1630s. This trend also had ramifications for the symbolic force of petitioning.

The very act of petitioning strengthened the bonds of loyalty and obedience which tied the subject to the monarch. Historians with a semiotic bent might note the physical construction of a petition. The symbolic power of the large letters of the King's title juxtaposed to 'humble' preceding the minutely written name of the petitioner and the tone of obsequiousness requisite throughout the address, intensified the conception of the petitioner as a supplicant dependent upon the grace of the sovereign. Indeed, the petitioners would often begin the summary section of their requests with the words 'and your subject humbly prayes'. However, like the Protestant critique of mediatory powers,[19] which claimed that by praying to saints, the worshippers were impugning on the honour and centrality of God, when the target of the appeal ceases to be the monarch, then the King may no longer appear potent, for the act of petitioning no longer reinforces the image of the King as the 'fount of justice', as the dispenser of patronage, or as the seat of power. Rather, some of the accoutrements, some of the charisma attached to these functions departs from the King and centres upon the person being petitioned. When petitions are addressed to the King, however, he is placed in the centre of government and is seen as the source of power and authority.

A considerable number of people underwent the experience of submitting petitions to the King. A conservative estimate is that over 10,000 people petitioned the King from 1661 to 1670;[20] 2,965 of these are preserved in the State Papers. This large number permits statistical analysis. The petitions were categorised using six variables: the date of the petition; the social status of the petitioner; the general type of request made; the specific nature of the request; and the reason offered which explained why the petitioner thought his request should have been granted; and the action the government took on that petition. Forcing petitions into this rigid format does tend to blur the distinctiveness of the individual petitions, but enough common ground exists to warrant generalisations about both the subjects' expectations of the King and the King's reaction to these expectations.

Charles's subjects seem to have been more eager to petition the King during certain years: 1661, 1662, 1665, 1666, and 1667 all occasioned an inordinate frequency in petitioning.[21] A number of factors explain this pattern. For instance, in 1662 eighty subjects requested positions in Queen Catherine's newly formed Court. In 1661 the numerous vacant ecclesiastical and court positions inspired many job hunters to try their luck. From 1665 to 1667 the Second Dutch War inspired petitions dealing with trade, debts, military jobs and captured Dutch ships. Yet these factors do not entirely account for such frequent petitioning.

Types of petitions which had little or no direct connection to the Dutch War or to the re-establishment of Church and State also flooded the throne in these years. For example, petitions dealing with trade or industry were frequent during 1661–2 as were requests for royal grants of money, leases, land titles, and discoveries. Furthermore, although requests for jobs might appear to have been particularly spurred on by those two crises, entreaties for jobs not connected with the vacancies in the government or Church were high in 1661 and 1662 as were requests for jobs not tied to the army or navy, in 1665–7.[22] Indirect as well as direct consequences of the war and the Restoration appear to have caused the frequent petitions in these areas.

To some extent such a high level of petitioning can be explained by those suffering economic hardship, expecting the King to bail them out. In 1661 and 1665 petitions for relief were particularly high. But the relatively small changes in attestations of poverty in petitions as a whole and in claims for arrears suggest that economic hardship played a minor role in spurring subjects to petition, or reflects a widespread belief that claims of hardship would not sufficiently move the King. More plausibly, either the general mood of expectation which spurred the many petitions dealing with the Dutch War (in the latter period), or the re-establishment of Church and State, acted as a catalyst, inspiring people to petition for unrelated requests, or perhaps during these years of political uncertainty people thought that the King needed support and that he would therefore strive harder to answer petitions favourably.

Charles II's administration did try to grant as many petitions as possible. At the beginning of his reign, Charles, confronted by obligations, vacancies and a flood of entreaties, dealt with a large number of petitions and replied favourably to many of them. By 1664 budgetary constraints seem to have set in and the number and percentage of petitions granted declined, but the percentage of petitions which received considerable attention remained high, suggesting that while the King was largely unable to answer petitions favourably the administration tried at least to show that they remained open to entreaties.

The argument that Charles II's administration purposely paid attention to a large number of petitions in order to appease the English people assumes that petitioners knew the status of their requests. A number of petitions specifically mention the place in the bureaucratic maze where a previous petition stopped. While the evidence is too scanty to be conclusive, some who mention the fate of their petition are of low status, which implies that information about a petition's fate could be obtained even by those who did not have contacts in the bureaucracy. For instance, Jane Palmer, a printer's widow, knew enough about the whereabouts of her petition to say that she 'was being tossed about like a tennis ball from one party to another to her utter ruin'.[23]

The theory of conscious policy, that the King tried to appease his subjects by showering attention upon them when he could not satisfy their demands, does not, however, seem to accord with the administrative activity of 1665. In this troubled year, almost three-quarters of petitions were largely ignored. The plague, which forced most of the King's servants to flee to Oxford surely helps to account for this low number. Yet the plague itself and the war with the Dutch occasioned a sharp rise in the number of petitions submitted. Because of the deluge of petitions, the King's servants did deal with a large number of petitions, only a smaller percentage of the larger whole. The great percentage of petitions which received attention in 1666 supports the theory of conscious policy. Only 23.5 per cent of petitions received favourable answers, but 47.6 per cent were dealt with.

From 1668 to 1670 it appears as though the administration adopted guidelines as to how many petitions it would grant or pay attention to. Regardless of the number of petitions submitted, the number which the administration granted or acceded to hardly wavered. Two explanations offer themselves. Perhaps only in times of military threats, as opposed to the strictly financial ones of the late 1660s, did the government strive to answer as many petitions as possible. Alternatively the new consistency may derive from Henry Bennet[24] instituting new guidelines for answering petitions.

Neither the King nor the populace thought all petitions were of equal weight. Certain requests, whether because of the nature of the petition, or the identity of the petitioner, were seen as deserving special attention. Although contemporaries made no explicit distinction, two general types of petitions seem to have been submitted petitions of right and petitions of grace. Petitions of right asked the King to act out of the strictures of justice. Petitions of grace asked the King to act out of his generosity.

Subjects submitting petitions of right felt that the very nature of their petition warranted the attention of the King. Inventors thought that establishing the originality of their discovery was all they needed to obtain a patent. Discoverers of property belonging to the King deemed a finders' fee their due as did officers asking for a portion of ships they captured. Petitioners seeking the resolution of disputes assumed that the King as the fount of justice would naturally desire to set things to rights.[25] Only 12 per cent of these petitioners cited their loyalty, suffering during the Civil War or other extraneous reason why their petitions should be granted.

A fear of impugning the King's honour may have restrained some petitioners of right from citing another explanation. Justifying their cause by extolling their loyalty could have been seen as implying that the King was not just, that he needed a personal political motive to uphold the law. While such an apprehension may have prevented some of his subjects from detailing their poverty or suffering during the Civil War, Charles did not take offence when they did. Petitions of right which recalled the subject's service to the King, or some other merit, fared far better than those which did not. Petitions of right without reason were granted 33 per cent of the time and received attention 51 per cent of the time. The King granted 47 per cent of those with reasons and the administration took notice of 65 per cent of those with reasons.

Petitioners of grace felt the need to justify their request. They expressed reasons far more often than average. Subjects asking for 'grants', 'jobs', and 'relief' frequently detailed why they merited the King's attention and money. The reasons expressed ranged from details of suffering in the Interregnum, to attestations of loyalty, to the avowal of Elizabeth Elliott, the daughter of the King's wet nurse, that she thought 'it the greatest happiness that could befall her to suck the same breast as so great a monarch'.

From such reasons offered by the populace we can glean something of perceptions of relationships to the King. The two most common claims, suffering during the Interregnum and loyalty, indicate that while people might have professed a general duty to the King, they clearly thought that he had a reciprocal and quite specific responsibility to regard those who stood by him. The King like any proper patron should reward his clients. This sentiment appears in literary form as well; a contemporary ballad, 'The Cavaliers' Complaint', bemoans the fact that while Charles tried to secure his position by spreading his bounty to powerful interests, he ignored his faithful followers. The emphasis on suffering during the Interregnum underscores the belief that the King had a responsibility to restore those who had fought on his behalf to their previous position.

Endorsement, the third most common argument for a petition, worked in two ways to convince the King that the petitioner merited the fulfilment of his request. The support of a prominent individual conveyed to the King the loyalty, valour or merit of the applicant. An endorsement also argued that the King had an obligation to his clients' clients. In other words, the suitors hoped that when a prominent individual supported one of their petitions, the King would feel obliged to grant it in order to maintain the support of that individual. Some petitions of grace claimed, in a limited way, right.

The administration's policy, however, did not accord with the expectation that the King would reward the loyal. Some people did benefit from their allegiance. Charles II drew up a list of everybody who helped him escape from Worcester in order to recompense them. But, generally speaking, attestations of loyalty or suffering on behalf of the King did not help a petitioner. Petitions which emphasised these 'reasons' did not fare any better than the average. It seems the Cavaliers were justified in their complaints. The one factor which helped a petition along was an endorsement. The response to Theophilius Hart's petition demonstrates the influence of a recommendation from a prominent figure like Monck. Petitions which had an endorsement on them consistently fared better than average.

One further group of petitions, those submitted by nobles, leading gentry and powerful interests, deserves note. These petitioners, like those submitting petitions of right, did not feel the need to express a specific reason for their request to be granted, even when appealing to the King's grace. To some extent, especially for courtiers and lords, the King's personal acquaintance with the petitioners would render enumeration of their suffering or loyalty redundant. But guilds, corporations, and gentry of whom the King and his administrators could not possibly have had detailed knowledge were equally likely to omit reasons. They, and probably the nobles as well, presumably thought that their status justified a rational hope of obtaining a favourable response. The powerful groups were not incorrect in their judgement. The administration tended to grant and pay attention to petitions from lords, gentry, large groups and courtiers more often than average; when the government faced fiscal difficulty this tendency became even more pronounced. From 1665 to 1667 the little patronage available went predominantly to the upper classes. During these years, the percentage of petitions from commoners which were granted fell from 44.9 to 14.4, and the percentage of petitions paid attention to dwindled from 60.6 to 28.1. In comparison the proportion of petitions from the lords which were granted declined only from 5.7 to 41.3 per cent and those responded to from 80.8 to 58.7 per cent.

Gervase Holles's records also reveal this shift of focus. Petitioners who went through the Masters of Requests came from a lower social class than those who used other methods; 19 per cent of the petitions in Holles's records came from people of a high status group (Lord, gentry, large groups or courtiers) as opposed to 48.8 per cent in the State Papers. The sharp decline in petitions granted from 1664 to 1668 suggests that the administration no longer desired or was able to placate or reward the commoners who made up the majority of the petitioners in Holles's records. Budgetary limitations forced the administration to limit the amount of money it could dole out, and it reserved its resources for the more powerful.

On the whole, Charles II's handling of petitions met his subjects' expectations. He remained accessible. Although Charles, when pressed, may have disappointed the loyal, he did not alienate those he needed to fear, for while occasionally parsimonious, the administration remained conscientious. This reflects Charles's general policy of using open access to build a broad bottom to his throne.

Notes

1. I would like to thank Professor Derek Hirst at Washington University and Dr Amanda Bebin at the Public Record Office for their aid in this paper.

2. See Mark Knights, 'London's Monster Petition of 1680', *HJ*, 36 (1993), 39–67.

3. The Act stated that no petition 'for alteration of matters established by law in Church or State' could have more than twenty signatures or ten presenters. A loophole existed whereby a petition with a large number of signatures was allowed to be presented if 'the matter thereof hath been first consented unto and ordered by three or more justices of that county or by the Major part of the Grand Jury of the County or division of the county where the same matter shall arise at their public assizes or general Quarter sessions or if arising in London by the Lord Mayor, Alderman and

Commons in Common Council assembled'. Only initiatives which did not have the backing of the local magistracy were suppressed. *The Statutes of the Realm* (London, Dawsons, 1963), p. 208. Charles II readily enforced this law. During the Exclusion crisis most delegates submitting large petitions were readily snubbed. But the representatives of Berkshire, who were sent by their grand jury were invited to drink a beer with the King. Mark Knights, *Politics and Opinion in Crisis: 1678–1681* (Cambridge, Cambridge University Press, 1994), p. 235; Victor L. Stater, *Noble Government: the Stuart Lieutenancy and the Transformation of English Politics* (Athens and London, University of Georgia Press, 1994), p. 140.

4. Some 91.7 per cent of all petitions came from individuals.

5. In comparison, the heading of petitions delivered to the Council of State in 1651 was roughly the same size as the rest of the petition. *Complete State Papers Domestic* (Brighton, Harvester Microfilm Press, 1981), *passim.*

6. PRO, SP 29, *passim.*

7. E.R. Turner, *The Privy Council 1603–1784* (Baltimore, John Hopkins Press, 1927–8), Vol. 1, p. 388.

8. The testimony comes from Edward Southwell who recorded how the Privy Council functioned during Charles II's reign. Turner, *The Privy Council*, Vol. 2, ch. xviii. Southwell was sworn as a Clerk of the Privy Council in 1664 (BL, Add. 38881, 1).

9. The petitions in the Secretary of State's possession include those which were handed directly to the King.

10. BL, Add. MSS 5759, 15632. Edward Hyde wrote to Sir Richard Fanshaw about the post of Masters of Requests in June of 1659: '. . . and if you were of my mind you would think it the finest place about the court, as in truth it is, and for a place of action inferior only to the Secretary of State, and from whence to be secretary is a very natural step, and that is Master of Requests, by which you have the King's ear three months in the year, as much as the secretary, and in which you would very honestly get six or seven hundred pound[s] a year though you should never make any suit for yourself'. However, Fanshaw later served as ambassador to Portugal, and how the Masters of Requests divided their work in his absence is unknown. HMC, *Heathcote* (50), p. 9.

11. Of the several hundred petitions examined there was only one instance of the compositor dating his petition and a prisoner scrawled the petition in question.

12. *CSPD, Charles II*, Vol. 3, p. 280.

13. Judith Richards, 'His Nowe Present Majesty: the Kingship of Charles I Before 1640', *Past and Present*, 113 (November, 1986), 70–96.

14. The Duke of Newcastle, William Cavendish, in his advice to Charles II urged the King to be restrictive of access to his person. T.P. Slaughter (ed.), *Ideology and Politics on the Eve of the Restoration: Newcastles's Advice to Charles II* (Philadelphia, 1984). Francis Bacon proposed similar steps to James I in 1621 and Shakespeare's Henry IV instructs Prince Hal on the merits of placing distance between monarch and subject. Starkey, *English Court*, pp. 6–7.

15. A. Garner Medwin, 'Views of King and People in Sixteenth and Seventeenth Century Ballads', in J.D. McClure and M.R.G. Spiller (eds), *Bryght Laternis: Essays on the Language and Literature of Medieval and Renaissance Scotland* (Aberdeen, Aberdeen University Press, 1989), pp. 24–32.

16. Ronald Hutton, *Charles II* (Oxford, Clarendon Press, 1989), pp. 358–9, 448.

17. BL, Add. MS 15632, pp. 41–8.

18. Bristol asserted that the Masters of Requests were not of a high enough social status to come in contact with the King on a regular basis. BL, Add. MS 15632, pp. 41–8.

19. Linda Levy Peck has found that suitors in James I's and Charles I's reigns referred to patronage brokers as saints and conversely 'systematically borrowed images of the Baroque court and its patronage to describe god, heaven and Christ'. Linda Levy Peck, 'Benefits, Brokers and Beneficiaries', in Kunze and Brautigam (eds), *Court, Country and Culture* (Rochester, University of Rochester Press, 1992), pp. 109–127, esp. pp. 114–15.

20. Penry Williams guesses that Henry VII received 3,000 petitions a year. Charles II may have received more than that. We do not have any record of the unsuccessful petitions which Gervase Holles and the other Masters of Requests handled. Furthermore, petitions from Irish and Scottish subjects were kept by the Lord Lieutenant of Ireland and the Secretary of State of Scotland. Penry Williams, *The Tudor Regime* (Oxford, Clarendon Press), p. 7.

21. In 1661 there were 565 petitions; 417 petitions in 1662; 378 petitions in 1665; 334 petitions in 1666; and 239 petitions in 1667.

22. In 1661 and 1662, 206 out of the 301 jobs (62.2 per cent) were for places in the Court or for ecclesiastical positions. But requests for jobs not connected to the re-establishment of government and Church were also quite high. In 1661–2 the average number of petitions per year for jobs unrelated to the Court or the Church were also quite high. In 1661 and 1662 the average number of petitions per year for jobs unrelated to the Court or the Church was 47.5. This number dropped in 1663 and 1664 to 35.5. In 1665 to 1667 it rose slightly to 37.6 and then dropped significantly in 1668–70 to 15. Likewise, in 1665–7 only 35 of the 154 jobs were related to the armed forces, as opposed to 1663–4 where 19 out of 66 were military jobs and 1668–70 when 10 out of 103 were army related.

23. *CSPD*, Vol. 3, p. 629. PRO, SP29:99:240.

24. After Clarendon's fall Henry Bennet controlled the machinery of patronage and he and Hyde had very different ideas about how to employ the government's resources. The competition between Arlington and Clarendon for control of the ministry through control of the House of Commons complicates the explanation of activity prior to 1667. Bennet consistently tried to establish a faction loyal to him through patronage, but Clarendon was much more stingy. Hutton, *Charles II*, p. 254; Paul Seaward, *The Cavalier Parliament and the Reconstruction of the Old Regime 1661–1667* (New York, Cambridge University Press, 1989), pp. 85–92.

25. These petitions surprisingly include a number which ask the King to interfere in current legal disputes. The legislation of 1641 severely curtailed the King's sway over civil judicial matters. The continuation of petitions asking for the King's aid in disputes shows either the steadfast nature of expectations or the belief that the King would use undue influence on the petitioners' behalf. Since art and literature depicted the King as a demi-god it seems quite likely that people did not understand the formal limitations on the King's prerogative and continued to believe, surely correctly, that he could influence the outcome of legal disputes.

12

A COUNTRY SEAT FIT FOR A KING: CHARLES II, GREENWICH AND WINCHESTER

Simon Thurley

The English republic dealt a devastating blow to the stock of royal residences which Charles I had enjoyed. Several, such as Richmond, were never to be occupied again, and others like Greenwich, notwithstanding plans to the contrary, were never to regain their former position. But in many respects the Commonwealth was only a catalyst in a process that had begun much earlier in the seventeenth century. Changing functional requirements, patterns of movement, modes of transport, aesthetic taste and standards of comfort had already begun to redraw the royal itinerary and redefine the functional denominations of the royal residences. The ending of the republic at the Restoration provided Charles II with an opportunity for a reassessment of royal residential requirements which he unhesitatingly seized. The King's plans were constrained by lack of sufficient finance and, with the single exception of the remodelling of Windsor Castle, remained incomplete. Two schemes, left unfinished at his death in 1685, were new palaces – Greenwich and Winchester. This chapter examines the nature and purpose of these in order to suggest some of the concerns which influenced royal residential building after the Restoration. It argues that the new palace at Greenwich was never intended to be a traditional standing house like its predecessor, rather a specialised residence with a specific diplomatic function, and that Winchester was designed to be the King's principal country residence. The arguments here are developed out of a reconsideration of the evidence for the design and use of the buildings in the light of what contemporaries thought to be their function.

The story of Charles II's Greenwich is closely bound up with that of the Restoration itself. Since the reign of Henry VII the house at Greenwich had been the second or third most favoured of royal residences, and during the reign of Charles I it had been designated as one of the King's three standing houses. Of all the royal houses it suffered the worst damage during the 1640s and 50s and was totally uninhabitable at the Restoration. In August 1661 the Dutch painter William Schellinks noted in his journal:

> The royal palace stands close to the water along the river. . . . It was damaged in the recent troubles and is at present in a badly ruined state; it was used by

> Oliver Cromwell as a prison during the war against the Dutch, of whom many died there of privation and disease. A little inland is the Queen's House or palace . . . this building too has suffered some damage in the recent war and is at present without furniture and pictures . . . There is a fairly large deerpark, surrounded by a wall, but the soldiers have killed all the game, which used to be there in large numbers. On a hill in this park are the ruins of a castle, which has been raised to the ground by the parliamentarians.[1]

Because of Greenwich's earlier popularity it was widely assumed that the palace would be brought back into a fit state quickly and resume its former role as a standing house. One of the reasons for believing this was the scramble for keeperships at Greenwich in 1660 which suggests that hopeful candidates thought posts there would be worthwhile.[2] Another reason, even more compelling, is that plans were afoot within months of the Restoration to completely rebuild the house in a new style.

In May 1661 Charles II ordered a survey of the much damaged palace and within two months the mason William de Keyser was drawing elevations for proposed new buildings.[3] On 19 October John Evelyn visited the Surveyor General of the King's Works, Sir John Denham, to discuss the siting of the palace, noting that Denham was already assisted by John Webb, the former pupil of Inigo Jones.[4] By December a wooden model of the new design had been made by John Turnor and late in January 1661 the King discussed with Evelyn his ideas on the new building.[5] Meanwhile, the demolition of the Tudor palace was put in hand and by the time of Evelyn's talk with Denham no more than the hall, chapel and eastern service buildings survived.[6]

The plans for Greenwich underwent two stages of development. The first is represented by the plans by de Keyser and model by Turnor which seem likely to be synonymous with two undated plans, in the hand of John Webb, of a U-shaped palace (one of which has a variant on a flap).[7] The first, at Worcester College, Oxford, shows a well-developed U-shaped building with a western range which can be confidently identified as the King's side with Guard, Presence, Privy and Withdrawing Chambers leading to a Bedchamber beyond which was a Gallery and Closets. The Guard Chamber led off a central domed staircase hall which had to its east two matching outer chambers answering to the King's (fig. 1, overleaf). What is curious about the east range is its omission of a matching suite of apartments for the Queen. In the plan there is clearly no provision for the Queen's Bedchamber with its characteristic alcove,[8] nor the requisite backstairs and closets. Rather, it contains a magnificent chapel and a series of grand assembly halls. The other design, now in the RIBA drawings collection shares these characteristics. In this plan the outer courtyard, with the King's range balancing the chapel, is the same as the Worcester College design in lacking any apartments for the Queen, but it includes two wings on the south side

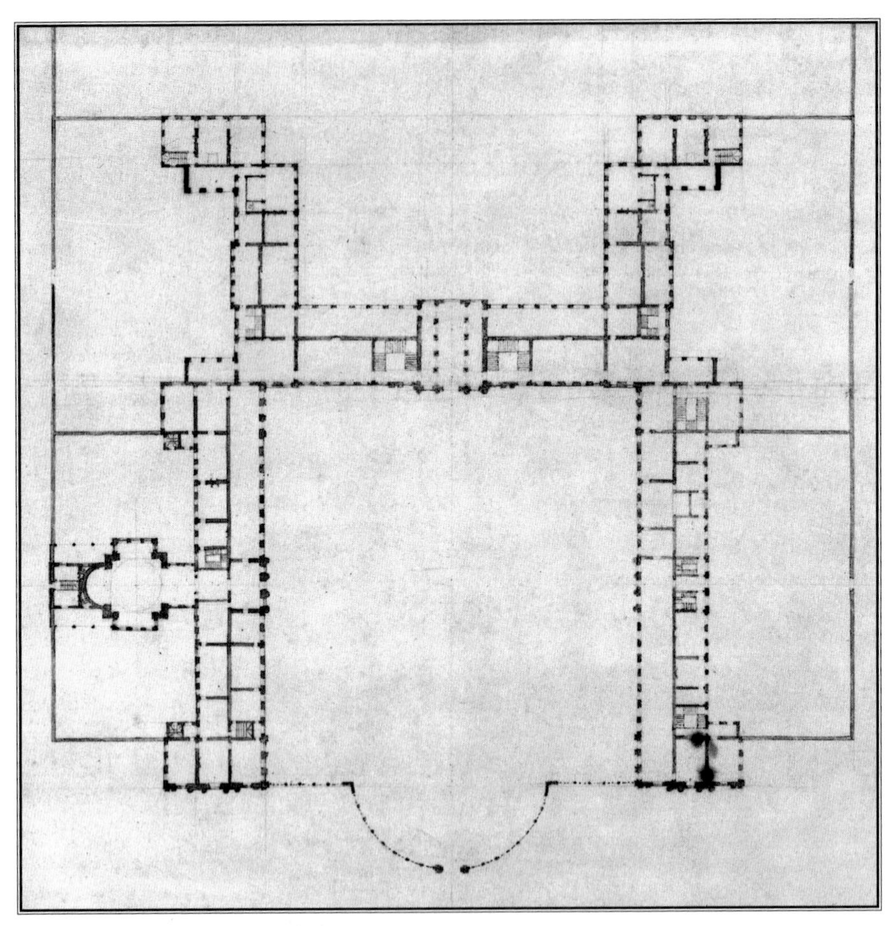

1. Greenwich Palace, first scheme for a new palace, 1661. (Reproduced with kind permission of the RIBA Library Drawings Collection, Burlington-Devonshire III/i(i))

each containing a set of apartments. This plan, it has been convincingly suggested, was prepared to illustrate that the Duke and Duchess of York could be accommodated within the palace.[9]

Together, these two plans embody a unique scheme, an English royal palace designed with provision only for the monarch and not his consort. It could be argued that the lack of the Queen's side reflected Charles's unmarried state at the Restoration, but as early as July 1660 he had been offered the hand of Catherine of Braganza with an enormous dowry and had started negotiations on that basis. It is therefore inconceivable that Greenwich was commissioned for a batchelor king – Charles fully intended to marry.[10] The reason behind Greenwich's unique plan almost certainly lies in Greenwich's position on the Thames, at the head of the estuary some four miles east of London. The river provided the principal means of access for foreign visitors to the capital and the King. From the reign of Henry VII Greenwich had played a singular role in the ceremonial reception of ambassadors and other visitors to the Court, and at the Restoration Charles II saw no reason not to revive Greenwich's highly individual part in State occasions. Before the Restoration a standard diplomatic reception procedure had been developed. Ordinary or resident ambassadors were greeted at Gravesend and then again at Tower Wharf before transferring to a coach for their reception at Whitehall. Favoured or important ordinary ambassadors and all extraordinary embassies and other important dignatories and their delegations likewise arrived at Gravesend but then were conveyed upriver to Greenwich where their preliminary reception would be held. There they transferred to the King's barge and were taken to Tower Wharf where a secondary reception took place; finally they were brought through the city by coach to Whitehall.[11] In February 1633 the King of Poland's ambassador, the twenty-year-old Janush Radzivil, son of the Duke of Birze, arrived at Gravesend where he was received by Sir John Finet, the Master of Ceremonies. The following day he was conveyed to Greenwich where he was met by Robert Rich, 2nd Earl of Warwick, Warwick's son, Thomas Hamilton, Lords Binning and Byres, William Paget, 6th Lord Paget and seventeen Gentlemen of the Privy Chamber. They accompanied him in the King's barge to Whitehall.[12] This ceremonial use of Greenwich persisted under the republic. In June 1658 the Duke of Crequi with a large French delegation was welcomed at Greenwich by Sir Oliver Flemming, the Master of Ceremonies and a large group of English grandees before being conducted, in the Protector's barge, to Tower Wharf and thence to their lodgings. At the Restoration the reception of the French ambassador the *comte* de Cominges followed the established pattern. Although he had been in England since December 1662 the Count only achieved his formal reception the following April 'landing' at Greenwich where he was received by the Master of Ceremonies and other officials. After being entertained there for an hour he was escorted in four barges by six Gentlemen of the Bedchamber to Tower Wharf.[13] Thus Greenwich had a particular ceremonial and diplomatic function intertwined with its primary use as a riverside palace. Precisely what the architectural requirements of this role were are unclear, but the reception of large and influential delegations by high-ranking courtiers clearly needed a suitable architectural stage. It has been convincingly suggested that the terrace and balconies on the south side of the Queen's House, as built by Henrietta Maria, were intended to form part of the auditorium of an ambassadorial reception.[14] Especially on the occasions when the monarch or his consort was involved in the ceremony a suitably splendid location was required. This was recognised after the death of Charles II by his niece, Queen Mary II,

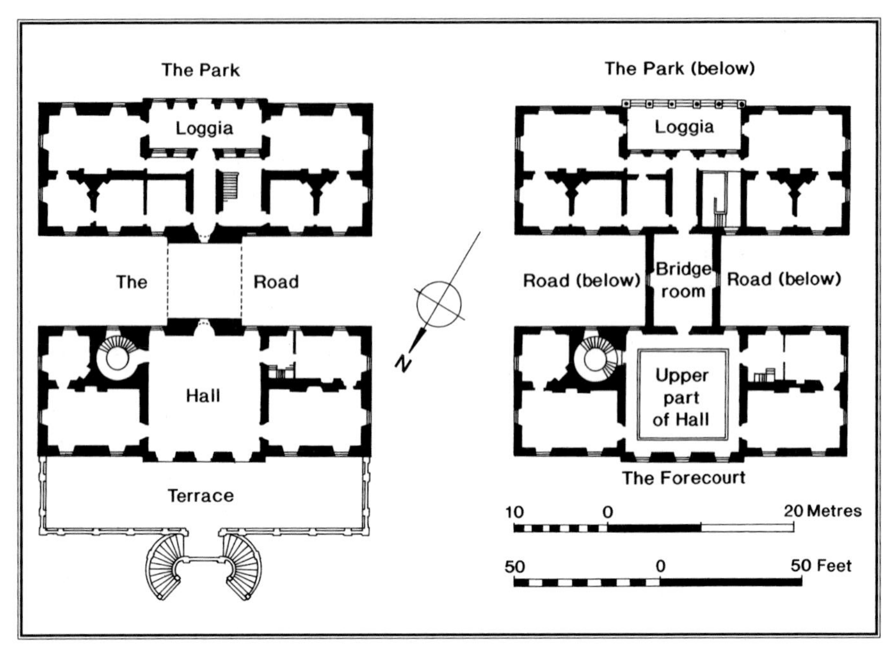

2. First-floor plan of the Queen's House in 1635 showing its original configuration.

who, according to Nicholas Hawksmoor writing in 1728, desired to make the Queen's House into a small retreat for herself and a place where 'Embassadors, or Publick Ministers might make their entry into London'.[15] This is in fact the key to understanding the role of Greenwich and the nature of its building. The two schemes devised in 1661 were specifically intended to provide a ceremonial gateway to the kingdom with its magnificent open courtyard facing the landing stage providing a spectacular disembarkation, the ceremonial stair and an entire wing full of reception halls creating first-rate reception space and, in addition, a set of ceremonial apartments for the King's own use.

As the King's plans for an ambassadorial palace progressed, the Queen's House underwent modification and enlargement between August 1661 and September 1662, presumably at first only to provide interim accommodation for the King, but later also for Catherine of Braganza. The Queen's House had been begun in 1617 by Anne of Denmark, who funded it out of her privy purse and continued by Henrietta Maria using the same source of income. The absence of any Office of Works accounts, together with an interruption shortly after the start of work, and lasting over a decade, make it difficult to ascertain either queen consorts' requirements for the building.[16] Yet a close look at its plan as completed for Henrietta Maria (fig. 2, p. 218) reveals that it could never have been intended for occupation. There is no room identifiable as a bedroom, with garderobe, closet, backstairs or the requisite antechambers for royal use. The important features were its terrace, a grand entrance and assembly hall, a fine staircase leading to two balconied rooms at the front then on to the loggia, and dining rooms on the park side with another stair leading down to the park. The remainder of the rooms and closets must have been withdrawing rooms and cabinets. The Queen's House may well have performed a role in diplomatic ceremonial but analogies with other early Stuart royal residences help to further illuminate its function. The Queen's apartments at Hampton Court on the east front looked out over the park in the same manner as the Queen's House and provided a large balcony for the Queen and her ladies to watch the hunt, just like Jones's loggia at the Queen's House.[17] But the Queen's House also performed a similar function to the Holbein and King Street gates at Whitehall, allowing courtiers and the royal family to cross a dirty and busy public highway from the residential side of the palace to the park, and like the Holbein gate it contained a number of private chambers and closets for royal use.[18] A final analogy can be made with any one of the many banqueting houses built in the parks and gardens of the greater houses, such as the one that still partially survives on the site of Nonsuch.[19] The structure allowed the production of a meal and exquisite, private and semi-outdoor surroundings to eat it in. Indeed, the structure was aptly described in 1659 as a 'House of Delight'.[20] Evidently, as originally conceived, the Queen's House was a grandstand, a bridge, a banqueting house – but never a residence.

The work on the Queen's House undertaken in 1661–2 transformed it into lodgings for royal use. The accounts for the conversion survive and leave no doubt that the aim was to create a king's side and a queen's side (fig. 3, overleaf). The conversion worked well, providing a Presence, Privy and Bedchamber with two Ante-rooms with a couple of lesser Closets.[21] But the principal rooms were tiny, the Presence Chambers measuring merely 32 ft × 18 ft, and the lack of service provision prevented the Queen's House from being used for little more than a temporary retreat.

The first occupant of the remodelled Queen's House was appropriately its pre-republic owner, Henrietta Maria, the mother of Charles II, who arrived in July 1662 and stayed the summer, pending the completion of works on the new royal dower house, Denmark House, on the Strand.[22] But even before Henrietta Maria moved in, a series of new orders were given which scrapped the scheme for a great unitary palace. In March 1662 orders were given to prepare a ground plan of the Queen's House as it stood.[23] Two months later the King, walking in St James's Park told one M. Batailler of his plans for developing Greenwich and expressed the hope of engaging the French garden designer André Le Nôtre, then employed by Louis XIV at Fontainebleau, to work on the gardens of the Queen's House.[24] It is possible that the idea of commissioning Le Nôtre

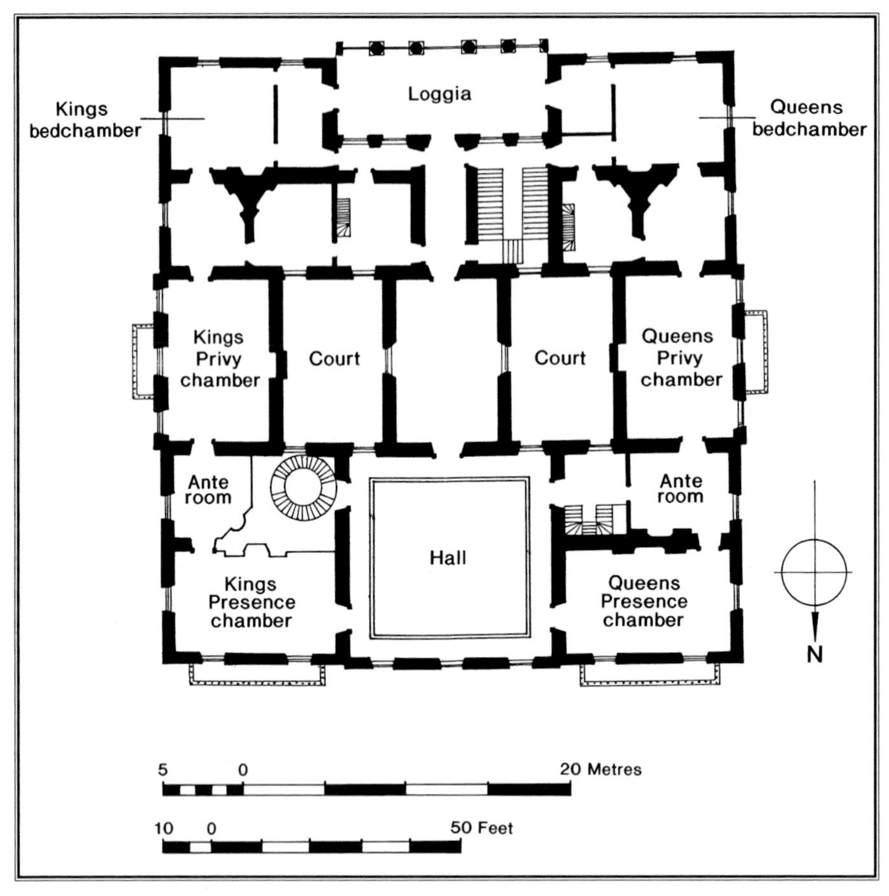

3. First-floor plan of the Queen's House as first modified by Charles II in 1662.

originated in August 1661 in a meeting between him and Henrietta Maria at the celebrations marking the opening of the revolutionary garden designed by him at Vaux le Vicomte. Certainly Le Nôtre believed that the commission emanated from the Queen Mother, annotating his sketch (fig. 4) 'la royne dangleter'. Henrietta Maria's chamberlain and Charles II's ambassador to France, the Earl of St Albans, was expected to bring Le Nôtre back to England in his entourage, shortly after being made Keeper of Greenwich in April 1662.[25]

But by the time Le Nôtre's involvement was mooted Webb had already started work on redesigning both the Queen's House and the gardens. Indeed, Samuel Pepys saw two avenues planted up the hill in the park in April 1662 and 'where it was too steep to climb up, steps had been cut into the ground to walk up in

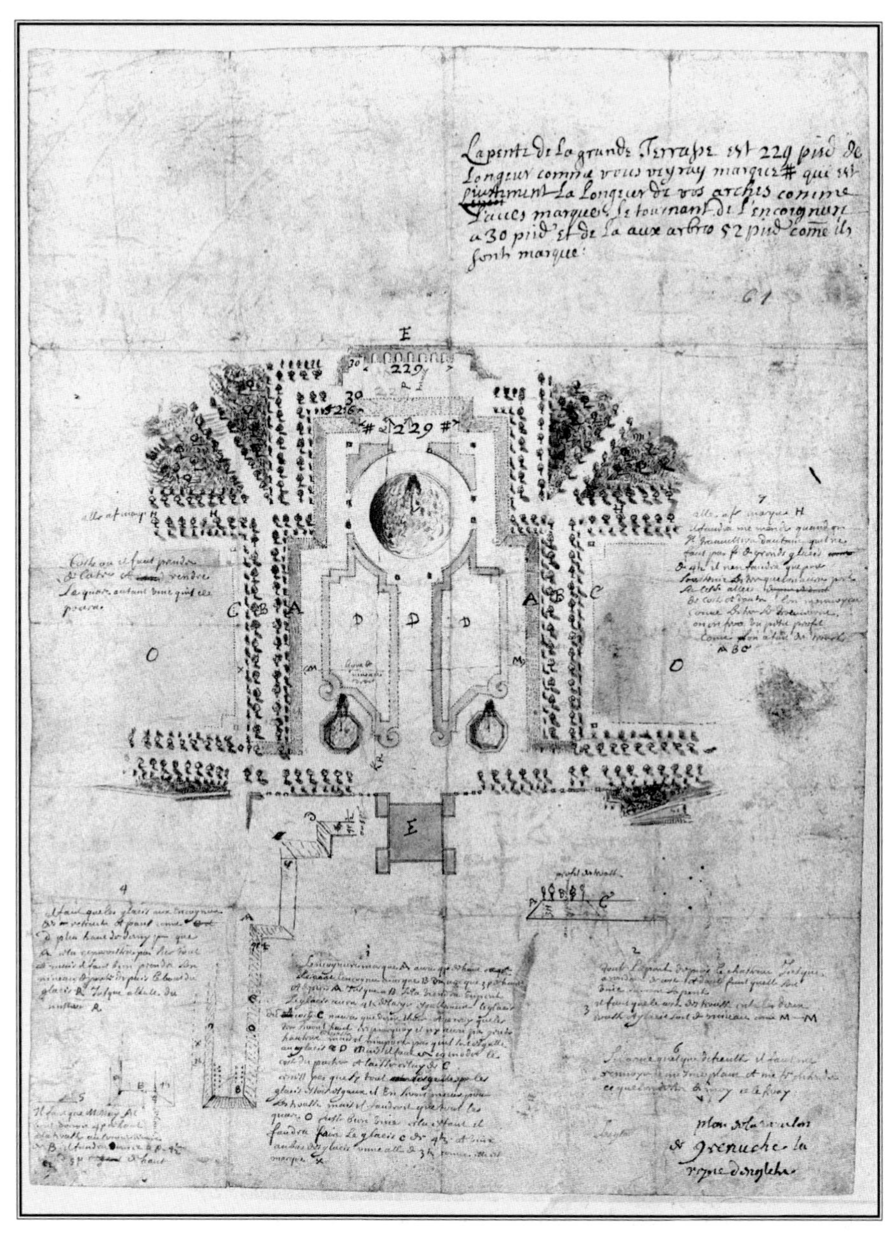

4. Le Nôtre's sketch plan for the gardens at the Queen's House. (Bibliothèque nationale de France, Portfolio No. 1605)

comfort'. These avenues were linked by a terrace raised up on seven arches designed by Webb, forming a focus for the central axis of the garden.[26] Webb was never to be joined in England by Le Nôtre although Louis XIV suggested that Le Nôtre might be able to travel to England at a later date. Yet what is certain is that a brief for the work at Greenwich was prepared for him and sent to France. In October 1664 the King was urging the Duchess of Orleans, his sister, to encourage Le Nôtre to complete his 'modell' of the gardens and he asked her to tell him to add a cascade of water to the hill. As an inducement Charles sent him a number of horses the same month.[27]

The only extant evidence of Le Nôtre's work at Greenwich is an undated plan in the Bibliothèque nationale de France showing his proposals for the site (fig. 4, p. 221). The Queen's House is shown with four pavilions, designed by Webb in the spring of 1662, and mentioned in Le Nôtre's brief of the summer. To its south is a parterre with three fountains and flanking terraces bordered by avenues focused on Webb's arches and specifically stated to be Le Nôtre's work.[28] Either side of the Queen's House to the east and west lay screen walls pierced by what were presumably intended to be ornamental iron panels in the manner of the later Tijou screen at Hampton Court. The road is not shown, presumably because it had been relocated further north.

Le Nôtre's sketch, together with Webb's Queen's House plans from 1662 to 1663,[29] and his plans for what was to become the King Charles Block, enable us to reconstruct Charles II's revised ideas for Greenwich (fig. 5, opposite). Evidently the Queen's House was to be enlarged by the addition of four corner pavilions to provide additional service and residential accommodation and the south range of the intended palace was to be abandoned. Webb's only extant ground-floor plan shows an arrangement in which the staircases in the corner pavilions are integral to them and lateral wings, or possibly walled terraces, related to Le Nôtre's screen walls, run out to the east and west. This failed to make the most of the space and the two first-floor plans, one with variants on flaps and the only (sketch) elevation, show a square link containing the staircases between the pavilions and the house (fig. 6, p. 224).[30] Essentially the bedchambers were to be in the pavilions approached by an ante-room, a large Privy or Withdrawing Chamber, another Antechamber at the stair top and a large outer or Presence Chamber in the old Queen's House. The stairs in the square link buildings enabled formal access to individual pavilions but had to double as service stairs too. The whole scheme was a fundamental change in use for the Queen's House. Le Nôtre's parterre meant that no longer was the loggia to be used for the observation of the hunt, rather the calm contemplation of a garden and a view of the hill. On the north side was a forecourt formed by the new flanking walls (fig. 5). The building now had four small but well-developed suites of royal apartments with appropriate service provision. The equality in size and status of the four suites rules out the possibility that one of them was generally intended to be used by the King.

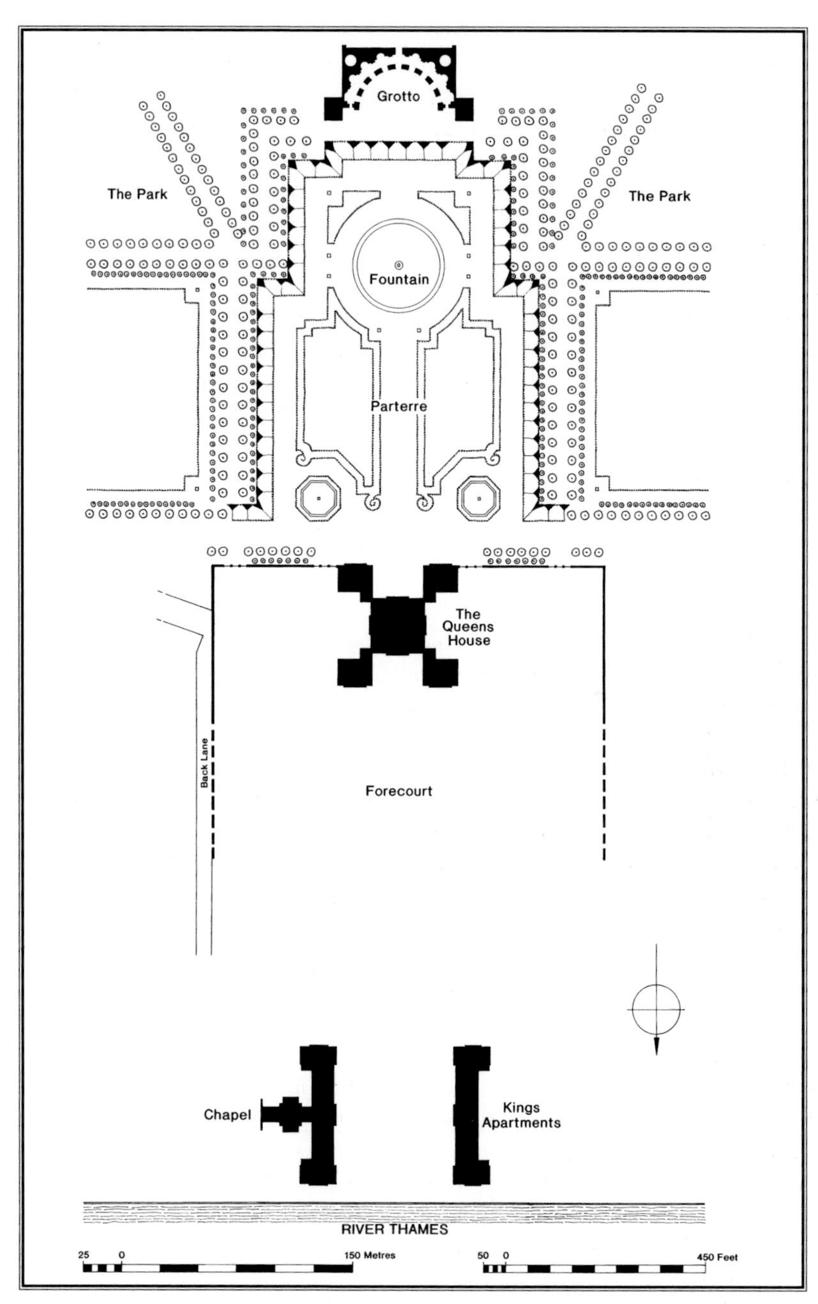

5. Reconstruction plan of Charles II's revised scheme for Greenwich as designed in spring 1662 and partially executed.

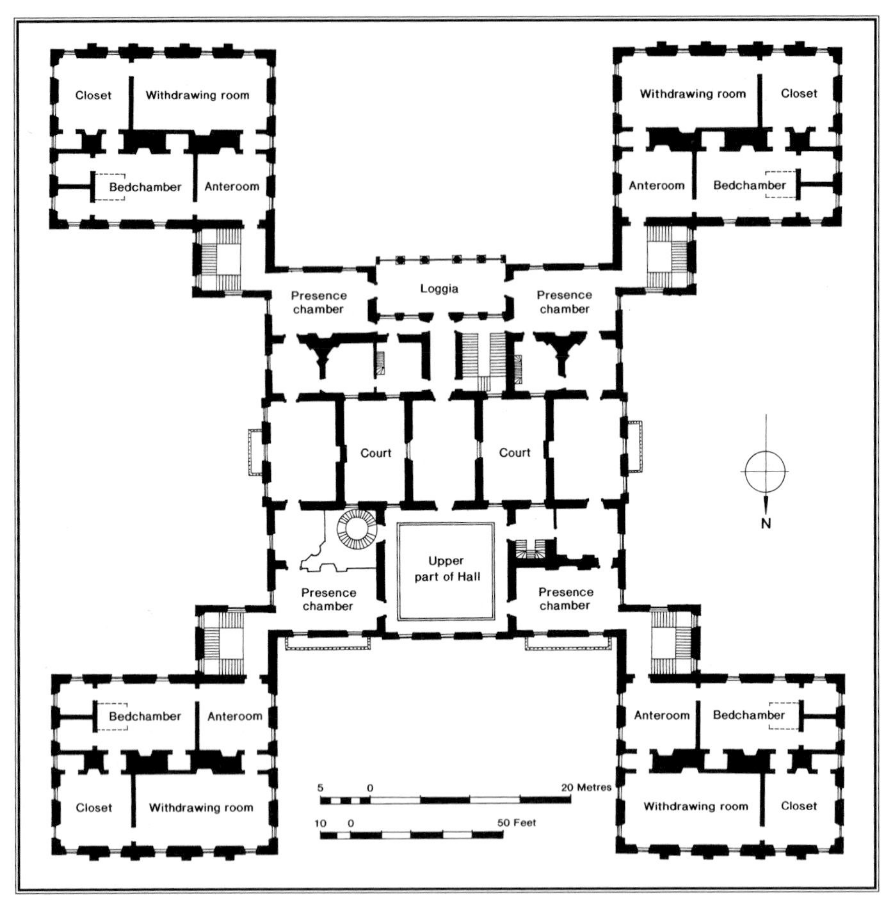

6. Reconstruction of the first-floor plan of the Queen's House as proposed by John Webb in early 1662.

Presumably they were intended for the Duke and Duchess of York and the Queen, or one of the King's mistresses. The King's own lodging was in the riverside block.

Pepys was present for the 'foundation laying of a very great house for the king', i.e. the riverside block, which, he observed, 'will cost a great deal of money'.[31] For this building over forty drawings survive, showing Webb's scheme in detail and dated between 1663 and 1666.[32] One of these show the first floor as executed with a Guard Chamber or 'grand chamber', as it is labelled on a drawing, at the head of the stairs and opposite a Presence Chamber which led on to a Withdrawing Chamber, Bedchamber, Cabinet and Gallery, at the end of which was another Drawing Room and a second Cabinet (fig. 7, overleaf). Some of the ground-floor rooms were set up for the King's private use and there was a kitchen at the south end near the entrance, with a slip stair joining the main stair to enable food to be brought up to the first floor.[33]

This building, like its predecessor, the U-shaped palace of 1661, was unique in concept. It was an entirely self-contained king's side only with space for the Gentlemen of his Bedchamber which would allow the King to conveniently conduct an audience, but little else. None of the extensive kitchen facilities for feeding any more than the royal mouth were included and no accommodation for any further members of the Court. It is possible, however, that more extensive kitchen arrangements may have been planned in the stillborn answering block which, as we have seen, was to contain a large number of reception halls and chambers.

The King Charles Block, as it is now known, was more or less completed by July 1669 but not before the King had revised his ideas on the Queen's House for a third and final time. Work had begun on one of the new pavilions in May 1663, and on another a few months later, but work soon ground to a halt as attention was focused on bringing up the King Charles Block.[34] As the riverside range reached roof height the King requested Webb to readdress the problem of lack of space in the Queen's House which he must have felt that the pavilions alone did not solve. In an estimate of 8 May 1667 Denham and Webb proposed work to the enormous value of £75,845 4*s* 0*d* on 'the 4 pavilions, with their Porticoes, and Raising ye palace belonging to the Queen Mother one story higher'.[35] This scheme, for which neither plan nor elevation survives, but for which a model was made by William Cleere, was intended to enlarge the Queen's House, not only by the pavilions, but also by the addition of another storey. Work, which included the underpinning of the house to take the extra storey, started on this scheme immediately.[36] But almost as soon as the work had begun it was stopped. By 1670 the lower windows of the King Charles Block were boarded up, the foundations for the pavilions of the Queen's House were filled in, Webb's last month's salary had been paid and the extraordinary account was theoretically closed. Notwithstanding the strains placed on Charles II's parlous finances, it was not realised immediately that work had effectively come to an end: there were several attempts to complete the King's side, to revive work on its corresponding wing, and a drawing for the chapel survives from 1670. As late as June 1673 a warrant to pay Philip Packer, paymaster of the works, £10,000 for ostensibly finishing the work then in suspension and starting the next stage was issued,[37] but it is more likely that this money was meant to cover the figure still outstanding from £26,433 7*s* 11*d* spent on building over four years up to February 1667.[38]

The important point about Charles II's plans for Greenwich is that right from the start the King had no intention of re-creating a traditional standing house.

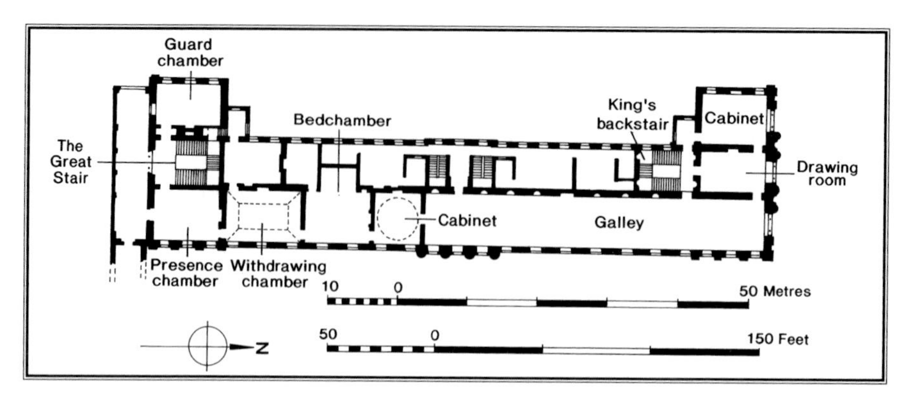

7. Reconstruction of the first-floor plan of the King's riverside block as planned and built for Charles II.

Charles's Greenwich was to be the ceremonial gateway to his kingdom, not a regular residence. But the King's interest in Greenwich seems to have been killed by the financial constraints on him in the late 1660s. He was to concentrate what sums became available to him in the 1670s upon the refurbishment of Windsor Castle, and it was not until work there was drawing to a completion that his mind turned once more to larger designs. By 1680 his finances were no longer precarious, and the expense of architecture was once again a possible pursuit.[39]

Winchester, in as much as a city can have a self-image, had always seen itself as royal. It was not only one of the two ancient royal seats of England, but it had played host to all the Tudor and Stuart monarchs before the Civil War, and in 1647 the Mayor and aldermen took the bold step of offering the civic mace to Charles I, as prisoner, when he passed through on his way to the Isle of Wight.[40] These facts alone would have been an attraction to Charles II but Winchester offered other delights such as good hunting and, importantly, racing. Racing had continued at Winchester through much of the Commonwealth and at the Restoration the corporation decided to try and obtain royal patronage for the sport, placing a notice in the *London Gazette* in July 1682 announcing that 'the inhabitants of this city being ambitious of the honour of his majesties presence' would establish a plate to be run on the downs at the end of August in the hope that the King and his Court would attend.[41]

The invitation was accepted and the King, Queen and much of the Court removed to Winchester at the end of August for the race.[42] During their brief stay the King was welcomed by large crowds, touched over sixty people for the king's evil and seems to have settled on the idea of a residence in Winchester. The city reacted with lightning speed, 'selling' the King the site of the medieval castle for 5*s*, promising him building timber and carriage, and even restricting the grants of new leases in the town subject to royal plans.[43] Behind the readiness of the corporation to oblige the King over his building plans lay the fear shared in the early 1680s by all incorporated boroughs, that of losing their charter and privileges. The city's obsequiousness, however, did not save it from having to surrender its charter in 1684, nor did it ensure a prompt replacement.[44] To compensate for this very real fear was the prospect of considerable financial returns for the city from the regular presence of the King and the Court. During the short 1683 summer visit to Winchester the Crown spent £1,755 19*s* 10*d* and in due course Charles was to outlay over £44,000 on building the palace, much of which flowed into local pockets.[45]

The King's initial reaction to Winchester and his future plans were widely reported. Just four days after the royal visit Sir Charles Lyttleton wrote to Christopher, 1st Viscount Hatton, that 'the King is mightily pleased at Winchester. . . . The Duke [of York] says tis abundantly better place for all sort of pleasure than Newmarket, and then tis neere ye forest for hunting.' But there was more to the attractions of Winchester than sport. Lyttleton continued: 'there is faction in this business too, ye Whig party being Lords at Newmarket, as hunting, got houses and possest themselves of ye best conveniences there'.[46] It was certainly true that many of the best houses around Newmarket belonged to Whigs, a fact which was at first inconvenient and distasteful and one which the events of 1683 proved to be positively perilous.

What happened during Charles II's visit of 1683 to Newmarket went towards the hardening of his resolve to build at Winchester. Conditions at Newmarket had been worsening for some years and the lodgings for courtiers had never been adequate.[47] What alienated the King was the depletion of game through over-hunting, and in March 1683 he attempted to remedy this by issuing a proclamation controlling hunting near Newmarket. *The Loyal Protestant* of 9 March reported that 'The country people have very much spoil'd and destroy'd His Majesties Game, which, together with the moross carriage to some gent. That attend the court, and the dirtiness of the town, tis said His majesty is not well pleas'd with; and it's discoursed that He will not for the future spend so much time in this place as formerly.'[48] The King's displeasure was compounded by the calamity of a fire which later that month reduced half of the town to ashes, narrowly avoiding the King's own house. John Evelyn believed that the fire 'made the King more earnest to render Wi[n]chester the seat of his Autum[n]al field diversions for the future'; it was, he tells us 'infinitely indeede preferable to New Market, for prospect, aire, pleasure and provisions'.[49] But more serious than this was the fact that the fire probably saved Charles's life as it caused the Court to leave Newmarket earlier than planned and thus inadvertently to foil not one, but two plots against the King: one to murder him planned by some Cromwellians from London, and another to capture him by a number of leading Whigs. What with limited accommodation, poor hunting, dirt, squalor, a major fire, a failed kidnap and high treason at Newmarket, Charles was even more eager to see work at Winchester advanced and to that end he moved there with the Court on 29 August and spent most of September lodging with local dignatories.[50] By this time the Hampshire grand jury had offered the shire hall (the medieval great hall of the castle) to the King and more ground nearby had been granted for building work. Land for the new hunting park, over 352 acres, was also bought at a cost of over £7,000.[51] At the end of the visit the Earl of Sunderland reported: 'We are like to be here twice a year, the King growing fonder of his building and the country every day.'[52] Pressure was brought to bear on Sir Christopher Wren to expedite the work. When asked by Charles II to say how soon it would be done, Wren answered two years to do the job properly but one year 'not so well, nor without great confusion, charge, and inconvenience'. The King insisted 'if it be possible to be done in one year, I will have it so, for a year is a great deal in my life'.[53]

In 1684 the King returned to the city twice, briefly in June and with the Court for four weeks in late August and September.[54] After the June visit a Dutch mat and a green damask travelling bed were ordered for the Queen and sent down in preparation for the longer autumn visit.[55] When the Court arrived, a substantial building must have been on site; most of the masonry was up and the roofs probably started. Shortly before his death on 6 February 1685 the King remarked to the Earl of Ailesbury: 'I shall be most happy this week, for my building will be covered with lead'.[56] Charles II's death was unexpected and it brought the building work at Winchester to an immediate halt, although it was another two years before James II decided to abandon the project. It was commonplace after Charles II's death to believe its purpose was merely to replace Newmarket. Evelyn tells us in 1685 that it was 'intended for a hunting house when his majestie came to these parts, and having an incomparable prospect'.[57] In about 1696 Celia Fiennes, on visiting the incomplete building, heard that it was for Charles II 'when he came to hunt, and for aire and diversions in the country'.[58] Wren's son in *Parentalia* also tells us that the 'best judges' esteemed it 'an excellent model of a royal hunting seat'.[59] And so does J. Mackay in his *A Journey through England*, commenting on the 'deliciousness of the country for all manner of country sports'.[60] Daniel Defoe, who wrote in the early 1720s, but perhaps visited Winchester earlier, also believed that the house's principal function was hunting, and that if finished it would have made 'that part of the country, the Newmarket of the ages to come'. However, unlike all other contemporary commentators he went on to observe that 'The Design included a noble Palace, sufficient like Windsor, for a summer residence for the whole court.'[61] The perspicacious Defoe realised that even in its incomplete state Winchester Palace was greater in size than any other royal hunting house, and was exceeded only by Windsor, Hampton Court and Whitehall, the three palaces designed to accommodate the entire Court for long periods of time.

A reconstruction of the plan of Winchester Palace (fig. 8, overleaf, and Appendix) leaves no doubt that it was meant to be a substantial royal residence. Its western façade was longer than the eastern façade erected in the 1690s at Hampton Court. Winchester was to have provided more royal accommodation than Hampton Court with both state apartments and privy lodgings for the King and Queen as well as for the Duke and Duchess of York and the Duchess of Portsmouth, the King's mistress, and both palaces had some 100 lodgings for courtiers. Importantly Winchester also had a council chamber and provision for Clerks of the Council. This latter point is a key one because the provision of so much well-thought out space for the King's Council sets the palace apart. Only Whitehall had such facilities; not even Hugh May's work at Windsor included a council chamber, Windsor being considered (as it still is) the principal suburban retreat. When Charles was at Windsor the Council would meet at Hampton Court and he would either walk or ride to Hampton Court to attend.[62] Even more so than the later Hampton Court, Winchester, in its layout and architectural pretension, clearly emulated Versailles as first enlarged for Louis XIV. Like Versailles it was set in a vast hunting park and was intended to have a magnificent broad approach which in Winchester's case, involved considerable urban demolition to create a mall aligned on the west front of the cathedral (fig. 9, p. 231).[63] All these features were a far cry from the diminutive scale of Newmarket and other royal hunting lodges where part of the attraction was the escape from many monarchical duties. These features create an unassailable presumption that at Winchester Charles II was building, at the time of his death, a significant new standing house rivalling Hampton Court or Greenwich before the Civil War.

The presumption that Charles II was creating a new standing house at Winchester and the rapidity with which, in 1683, the choice was made and with which the project proceeded, suggests that he had been considering potential sites for a new standing house for some time. Certainly the King had developed a distaste for London, which had played such a large role in the downfall of his father, and the events of the early Restoration did little to endear the metropolis to him. The Bawdy House riots of 1668, the first major political riots in London of the reign, were accompanied by slogans such as 'ere long we will come and pull Whitehall down'. But much more serious and certainly the spur for the decision to build at Winchester was the extreme ferment in the capital caused by the Exclusion crisis. The decision to summon Parliament to Oxford in March 1681 had been an expression of royal unease with London, which was to be borne out by the Exclusion riots of November 1682. It is almost certainly no coincidence that within nine months Charles had decided on a new standing palace far from the metropolis.[64]

The decision to build a new palace at Winchester broke with two-hundred years of royal building which had located the Crown's standing houses in the

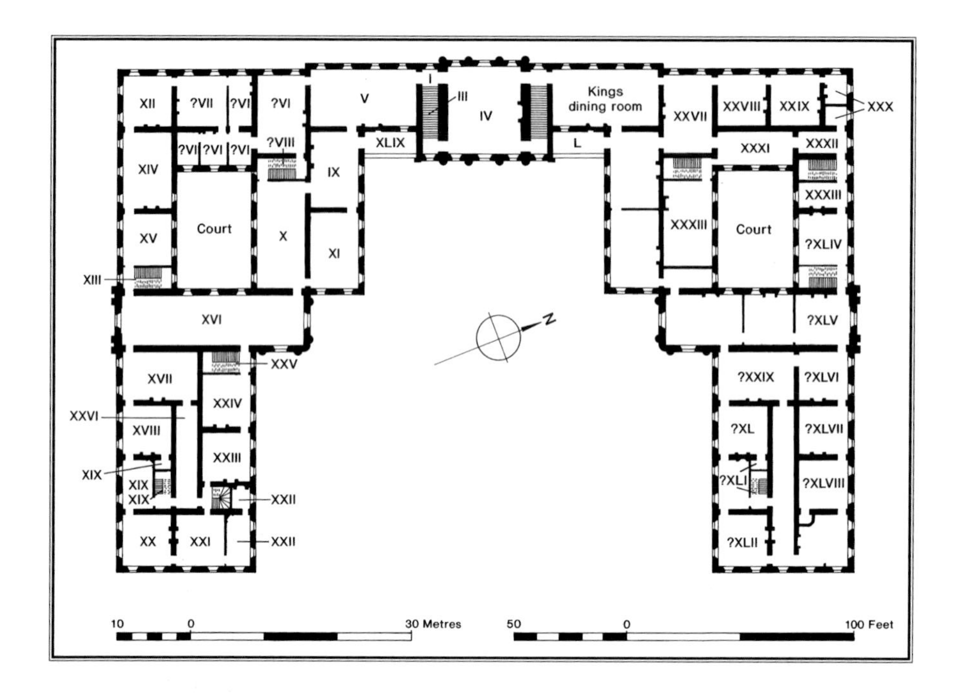

KEY

I. Entrance for the King's Coach
II. Garde-chamber below Staires
III. Principal Staires (The rest represents the plan of the second storey)
IV. Lobby

King's Side

V. Presence
VI. Passage and Ante-Chappell and Closet above the skreene
VII. Chappell
VIII. Staires to the Closett
IX. Privy Chamber
X. Drawing Room
XI. Lobby, or Dining-room, on the King's side
XII. Anteroom to the Councill-chamber and ye Clerkes Seates
XIII. Staires to the Councill
XIV. Council Chamber
XV. Closet to the Councill-chamber
XVI. Privy-Gallery
XVII. Ante-Roome
XVIII. Bed-chamber
XIX. Lobby, Stoole-roome and private Staires
XX. Cabinet
XXI. Inner Bed Chamber
XXII. Dressing-roome, Closett and Staires to the inner Bed-chamber
XXIII. Inner roome of the Back Staire
XXIV. Waiting-room of the Back Staire
XXV. Back Staires
XXVI. Passage with light from above

Queen's Side

XXVII. Presence
XXVIII. Drawing-Roome
XXIX. Bed Chamber
XXX. Closett and Stoole-room
XXXI. Dressing-roome, Robes and private Staires
XXXII. Waiting-Roomes and Back Staires
XXXIII. Chapell

Duke's Side

XXXIV.	Staires out of the Garde-chamber
XXXV.	Presence
XXXVI.	Privy-chamber
XXXVII.	Bed-chamber
XXXVIII.	Garderobe, Cabinet, Stoole-roome

Duchesse's Side

XXXIX.	Presence
XL.	Bed-chamber
XLI.	Dressing-room, Stoole-roome, Back Staires
XLII.	Garde-robe and Cabinet
XLIII.	Passage and Trunk roome

Another Apartment

XLIV.	Great Staires and Anteroome
XLV.	Dining-roome
XLVI.	Drawing-roome
XLVII.	Bed-chamber
XLVIII.	Dressing-roome, Cabinet, Garde-robe, Back Staires
XLIX.	Belcony
L.	Belcony

Over the Garde-chamber II, is the King's Dining-roome on the Queen's side. Over the passage I is a Gallery joining the King and Queen's side with the Duke and Duchesse.

8. Reconstruction of the first-floor plan of Winchester Palace.

Thames valley. From the fifteenth century there had been an increasing concentration of royal, noble and episcopal houses along the Thames between Greenwich and Windsor. The river not only provided a quick, safe and comfortable way to travel between houses but also cheap transport for building materials and a free sewerage system.[65] The last standing house to be built outside the Thames valley was Henry VIII's manor of New Hall in Essex, notably the least successful of his residences, visited a mere thirteen times during his reign and not at all after 1530.[66] In practice during the sixteenth century

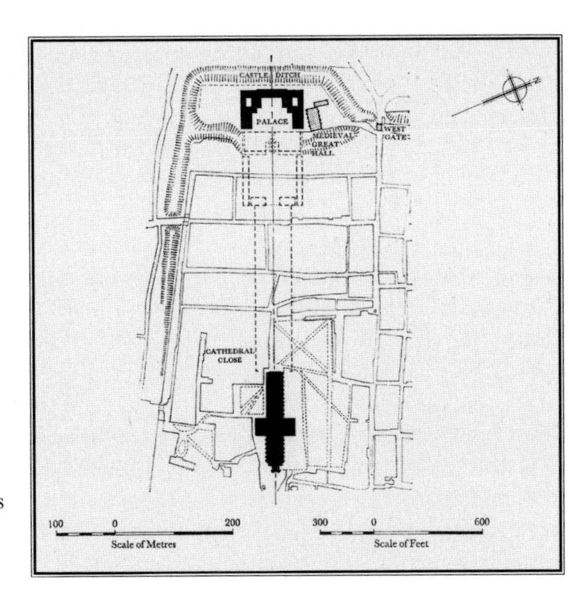

9. Reconstruction of the town of Winchester and the palace as intended by Charles II. (Crown Copyright)

standing houses, designed to be used by the full Court in the winter months, could not be sustained if they were not on the Thames. Eltham, for instance, was a substantial, but landlocked residence which lost its precedence to Greenwich for that very reason.[67] But during the early years of the seventeenth century a significant change began to take place in modes of royal transport. By the 1630s travel by coach had become normal for Charles I and a network of royal roads was built up between the major royal palaces to ensure quick and comfortable transport between them.[68] From at least the time of Charles I one of these private roads had linked Lambeth to Greenwich, allowing rapid access by coach from Whitehall. The disadvantage of this particular route was that it was necessary to take the ferry at Lambeth to cross the Thames. During Charles II's peak enthusiasm for Greenwich in 1664, and in anticipation of the completion of the new works there, the possibility of a bridge being built across the Thames at Westminster to improve access by land was considered.[69] Thus for Charles II the primary access to Greenwich was to be by road, not river. The Winchester project illustrates almost better than anything else the tangible consequence of the change in the Crown's attitude to transport between its residences. In choosing a new site a good road with appropriately placed bridges had become more important than proximity to the River Thames. The fact that Hampshire had good, ancient road links with London, the state of the London to Winchester road being described in 1675 by John Ogilby as 'very good', must have greatly influenced the choice of Winchester for a new standing house. At Winchester the King and Court were at a comfortable distance from London, but even so remained conveniently accessible at all times.[70] If good road access allowed Charles II to contemplate building at Winchester, the city, as a traditional royalist stronghold, was politically an obvious option. During the Exclusion crisis the city's royalist sympathies were confirmed when its members, in conjunction with the majority of the Hampshire MPs, stood firm in their support for the Duke of York whom, together with the King, Winchester made honorary freemen. After the dissolution of the Oxford Parliament Hampshire dignitaries rallied to the Crown.[71] In October 1682, on the announcement of the choice of Winchester, it was said that the King was 'extremely satisfied with the loyalty of that city'. As well he might be in light of the growing tension in Newmarket and London.[72]

Another factor in Winchester's favour was the excellent accommodation it could offer for the supernumeraries of the Court and the administration, in telling contrast with Newmarket. A year after Charles II's death, Winchester could provide bedding for 336 persons and stabling for 1,048 horses, only five other places in the kingdom being better supplied.[73] In addition to these merits Winchester's geographical position had much to commend it, being only a short distance from the increasingly important naval base at Gosport, which preoccupied much of the King's time. In 1665 he had begun extensive improvements to the fortifications there and in the summer of 1683 rode from

Winchester to inspect the continuing work with the Duke of York and Prince George.[74] It is difficult to imagine that the two projects, geographically so close together, were far separated in the royal mind.[75]

The ravages of the republic on the ancestral properties of the Crown enabled Charles II to reappraise his houses in the light of his needs and the pressures of Restoration England. His fear and suspicion of London led him to seek an alternative standing house to either Greenwich or Hampton Court, the principal suburban seats of his father. Greenwich he intended to rebuild as a focus for diplomatic activity and Hampton Court was to become home to the Duke and Duchess of York and his mistresses. Winchester was chosen as a new standing house, marrying the city's aggressive civic ambition and the King's specific requirements. Neither Greenwich nor Winchester reached fruition and because of this the royal map of England was never redrawn. After 1688 William re-affirmed London as the focus of royal building, reconstructing Hampton Court to fulfil the role that Winchester so nearly took on. As for Greenwich, although it retained a residual role in diplomatic activity into King William's reign, all but the Queen's House was abandoned by James II as early as 1687. The refitting of Windsor Castle alone entered the eighteenth century as a reminder of the Restoration of Charles II.

Appendix: A Reconstruction of Winchester Palace

Although a plan of the first floor of Winchester has survived,[76] and a list of rooms, being the key to another (lost) first-floor plan exists,[77] no one has hitherto tried to reconstruct the first-floor plan of the palace. This reconstruction (fig. 8) makes the reasonable presumption that the key follows a logical order, and that the privy gallery was the 80-ft long gallery running north–south across the centre of the King's apartments. If these two premises are correct, the sequence that emerges is as follows. An ante-room (XVII) separated the gallery (XVI) from the King's great Bedchamber (XVIII). This room had, as is normal with a bedchamber a small stool room (XIX) adjacent. Beyond were the privy stairs (XIX) at the head of which was a lobby (XIX), which separated the public part of the bedchamber open for levees from the private part reserved for the King. Beyond the lobby at the corner of the block with windows looking out south and east was the King's Cabinet (XX) or closet (his private study). Then came the King's little or Inner Bedchamber (XXI), the one where he actually slept. Next to this was his Dressing Room (XXII) and a small Closet, probably again for washing (XXII). The King's Inner Bedchamber was served by the 'staires to the inner bedchamber', (XXII) next to which was a room for his Gentlemen – the inner room of the backstairs (XXIII) – and to that a Waiting Room (XXIV) to provide an ante-room for visitors who had ascended the backstairs (XXV). Linking the Ante-room (XVII), the Lobby (XIX) and the rooms of the backstairs

(XXIII–XIV) was the 'passage with light from above'. This allowed the Gentlemen and Grooms of the Bedchamber to reach all the ancillary rooms with ease. The King's outer rooms were to the west of the Privy Gallery and began with a Guard Chamber on the ground floor (II). From here a straight run of stairs (III) led to a small lobby at the stair top (I) before entering the Presence Chamber (V). From the Presence Chamber, to complete the normal sequence of state rooms one would expect three rooms: a principal audience chamber – a Privy Chamber – a Dining Room, often called an Ante-room as it was only set up when required, and a Withdrawing Room. These rooms would need to be consecutive and lead to the Privy Gallery so as to enable courtiers to process through the sequence for a levee. In terms of the key this means that rooms VI, the passage, Ante-chapel, etc., must lie to the south of the Presence Chamber and the room to the east must be the Privy Chamber (IX). Next door to the south lay the Drawing Room (X), a major reception room with four great south-facing windows and direct access to the Privy Gallery (XVI). The Dining Room, or Ante-room (XI) was cleverly positioned in the corner of the block in such a way that it could be circumnavigated when not in use for public dining. When it was set up the room could easily be included in the circuit between the Privy and Withdrawing Rooms.

To the south of the Presence Chamber, if we are to follow the logic of the key, was the Chapel. *Parentalia* seems to indicate that the Chapel was on the ground floor, but the key firmly puts it on the first floor with a cloister or passage running beneath it. The rooms involved, the Chapel (VII), Passage and Antechapel, and Closet above the screen (VI) and stairs to the Closet (VII) cannot be fitted into the plan as we have it now, but there was a stair and enough space on both floors to accommodate all the spaces mentioned. Additionally the first-floor area lies over one of the areas of passage or cloister below. Having placed the Chapel and its ancillary rooms on the west, this helps to identify the three large rooms and a stair with a lobby on the south as the three Council rooms (XII, XIV and XV) and the stairs to the Council (XIII). The rooms are not listed in an order so as to fit the present plan but spatially and in terms of usage[78] they fit perfectly.

The reconstruction of the Queen's side poses some difficulties. Four sets of apartments were located here and the plan fails to furnish the requisite number of staircases listed in the key so that only two bedchambers can certainly be fixed. It is known that the King's Dining Room was sited over the ground-floor Guard Chamber (II): despite its nomenclature this was the royal joint public dining room, and habitually it was on the Queen's side, not the King's.[79] Although the precise location of the Guard Chamber on the ground floor is not known it can be assumed that it was close to the foot of the stairs, thereby enabling the King's guard to control visitors going upstairs. Therefore it is likely that this room was the chamber which balanced the King's Presence Chamber across the great staircase.[80]

Beyond this room to the north was one of the two clearly defined apartments on the Queen's side. Two outer rooms, a Bedchamber, a Closet, a Stool Room and various ancillary rooms. As this apartment cannot be satisfactorily identified with those meant for the Duke or Duchess of York or the 'other' apartment, it follows that these were the Queen's. The Queen's Presence Chamber (XXVII), Drawing Room (XXVIII), Bedchamber (XXIX) Closet and Stool Room (XXX) ran along the west front of the palace. Her ancillary rooms including her backstairs and privy stairs and her robes (XXXI–XXXII) all lay behind these to the east (over the passage below, as stated by the key). Her chapel (XXXIII) probably led off her privy stairs and looked out into the inner courtyard. The identification of this room is confirmed by the off-centre position of its fireplace, sited beside the royal pew at the west end of the chapel.

From this it follows that the large rooms corresponding to the Privy and Dining Chambers on the King's side were probably intended for the Duke of York. This is confirmed by the fact that the apartment began with 'stairs out of the guard chamber' (XXXIV), which place it at the westernmost part of the wing. There was perhaps a staircase leading up to the Duke's apartment which was not recorded. How the rooms listed in the key precisely fit into the plan is not at all clear. The Duchess, it is suggested here, occupied the only other identifiable bedchamber, together with the apartment which adjoined it. The Duchess's rooms (XXXIX–XLIII) fit the spaces on the plan almost exactly. This means that the 'other' apartment occupied the north side of the range. A staircase leading up from the court can be identified as 'great stairs and Ante-room' (XLIV), the Dining Room (XLV), Drawing Room (XLVI), Bedchamber (XLVII), Dressing Room, etc. (XLVIII).

ACKNOWLEDGEMENTS

Several people have been kind enough to help with the preparation of this chapter. I would like to thank Alasdair Hawkyard, John Newman, Eveline Cruickshanks, David Jacques, Richard Flenley, Peter Barber, Clare Murphy, Anna Keay and Kay Ford.

Notes

1. *CSPD, 1635–6*, p. 569; *CSPD, 1636–7*, p. 130; *CSPD, 1654*, p. 373; M. Exwood and H.L. Lehmann (eds), 'The Journal of William Schellinks' Travels in England 1661–1663', Camden Society, 5th Series, Vol. 1 (1993), p. 47.
2. *CSPD, 1660–6*, pp. 101, 238; *CSPD, 1661–2*, pp. 75, 77, 293, 348, 535; A.G. L'Estrange, *The Palace and the Hospital or Chronicles of Greenwich* (London, 1886), pp. 63–4.
3. Colvin, *King's Works*, Vol. V, p. 140.
4. Evelyn, *Diary*, Vol. III, pp. 300–1.

5. Ibid., p. 313. It is also noted that work on the model may have been going on since August 1661 (Colvin, *King's Works*, Vol. V, p. 140 n.).

6. PRO, Work 5/2, ff. 379–450; Work 5/3, ff. 407–62.

7. The first scheme is found in two forms, first in the hand of John Webb, Worcester College, Oxford, Inigo Jones Collection, Vol. IV, p. 20 (J. Harris and A.A. Tait, *Catalogue of Drawings by Inigo Jones, John Webb and Isaac De Caus at Worcester College, Oxford* (Oxford, 1979), p. 37 and pls 69–70), and then in another, unknown hand, All Souls College V.21, 25–6 (*Wren Society*, 20 vols, 1924–43, VIII, (Oxford, 1931), pl. XX). The second scheme, in Webb's hand is RIBA Drawings Collection, Burlington-Devonshire III/I(I) (J. Harris, *Catalogue of the Drawings Collection of the RIBA, Inigo Jones and John Webb* (Farnborough, 1972), p. 24 and fig. 119). There is some debate over the date of these plans. The present writer concurs with the view expressed by John Newman in the *History of the King's Works* (Vol. V, pp. 140–1) which dates them to 1661 on the basis of Webb's known involvement in the Office of Works, his plans dated 1661 for Whitehall, and of the reduction of the scheme at a later date (see also S. Thurley, *The Royal Palaces of Stuart England* (forthcoming)). J. Bold, *John Webb, Architectural Theory and Practice in the Seventeenth Century* (Oxford, 1989), p. 127, rejects this view, dismissing Evelyn's comments and claiming a date of 1663.

8. As seen on the alternative scheme in the RIBA (fig. 1) or in the subsequent plans for the King Charles Block.

9. *HKW*, Vol. V, pp. 141–4.

10. Ronald Hutton, *Charles II* (Oxford, 1989), pp. 158–60.

11. For an example of Tudor diplomatic activity see D. Starkey (ed.), *Henry VIII, A European Court in England* (London, 1991), pp. 54–86; for Stuart procedures, A.J. Loomie (ed.), *Ceremonies of Charles I, The Note Books of Sir John Finet 1628–1641* (New York, 1987), pp. 26–30.

12. Ibid., pp. 134–5.

13. R. Sherwood, *The Court of Oliver Cromwell* (Cambridge, 1989), pp. 74, 100, 120; J.J. Jusserand, *A French Ambassador at the Court of Charles the Second* (London, 1982), pp. 80–1.

14. John Harris and Gordon Higgott, *Inigo Jones, Complete Architectural Drawings* (Royal Academy of Arts, London, 1989), pp. 226–7.

15. C. Wren, *Parentalia, or Memoirs of the Family of Wrens* (London, 1750).

16. The most detailed analysis of the surviving information can be found in *HKW*, Vol. IV, pp. 113–32.

17. Illustrated in Thurley, *Royal Palaces*. It should be noted that at a number of other houses, including Oatlands and St James's, balconies were a feature of the Queen's drawing room. *HKW*, Vol. IV, pp. 216, 249.

18. S. Thurley, *Whitehall Palace, An Architectural History of the Royal Apartments 1240–1698* (Yale, 1999), pp. 43–6.

19. John Dent, *The Quest for Nonsuch* (London, 1962), pp. 125–30.

20. G.H. Chettle, *The Queen's House, Greenwich*, Survey of London Monograph XIV (1937), p. 35.

21. The work is described in great detail in PRO, Work 5/2, ff. 313–477 and Work 5/3, ff. 407–75.

22. Raymond Needham and Alexander Webster, *Somerset House Past and Present* (London, 1905), pp. 142–9.

23. PRO, Work 5/3, f. 474.

24. Evelyn Cecil, *A History of Gardening in England* (London, 1910), p. 186.

25. *CSPD, 1661–2*, p. 403; Charles II's sister, the *duchesse* d'Orleans, had also visited Vaux in July 1661 and may have written to Charles about its merits. R. Norrington (ed.), *My Dearest Minette, The Letters Between Charles II and his Sister, Duchesse d'Orleans* (Guildford, 1996), pp. 51–2.

26. Pepys, *Diary*, Vol. III, p. 63; Bold, op. cit., p. 129.

27. Norrington (ed.), op. cit., p. 93.

28. The best analysis of this plan with transcriptions of the annotations and discussion on its date can be found in The Royal Park's *Historical Survey of Greenwich Park* (Land Use Consultants, January 1986), pp. 10–13, 149–52. I am grateful to David Jacques for pointing this out to me and to Richard Flenley for supplying me with a copy of the report. See also F. Hamilton Hazlehurst, *Gardens of Illusion, The Genius of Andre Le Nostre* (Nashville, 1980), pp. 3, 377–8; David Jacques and Arend Jan van der Horst, *The Gardens of William and Mary* (London, 1988), pp. 20–1.

29. Harris, op. cit., p. 27, cats 166–9, figs 165–8 (a printing error means that cat. 167 is illustrated by fig. 167 and cat. 168 is fig. 166).

30. Harris, op. cit., p. 25, figs 165–8.

31. Pepys, op. cit., Vol. V, (1971), p. 75.

32. Harris, op. cit., cats 122–63, pp. 24–5.

33. My identification of the rooms in this building relies on the annotations on Webb's drawings: Harris, op. cit., cats, 129, 144, 148, 150, 153, 155, 160 (which gives dimensions), 162. For downstairs, cats, 123, 163 and PRO, Work 5/5, ff. 226, 398. It differs from that printed in Bold, op. cit., fig. 10.

34. PRO, Work 5/4, ff. 349v, 351v–352, 355v, 356, 391.

35. A note for Hawksmoor on a plan of 1723 at Wilton House. See K. Downes, *Hawksmoor*, (London, 1959), pp. 94–5 and cat. 358.

36. PRO, Work 5/10, Ordinary account, May.

37. *CSPD, 1673*, p. 358; *CTB, I (1672–5)*, p. 160. Evidence for other attempts to continue the work appear in 1665 when Webb designed a 'grotto and ascent' for the hill behind the Queen's House (J. Bold, 'Greenwich: "the Grott and Ascent by Mr Webb"', *Burlington Magazine*, 129 (1982), 149–50), and in 1667 when work restarted on the construction of the four corner pavilions (*HKW*, Vol. IV, p. 146).

38. *CSPD, 1667*, p. 65; Bold, *John Webb*, p. 146; *HKW*, Vol. V, pp. 39–42, 149–50.

39. J. Miller, *Charles II* (London, 1991), p. 66; *HKW*, Vol. IV, pp. 315–29.

40. Adrienne Rosen, 'Winchester in Transition, 1580–1700', in P. Clark (ed.), *Country Towns in Pre-Industrial England* (Leicester, 1981), pp. 162–9.

41. *London Gazette,* 31 July 1682; Rosen, op. cit., pp. 169, 180.

42. *CSPD, 1682*, p. 356; *True Protestant Mercury*, 30 August and 1 September 1682, nos 172–5.

43. *True Protestant Mercury*, no. 174; *Loyal Protestant*, no. 228. 'Correspondence of the Family of Hatton Being Chiefly Letters Addressed to Christopher First Viscount Hatton 1601–4', ed. E.M. Thompson (Camden Society, 1878, 2 vols), Vol. II, p. 18; Rosen, op. cit., p. 180.

44. *HC 1660–1690*, Vol. 1, p. 260; J. Levin, *The Charter Controversy in the City of London 1660–1688, and its Consequences* (London, 1969), pp. 61, 91.

45. A.M. Coleby, *Central Government and the Localities: Hampshire 1649–1689* (Cambridge, 1987), p. 215; *HKW*, Vol. V, p. 311.

46. 'Correspondence of the Family of Hatton being Chiefly Letters Addressed to Christopher, First Viscount Hatton 1601–4', ed. E.M. Thompson (Camden Society, 1878, 2 vols), Vol. II, p. 18. Note also James II's remarks on the countryside to his niece the Countess of Litchfield in 1683: 'This country is a very proper place for women to ride in, for I never saw a finer, for all field sports, the duchesse and my daughter have been several tyms a hare hunting with little beagles'. Viscount Dillon (trans. and ed.), 'Some Familiar Letters of Charles II and James, Duke of York addressed to their daughter and niece the Countess of Litchfield', *Archaeologia*, 58 (1902), 181.

47. N. Luttrell, *A Brief Relation of State Affairs* (Oxford, 1857), Vol. I, p. 172.

48. *Loyal Protestant*, no. 244, 9 March.

49. Evelyn, *Diary*, Vol. I, p. 341.

50. *London Gazette*, no. 1855; *CSPD, July–September 1683*, pp. 334, 352; the Court returned to Whitehall on Tuesday 5 September (*London Gazette*, no. 1863).

51. *CSPD, January–June 1683*, pp. 32–3, 99; *CTB*, Vol. VII, pp. 972–4.

52. *CSPD, July–September 1683*, pp. 410–11.

53. Roger North, *Lives of the Norths*, ed. Jessop, Vol. II (1890), p. 207.

54. *CSPD, 1684–5*, pp. 43, 120; HMC, *7th Report*, p. 315.

55. PRO, LC5/67, pp. 26–7.

56. J. Bruce, Earl of Ailesbury, *Memoirs*, ed. W.E. Buckley (Roxburgh Club, 1890) (I), pp. 23, 92–3.

57. Evelyn, *Diary*, Vol. I, p. 471.

58. C. Morris (ed.), *The Journeys of Celia Fiennes* (London, 1949), pp. 46–7.

59. *Parentalia*, p. 325.

60. J. Mackay, *A Journey through England* (2 vols, London, 1722), Vol. II, p. 21. Another later account further corroborates this view: 'A Journey through Hampshire . . . 1738', HMC, *Portland*, VI, p. 174.

61. D. Defoe, *A Tour through the Whole Island of Great Britain* (2 vols, London, 1928), Vol. I, p. 185.

62. For example, 'His majesty having been pleased to appoint that, during his residence at Windsor, his privy Council should meet every Wednesday at Hampton Court . . .', *London Gazette*, no. 890, 29 May 1674.

63. For the building's French precedents see *HKW*, Vol. V, pp. 305, 308; J. Summerson, *Architecture in Britain 1530–1830* (London, 1983), pp. 243–4; E.F. Sekler, *Wren and his Place in European Architecture* (London, 1956), pp. 157–9.

64. Tim Harris, *London Crowds in the Reign of Charles II: Propaganda and Politics from the Restoration until the Exclusion Crisis* (Cambridge, 1987), pp. 82–9, 108, 157, 174, 186.

65. Thurley, *Royal Palaces*, pp. 75–8.

66. S. Thurley, 'English Royal Palaces 1450–1550', Ph.D. thesis (Courtauld Institute of Art, London, 1991), Vol. II, p. 123.

67. Thurley, *Royal Palaces*, p. 76.

68. *HKW*, Vol. V, p. 459.

69. And also access to Nonsuch and Hampton Court. *CSPD, Charles I, 1630*, p. 363; *CSPD, 1664–5*, p. 145.

70. It should be noted that the road from Windsor to Winchester was particularly good. John Ogilby, *Britannia* (London, 1675 reprinted), with an introduction by J.B. Hartley (Amsterdam, 1970),

pp. 193, 101; E.G. Box, 'Hampshire in Early Maps and Road Books', *Hampshire Field Club Papers Proceedings*, 12 (1931), 223.

71. A.M. Coleby, op. cit., pp. 211–4, 235. See also G.N. Goodwin, *The Civil War in Hampshire 1642–4* (Southampton, 1904) for the earlier history of Royalism in the area.

72. *Loyal Protestant*, no. 228.

73. Rosen, op. cit., p. 172.

74. *CSPD, 1664–5*, p. 510; G.H. Williams, 'The Western Defences of Portsmouth Harbour 1400–1800', *Portsmouth Papers*, 30 (December 1979), pp. 15–17.

75. HMC, *15th Report*, Appendix, Part 1 (1896), pp. 122–4.

76. The first-floor plan used here largely follows that given in Newman, *History of the King's Works*, Vol. VI, figs 25–6. It is based on All Souls College, Oxford, Wren Drawings II, 98 (*Wren Society*, Vol. VII, pl. I), RIBA Drawings Collection AF 2/17 (J. Harris, *Catalogue of the Drawings . . .* , Cat. 17) and a later eighteenth-century plan helps corroborate many details; Bodl. Lib. MS Top. Gen. a.7, no. 8 (Alan Cook, 'Wren's Design for Winchester Palace', in H. Colvin and J. Harris (eds), *The Country Seat*, (London, 1970), pp. 58–63).

77. Printed in *Wren Society*, Vol. VII, pp. 17–19.

78. Council chambers are almost always sited off the privy gallery as at Whitehall (*HKW*, Vol. V, fig. 23). A similar symmetrical arrangement of Council suite balancing the King's own rooms is found at St James's (*HKW*, Vol. V, fig. 20).

79. As at Hampton Court where the 'Public Dining Room' was on the east front in the King's apartments (*HKW*, Vol. V, fig. 5, the room labelled 'Music Room' was for public dining.

80. It is anyway likely that such a public room as the public dining room would be an outer chamber readily reached from the great stairs.

13

THE JACOBITE COURT AT SAINT-GERMAIN-EN-LAYE: ETIQUETTE AND THE USE OF THE ROYAL APARTMENTS

Edward Corp

The political importance of the Jacobite movement has received considerable attention from historians in recent years. But the Jacobite Court in France, and the way that it was organised, is still relatively unknown.[1] It will be the aim of this chapter to consider various aspects of its structure, and in particular its ceremonial and etiquette.

The Stuart Court at Saint-Germain-en-Laye was by no means the only royal or princely court established in exile during the seventeenth, eighteenth and nineteenth centuries. But it is of especial interest because it was one of the very few, and certainly the most important, established following a usurpation of the throne.[2] It maintained close links with loyalist supporters in Great Britain, and was expected by many to return after an eventual restoration. But until that restoration actually took place, the Court's future was uncertain. It could not depend on the support of all Royalists, or monarchists, in Great Britain, and was in direct competition with a rival court, inevitably more impressive, and presided over by the successful usurper. It therefore had to be seen to represent legitimacy, to be manifestly royal, and to lay emphasis on continuity.

The desire for continuity at Saint-Germain-en-Laye was complicated by recent developments in England. James II had started his reign in 1685 by introducing some important administrative reforms in the organisation of his Court. William III had, therefore, made a particular point of reversing all these reforms when he took the Crown in 1689, thus attempting in his Court, as in his policies and government, to establish the illegitimacy of the rule of James II, and a continuity with the reign of Charles II.[3] In studying the exiled Court of James II we must therefore consider the extent to which James II chose, or was obliged, to reverse his own earlier reforms.

The Court of James II at Saint-Germain-en-Laye was much smaller than it had been at Whitehall. The King's Household was comparable in size to the household that he had previously had when Duke of York.[4] Nevertheless, the Stuart Court in exile remained very consciously a royal court. It also contained a significant percentage of people who had previously served the King in England. At Whitehall the King's Household had numbered approximately 600 people.

Of these 600 only about 50 followed James II into exile, but as his Household at Saint-Germain only contained about 100 people, these 50 provided the new Court with a considerable degree of continuity – even more so when it is remembered that the newly recruited servants were mainly employed in subordinate positions, below stairs and in the Stables.[5] We may note then that, although exile involved a change of location, it did not involve an important break as regards the personnel of the Court.[6] James II had himself favoured a smaller and cheaper Household when still in England, and many of the posts now dropped were inseparable from the palaces and properties which had been left behind.

A problem confronting all exiled courts, and particularly that of the Stuarts, was the need to make use of a château that had been built to house a foreign court, with a different organisation and ceremonial. This chapter will therefore begin by making some preliminary points about the Château de Saint-Germain, which was obviously never designed to welcome an English court, and then draw attention to various ways in which the exiled Stuarts were obliged to modify the organisation and etiquette of their Court, to take account either of the architectural problems they encountered, or else simply the fact of being in exile. The chapter will then consider the ceremonial developed by the Stuarts during their frequent meetings with the family and courtiers of Louis XIV. It will show to what extent James II and Mary of Modena chose to adopt French practices during the twenty-five years that their Court was in France at Saint-Germain, only a few miles away from Versailles.

The Château de Saint-Germain had been used by Louis XIV as his principal residence from 1666 to 1682.[7] It consisted of an irregular pentagon around a central courtyard. One wing was occupied by a chapel; another contained a magnificent theatre. The remaining three each had a ground floor and three storeys above. At the five corners of the château a pavilion had recently been added, and each of these contained four storeys above the ground floor.[8] The Stuarts themselves occupied most of the second floor, in the three wings not given up to the chapel and the theatre. They had the apartments previously used by the French royal family, now extended into the recently added pavilions. The other floors of the château were divided up into apartments of various sizes, which were allocated among the most important courtiers and the most essential Household servants.

Louis XIV had moved the French Court from Saint-Germain to Versailles in 1682. The château had then remained unoccupied, and for that reason was available for James II and Mary of Modena when they arrived in the winter of 1688–9. In a way they were very lucky to be able to use it. After all, it had been Louis XIV's principal residence, and was conveniently close to both Versailles and Marly. But the inconveniences which had eventually forced Louis to leave were now encountered by the Stuarts. There was insufficient accommodation in the château itself, so that the majority of the Jacobites, like the French courtiers before them, had to find lodgings in the town. The shape of the château, with narrow wings built around a central courtyard, created serious problems of circulation, with the need to go up and down stairs, and even out of doors, to get from one apartment to another. But most serious of all, from the point of view of James II, was the shortage of space in the King's apartment.

We have to remember that access to the Bedchamber of the King of France was granted to most of his courtiers, whereas in England it was a privilege enjoyed by very few. Rank in France was revealed by how long a courtier spent in the King's antechamber, and by how quickly he was allowed to proceed to the Bedchamber. Rank in England, on the other hand, was revealed by how far a courtier was permitted to proceed in the sequence of state rooms: to the Guard Chamber only, or to the Presence Chamber, or beyond that to the Privy Chamber, or beyond that to the Withdrawing Room. In 1685 James II had restricted access to the Bedchamber to a mere handful of people: the Secretaries of State, and two or three other ministers. This hierarchical organisation by *time* in France, and by *space* in England, affected the architecture of the royal palaces: the King of France needed only one antechamber between the Guard Chamber and his Bedchamber, whereas the King of England needed at least two, and by the late seventeenth century was accustomed to having three or more.[9]

In all his other residences Louis XIV had actually introduced another antechamber in his apartments, to avoid having to eat his evening meal *en famille* (the 'souper') in his main antechamber – hence the distinction at Versailles between 'la première antichambre' beyond the 'Salle des Gardes', called 'l'antichambre du grand couvert', and 'la seconde antichambre' immediately before the 'Chambre du Roi', called 'l'antichambre des nobles'. In 1689, when James II and Mary of Modena arrived in France, the Château de Saint-Germain was the only French royal residence which still had *one* antechamber in the King's apartment.[10] James II was obliged to use it as both Presence Chamber and Privy Chamber. He had no Withdrawing Room, no Privy Gallery, and no separate Eating Room; and, in the secret lodgings, no separate Council Chamber.

The available documentary evidence does not tell us how James II coped with this situation during the eleven years that he lived at Saint-Germain. But it is clear that it must have profoundly affected the daily life of the Court. The King did not employ a Groom of the Stole, and he merged the Bedchamber department into the Chamber, under the control of the Lord Chamberlain. This involved winding up the Bedchamber as a separate department for the first time since 1603. James II also made no reference to any particular room in the employment of his Gentlemen Ushers.[11] It is not clear to what extent he permitted greater access to his Bedchamber. It had to be used by his councillors in order to gain access to his Closet, which lay beyond it in the north-east pavilion, and seems to have been used as a Council Chamber. It was also used for receiving secret visitors from England (such as Lord Ailesbury), who came up the private staircase.[12] Moreover, James II refused to give any formal diplomatic audiences, insisting that any ambassadors who wished to be received would have to meet him privately in his Bedchamber.[13] The antechamber was used for the King's levee, for the daily assemblies before processing to the chapel, and for court balls. It probably contained a canopy and a throne, but no positive evidence of this has yet emerged.

Access to the King's apartment was via the grand staircase in the middle of the north wing. The Queen had a separate oval staircase in the south-east pavilion, and an apartment which contained two antechambers. Mary of Modena was therefore able to have both a Presence Chamber and a Privy Chamber. Her apartment was laid out in such a way that it converged with that of the King in

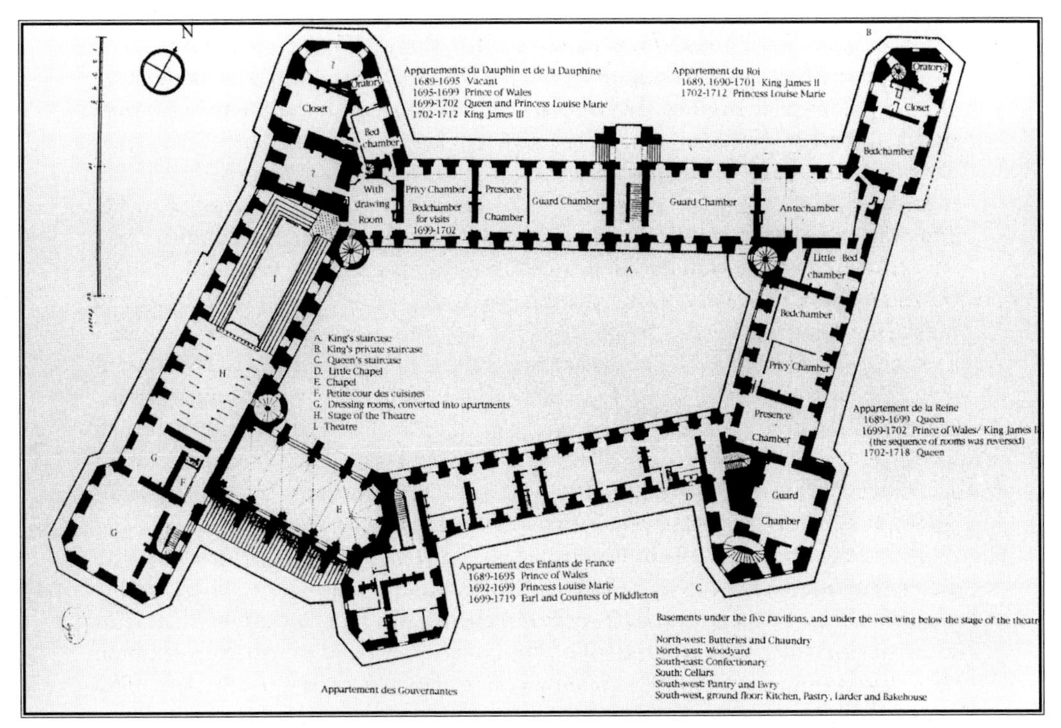

1. The second floor of the château-vieux de Saint-Germain-en-Laye, showing the royal apartments as they were used by the Stuarts. The château-vieux contained three floors above the ground floor, with an additional fourth floor in each of the corner pavilions. The basements of these pavilions, and the ground floor of the one in the south-west corner, contained the subdepartments of the Household Below Stairs. (Edward Corp/Bibliothèque nationale de France, Est. B.8553)

the north-east corner of the château. The King and Queen each had a separate formal Bedchamber, with a bed surrounded by a balustrade. They also shared a common Bedchamber, referred to at Saint-Germain as the 'little bedchamber'.[14] which lay beyond the Queen's formal Bedchamber, and was accessible to the King through a small corridor.

The two children of the King and Queen (the Prince of Wales, born in London in 1688, and the Princess Louise Marie, born at Saint-Germain in 1692), were brought up in the south wing of the château, in the apartment previously used by 'les Enfants de France'. It was in 1695 that the seven-year-old Prince was 'put into men's hands', and given his own apartment.[15] This was the former apartment of the Dauphin, in the north wing, entered from the other side of the King's grand staircase. For reasons which are not clear, this apartment was larger than that of the King. It contained two antechambers, in addition to the Guard Chamber and the Bedchamber, and thus permitted its occupant to have both a Presence Chamber and a Privy Chamber. One is bound to ask why Louis XIV had not used it himself. If he had remained at Saint-Germain after the death of Queen Marie-Thérèse perhaps he might have done so. Beyond the apartment of the Dauphin was a much smaller one used by the Dauphine, which was not large enough for the Queen, but which could have been used as *cabinets intérieurs*. As for James II, his prestige probably required him to use the apartment of Louis XIV, and the shortage of space eventually became a convenient excuse. It allowed him to withdraw into a life of spiritial meditation, and religious observance, in his Closet and Oratory, or in the little rooms he also used on the floor above.[16] All of these enjoyed spectacular views east, over the River Seine, towards Paris.

At first, no doubt, there was another reason: the 'little bedchamber' was situated where the apartments of the King and the Queen converged in the corner of the château. If so, this reason had ceased to apply by 1699. In the autumn of that year, while James II and Mary of Modena were enjoying their annual visit to Fontainebleau, the royal apartments at Saint-Germain were rearranged and redecorated. The Queen and the Prince of Wales changed places, and the young Princess Louise Marie, now seven years old, was moved to the former apartment of the Dauphine in the north-west pavilion. In effect, father and son now lived on one side of the grand staircase, and mother and daughter on the other side. The sequence of rooms in the apartment of the Prince, previously the apartment of the Queen, was reversed: the oval staircase because the backstairs, and the apartment was now entered from the King's antechamber.[17]

None of this information about the château is to be found in any of the biographies of either James II or Mary of Modena. Yet it is surely of some biographical interest. The fact that the King and Queen now occupied apartments which started at the same place, and then progressively separated, meant that there could be no possible direct contact between either their

Bedchambers or their *cabinets intérieurs*. This must have been obvious to anyone living at the Jacobite Court.[18]

Apart from the occasional reference in the Jacobite archives, the documentary evidence for these changes is almost exclusively French, particularly the memoirs of the Baron de Breteuil[19] (who visited the Court of Saint-Germain and commented on its ceremonial), and the detailed archives of the 'Secrétariat de la Maison du Roi', and of the 'Surintendance des Bâtiments du Roi'.[20] These papers give us precise details of when and how the Stuart apartments were furnished and decorated, and refurnished and redecorated, including the number of *fauteuils*, *sièges pliants* and *tabourets* in each room, essential information for understanding the etiquette of the Court. It is impossible to examine all this information in the present chapter. But a single example will suffice to demonstrate its potential interest. When James II died in September 1701 every article of furniture and interior decoration in the royal apartments was removed, and replaced with temporary substitutes in the colours of mourning: violet for the new King, grey for the Queen and Princess. The 'Journal du Garde Meuble'[21] takes each room in turn, and then lists every item. The rooms of the apartment of the Queen in the north wing, where she had lived since 1699, are analysed as follows: 'Salle des Gardes' (her Guard Chamber); 'Antichambre de la Reine' (presumably her Presence Chamber); and then 'Chambre ou la Reine reçoit ses visites'. This ought to be her Privy Chamber, but the 'Journal' makes it clear that it contained a bed, and was therefore a *chambre d'apparat*. The next room is described simply as 'la Chambre', but it also contained a bed. Each room had three armchairs, and a large number of *sièges pliants* (or folding seats). It seems that Mary of Modena had by then decided to introduce French court etiquette into her apartment at Saint-Germain. Visitors would be received, as they would be at the French Court, in the royal Bedchamber. But English etiquette would also be respected. The second, or real Bedchamber, would remain private, with access strictly limited to the Queen's own ladies, the Princess, the new King and his Governor, and perhaps the Secretaries of State.[22]

This point is well illustrated by the description we have of the state visit of King Philip V of Spain to the Jacobite Court in November 1700.[23] James II escorted him to his antechamber, 'la chambre qui est après la salle des gardes, dans laquelle il n'y avait point de lit'. Mary of Modena then escorted him to the first of her two Bedchambers, the one where she received her visits, described in the account as her 'chambre à coucher'.

When the Court came out of mourning in 1702, James III, the new King, decided not to occupy his father's old apartment. He returned to the much larger apartment of the Dauphin, but also used the apartment of the Dauphine to add a Withdrawing Room and a Closet. He re-created the Bedchamber department, by separating it from that of the Chamber, and more than doubled the number of Gentlemen and Grooms employed in both the Bedchamber and the Chamber.

The Ushers were now specifically allocated to either the Presence or the Privy Chamber.[24] Meanwhile, the Queen returned to her old apartment in the east wing, where she continued to have two Bedchambers, and the Princess (still only ten years old) maintained direct access to her mother by occupying the former apartment of James II. We may conclude, then, that whereas James II, and particularly Mary of Modena, made compromises in the organisation and etiquette of their Court, the young James III, who had no first-hand experience of the English royal palaces, was keen to make his apartment as English as possible. He also began to give formal diplomatic audiences, receiving the ambassadors in ceremony in his Privy Chamber.[25]

These changes in the royal apartments were not the only ways in which the Stuart Court at Saint-Germain differed from the Court in England. There were also changes in the catering arrangements. In general terms, the Household below stairs at Whitehall, under the Lord Steward, contained many more sub-departments than the French 'Maison du Roi', under the 'Grand Maître d'Hôtel'. At Whitehall there were fifteen subdepartments, whereas the French system involved only seven, known as 'les sept offices'. They were divided into 'la Bouche du Roi' and 'la Bouche de la Reine', situated in the château itself (whether at Saint-Germain or Versailles), and 'les Offices-Commun' in a building adjacent to the château. At Saint-Germain this was the building surrounding the 'Cour des Cuisines', outside the west wing. The 'Bouche du Roi' and the 'Bouche de la Reine' provided food for the royal tables, and were the equivalent of the Privy Kitchens. The 'Offices-Commun' provided food for the Household, and were thus the equivalent of the Household Kitchen.[26]

Communal dining at the English Court had been abolished in 1663, with only a few tables remaining for various servants in immediate attendance on the King and Queen. After a while these had included, among others, the King's Gentlemen Waiters, but their table had been suspended in 1679 and never reintroduced. Under Charles II the food for these remaining tables had been prepared by the Household Kitchen. James II had abolished the Household Kitchen in 1685, and transferred its functions to the Privy Kitchen.[27] At Saint-Germain the Household Kitchen was never re-established, which meant that part of the accommodation of the French 'Offices-Commun' in the 'Cour des Cuisines' could be used for other purposes.[28] But despite this there was an increase in communal dining at the Court of Saint-Germain. In part this was merely because the proportion of people having diet there was very much greater, in a court that was itself very much smaller. But the main reason was that the Gentlemen Waiters' table was reintroduced by James II, and subsequently continued and expanded by James III.[29] The Privy Kitchen at Saint-Germain was thus required to produce more food than it had done in England, under more difficult circumstances. Some of the subdepartments of the Household at the exiled Court were abolished, because they were no longer needed in exile;[30]

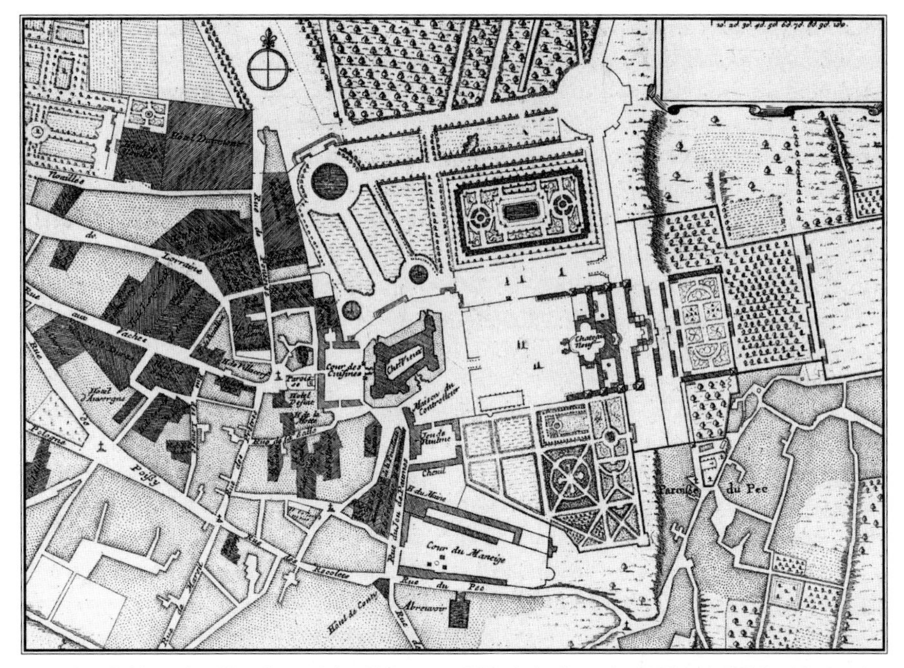

2. A detail from the *Plan Général des Châteaux et Ville de St Germain en Laye*, published by Nicolas de Fer in 1705. The château-vieux can be seen in the centre, surrounded by the grand parterre (north), the château-neuf and hanging gardens (east), the Jeu de Paume, chenil, manège and stables (south), and the 'cour des cuisines' and parish church (west). (Bibliothèque nationale de France, Est. C.79045)

the remaining ones were moved into the basements of the château which had previously housed the 'Gobelets' of the French royal family.[31]

James II's Privy Kitchen was on the ground floor of the west wing of the château, beneath the theatre. It was organised on English lines, whereas the Queen's Privy Kitchen, in the basement immediately below,[32] was identical in its staffing structure to the French 'Bouche de la Reine'.[33] Later, the Queen's kitchen moved upstairs, and shared the same accommodation as the King's, which suggests that after the death of James II the King and Queen Mother rarely took separate meals.[34] Either way the royal kitchens at Saint-Germain were not very conveniently situated. Although they were in the château itself, it was virtually impossible to transport the food to the royal apartments without going out of doors and across the interior courtyard, an obvious inconvenience in bad weather. By contrast, the former apartment of the Dauphin, used by James III, could be reached directly via the staircase in the south-west pavilion, followed by a procession through the theatre. This is perhaps another reason why Mary of Modena had used that apartment in the two years before her husband's death.

It is not clear in which rooms James II and Mary of Modena took their meals. The records suggest that they normally took dinner privately, at midday, in the Queen's Bedchamber, and that when eating alone the King used his own Bedchamber.[35] After the Queen moved into the apartment of the Dauphin in 1699 she could have used the extra space to create a separate Eating Room, which James III might subsequently have maintained.

James II and Mary of Modena probably dined together in public in the Queen's Privy Chamber. There is evidence that the King ate publicly by himself in his own antechamber.[36] One of the 'Introducteurs des Ambassadeurs' at the French Court noted in 1689 that when the King and Queen first dined in public they did so with the same ceremonies observed for Louis XIV,[37] but they reverted to English ceremonial as soon as enough English servants had arrived to make that possible. Thereafter they continued to dine in public with English ceremonies.[38] The detailed inventory of the King's possessions, drawn up after James II's death, gives us precise information about the objects the King and Queen used at table.[39] The Stuarts owned their own *caddinets*, and all their own plate and cutlery. They also owned their own tablecloths and napkins, unlike Louis XIV who always rented his.[40]

The Stuarts in exile were probably served at table in the same manner as they had been in England.[41] But there are no archives which give us details of this type. There is, however, an interesting letter from the Duke of Perth, the young King's Governor and Gentleman of the Bedchamber, who comments that James III normally ate with Mary of Modena on his right, and with Perth himself on his left.[42]

We know a great deal more about the ceremonial developed by the Stuarts when receiving, and being received by, the French royal family. All three 'Introducteurs des Ambassadeurs' at the French Court (the Seigneur de Bonneuil, the Marquis de Sainctot, and the Baron de Breteuil) have left very detailed accounts of where and how the two families received each other, how they walked together through the state apartments, and the way they sat together, whether at table, in the chapel, or at the court theatre.[43] James II and Mary of Modena were always given precedence over the Dauphin, just as the Prince of Wales was always given precedence over the Dauphin's three sons – until, of course, one of them became King Philip V of Spain. As there was neither a Queen of France, nor (after 1690) a Dauphine, Mary of Modena's claim to be the first lady of the French Court was beyond question. When James II died in 1701 his son James III was given exactly the same honours: equality with Louis XIV and precedence over the Dauphin. When Princess Louise Marie came of age, and began to visit Versailles and Marly without her mother, *she* became the first lady at the French Court. As the daughter of a King, she outranked even Louis XIV's favourite, Marie-Adelaide de Savoie, Duchesse de Bourgogne, who only counted as the granddaughter of a king. This changed in 1711, after the death of Monseigneur, when the Duchesse became the new Dauphine.[44]

From the very beginning James II and Mary of Modena were keen to play down these awkward questions of precedence, particularly when the Dauphin visited Saint-Germain. Because James II could not offer him an armchair, he made a point of always receiving him standing up.[45] Mary of Modena discovered that Queen Henrietta Maria, in exile during the 1640s and 1650s, had given an armchair to both Gaston, duc d'Orléans and Louis XIV's brother Philippe, and she used that precedent to give one to the Dauphin when he visited her. But when James II was present in the Queen's apartment she could not do this, so all three sat on *tabourets*.[46] James III adopted the same tactful approach, and even insisted on extending it to the French Court. When Louis XIV was not actually present, as regularly happened in the Court theatre at Fontainebleau, James III insisted that the Dauphin and his family should all have armchairs, and not merely *tabourets*, and thus be treated as his equals. Otherwise, he argued, he would not be prepared to attend any performances himself.[47]

At a slightly lower level, the Stuarts had to reconcile the differences between English and French ceremonial. When the Princesses of the Blood first visited the Queen she greeted each of them with a kiss in the English style, and then gave them *sièges pliants*. This was a sensitive point at the French Court, because the Queens of France only kissed their immediate families, their brothers-in-law, and the granddaughters of a king, but never the Princesses of the Blood. The ordinary princesses and the duchesses then demanded the same treatment. Mary of Modena was reluctant to agree, but consulted Louis XIV. With his support she then made them choose: either to be treated according to English ceremonial, by which they would be kissed only; or according to French ceremonial, which was to sit down on *sièges pliants*, and be allowed to enter the interior courtyard of the château in their carriages, but not to be kissed. The ladies preferred the conveniences of French ceremonial, which then became normal at the Court of Saint-Germain.[48]

According to French ceremonial the ladies were only entitled to *sièges pliants* if they had the rank of princesses or duchesses. So Mary of Modena had to ensure that there were always ladies of similar rank at the English Court, who could accompany her to Versailles. For the first few years there were Lady Sussex and Lady Waldegrave, the natural daughters of Charles II and James II, who were treated as princesses. But the Queen initially wanted four of her ladies to be allowed to sit down, and she had no duchesses. The Marquess of Powis, therefore, had to be created a duke, so that Lady Powis could be a duchess.

But that only made three. An exception had to be made for one of the other Ladies of the Bedchamber. At first this was Vittoria Davia. She was the niece of the great general Montecucculi, an imperial prince and neapolitan duke, but she had no title of her own so had to be given a Scottish peerage (as Countess of Almond) to make the arrangement more acceptable.[49] Thereafter, the Queen tried to make sure that there was always at least one duchess at Saint-Germain; and the subsequent Jacobite dukedoms were perhaps partly made for this reason.[50] The remaining Ladies of the Bedchamber at Saint-Germain were always countesses, or the daughters of peers.[51] They were allowed to sit in the Queen's presence at the Jacobite Court, but not when they went to Versailles. It was noticed that an exception was made when the Stuarts paid their state visit to King Philip V of Spain. As a purely Anglo-Spanish occasion, the English ladies were all allowed to use *tabourets*.[52]

Contrary to what is often thought, the Stuart Court in exile was not short of money. James II, and then James III, received a regular annual pension of 600,000 livres from Louis XIV. Jacobite supporters in England and Scotland made secret donations, as also did some of the Italian princes, the Dukes of Modena and Mantua, and the Pope. The Queen had important investments in both France and Italy, inherited from her mother, a niece of Cardinal Mazarin. Many of the leading courtiers managed to safeguard their estates in England and Scotland, and have their incomes transmitted to France, as of course the Italian courtiers did from Modena.[53] The English Catholics were closely linked with the English convents on the Continent, and some already had investments in France.[54] These people were not, therefore, totally dependent on the salaries and pensions paid by James II and his son. The Stuarts also received presents every so often from the French Court, sometimes disguised as winning lottery tickets.[55] But these sources of income were not all: there were also the various expenses which did not have to be met. These included all the furniture and decorations; and all the guards, who were provided and paid for by Louis XIV. The King of France also paid for the maintenance and repair of the château, and the upkeep of all the gardens.[56] These things meant that the Stuarts could use their available money to pay for a respectable Household, and provide pensions for a large number of additional courtiers.[57] The rest of their money, which was never in short supply, was freely spent on precisely those things which emphasised the regality of their Court: paintings, gold and silver medals, and musical entertainment.[58]

By going abroad into an extended and (as it turned out) permanent exile, the Stuart Court was forced to adapt itself to changing circumstances. In so doing the King and Queen, and their leading Household servants, were obliged to take careful decisions about which aspects of the Court at Whitehall had been essential, and which could be safely discarded. The King made changes because he had to; the Queen was prepared to go further than was necessary. But on one point they were both agreed: the ceremonial and etiquette, whether English or French, should emphasise that the Court at Saint-Germain was royal, in the great tradition of the Stuart Courts in England.

Notes

1. For the Jacobite Court at Saint-Germain-en-Laye, see E. Corp and J. Sanson, *La Cour des Stuarts à Saint-Germain-en-Laye au Temps de Louis XIV* (exhibition catalogue, Réunion des Musées Nationaux, Paris, 1992). See also the papers presented at the Stuart colloquium at Saint-Germain in 1992, published in E. Corp (ed.), *L'Autre Exil: les Jacobites en France au Début de XVIIIe Siècle* (Montpellier, 1993), and E. Cruickshanks and E. Corp (eds), *The Stuart Court in Exile and the Jacobites* (London, 1995). Other papers presented at the same colloquium were included in a special issue of the *Revue de la Bibliothèque Nationale* entitled 'Les Jacobites' (Winter 1992, no. 46).

2. Exiled courts may conveniently be divided into four categories, depending on the status of the prince: in exile following abdication (e.g. Queen Christina of Sweden, 1654–89); in exile as a result of military occupation (e.g. the Elector of Bavaria, 1704–14); deposed by revolution (e.g. Charles II of England, 1649–60); deposed by usurpation (e.g. James II and James III, 1689–1766). Other examples of the last category are Stanislas Leszczynski of Poland, 1704–9, but he was only an elected king; and perhaps Louis XVIII after 1804, but he had previously been deposed by revolution. National unification in the nineteenth century provides a different form of usurpation.

3. A.P. Barclay, 'The Impact of King James II on the Departments of the Royal Household' (unpublished Cambridge University Ph.D. thesis, 1993), particularly chapters 3 and 7. James II abolished the Household Kitchen, and with it any hope of an increase in communal dining at Court; he abolished the payment of boardwages in addition to normal wages, and introduced a single salary payment for all royal servants; he reduced the size of the Household (Chamber, Stables and Household); and he made the Bedchamber more independent of the Chamber.

4. Barclay, op. cit., p. 212.

5. Barclay, op. cit., pp. 211–12, gives the names of the King's servants who followed him to France. For an incomplete list of the newly recruited servants, see Marquis de Ruvigny et Raineval, *The Jacobite Peerage* (Edinburgh, 1904), pp. 216–17. This list can be supplemented by using the list of the King's Household in 1696 (Sizergh Castle, Strickland Collection R.4), and the parish registers of Saint-Germain-en-Laye (kept at the Hôtel de Ville de Saint-Germain-en-Laye and reproduced in C.E. Lart, *Jacobite Extracts: the Parochial Records of Saint-Germain-en-Laye* (2 vols, London, 1910 and 1912)). The servants at Saint-Germain were both Anglican and Catholic. In percentage terms, the King employed twice as many Anglicans at Saint-Germain as he had employed Catholics at Whitehall.

6. The proportion of people who followed the Queen into exile was very much higher. Her Household at Saint-Germain in 1689–91 contained approximately eighty people, the great majority of whom had served her in England. (It seems, however, that only three were Anglicans.)

7. B. Saule, *Louis XIV à Saint-Germain, 1638–1682: de la naissance à la gloire* (exhibition catalogue, Saint-Germain-en-Laye, 1988).

8. Plans of the ground floor, first floor, second floor, and second-floor entresols are reproduced in the *Revue de la Bibliothèque Nationale* (Winter 1992, no. 46), pp. 6–7, 10–11. Plans of

the third floor, and the fourth floor in the pavilions, are in the BN, Cabinet des Estampes, Va. 448e and 78c.

9. H. Murray-Baillie, 'Etiquette and the Planning of State Apartments in Baroque Palaces', *Archaeologia*, 101 (1967), 169–99.

10. The Louvre, the Tuileries, and the châteaux at Versailles, Vincennes, Fontainebleau, Chambord and Compiègne all had two antechambers in the King's apartment.

11. Corp, *L'Autre Exil*, pp. 57–9.

12. T. Bruce, Earl of Ailesbury, *Memoirs*, ed. W. Buckley (London, 1890), p. 323 ff.

13. Corp, *L'Autre Exil*, pp. 58–9, 73–4.

14. It is referred to in the journal of David Nairne (National Library of Scotland MS 14266), on various occasions between 15 April 1693 and 26 June 1697. Further references to this diary will be cited as 'Nairne'.

15. Nairne, 4 June 1695; J. Guiffrey (ed.), *Compes des Bâtiments du Roi sous le Règne de Louis XIV* (*CBR*), Vol. 3 (Paris 1891), cols 1158–61, 1195; Archives Nationales, 0/1/3306, 'Journal du Garde Meuble' (20 July 1695).

16. There was no apartment above that of the King in the north-east pavilion, in part because the ceilings of the King's Bedchamber and antechamber were too high. But some small rooms were accessible via the private staircase. For James II's spiritual life at Saint-Germain, see Corp and Sanson, *Cour des Stuarts*, pp. 131–8.

17. Archives Nationales 0/1/1716, 'estat de ce qu'il est proposé . . . de payer aux ouvriers qui ont travaillé au chateau . . . de Saint Germain en Laye, suivant l'ouvrage qu'ils ont fait pendant les 2 semaines finies le samedy 17 jour octobre 1699'; *CBR*, Vol. 4 (Paris, 1894), cols 502–5, 562–4, 18 October to 15 November 1699. (There is no reference in Nairne because he was away from Saint-Germain at the time.)

18. There seems to have been one precedent for this arrangement: at Greenwich the King and Queen had apartments that progressively separated from a common Presence Chamber. (I am grateful to Simon Thurley for this information.)

19. Bibliothèque de l'Arsenal MS 3862, 3863, 3864. Extracts have been published in E. Lever, (ed.), *Mémoires du Baron de Breteuil* (Paris, 1992).

20. Archives Nationales 0/1/1716, 0/1/2004, 0/1/3306–8; *CBR*, Vols 3, 4, 5 (Paris, 1891, 1894, 1901).

21. Archives Nationales 0/1/3307, 'estat des meubles de Deuil faire pour la Cour d'Angleterre pour le Deuil du Roy d'Angleterre deffunt Jacques 2e decedé a St Germain en Laye le 16e septembre 1701, et livré . . . pendant le moi d'octobre denrier'.

22. The apartment of Princess Louise Marie contained an antechamber, a Bedchamber, and a private chapel, the last of which was decorated between 16 January and 5 June 1701. (*CBR*, Vol. 4, cols 754–9, 810). The chapel was subsequently used by James III.

23. *Mémoires du Baron de Breteuil*, pp. 268–9; BN MS Fd. Fr. 6679, 'Journal du Marquis de Sainctot'. (The visit took place on 23 November 1700.)

24. Ruvigny et Raineval, op. cit., pp. 219–23; BL, Egerton MS 2517, 'The Establishment of our Household commencing in the month of January 1709'. The 'Journal du Garde Meuble' refers to these rooms beyond the Salle des Gardes as 'l'anti-chambre du Roy' (26 February 1703), 'Grand Cabinet du Roy' (22 June 1706), and 'Grande Chambre du Roy' (28 December 1702).

25. Nairne specifically states this in his journal on 23 April 1702. But there is a letter from the Queen, written a few months later, which suggests that James III later reverted to the practice of his father: BL, Add. MS 20293, f. 57, Mary of Modena to Cardinal Gualterio, 9 August 1702.

26. The details of the French catering system are clearly explained in the article by B. Saule in *Les Tables Royales* (exhibition catalogue, Réunion des Muséees nationaux, Paris, 1994), p. 42.

27. Barclay, op. cit., p. 62. (For the abolition of communal dining in 1663, see Andrew Barclay's chapter on 'Charles II's Failed Restoration'.) The only royal servants who continued to have diet in England were the Queen's Waiters, the Maids of Honour, the Chaplains, the officials of the Greencloth, the Clerk of the Kitchen, the Master Cook, the Pages of the Backstairs, and the Yeomen of the Guard. The remaining servants were given boardwages, an additional cash payment to compensate them for the loss of diet. Boardwages had been abolished in 1685 by James II, who had given his servants a single salary.

28. The Guards at the Château de Saint-Germain were provided by the King of France. There were three types: 'Gardes du Corps', 'Gardes de la Porte', and 'Gardes de Cent Suisses'. It is not clear what catering arrangements were made for them.

29. It was generally referred to as the Gentlemen's Table, because it was not only used by the Waiters. The list of people who had diet at Saint-Germain included all those who had had it in England, (excluding the Yeomen of the Guard), and in addition the Esquires of the Body, the Gentlemen Ushers of both the Presence and Privy Chambers, the Gentlemen Waiters, the Groom of the Privy Chamber, and the Confessors, and no doubt also the Governors and Governesses of the Prince and Princess. Those who lived in the château itself, without cooking facilities, were possibly also catered for.

30. The Accatry and Scaldinghouse were never introduced; the Spicery was abolished in 1695; and the Pastry was made part of the Kitchen.

31. The Chaundry was merged with the Buttery; and the Ewry was merged with the Pantry. The Larder, the Confectionary, the Bakehouse, the Silver Scullery, the Cellar and the Woodyard remained as separate subdepartments. (The Pantry, Buttery and Cellar equated to the 'Gobelet du Roi' which, with the 'Cuisine', formed the 'Bouche du Roi'. The Confectionary and Woodyard were part of the 'Offices-Commun'. In the French system there was no separate Pastry, Bakehouse or Silver Scullery). There were (and are) no basements in the Château de Saint-Germain, except below the five corner pavilions. The south-west pavilion had been designed for the 'Cuisine de la Reine', and the basements in the other four for the 'Gobelets' of the King, Queen, Dauphin and Dauphine.

32. The south-west pavilion was the largest of the five, and eventually housed the Pantry (and Ewry), the Pastry, the Larder and the Bakehouse, as well as the Privy Kitchens.

33. The Queen had her own Pantry and Wine Cellar as well as her Privy Kitchen. The staff of the Privy Kitchens of the King and the Queen was predominantly English, with several French servants, some of whom had already worked at Whitehall. The King's Master Cook was always English; two of the Queen's three cooks were always French. There was clearly close contact with the 'Bouche du Roi' at Versailles, because some of the servants and their children at Saint-Germain married into the families of their opposite numbers at the French Court.

34. After James III's departure Mary of Modena complained about having to eat alone in public, and avoided having to do so by going to Chaillot. See M. Haile, *Queen Mary of Modena, Her Life and Letters* (London, 1905), p. 440.

35. Nairne, 8 May 1698; *HMC, Calendar of the Stuart Papers Belonging to His Majesty the King, Preserved at Windsor Castle* (*HMC, Stuart*), Vol. VI (London, 1916), p. 59, 'historical account' by Thomas Sheridan. The Prince of Wales began to eat with the King and Queen on 22 March 1699, according to Nairne: 'Ye Pce began for ye first time to dine wth ye K and Q regularly and to have no more table for himself but only for supper.'

36. Nairne, 13 December 1699; Helmut Lahrkamp (Hg.), 'Lambert Friedrich Corfey, Reise Tagebuch, 1698–1700', in *Quellen und Forschungen zur Geschichte der Stadt*, Münster, N.F. Bd 9 (Münster, 1977), p. 66: 'Den 24 September haben wir zu St Germain en Laye Mittag gehalten und den König Jacob von Engeland speisen gesehen. Das Taffelzimmer war mit grunen Sammt behangen. Er speiset recht auf sein Englisch und haben die Hunde eine grosse Libertet an seiner Taffel.'

37. BN MS Fd. Fr. 16633, 'Journal des Cérémonies' 1666–91. The 'Introducteur' was Etienne Chabenat, Seigneur de Bonneuil, and the note is dated 13 January 1689.

38. This aspect of the Court, including the plate and cutlery specially commissioned by James II in Paris during the 1690s, is discussed in detail in E. Corp, 'James II and James III in Exile: the English Royal Table in France and Italy, 1689–*c.* 1730', in *Royal and Princely Tables of Europe: Commissions and Gifts*, ed. L. d'Orey (Institu Portugués de Museus, Lisbon, 1999), pp. 112–19.

39. Brotherton Library, University of Leeds, MS Dep. 1984/3/5, Inventory of James II, 1703.

40. Mary of Modena also made a collection of Imari and Kakiemon porcelain, some of which still exists. It is referred to by Nairne on 12 December 1704: 'I write a memoire for the Queens china ware.'

41. Dishes were passed from the Pages to the Grooms, who passed them to the Gentlemen, who presented them to the King. The Gentlemen of the Bedchamber acted as Cupbearer and Carver, and the Groom of the Bedchamber as Sewer.

42. N. Hooke, *Correspondence, 1703–1707* (2 vols, London, 1870–1), Vol. 1, p. 194, Perth to Hooke, 8 June 1705. When James III embarked on the attempted invasion of Scotland in 1708, we are told that 'la table du Roy' had 'douze Couverts, magnifiquement servie'. (Claude, comte de Forbin, *Mémoires* (Paris, 1729), Vol. 2, p. 325.

43. There were two 'Introducteurs': Breteuil succeeded Bonneuil in 1698. For Bonneuil see above, n. 37; for Sainctot see n. 23; for Breteuil see n. 19. See also the accounts of the Duc de Saint-Simon and the Marquis de Dangeau in *Mémoires de Saint-Simon*, new edition by A. de Boilisle (39 vols, Paris, 1879–1927), Vol. 9, pp. 296–7 and Vol. 12, p. 439.

44. *Mémoires de Saint-Simon*, Vol. 22, pp. 12–13. Cf. *Mémoires du Baron de Breteuil*, p. 245.

45. Bibliothèque de l'Arsenal MS 3862, pp. 155–6. ('Mémoires de Breteuil'.)

46. Ibid., p. 156.

47. BN, MS Fd. Fr. 6679, ff. 667–72, 'Journal de Sainctot'; Bibliothèque de l'Arsenal MS 3862, pp. 157–8, 'Mémoires de Breteuil'.

48. BN, MS Fd. Fr. 16633, 10–11 January 1689, 'Journal de Bonneuil'; B.N. MS n.a.fr. H.751, 'Journal de Dangeau', 9–10 January 1689; *Mémoires de Saint-Simon*, Vol. 9, p. 270.

49. A. Strickland, *Lives of the Queens of England* (London, 1846), Vol. 9, pp. 294–5 for 1689, and pp. 352–3 for 1695. For Lady Almond, see BN, MS Fd. Fr. 6679, ff. 1–5, 'Journal de Sainctot';

Nairne, 22–3 April 1698; and *Mémoires de Saint-Simon*, Vol. 11, pp. 92–3: 'C'était une grande femme très bien faite, et de beaucoup d'esprit, dont notre cour s'accommodoit extrêmement. La reine l'aimoit tant, qu'elle lui avoit fait donner un tabouret de grâce.'

50. Dukedoms were given to Tyrconnell in 1689, Melfort in 1694 (but kept secret until 1705), and Perth in 1701. The Duke of Berwick married twice, in 1695 and 1700; his brother the Duke of Albemarle married in 1700. (The widowed Duchess of Albemarle married the eldest son of the Duke of Melfort in 1707.) See the *Mémoires de Saint-Simon*, Vol. 12, p. 451: 'Melfort . . . et sa femme eurent en France le rang et les honneurs de duc et de duchessse comme tous ceux qui l'avoient été faits à Saint-Germain, ou qui y étoient arrivés tels.'

51. They included Lady Sophia Bulkeley, the Countess of Middleton, Lady Charlotte Talbot, and the Countess of Clare.

52. BN, MS Fd. Fr. 6679, ff. 598–9, Sainctot; and *Mémoires du Baron de Breteuil*, pp. 260–2, both describing the visit of James II and Mary of Modena on 17 November 1700.

53. Corp, *L'Autre Exil*, pp. 63–7; Haile, op. cit., pp. 317, 326, 341, 426.

54. The best example is probably Lord Caryll.

55. Haile, op. cit., p. 372, Rizzini to the Duke of Modena, May 1703.

56. The money spent on the Château de Saint-Germain is shown in *CBR*, Vols 3, 4, 5. Between 1689 and 1695 the expenditure on Saint-Germain was about the same as on the Château de Fontainebleau (Vol. 3, cols 1208–9); from 1696 to 1705 it was rather more than half the expenditure on Fontainebleau (Vol. 4, cols 1256–7); and between 1706 and 1715 it rose again to be very much more than half (Vol. 5, cols 943–4).

57. The number and amount of the pensions at Saint-Germain had to be substantially reduced in the spring of 1695, in order that the salaries of the Household should remain unaffected. Because a large number of the people receiving pensions had been Protestants, this retrenchment gave rise to the legend that Protestants were not welcome at Saint-Germain. (Nairne, 9 March and 11 May 1695; Bibliothèque de l'Arsenal MS 10533, Stafford to Bromfield, 10 August 1695; A.C. Biscoe, *The Earl of Middleton* (London, 1876), p. 204, Middleton to Bruce, 23 December 1695). See also E. Corp, *James II and Toleration: The Years in Exile at Saint-Germain-en-Laye*, Royal Stuart Society Paper LI, 1997.

58. Corp and Sanson, *Cour des Stuarts*.

14

THE VICEREGAL COURT IN LATER SEVENTEENTH-CENTURY IRELAND

Toby Barnard

Dublin Castle housed the local head of the Irish government, and some of the most important departments of state. The castle also served as citadel, arsenal and gaol. The former functions made it resemble Whitehall until 1688; the latter, the Tower of London. Because of its several uses the castle offered a tempting target to those discontented either with the current viceroy or with the English rule and ruler whom he represented. So it was that an alleged conspiracy to capture the castle inaugurated the long war of the 1640s.[1] In 1647, Charles I's Lord Lieutenant, Ormonde, ensured lasting English control over Ireland by rendering up the stronghold to commissioners sent from the Westminster Parliament.[2] In 1659 the taking of the bastion precipitated the collapse of the military rule improvised after the fall of the Cromwellian Protectorate.[3] Again, in 1663, aggrieved Protestants planned a coup, closely modelled on that late in 1659, in which the centrepiece would be the seizure of the castle.[4] At other times, the castle, so assertive and yet so rickety, a symbol and an affront, tempted the disaffected to scheme how best they might take it.

The castle, sited on rising ground south of the River Liffey and close to Dublin's two main religious foundations, St Patrick's and Christ Church cathedrals, suffered from the benefits and problems of centrality. As Dublin started to grow rapidly, from the 1630s, the building's insecurity and cramped site proved to be drawbacks.[5] Despite these inconveniences, the viceregal court did not withdraw from the city, even to the extent that Whitehall was separated from the city of London, let alone Versailles from Paris. Residential and commercial Dublin hemmed in the castle. From time to time terrified Dubliners fled lest the store of gunpowder be detonated by one of the frequent fires. However, the business generated by the establishment and its inmates compensated for any attendant risks.[6] But if, for the most part, the citizens were happy to keep the court in their midst, successive viceroys fretted at their cramped quarters. Moreover, as the work of the government expanded and diversified, the difficulties of accommodating it within the confines of the castle increased. In turn, the meetings of Council and Parliament were removed to nearby premises.[7] Also, even before Wentworth landed, the deputies themselves required higher standards of comfort and order. In the 1620s, Viscount Falkland created a gallery which first introduced a degree of classical symmetry into the ramshackle muddle.[8] In the 1650s the discomfort of Henry Cromwell was alleviated by purchasing for his use a part of the adjacent Cork House.[9] After 1660, the feeling that the power of the restored monarch should be reflected in the new dignity surrounding the Irish viceroy stimulated numerous proposals for modernising and enlarging the castle. Architectural pundits, from the amateurs Petty, Orrery and Sir Francis Brewster to the adepts Westley, Robinson and Burgh, pontificated about improvements in the classical idiom.[10]

Yet, though the Lord Lieutenant was short of space, his administration was shorter still of cash. Increasingly success or failure in the government of Ireland was judged by the viceroy's ability to convert the Irish deficit into a surplus. In this spirit, during the 1670s money was creamed from the Irish customs to help Charles II and Hugh May to engage in dynastic triumphalism at a revamped Windsor Castle, but little could be spared for Dublin Castle.[11] Serious fires necessitated repairs. One, in 1671, was said to have been started by a rat carrying a lighted candle;[12] a second, in 1681, immolated an elephant and its attendant in their makeshift timber shelter;[13] a third allowed the Lord Deputy, Ormonde's son, Arran, to engage in the same heroics as Charles II had earlier displayed during the Great Fire of London.[14] Immediately after the last Arran reported, 'there are a hundred projectors at work already about framing proposals'.[15] Most of the little money which could be spared for architectural display in Dublin was devoted to another project, the royal hospital of Kilmainham. Its completion gave the city a series of impressive baroque interiors and enabled the stores of gunpowder to be removed from a tower of the castle.[16]

Later seventeenth-century Lords Lieutenant, being political realists, rather than undermine their shaky political positions by nagging for a new castle, pressed for a modest haven away from the noise and disease of the city. Strafford in the 1630s had first seriously argued for a rural retreat, and began to build one, at Jigginstown, some twenty miles from Dublin. The remains testify alike to the scale of his ambition and the novelty of the style for, throughout the eighteenth century, Jigginstown was attributed to Inigo Jones. Wentworth persistently denied any wish for self-aggrandisement, and so explained the pretensions of Jigginstown as appropriate to its intended function as a residence for the King, not for himself.[17] Astute successors repeated this argument. Accordingly, in the 1670s Essex recommended possible country seats as habitations suitable for the Governor if, as was frequently rumoured, Charles II commissioned his son, Monmouth, as Irish viceroy.[18] Such projects came to little. The abandoned shell of Jigginstown decayed, its fittings cannibalised for other houses: at best an inspiration for Anglo-Irish virtuosi.[19] Meanwhile, jaded Lords Lieutenant refreshed themselves at the hunting lodge of the Phoenix, only two or three miles from Dublin Castle on the north bank of the Liffey. This retreat, enlarged in the 1660s, boasted the sizeable complement (for Ireland) of thirty hearths. A second refuge at Chapelizod, further from Dublin but still on the river, was increasingly favoured.[20] Although its furnishings and gardens were improved, Chapelizod remained a modest country house rather than a sumptuous royal palace. In the 1660s taxed on only thirteen hearths, even in the 1730s it could still be dismissed by a visitor, who sneered, 'the house belongs to the government. It makes no figure at all, being a very plain single brick house, but pleasantly situate.'[21] Certainly this viceregal box could not compare in scale or grandeur with the residences of local notables at Carton and Castletown.

Ambitious plans to rehouse the Dublin government were frustrated by lack of funds, political uncertainty, and the ambiguous and awkwardly dependent position of the kingdom of Ireland on England, and so of the Dublin court on London. Wentworth believed that this dependency might be deepened, and the Irish elites more thoroughly assimilated to English ways, through improvements in the physical setting of the Irish administration. Ormonde, in some senses Wentworth's ideological heir, thought similarly. Back in 1633, Wentworth, fresh from England, worried as he contemplated the casual arrangements in Dublin Castle lest 'the king's greatness, albeit but in the type, become less reverenced than truly it ought to be'. To remedy these defects he sought to improve the setting and ceremonial of the viceregal establishment.[22] Ormonde, three times viceroy between 1643 and 1685, resumed this endeavour to invest the office with greater majesty. In the 1660s observers noted that his 'court is small, but the lodgings although very ancient are very handsome, and worthy of being the dwelling of a viceroy', and that he maintained 'a fine court and a suite altogether royal'.[23] Ormonde, in this yearning for physical splendour, may have continued the tradition of Wentworth. However, his appointment, and that of his grandson, 2nd Duke of Ormonde (Lord Lieutenant in 1703–7 and 1710–13) and the Catholic Tyrconnell (between 1687 and 1690), marked a regression to the older practice of entrusting Ireland's government to a leading Irish nobleman.[24]

For the Dukes of Ormonde, the lack of a spacious viceregal retreat, even of an adequate Dublin palace, mattered little since they used their own properties, particularly Kilkenny Castle, but occasionally Dunmore, Carrick and Clonmel, for sport, entertaining and official duties. Dublin Castle was certainly invested with new grandeur. Two chairs of state now stood in the Presence Chamber. Into their construction went 56 yd of branched velvet and 525 oz of gold and silver fringe. One was embroidered with the sovereign's arms, badges and supporters. These thrones proclaimed the monarch, on whose behalf Ormonde ruled Ireland; they had been paid for by, and so belonged to, the State. But much else in the castle, even in the Presence Chamber, was Ormonde's: the gilded sconces which glittered on the walls, the tables, the upholstered chairs and woven hangings.[25] To a bewildering extent the Ormondes regularly swopped their own props between their mansions and the castle.[26] Furthermore, by holding court frequently at their own Kilkenny – itself reordered and embellished after 1660 – they irretrievably confused the private and public.[27] The state maintained by the

Ormondes set a standard by which their successors from England were judged. For the stranger pitched into life at the castle and without an Irish country house to which to retire, this amplitude was difficult to emulate.[28] The jaundiced newcomer remarked on the similarities between the castle and a prison (for which purpose it was still used) rather than its palatial qualities. The Robarteses, who had succeeded the Ormondes in 1669, at a loss how best to manage, were rescued by the Duchess of Ormonde. The latter, with unwonted generosity, offered her surplus chattels at a special price.[29]

The Ormondes occupied a level of their own in later seventeenth-century Ireland. Indisputably among *les grands*, they equalled and mingled with the ducal families of England, like the Beauforts, Somersets and Newcastles. Ireland could boast only one other family of comparable wealth – with rentals worth perhaps £25,000 annually – the Boyles. The members of that dynasty lacked any long or special intimacy with the soverign.[30] Ormonde, in contrast, Charles II's companion in exile, Ireland's sole duke and, from 1682, an English duke as well, could claim kinship through the Boleyns with Queen Elizabeth and attended the restored king as Lord Steward. Had Ormonde not been an instinctive loyalist, the Stuarts might have hesitated to entrust so much power to one so well equipped to play the overmighty subject. As it was the Ormondes threw their great territorial influence, their considerable (but not considerable enough) wealth and their credit into the service of the English Crown in Ireland. This loyalty, based in part on a personal fealty, culminated in the 2nd Duke following the Stuarts into exile in 1715.

The Ormondes spent recklessly and ran heavily into debt.[31] Since many of these expenses had been incurred on behalf of the Stuart monarchy, they recompensed themselves as best they could. Yet, as the Ormondes' predecessors and successors also discovered, the scope for personal enrichment from the Lord Lieutenancy was disappointing. Many of the best posts in Ireland, as judges, bishops and government functionaries, were reserved to the Crown, so that the viceroy, if he wished to influence their distribution, had to compete against, and was often outmanoeuvred by, English courtiers.[32] By the 1720s, it has been calculated, about 150 positions remained in the viceroy's gift.[33] For Ormonde's numerous dependants after 1660 commissions in the army offered welcome out relief. However, by the 1680s these, together with the most attractive jobs in the Irish revenue, were dispensed from London.[34] The Ormondes, therefore, tended to gratify their large and greedy affinity with offices in the lower reaches of government or in their palatinate, with preferential treatment in the disposal of lands and with unofficial ploys, such as transferring some of their personal servants to the State's payroll. The limited opportunities to profit from the viceroyalty contrast sharply with Dr Gerald Aylmer's findings about the ready cash for which, as Lord Steward, Ormonde sold places in the royal Household in England.[35]

The viceroyalties of the Ormondes exemplified a style of government which, by the early eighteenth century, looked anachronistic if not dangerous. Always popular among a circle of allies and clients, the Ormondes enlarged their following through ample hospitality and an odd mixture of hauteur and bonhomie.[36] In England, the economical nature of their government for long outweighed any risk of Irish particularism until, after 1715, the Butlers acquired the forbidden allure of Stuart allegiance and Irishness. Even before this, a sequence of episodes between 1685 and the 1720s reminded English politicians of the perils posed by a waywardly assertive Ireland. The need for Lords Lieutenant docile to London was better appreciated. By the early eighteenth century, Ireland, apparently pacified and seemingly anglicised, no longer needed a royal deputy capable of leading armies into battle against the rebellious Irish, of energetically touring the island in order to advertise the strength of English authority and the superiority of English culture, or indeed of intimidating the troublesome who were summoned before the Dublin Council.

After the demise of the 2nd Duke of Ormonde, the Lord Lieutenant typically camped out in Dublin Castle for a few months while Parliament was sitting and, if he ventured into the hinterland, did so for social rather than strategic purposes.[37] The chief duty of the viceroy was now to identify and organise the politicians who undertook to manage the business of Parliament, and so to guarantee the passage of money bills and other essential measures. As early as the 1660s, Ormonde, disdaining 'those small arts of familiarity and caressing which the men of many designs could not be without', relied on others to guide Parliament.[38] By the 1690s, when Parliament became a regular event in the Dublin calendar, viceroys had either to devote themselves more wholeheartedly to this drudgery or find surrogates who would do so.[39] Even the 2nd Duke of Ormonde deployed social and political arts to convert the Butler affinity into a larger political interest, markedly Tory in outlook, through which government and parliamentary measures could be accomplished.[40]

These regular meetings of Parliament altered the social as well as political tasks of the viceroy. Already many from provincial Ireland gravitated towards Dublin; the sessions brought more, and obliged some to stay longer. The presence in the capital of so many who governed in the localities afforded an expansive viceroy and vicereine wonderful opportunities to set or popularise fashions, which might have political, economic or cultural implications, and all of which could hasten the anglicisation of Ireland. But too often, an English Lord Lieutenant, charged with the implementation of unpopular courses, unfamiliar with or insensitive to local worries, strained the already tense relationship with England. Since Lords Lieutenant were seldom empowered to initiate new or alter old policies and, absent from London, lacked great influence over the formulation of measures for Ireland, they contented themselves with more trivial achievements. The viceroy and vicereine, by buying or wearing only Irish manufactures, spread the craze, in turn, for Irish frieze, linen and poplin.[41] Wentworth and his successors, interested in adorning Dublin and its environs with classical buildings, invested architecture with ideological and anglicising intentions, since it would substitute for the notoriously primitive habitations of the Irish those which met international standards.[42] In the 1670s, the Lord Lieutenant, Essex, eagerly attended horse races. He justified this pastime, not as a simple escape from unhealthy Dublin, but as a way of meeting those who counted in local society. Furthermore, by presenting valuable prizes in the King's name, he hoped to promote selective breeding and so improve the bloodlines of Irish horses to the permanent benefit of Irish agriculture.[43]

Until the mid-eighteenth century when Dublin Castle was ambitiously enlarged, its physical constriction and dereliction aptly reflected its tangential place even in Irish Protestant society.[44] Successive English monarchs and ministers stinted on what was allowed to the royal deputy in Dublin. Despite the protests of the perceptive, such as Wentworth and Ormonde, that this parsimony lessened the regard in which the monarchy itself was held and that the viceregal establishment, if properly housed and regulated, could be the physical and symbolic embodiment of the constitutional tie between the two kingdoms, the Dublin court was never systematically developed as a means to bind the Irish elites to England. This half-heartedness accurately reflected the ambiguous dealings between the two kingdoms. Proximity, assisted by the well-established and continued connections of many in Ireland with their kinsmen and compatriots in England, enabled the ambitious, the angry and the idle to frequent London.[45] The Governor in Dublin wielded too little power over policy or patronage to draw many to the capital. Even that valuable adjunct of viceroyalty, the right to dub knights, promiscuously bestowed in the seventeenth century, was very sparingly exploited in the eighteenth.[46] Those who could resorted instead to the Court and ministry in London. Even in the matters of fashion and taste, the easy and regular traffic between Ireland and England meant that novelties were lifted directly from the metropolis rather than being introduced by visiting notables. At best eighteenth-century viceroys, by staging smart entertainments at the castle, allowed the modish to show off the elegant accomplishments and accoutrements that they had picked up for themselves in London.[47]

In the attenuated Dublin court few attractive posts fell to locals. Instead, English noblemen rewarded their own connections.[48] English clergymen imported as chaplains to the viceroy often stayed on as bishops: a method of conforming the Church of Ireland more closely to English norms which did little to endear Anglicanism to Irish Protestants.[49] A few who had come first in the viceregal retinue might settle: for example, Jeremy Hall and the Carpenters who had arrived with Wentworth.[50] Cultivated aides, such as Andrew Fountaine who had accompanied Lord Pembroke in 1707, or Joseph Addison who acted as secretary to Wharton, struck up friendships with the congenial and impressionable in Dublin which might outlast their own tours of duty in Ireland and allow for a continuing exchange of ideas.[51] Others in the castle set, such as Sir Cyril Wyche and Sir William Ellis, successively secretary to the Lord Lieutenant between 1676 and 1685, grasped the opportunities to profit from property speculation.[52] In cases such as those of Wyche and Ellis it is difficult to distinguish between followers of the viceroy and the larger group which was colonising the upper levels of the Irish administration.

Energetic or enlightened Lords Lieutenant assisted anglicisation through patronising institutions like the short-lived Court of Wards or Dublin University and encouraging promising initiatives such as the Dublin Philosophical Society in the 1680s and 1690s or the Dublin Society of the 1730s.[53] Such interest, while welcomed in the rarefied Irish circles which looked to the castle for a lead, contributed little to the undoubted assimilation of Ireland to English rule which occurred during the seventeenth and eighteenth centuries. Even within Dublin itself, the chief redoubt of English and Protestant influence in the island, the viceregal establishment occupied an uncertain place. A viceroy pleased the gossipy and ever critical Dubliners only when he listened to and advanced local favourites, shopped in the city, hired menials from Dublin's inhabitants, and awarded to nearby tradespeople the lucrative contracts to supply the castle's tables with cream, milk, samphire, sturgeon, and black and white puddings.[54] So, in the course of the sixteenth to eighteenth centuries, the Dublin court, having expanded from a rudimentary noble household into a blaze of ducal prodigality under the Ormondes, contracted again into a makeshift court preoccupied with the minutiae of parliamentary bills, where best to buy sausages and how most speedily to return to England.

Notes

1. *The Copie of a Letter Sent from the Lord Chiefe Justices and Privie Councellors in Ireland . . . Together with a Discoverie of the Plot* (London, 1641).

2. *Articles of Agreement Between the Lord Marq. of Ormond and Arthur Annesley . . .* (London, 1647).

3. Staffordshire County Record Office, Bridgeman MS, D (W) 1778/1/i/75; [John Bridges], *A Perfect Narrative of the Grounds & Reasons Moving Some Officers of the Army in Ireland to the Securing of the Castle of Dublin for the Parliament, on the 13 of December Last* (London, 1660).

4. Trinity College, Dublin, MS 844, ff. 223–4; *The Horrid Conspiracie of Such Impenitent Traytors as Intended a New Rebellion* (London, 1663).

5. N.T. Burke, 'Dublin 1600–1800: a study in urban morphogenesis' (unpublished Ph.D. thesis, Trinity College Dublin, 1972); R. Gillespie, 'Describing Dublin: Francis Place's visit, 1698–99', in A. Dalsimer (ed.), *Visualizing Ireland; National Identity and the Pictorial Tradition* (Winchester, Mass., 1993), pp. 99–118; C.L. Falkiner, *Illustrations of Irish History and Topography* (London, 1904), pp. 380–1; W. Knowler (ed.), *The Earl of Strafforde's Letters and Dispatches* (2 vols, London, 1739), Vol. I, pp. 131–2.

6. J. Petty to W. Petty, 20 May 1671 (Petty Papers 13/3, formerly at Bowood, now in the British Library); W. Petty to Lady Petty (ibid., 5/126); R. Curtis to Jane Bonnell, 17 April 1711 (National Library of Ireland, PC 435); HMC, *Ormonde MSS*, New Series, VII, p. 221.

7. J.T. Gilbert, *An Account of the Parliament House, Dublin* (Dublin, 1896), pp. 4–8; J.L.J. Hughes, 'Dublin Castle in the Seventeenth Century: a Topographical Reconstruction', *Dublin Historical Record*, II (1940), 87, 90.

8. Knowler, *Strafforde's Letters*, Vol. I, pp. 102, 131.

9. Cambridgeshire County Record Office, Cromwell-Bush MS, 731 dd Bush, no. 31; Chatsworth House, Derbyshire, Lismore MS, diary of 2nd Earl of Cork, 23 April 1657, 9 February 1657[8], 15 January 1660[1].

10. R. Loeber, 'The Rebuilding of Dublin Castle: Thirty Critical Years, 1661–1690', *Studies*, LXIX (1980), 45–68; R. Loeber, *A Biographical Dictionary of Architects in Ireland 1600–1720* (London, 1981), pp. 26, 34–5, 84, 94, 112–13.

11. Colvin, *King's Works*, Vol. V, *1660–1782*, pp. 312, 322–8.

12. Petty Papers, 13/3; *CSPD, 1671*, p. 256.

13. W. Ellis to C. Wyche, 2 June 1681 (National Archives, Dublin, Wyche MS, 2nd Series, 141); A. Mullen, *An Anatomical Account of the Elephant Accidentally Burnt in Dublin on Fryday June 17 in the year 1681* (London, 1682).

14. Petty Papers, 5/126; HMC, *Ormonde MSS*, New Series, VII, pp. 209–10, 220–1.

15. HMC, *Ormonde MSS*, New Series, VII, p. 210.

16. Ibid., p. 225; Loeber, 'Rebuilding Dublin Castle', pp. 45–6; E. McParland, *The Royal Hospital Kilmainham, Co. Dublin*, reproduced from *Country Life*, 9 and 16 May 1985.

17. M. Craig, 'New Light on Jigginstown', *Ulster Journal of Archaeology*, XXXIII (1970), 107–10; H.G. Leask, 'Early Seventeenth-century Houses in Ireland', in E.M. Jope (ed.), *Studies in Building History* (London, 1961), p. 245.

18. Bodl. Lib., Add. MS C.34, f. 90v.

19. The architect Earl of Burlington commissioned one of the surviving eighteenth-century surveys of the ruins. By this date much of the adjacent land belonged to Thomas Burgh, a leading Irish architect.

20. G.S. Cary, 'Hearth Money Roll for County Dublin, 1664', *Journal of the Kildare Archaeological Society*, XI (1930–3), 456; M. Craig, *Dublin 1660–1860* (London, 1952), pp. 13–16; Chatsworth, Cork's diary, 6 and 10 August 1655.

21. Cary, 'Hearth Money Roll', p. 439; S. Markahm, *John Loveday of Caversham 1711–1789: the Life and Tours of an Eighteenth-century Onlooker* (Salisbury, 1984), p. 161; T.C. Barnard, 'Gardening, Diet and "Improvement" in Later Seventeenth-century Ireland', *Journal of Garden History*, X (1990), 79.

22. Knowler, *Strafforde's Letters*, Vol. I, pp. 200–1. See also BL, Add. MS 29587, ff. 17–22, 24–5. Dr David Howarth, of the University of Edinburgh, is studying Wentworth's architectural activities. I am fortunate in having heard a paper which he delivered on this subject in Oxford in November 1994 and for discussions with him.

23. Falkiner, *Illustrations*, pp. 24, 413.

24. T.C. Barnard, 'Scotland and Ireland in the Later Stewart Monarchy', in S.G. Ellis and S. Barber (eds), *Conquest and Union: Fashioning a British State 1485–1725* (London, 1995), p. 258.

25. They cost £447. Bodl. Lib., Carte MS 53, f. 134; National Library of Ireland (NLI), MS 2554.

26. NLI, MS 2522, ff. 82–119; 2527/2; HMC, *Ormonde MS*, New Series, III, pp. 448, 454.

27. NLI, MS 2522/12, 2527/1 and 2; 2554/6; J. Fenlon, 'The Ormonde Inventories: a State Apartment at Kilkenny Castle', in A. Bernelle (ed.), *Decantations: a Tribute to Maurice Craig* (Dublin, 1992), pp. 47–59. Fenlon, 'Episodes of Magnificence: the Material Worlds of the Dukes of Ormonde', in T.C. Barnard and J. Fenlon (eds), *The Dukes of Ormonde 1610–1715* (Woodbridge, 1999), pp. 137–59.

28. PRO, SP30/24/50, 23; PRONI, D638/14/39 and 40; NA, Wyche MS, 2nd Series, p. 142; Royal Irish Academy, MSS 24 G 4/42, 24 H 22; Bodl. Lib., Clarendon MS 88, ff. 171–80.

29. HMC, *Ormonde MSS*, New Series, III, pp. 443–4, 445.

30. T.C. Barnard, 'Land and the Limits of Loyalty: the Second Earl of Cork and First Earl of Burlington (1612–98)', in T.C. Barnard and J. Clark (eds), *Lord Burlington: Architecture, Art and Life* (London, 1995), pp. 167–99.

31. For varied estimates of the Ormondes' debts: G.E. Aylmer, 'The First Duke of Ormonde as patron and administrator', in Barnard and Fenlon (eds), *Dukes of Ormonde*, pp. 118–19; T.C. Barnard, 'The Protestant Interest, 1641–1660', in J. Ohlmeyer (ed.), *From Independence to Occupation: Ireland 1640–1660* (Cambridge, 1995), p. 227; T. Power, *Land, Politics and Society in Eighteenth-century Tipperary* (Oxford, 1993), pp. 76–8.

32. T.C. Barnard, *Cromwellian Ireland; English Government and Reform in Ireland 1649–1660* (Oxford, 1975), p. 21, n. 21; Barnard, 'Scotland and Ireland in the Later Stewart Monarchy', pp. 254–7; R.T. Dunlop, *Ireland under the Commonwealth* (2 vols, Manchester, 1913), Vol. II, p. 442.

33. PRO, SP63/371/75–80; P.S. McNally, 'Patronage and Politics in Ireland, 1714 to 1727' (unpublished Ph.D. thesis, Queen's University, Belfast, 1992), p. 23.

34. Barnard, 'Scotland and Ireland under the Later Stewart Monarchy', pp. 269, 272; J. Childs, *The Army of Charles II* (London, 1976), pp. 207–9; J. Childs, *The Army, James II and the Glorious Revolution* (Manchester, 1980), pp. 58–76; S. Egan, 'Finance and the Government of Ireland, 1660–1688' (2 vols, unpublished Ph.D. thesis, Trinity College Dublin, 1983), Vol. II, pp. 118–32, 145–79, 199–207; P. Kelly, 'Ireland and the Glorious Revolution: from Kingdom to Colony', in R.A. Beddard (ed.), *The Revolutions of 1688* (Oxford, 1991), p. 167.

35. Bodl. Lib., Carte MS 59, ff. 110–13v, 121–2; Aylmer, 'Ormonde as patron and administrator', in Barnard and Fenlon (eds), *Dukes of Ormonde*, pp. 119–20.

36. Pearse Street Public Library, Dublin, Gilbert MS 207, pp. 2–4, 34–7; Barnard, 'The Protestant Interest'.

37. D.W. Hayton, 'Ireland and the English ministers, 1707–16' (unpublished Oxford D.Phil. thesis, 1975), ch. 6; T. Gogarty (ed.), *Council Book of the Corporation of Drogheda*. I. *1649–1734* (Drogheda, 1915), pp. 289, 375; NLI, MS 2714, pp. 134–5; PRO, SP63/363/373, 384, 393; J. Evelyn, Jr. to J. Evelyn, Sr., 29 May 1693 (Christ Church, Evelyn Letters, f. 660).

38. Pearse Street Public Library, Gilbert MS 207, p. 37.

39. D.W. Hayton, 'The Beginnings of the "Undertaker System"', in T. Bartlett and D.W. Hayton (eds), *Penal Era and Golden Age: Essays in Irish History 1690–1800* (Belfast, 1979), pp. 32–54; Hayton, 'Walpole and Ireland', in J. Black (ed.), *Britain in the Age of Walpole* (London, 1984), pp. 95–119.

40. BL, Add. MSS 38150, f. 127; 38155, f. 27; 38157, f. 85; PRO, SP63/359/375; 63/360/265; 63/363/252; 63/364/13; 63/365/98; BL, Loan 37/8; NLI, MS 2548; Hayton, 'Ireland and the English Ministers', pp. 155–7, 167, 171.

41. Kent Archives Office, Maidstone, Sackville MSS, U269, C18/6; PRO, C110/46/729; M. Dunlevy, 'Samuel Madden and the Scheme for the Encouragement of Useful Manufactures', in Bernelle, *Decantations*, pp. 21–8.

42. Knowler, *Strafforde's Letters*, Vol. I, pp. 131–2; Vol. II, pp. 105–6; T.C. Barnard, 'The Political, Material and Mental Culture of the Cork Settlers, *c.* 1650–1700', in P. O'Flanagan and N.G. Buttimer (eds), *Cork: History and Society* (Dublin, 1993), pp. 309–10.

43. Bodl. Lib., Add. MS C.34, f. 81; NA, Wyche MS, 1/1/38; M.3070; Warwickshire County Record Office, Newdegate MSS, Cr 136/ B 285, B 286; W. Temple, 'An Essay upon the Advancement of Trade in Ireland . . . 22 July 1673', in W. Temple, *Miscellanea* (London, 1980), pp. 134–5.

44. Craig, *Dublin*, pp. 164–7.

45. Barnard, 'The Protestant Interest'; J.G. McCoy, 'Local Political Culture in the Hanoverian Empire: the Case of Ireland 1714–60' (unpublished D.Phil. thesis, Oxford, 1993), p. 15.

46. W.A. Shaw, *The Knights of England* (2 vols, London, 1906), Vol. II, *passim*, but esp. pp. 285, 286, 288, 289, 291, 292.

47. BL, Add. MS 38154, f. 154; PRO, C.110/46/404, 414, 470–1, 496, 916; R. Howard to H. Howard, 6 January 1731[2] (NLI, PC227); A. Crookshank and D. Fitzgerald, Knight of Glin, *The Painters of Ireland,* c. *1660–1920* (London, 1978), pp. 60–1.

48. NLI, Inchiquin MSS, no. 983; NA, Wyche MS, 2nd Series, p. 161.

49. J. Falvey, 'The Church of Ireland Episcopate in the Eighteenth Century: an Overview', *Eighteenth-Century Ireland*, VIII (1993), 110; Hayton, 'Ireland and the English Minister's', p. 263; McNally, 'Patronage and Politics', pp. 145–8.

50. PRO, PROB 11/405/100; Barnard, 'Cork Settlers', pp. 340–2; Barnard, *Cromwellian Ireland*, pp. 213–14; R. Lascelles, *Liber munerum publicorum Hiberniae* (2 vols, London, 1824–30), Vol. II, pp. 69, 86–7; E. Wilson, 'Dr Jeremiah Hall and his Charities', *Transactions of the Halifax Antiquarian Society* (1956), pp. 1–10.

51. R. Howard to H. Howard, 15 July 1707?, 18 September 1707; H. Howard to R. Howard, 21 May 1726 (NLI, PC227); J. Clark, '"Lord Burlington is here"', in Barnard and Clark, *Burlington*, pp. 251, 270, 285.

52. NA, Wyche MSS, 1/1/22, 35, 38; 2nd Series, pp. 141, 142, 158, 160; Lascelles, *Liber munerum publicorum Hiberniae*, Vol. II, pp. 104, 112, 133, 136.

53. R. Howard to H. Howard, 18 September 1707 (NLI, PC227); N.L.I., MS 2493/383; Barnard, *Cromwellian Ireland*, pp. 198–212; T.C. Barnard, 'The Purchase of Archbishop Ussher's Library in 1657', *Long Room*, Bulletin of the Friends of the Library, Trinity College, Dublin, 4 (1971), 9–14; H.F. Berry, *A History of the Royal Dublin Society* (London, 1915), p. 13; K.T. Hoppen, *The Common Scientist in the Seventeenth Century: a Study of the Dublin Philosophical Society* (London, 1970), pp. 97–8, 175, 192–3; M. Pollard and S. Ó'Seanóir, '"A Great Deal of Good Verse": Commencement Entertainments in the 1680s', *Hermathena*, CXXX, CXXXI (1981), 12–13; V. Treadwell, 'The Irish Court of Wards under James I', *Irish Historical Studies*, XII (1960), 1–27.

54. J. Evelyn, Jr. to J. Evelyn, Sr., 14 January 1692[3], 5 May 1694, 15 November 1694 (Christ Church, Oxford, Evelyn Letters, ff. 657, 667v, 669); Royal Irish Academy, MS 24 H 22; BL, Add. MS 21122, f. 36v; R. Howard to H. Howard, 15 July 1707?, 25 April 1730, 12 October 1731, 2 November 1731, 23 December 1731, 22 April 1732.

15

'From Thames to Tweed Departed': the Court of James, Duke of York in Scotland, 1679–82

Hugh Ouston

When Charles II's brother James was sent to Scotland in October 1679 to remove him from the Exclusionist Parliament in London, he created the first royal court at Holyrood Palace, outside Edinburgh, for forty-six years and only the third since the departure of his grandfather James VI in 1603. This fact was in itself the most important feature of that Court. It can largely account for answers to the most significant questions about James's Court in exile: what were its purposes? What was its nature? How effective was it?

For running through the way that James used the Court in Holyrood to deal with the exigencies of the political circumstances in which he found himself was the theme of loyalty to the establishment and the Stuart monarchy. The Court in Edinburgh between 1679 and 1682 was an instrument of policy, a policy which was an important factor in enabling the Stuart brothers to weather the Exclusion crisis and regain, albeit temporarily, the political initiative. James was not just pushed out of London to get him away from Shaftesbury and his Bills; he was pulled to Edinburgh by the need to ensure Scottish loyalty and the advantages to be had from setting up a supplementary power base and proving that he could run part of his brother's dominions without threatening the establishment. This chapter will look at the role of the Court at Holyrood in this process.

James had already spent the summer of 1679 in exile, in Brussels.[1] His return in September was generally accepted and when he went abroad again in the autumn he could look to a growing band of personal supporters. James wanted to stay in London, using his wife's illness as an excuse, but was encouraged by Charles to go to Scotland, as a compromise destination where his work might prove a useful foundation for any strategy Charles would wish to develop against Exclusion.

James left London on 27 October and travelled overland, finding mixed support among the aristocracy of the shires he passed through. He reached Scotland on 24 November. He returned to London in late February 1680 but the long, hot political summer persuaded him to leave again on 20 October, pessimistic about his chances of succession. With the rejection by the Lords of the Exclusion Bill on 15 November and the dissolution of Parliament in the new year, the royal counter-attack began; however, the prospect of another Parliament meant James had to stay in the north. Even when the Oxford Parliament had also been dissolved there remained the possibility of another one being called to provide a subsidy for William of Orange. Nor did all the English Court wish for his return. The Duchess of Portsmouth, for example, was afraid she would not be forgiven for supporting Exclusion.

The prospect of some revenue from the Post Office changed her mind and Louis XIV's withdrawal from Luxembourg meant a new Parliament was less likely. However, James's work in Scotland was not yet finished: he was appointed High Commissioner to the first Parliament since 1673. He used both ceremonial and legislation to consolidate the royalist hold on Scotland. One of the main reasons for James's final return from Scotland in late February 1682 (apart from the voyage north to fetch his wife in May) was that the English Tories saw his work there on behalf of the dynasty as proof that the established Church was safe in his hands.

When he became King, James was to put a different and more destructive interpretation on the popularity he had gained in Scotland. Nevertheless, the creation of an image for himself as a loyal supporter of the establishment was a purpose of his exile in Scotland from the start. The unsympathetic Gilbert Burnet remarked that James 'would study to make himself acceptable to that Nation, and bring things among them into order and temper'.[2] As James put it himself: 'I live here as cautiously as I can and am careful to give offence to none and to have no partialities and preach to them laying aside all private animosities and serving the King his own way.'[3]

Sunderland commented on James's handling of his brother's affairs in Scotland: 'we apprehended he would have disordered them, but we find quite the contrary'.[4] For James read the Scottish political scene well and disappointed Shaftesbury who had believed 'the Mass and the Presbytery would make but a mad medley together'.[5]

The role of a Stuart prince restoring past glories to Holyrood was important in defusing tensions in Scotland in both politics and religion. In politics, the 1670s had seen the growth of an aristocratic opposition amid general discontent with the Chancellor, Lauderdale. Burnet believed that James was popular because 'the nobility and gentry, who had been so long trodden on by Duke Lauderdale and his party, found a sensible alteration'.[6] The presence of James himself in Edinburgh helped to stop the mutual tale-bearing to Whitehall and Lauderdale, now ill, was allowed to retire without having to be dismissed.

In religion, the murder of Archbishop Sharp in 1679 had encouraged a military rising by the remnant of the Presbyterian party who had not been brought into the established Church by the previous decade's mixture of leniency and violence directed against them. Monmouth was sent to command the troops against them and won the skirmish at Bothwell Brig. Ironically, his tight control of the troops was attacked by James as 'courting the people' but it was a lesson James learned well after Monmouth was sent abroad and he took over responsibility for law and order in Scotland.[7] James argued wherever possible for a political interpretation of rebellion and went out of his way to commute the death penalty for conventiclers.[8] A tolerance of dissent was obviously in his own interest but he was also trying to lower the religious temperature and develop a reputation for royal beneficence. The basis of his ability to do this was his royal status; as the dedication of a book published in Edinburgh in 1682 put it:

> neither his interest nor inclination can incite him to those enormities that commonly attend, and are to be feared, from the lower persons in such a Ministry: For, he has no poor Kindred to inrich with our spoils, nor Party to raise by our ruine . . .[9]

James was also able to appeal to a royalist political and social ideology in which the Court played a central part. This was most clearly articulated in the writings of the Lord Advocate, Sir George Mackenzie of Rosehaugh, but was echoed in various ways in Scottish society – by loyal addresses, eulogies and seekers after patronage, by Privy Councillors and MPs, and by the nobility and gentry who made up the courtiers and dominated the political classes in Scotland. Mackenzie argued for the divine right of kings and for feudal law. His argument though thorough was not as original as that of his great legal rival the Earl of Stair; the main lines of his beliefs had been well laid out in the reign of James VI by the King himself and by the jurist Sir Thomas Craig. This itself, however, lent them validity in royalist eyes: royalist ideology as well as social life tended to look back with nostalgia to James VI's Court. The nadir of this world view was the execution of Charles I, the low point of disorder which was invoked as a consequence of any kind of opposition to the monarchy in Scotland as frequently as in England during the Exclusion crisis.

The reason why monarchs derived their power from God and not from the people is that His design was to create 'a World, so Vast and regular as this is' to which end it was natural that 'he should have reserved to himself the immediate dependence of the supream Power'.[10] Mackenzie followed his legal-historical thesis through to argue that social order consisted of a hereditary landowning aristocracy owing its security to 'positive law' promulgated by the absolute monarch; 'government is the King's, and property the subject's birthright' he argued.[11] Parliament was only needed for the monarch to obtain assistance in the defence of his kingdom from those to whom he had originally given land away. The memory of physical rebellion, and the threat of its repetition, whether by conventiclers in Scotland or Exclusionists in England, was a continual reminder of the need to maintain a cohesive establishment underpinned by, and also reflecting, an ideology of order.

In addition Mackenzie spent much time working on questions of heraldry, antiquities and precedency, questions central to the ceremony and symbolism of court life. He saw heraldry as part of the law, a description of the established social order. Contemporary antiquarians looked for a past which mirrored the present, especially in the glorification of Scotland and her royal house, just as natural historians such as Dr Robert Sibbald searched for evidence of order in nature, or exceptions which threw it into relief. Such 'virtuosi' looked to James for patronage, both before and after 1682. James took a particular personal interest in the establishment of the Royal College of Physicians in 1681. This proposal met with serious opposition which Sibbald was able to overcome by showing James a supportive paper signed by James VI: 'As soon as he saw it superscribed by King James, [he] said with much satisfaction "he knew his grandfather's hand and he would see our business done" and from that moment acted vigorously for us.'[12] James's personal patronage of the doctors was typical of his improving on an opportunity to create a positive image for himself, but the link with James VI was a major ingredient in this image.

The Royal College of Physicians, and other intellectual organisations such as the Faculty of Advocates' Library, emulated the structure and status of contemporary loyal social organisations such as the Royal Company of Archers (1677) and the Order of the Thistle (1687). An obsession with genealogy was another manifestation of the same concerns; the portraits of 111 Scots kings which still adorn Holyrood House were commissioned shortly after the departure of James. Their significance after the Exclusion crisis would not have been lost on the Stuarts' supporters. Precedency had its most important day at the Riding of Parliament from Holyrood to the Parliament House in 1681, but it also, of course, informed court ceremony at all times. Such interests declined notably after the revolution of 1688 took away their lynchpin.

This mixture of pragmatic and prescriptive conservatism was brought into focus by the arrival of James and the setting up of his Court.[13] Thus the Privy Council wrote to Charles on 11 December 1679 that they were happy to have 'your Royal Brother amongst us; who have not for many years seen any of the Royal Family in this your Majestie's Antient Kingdom; and as he will certainly be a Pattern for our loyalty to imitate . . . .'[14] and so on. James knew well what to do with such loyalty. A copy of the London Gazette reprinted in Edinburgh on 31 January 1681 reported that James had told the Privy Council 'that the Nobility and Gentry here were not only able and ready to keep those unquiet people in order, but also he saw them generally so firmly attached to the Royal Interest as he doubted not but the good Condition of the Kingdom'[15] would be maintained. There was much mutual expression of determination to maintain the legitimate succession, too.[16]

Councillors were by definition courtiers too; the Privy Council had its own chamber in Holyrood where James was present at thirty or more meetings. The Council as executive and Parliament as legislature were personally and constitutionally linked to the Court. The role that James assumed from his first joining the Privy Council in 1679 and later as High Commissioner to Parliament was essentially viceregal. Similarly, his Court can be seen as an extension of Charles's Court in London, both in what it stood for and in the way it worked. The Scottish political classes could now become courtiers in numbers previously denied to them and mingle with those of his own retinue whom James brought north. It was this physical intensification of the experience of being at Court which gave such a fillip to James's assumption of political leadership in Scotland and his drive towards unifying the political life of Scotland behind the throne.

The purpose of James's Court in Edinburgh was evidently political, but what was it like and how did its characteristics help the Stuart cause? It is not clear precisely how many courtiers James took north. On 26 December 1679 the Town Council admitted the Duke and 117 persons of his following to the freedom of Edinburgh.[17] On his departure from London in 1681 he took leave of 'his Majestie and the whole Court, attended by a splendid train of Nobility' but it is ambiguous whether they stayed or went.[18] More evidence of which elements of his English establishment accompanied him is found in the stories surrounding the wreck of the *Gloucester*, the ship in which James was sailing to Scotland on his final visit in May 1682.[19] It had taken two hours 'to dispose of his Royal Highness's Retinue and Goods' as the flotilla of frigates and yachts lay at anchor in the Thames on Friday 3 May. The *Gloucester* struck the Lemon sand off Yarmouth at 5.30 the following morning. When pumping was seen to be ineffective, James agreed to launch his 'barge' and evacuation was organised by social status. Unfortunately, the seas moved the ship into deeper water as this was going on and 150 men were drowned, including some of James's servants. 'All the persons of Quality were saved', except for five. James is said to have called particularly for Sir George Gordon of Haddo, who he was about to make Chancellor, to continue his policy in Scotland. Other tales suggested that his dogs were also rescued as a priority as were some unknown members of his retinue; it was presumed these were his priests by opposition pamphleteers.[20]

James's second wife, Mary Beatrice, accompanied him on his stay in Scotland. As their coaches arrived at the border on 20 November 1679 and they were formally greeted by the Scots nobility, the Duchess remained in her coach but James descended from his. The Duchess certainly brought her Chaplains and Ladies-in-Waiting to Holyrood. James's younger daughter, Lady Anne, travelled north in July 1681 with her own Maids of Honour and played a full part in the social life of the Court. They were reputed to have introduced the Scots courtly women to tea drinking; at any rate the English members of the Court created an important element of glamour which enhanced the status of the Duke himself, even if we do not believe the English tourist Ralph Thoresby's diary entry for 15 September 1681: 'At Holyroodhouse, observing the state of the building and attendants, where many judge is as great a court as at Whitehall.'[21]

The 'state of the building' of Holyrood was that it had recently been largely rebuilt to the designs of Sir William Bruce, carried out by the royal master mason Robert Mylne.[22] This had been initiated after the Restoration, when only the west range of the palace was left inhabitable by the ravages of fire and Cromwell's troops quartered there. It was important that the restored monarchy should have a restored palace. A survey was carried out in 1663, money finally voted by the Privy Council in 1670 and a design agreed after Bruce's first suggestions were rejected by Charles II. Both the Queen's and the King's apartments were designed in a ceremonial sequence: Guardhall, Presence Chamber (with the canopied chair of state), Privy Chamber, Antechamber, Bedchamber, with the genuinely private Closet behind. The rest of the palace 'was designed to provide lodgings to be occupied normally by officers of state, in which the King's retinue could be billeted during a royal visit'. Thus Holyrood palace was intended to be the outward and visible sign of Stuart power and security. Officers of state such as the Lord Treasurer Depute, who was Lauderdale's brother, and the Marquess of Atholl, Lord Privy Seal, were granted lodgings in the palace in 1675. The exterior was finished in 1678–9, though the clock face on the crowned cupola above the west front, accompanied by Scottish royal symbols, is dated 1680.[23]

The aspects of courtly social life about which there is most evidence are those most commented on because they were unusual. The day-to-day rituals of the Court would have mirrored those of Whitehall. Theatricals, dancing and games each aroused the interest of Scots commentators and Stuart propagandists. Balls, plays and masquerades were given for the nobility and gentry. The sycophantic Michael Livingstone wrote:

> Let these be repute rebels to their KING
> Who won't concurr to laugh, play, dance and sing[24]

and certainly the pleasures of the Court themselves could be described as a test of political loyalty. Lauder of Fountainhall, for example, wrote disgustedly in November 1681: 'Not only the canonists, both Protestant and Popish, but the very heathen Roman lawyers, declared all scenic and stage players infamous, and will scarce admit them to the sacrament of the Lord's supper.'[25]

There had been theatrical performances in Edinburgh since the Restoration, and one family had the post of 'Masters of the Revells'; a troupe of Irish actors had to be given special permission to import their costumes when they came to Scotland on tour during James's stay.[26] It was courtly theatre which was new. As was done elsewhere in Europe, the tennis court at Holyrood was tricked out as a theatre. Nathaniel Lee's play *Mithridates, King of Pontus* was acted privately on the Queen's birthday, 15 November 1681, 'keept with great solemnitie by canons, bonefires and a comedie at the Abbey'.[27] The actors were Lady Anne and her Maids of Honour. Dryden's play about Montezuma, *The Indian Emperor*, was one of the productions by a part of the Duke's own company of players who came north. Dryden himself took the opportunity to have a dig at them, and at the Scots in general, in a prologue he wrote to a play performed in Oxford at the time:

> Our brethren are from Thames to Tweed departed
> And of our sisters all the kinder-hearted
> To Edinburgh gone, or coached or carted.
> With bonny Blue-cap there they act all night,
> For Scotch half-crown, in English threepence hight.
> One nymph to whom fat Sir John Falstaff's lean
> There with her single person fills the scene.
> Another, with long use and wont decayed
> Dived here old woman, and there rose a maid.
> Our trusty doorkeepers of former time
> There strut and swagger in heroic rhyme.
> Tack but a copper lace to drugget suit,
> And there a hero's made without dispute,
> And that which was a capon's tail before,
> Becomes a plume for Indian emperor.
> But all his subjects, to express the care
> Of imitation, go like Indian bare:
> Laced linen there would be a dangerous thing,
> It might perhaps a new rebellion bring –
> The Scot who wore it would be chosen king.[28]

There were more intellectual meetings at Holyrood, too, in an echo of Charles's interest in the Royal Society. Dr Sibbald gave a discourse of personal thanks to the Duke after the foundation of the Royal College of Physicians. This 'occasioned much envy to me, that I was taken notice of at the Court'.[29] Outdoor activities included golf and horse racing. It is no longer possible to extract much reliable information about the golf from the encrustation of legend around it, but there appears to have been an element of international rivalry and James certainly played himself. Livingston extended his paeon on the life of the Court to the links:

> let Clubs be pliant, each rest be a tease
> Unto the leaping Ball, and both accord
> T'obey his nod, and pleasure to afford.[30]

The Duke's interest in horses was pandered to by the Town Council of Edinburgh, who brought forward a cup race at Leith from the spring to 12 February 1680 because the Duke and Duchess would be leaving soon.[31]

Four editions of the *London Gazette* were reprinted at Edinburgh in the winter of 1679 to describe James's arrival. Four more were printed the next winter as the *Edinburgh Gazette*. 'Published by authority', they give a picture of court life as it was hoped the English and Scottish public would see it. The first describes the nobility and gentry's presence at Holyrood and emphasises their political loyalty. The next praises the Duke's 'gentleness of Temper in Private Conversation and that justice tempered with Clemency and Moderation in his public appearances at the Council Board'. The apprehension of rebels, the death of one of Montrose's lieutenants and the latest news from the London Parliament formed the context for descriptions of court life. At Christmas many of the courtiers went home to their country houses 'with a full resolution to return and wait on their Royal highnesses after the holy dayes are over'. This illuminates the social reality of the Court as a gathering place for landowners, whose presence waiting on James was a mark of loyalty to the political structures which defended their status.[32] In George Mackenzie's words, 'Government is the King's and property the subject's birthright.'

In Scotland, with its poor communications, the contrast between court and country was geographical, although there were certain nobles and gentry who qualified for court life who rarely appeared for political reasons. Livingstone may have had them in mind when he hoped that 'all prefer the court to solitudes' and George Mackenzie wrote on the same well-worn dichotomy. More interesting was the controversy over the removal of the summer Session of the Law Courts in Edinburgh, ratified by an Act of the 1681 Parliament. The magistrates feared a loss of trade but the landowning lawyers wanted to be at home improving their estates in the good weather. Once again the importance of landownership in the political structure of Scotland was revealed; life at the court was bound to reflect this. This controversy also shows how court life was integrated into the wider social life of the city, as it was becoming in London at the same time. In this sense the Court at Holyrood was modern.

One way for the geographical problem to be overcome was by royal progresses. As with the static Court, there was a ceremonial structure to the Duke's travel, which is in fact better documented. Edinburgh was his main concern at all times. His first arrival overland has been mentioned. In November 1679, after being met at the border north of Berwick, he went to Lauderdale's house in the Borders before travelling on to make a formal entry into Edinburgh.[33] The standing forces were drawn up for the Duke and Duchess to pass through; the magistrates and 200 burghers and 'ladies of Quality' attended. The Provost made a loyal speech and presented the Duke with the city keys. Bonfires and free wine were standard on such an occasion. The Town Council had arranged for beggars to be cleared from the streets back in October 'considering that his Royall Highnes the Duke of Albanie and York and many of the Inglish nobility and gentry are to come to this place shortly'. Later they were to spend £14,000 (Scots) on a 'treat' for the Duke and Duchess.[34] It was vital for James's security that Edinburgh should be well under loyal control; conversely, the presence of the Court in nearby Holyrood was a tremendous economic boon to the city.

On his return the following year, James landed at Kirkcaldy and crossed to Leith after staying with the Earl of Rothes in Fife, where nobles and gentry began to join him. A contemporary pamphlet describes the crowds, the guns fired from Edinburgh Castle, the troops of guards, the aristocracy, the long train of coaches. Trainbands and militia made an avenue up to Holyrood; James was given the keys of the city again and, in the palace, the keys to the castle. During the following week the clergy and members of the College of Justice came to kiss his hand. These welcoming ceremonies were intended to deliver two messages: that Scotland was peaceful and loyal and that an ordered hierarchy depending on the monarchy was the natural form of society. The Duke's position as the personification of the monarchy was the basis of his political policy.

Evidence from other formal occasions reinforces this picture. James was present at the coronation of the new Lord Lyon, King-at-Arms in July 1681 when an order to be observed was published, understandably for this key post in defining social status.[35] He also made two progresses to other parts of the lowlands, both at short notice, which saw the local dignitaries scampering to replicate the rituals they had attended or heard about in Edinburgh. In February 1681 a spell of fine weather induced James to visit Stirling and Linlithgow; the weather proved to be deceptive and snow made attendance by more remote lairds difficult. He was escorted by the nobility and gentry of each shire as far as its boundary, where those of the next shire took over. Linlithgow mimicked the reception he had had at Edinburgh; Stirling Castle that at Holyrood.[36]

On 8 October James went to Glasgow and Dumbarton 'attended with a very splendid train of the prime Nobility and Gentry'.[37] The Archbishop, local landowners, a military escort and a youth display formed the elements of his welcome, and a series of banquets and speeches included several of the latter at the College of Glasgow. All attendances on the Duke were a serious social and political duty, as can be seen from the instructions given by Rothes in October 1680 that all the Privy Councillors south of Aberdeen should come to Edinburgh to receive James, and that standard letters should be sent out to all the gentry telling them to make their way to Leith.[38]

It was, however, the Scottish Parliament of 1681 which saw the climax of James's symbolic role and of his political programme. The Parliament met in July, August and September, after the Oxford Parliament and the royal counter-attack on the Exclusionists but while there was still a threat to the dynasty. Charles had a clear idea of how to extract what was wanted from Parliament; bearing in mind the problems caused by the aristocraic opposition in 1673, he gave James private instructions 'to Take specaill care to suppress all motions for proposeing, voteing or caerrieing on anie thing in parliament in ane unparliamentaire method . . . so the antient and laudable methods and order of preceeding, may be duly observed . . . .'[39] What this meant was the protection of the power of the Lords of the Articles to prepare and vet carefully parliamentary business. Charles particularly warned his brother about extraordinary cabals and about any rising of the rebels, for it was the combination of popular and parliamentary opposition, as in England but of a different origin, which posed the greatest threat to the Stuart establishment. Charles's letter to Parliament, read out at the opening on 28 July, stressed the indivisibility of loyalty to the Crown and the peace and security of people and property. The Duke in his speech emphasised the established religion, law and the succession.[40]

James was now able to cash in on eighteen months of work in Scotland. Laws were passed confirming the established religion and the lawful succession, offering increased supply to deal with conventiclers, securing the peace of the country by giving landowners powers to evict tenants for crimes against the Church government. Above all the Test Act was used to smoke out forty ministers still disaffected to episcopacy and to condemn (and later execute) the Earl of Argyll. The Test Act was undermined by Viscount Stair, who managed to add a clause agreeing with the 1567 Confession of Faith; this introduced a contradictory element into the oath. Stair wrote in 1690:

> the then Duke of York did, the very night the Act passed, declare to the late Earl of Argyle that I had ruined all honest men [meaning Papists] by bringing in that confession. . . .'[41]

In 1681 Stair retreated to his estate and later to Holland.

It had been no coincidence that Stair had failed to meet James on the road on his first visit to Scotland, pleading pressure of work, for the political programme of 1679–82 was bound up with the ritual of the Court. Thus the Riding of Parliament on 28 July 1681 was the high point of court as well as political life during James's stay in Scotland. The order of the Riding – from Holyrood to the Parliament house – was established by an Act of the Duke himself.[42] It was to follow precisely the order established by the 1663 Act and only included minor changes due to the fact of the Commissioner being the King's brother. The details included who was to ride and who was to walk, who was to be bareheaded, how many servants the different ranks could have, and the distance apart they should walk. The procession was in effect a masque of Scottish society, including in the courtly ritual not only clergy and lords but also the third estate, elected representatives of the shires and burghs. One novelty was the presence of the Duchess and ladies of the Court.[43] James took his place as the leader and protector of this display of heraldry, precedency, stability and order, the only thing more important than himself being his Commission from the King, 'carried before him in a Velvet Bagg'. Each day Parliament met, a similar procession took place. The English traveller Ralph Thoresby spent the morning of 14 September 'standing in the yard of the parliament house, observing the several members and nobles as they went to the House, and after them, the Duke of York and Albany, in great state'.[44] By the time of the Act of Adjournment on 17 September James had secured Scotland for his brother and done much to ensure his own peaceful succession to the throne.

This achievement should not be portrayed as automatic or even easy. The Duke of Hamilton had led forty MPs in an argument that James could not be Commissioner without taking the oaths, which of course his Catholicism made him unable to do. A legal argument countered this – that a Commission was not an office of state – and Hamilton desisted. Most Bills were opposed; the Test Act itself only passed by seven votes. Burnet claimed that James gained advantage from the death of Rothes the day before Parliament opened, because many were seeking his posts; however, he also made it clear that it was James's own leadership which pushed forward so much favourable legislation so quickly, and he actually refers to the 'Court party' in his description of the politics of the 1681 Parliament.[45]

Parliamentary opposition was thus dealt with by the Duke of York's determination and his exploitation of loyalty to the Crown; the Court played an important part in this strategy. James was also able to make capital out of such physical threats as the conventiclers; he did the same with the students who rioted on Christmas Day 1680, burning an effigy of the Pope and fighting the Duke's supporters, the cries on each side being 'No Pope, No Priest, No Bishop, No Atheist' against 'I am no fanatic'.[46] However, the Privy Council ordered the magistrates to close the College (Edinburgh University) and ban the students for fourteen months 'considering how disloyall and mutinous persons did in the last age bring on their dreadfull rebellion from such a beginning'.[47] The whole incident 'The Duke of York took ill, as a reflection on him, being then at the Abbey of Holyrood House.'[48] Though old General Tam Dalywell was led a merry dance by the rioters, it was doubtful whether this disturbance was any more of a threat to the Duke and Court than the comet which appeared that month or the Edinburgh merchant and his country friend who saw a fire descend the Royal Mile and a voice say 'This is the sword of the Lord.'[49] There was a move to take James to a safer location, but in February he intervened on the students' behalf and modified the conditions under which the College could reopen.[50] Similar disturbances in 1686 and 1688 were much more serious, as by then James had forfeited much of the support he had built up in 1680–1.

The Privy Council's reaction to the student riot is a reminder of the political terms of reference in Scotland and England at the time of the Popish Plot.

Royalist ideology, though unoriginal, was not merely academic; it had a continuing and serious function in contemporary political reality. The Court in all its manifestations – buildings, ceremony, social life, progresses, propaganda or the Riding of Parliament – was an important means of reinforcing this ideology in contemporary politics. To return to the original questions: the Court was both a medium of political power and a symbol of stability and order. It was used by James as part of a British strategy to save the Stuart dynasty: he intended to develop a loyal power base in Scotland and he had largely succeeded by 1681. He had turned the ideas of status, order, security and peace into the more tangible benefits of loyalty to the establishment, legal security for the succession, money and troops.

One key to his success was his role as a Stuart prince at the head of a Stuart court. A propaganda tract in the form of 'A letter from a Person of Quality in Scotland to a Person of Honour in London' puts this clearly: 'But you see that he himself, by his actions and converse, in a little time, has been able to do more than all the words and arguments in the world could do.'[51] James's acceptance on his return to England and the celebrations in Edinburgh on his succession in 1685 were evidence of the success of his Scottish policy.

What then happened in Scotland was an echo of his policy in England. He mistakenly thought he could build on the loyalty of his subjects, and his support from the establishment, to effect a revolution which undermined that very establishment. Holyrood palace continued to be a focus for James's policy once he became King. He set up a Catholic chapel in the Council Chamber in 1686, revived the Order of the Thistle and took over the Abbey Church as its headquarters, and finally set up a Jesuit school in the Chancellor's lodging. By 1688 James's policy had systematically alienated all of the institutions and political classes which he had so successfully drawn into the orbit of his Court during his stay in Scotland. So it was the Town Council and the lawyers who drew up the address to William of Orange on 31 December 1688, the rump of the Privy Council who decided to publish William's declaration, the Lords of Session who re-established order during January 1689 and the indulged Presbyterian clergy who led the revolution in the Church which followed. And it was towards Holyrood Palace that the mob directed their anger, sacking the Abbey Church in December 1688. When the last Stuart set up a court at Holyrood, in 1745, he could see the Abbey Church ruins standing to show how in the end James had not recreated but destroyed the Stuart Court in Scotland.

Notes

1. John Miller, *James II: a Study in Kingship* (London, Methuen, 1978), ch. 7.
2. Gilbert Burnet, *History of My Own Time* (London, Thomas Ward, 1724), Vol. I, p. 477.
3. Miller, op. cit., p. 107.
4. Malcolm V. Hay, *The Enigma of James II* (London, Sands, 1938), p. 26.

5. Maurice Ashley, *Charles II* (London, Panther Books, 1973), p. 262.

6. Burnet, *Own Time*, p. 510; William Ferguson, *Scotland's Relations with England: a Survey to 1707* (Edinburgh, John Donald, 1977), p. 160. See also John Patrick, 'A Union broken? Restoration politics in Scotland', in Jenny Wormald (ed.), *Scotland Revisited* (London, Collins and Brown, 1991), pp. 119–28.

7. Burnet, *Own Time*, pp. 473, 511.

8. Miller, op. cit., p. 107.

9. Christopher Irvine, MD, *Historiae Scoticae Nomenclatura Latino-Vernacular* (Edinburgh, Anderson, to be sold by G. Shaw, January 1682).

10. Sir George Mackenzie of Rosehaugh, *Jus Regium, or the Just and Solid Foundations of Monarchy* (Edinburgh, heir of A. Anderson, 1684), p. 21.

11. Ibid., p. 50.

12. Sir Robert Sibbald, *Remains, Containing his Autobiography etc.* (Edinburgh, Thomas Stevenson, 1833), p. 30.

13. Cf. J.G.A. Pocock, 'Time, Institutions and Action: An Essay on Traditions and their Understanding', in P. King and B.C. Parekh (eds), *Politics and Experience* (Cambridge, Cambridge University Press, 1968), p. 234.

14. P. Hume Brown (ed.), *Register of the Privy Council of Scotland*, Vol. VI, (HMSO, 1914), p. 345; Anon., *Some Historical Memories of the Life and Actions of his Royal Highness . . . James, Duke of York . . . to this Present Year, 1682* (London, Daniel Brown, 1683), pp. 113–14.

15. *London Gazette*, No. 1485 ('Published by Authority'; Edinburgh, reprinted by Anderson's heirs, 1680/1).

16. For example, in the letter from the Privy Council to the King on 2 November 1680. *Register of the Privy Council of Scotland*, Vol. VI, pp. 567–8, and in the Duke's speech to Parliament on 28 July 1681: *The King's Majestie's Gracious Letter to his Parliament of Scotland, 28 July, 1681* (Edinburgh, Anderson's heirs, 1681).

17. Margeurite Wood (ed.), *Extracts from the Records of the Burgh of Edinburgh, Vol. X, 1665–1680* (Edinburgh, Oliver and Boyd, 1850), p. 388, 26 December 1679.

18. Anon., *Some Historical Memoires . . .*, p. 119.

19. Ibid., pp. 129–34.

20. Robert Chambers, *Domestic Annals of Scotland, Volume II* (Edinburgh, Chambers, 1858), pp. 403 ff.

21. P. Hume Brown (ed.), *Tours in Scotland 1677 and 1681* (Edinburgh, David Douglas, 1892), p. 52, 14 September 1681.

22. John Gifford, Colin McWilliam and David Walker, *The Buildings of Scotland: Edinburgh* (London, Penguin, 1984), p. 127.

23. Ibid., p. 143. See also John Harrison, *The History of the Monastery of . . . Holyrood* (Edinburgh, Blackwood, 1919), pp. 197–205.

24. Michael Livingstone, *Albion's Congratulatory* (Edinburgh, Anderson's heirs, 1680), p. 3.

25. As quoted in Chambers, *Domestic Annals*, p. 404.

26. Ibid., p. 405.

27. Sir John Lauder of Fountainhall, *Chronological Notes of Scottish Affairs from 1680 till 1701*, ed. Sir Walter Scott (Edinburgh, Constable, 1822), p. 20. As quoted by James C. Dibdin, *The Annals of the Edinburgh Stage* (Edinburgh, Richard Cameron, 1888), p. 28.

28. Chambers, *Domestic Annals*, pp. 404–5.

29. Sir Robert Sibbald, *Remains*, p. 33.

30. Livingstone, *Albion's Congratulatory*, p. 4. See also the stories in James Grant (ed.), *Cassell's Old and New Edinburgh* (Edinburgh, Cassell, Petter, Galpin, 1882), Vol. II, p. 75.

31. Wood, *Records of the Burgh of Edinburgh, Vol. X*, p. 390.

32. *Edinburgh Gazette* (Edinburgh, Anderson's heirs, November–December 1680).

33. Anon., *Some Historical Memoires*, p. 112.

34. Wood, *Records of the Burgh of Edinburgh, vol. X*, pp. 381 (29 October 1679), 398 (21 February 1680).

35. *Cassell's Old and New Edinburgh*, Vol. I, p. 371.

36. *A True and Exact Relation of his Royal Highness' Progress Upon the 3rd, 4th and 5th February Instant* ('Published by Authority'; Edinburgh, Anderson's heirs, 1681).

37. Anon., *Some Historical Memories*, p. 123.

38. *Register of the Privy Council of Scotland , 3rd Series*, Vol. VI (1914), p. 566 (23 October 1680).

39. 'Charles R. Privat Instructions to our intirelie beloved Brother James Duke of Albanie and York our Comissioner in Scotland' (BL, MS 11,252.8).

40. *The King's Majestie's Gracious Letter to his Parliament of Scotland, 28 July, 1681* (Edinburgh, Anderson's heirs, 1681).

41. 'An *Apology* for Sir James Dalrymple of Stair . . . by himself' (Edinburgh, 1690, reprinted by the Bannatyne Club, 1825), pp. 4–5.

42. *Register of the Privy Council of Scotland*, Vol. VII (1915), pp. 167–70: 'An Act by his Royal Highness . . . Establishing the Order of Ryding &c.' (at the opening of the ensuing Parliament).

43. Lauder, *Chronological Notes*, p. 19.

44. Hume Brown, *Tours in Scotland*, p. 51 (14 September 1681).

45. Burnet, *Own Time*, pp. 514–15.

46. *A Proclamation Concerning the Students in the College of Edinburgh* (Edinburgh, Anderson's heir, 21 January 1681); Chambers, *Domestic Anmals*, p. 413.

47. *Register of the Privy Council of Scotland*, Vol. VII (1915), p. 24. See also n. 45.

48. J.G. Fyfe (ed.), *Scottish Diaries and Memoirs 1550–1746* (Stirling, Mackay, 1928), p. 264. The diarist was Robert Law. *The History of the Late Proceedings of the Students of the College at Edenborough . . . in Three Several Letters to a Worthy Citizen of London* (London, for Richard Janeway, 1681).

49. Chambers, *Domestic Annals*. p. 412.

50. *Records of the Privy Council of Scotland, 3rd Series*, Vol. VII, pp. 28–30, 39. *The History of the Late Proceedings of the Students*, p. 4.

51. *A Letter from a Person of Quality in Scotland to a Person of Honour in London, Concerning his Royal Highness James, Duke of York*, in Walter Scott (ed.), *Somers Tracts* (New York, AMS Press, 1965).

SELECT BIBLIOGRAPHY

Except where otherwise stated, the place of publication is London.

Adamson, John (ed.). *The Princely Courts of Europe: Ritual, Politics and Culture Under the Ancien Regime 1500–1750*, 1999

Akrigg, G.V.P. *Jacobean Pageant & the Court of James I*, Cambridge, Mass., 1952

Ash, Ronald G. and Birke, Adolf M. (eds). *Princes, Patronage, and Nobility: The Court of the Beginning of the Modern Age, c. 1460–1650*, Oxford, 1991

Ashley, Maurice. *Charles II*, 1973

——. *The House of Stuart*, 1980

Ashmole, Elias. *The Institution, Laws and Ceremonies of the Most Noble Order of the Garter*, 1972

Ashton, Robert. *James I by His Contemporaries*, 1969

——. *The City and the Court 1603–1643*, Cambridge, 1979

Aylmer, G.E. *The King's Servants: The Civil Service of Charles I 1625–1642*, 2nd edn 1974

Berrington, D. and Holbrook, P. (eds). *The Politics of the Stuart Court Masques*, Cambridge, 1998

Birch, Thomas (ed.). *The Court and Times of Charles I*, 2 vols, 1849

Brookes-Davies, Douglas. *The Mercurian Monarch: Magical Politics from Spencer to Pope*, Manchester, 1983

Brown, Keith. *Kingdom or Province? Scotland and the Regal Union, 1603–1715*, New York, 1992

Bucholz, R.O. *The Augustan Court: Queen Anne and the Decline of Court Culture*, Stanford, Calif., 1993

Butler, Martin. *Theatre and Crisis 1632–42*, Cambridge, 1984

Cannadine, David and Price, Simon (eds). *Rituals of Royalty: Power and Ceremonial in Traditional Societies*, Cambridge, 1987

Carlton, C. *Charles I: The Personal Monarch*, 1983

Clarke, J.S. (ed.). *The Life of King James II*, 2 vols, 1816

Coward, Barry. *The Stuart Age: England 1603–1714*, 2nd edn 1994

Cruickshanks, Eveline and Corp, Edward (eds). *The Stuart Court in Exile and the Jacobites*, 1995

Davies, Julian. *The Caroline Captivity of the Church: Charles I and the Remoulding of Anglicanism 1625–1641*, Oxford, 1992

Dickens, A.G. (ed.). *The Courts of Europe, Politics, Patronage and Royalty, 1400–1800*, New York, 1977

Donald, P. *An Uncounselled King: Charles I and the Scottish Troubles, 1637–1641*, Cambridge, 1990

Dutton, R. *English Court Life from Henry VII to George II*, 1973

Elliott, J.H. and Brockliss, L.W.B. (eds). *The World of the Favourite*, New Haven, Co., 1999

Erskine-Hill, Howard. *Poetry and the Realm of Politics: Shakespeare to Dryden*, Oxford, 1996

Figgis, John Neville. *The Divine Right of Kings*, New York, 1965

Fincham, Kenneth. *The Early Stuart Church*, Stanford, Calif., 1993

Fraser, Lady Antonia. *King Charles II*, 1979

——. *Royal Charles: Charles II and the Restoration*, New York, 1979

Gaunt, W. *Court Painting in England from Tudor to Victorian Times*, 1980
Glassey, L. (ed.). *The Reigns of Charles II and James VII & II*, 1997
Goldberg, Jonathan. *James I and the Politics of Literature*, Baltimore, 1983
Gregg, Pauline. *King Charles I*, Berkeley, Calif., 1981
Harris, T., Seaward, P. and Goldie, M. (eds). *The Politics of Religion in Restoration England*, Oxford, 1990
Harris, Tim. *Politics Under the Later Stuarts: Party Conflicts in a Divided Society*, 1993
Hart, Vaughan. *Art and Magic in the Courts of the Stuarts*, 1997
Heal, Felicity. *Hospitality in Early Modern England*, Oxford, 1990
Healy, Thomas and Sawday, Jonathan (eds). *Literature and the English Civil War*, 1990
Henderson, T.F. *James I and VI*, 1904
Hibbard, Caroline M. *Charles I and the Popish Plot*, Chapel Hill, North Car., 1983
Hirst, Derek. *England in Conflict 1603–1689*, 1999
Howarth, David. *Lord Arundel and his Circle*, New Haven, Co., 1985
—— (ed.). *Art and Patronage in the Caroline Court: Essays in Honour of Sir Oliver Millar*, 1993
——. *Images of Rule: Art and Politics in the English Renaissance 1487–1649*, 1997
Hughes, Joan and Ransom, W.S. (eds). *Poetry of the Stewart Court*, 1982
Hutton, Ronald. *The Restoration*, Oxford, 1985
——. *Charles II: King of England, Scotland and Ireland*, 1989, reprinted 1992
Jones, J.R. (ed.). *The Restored Monarchy, 1660–1688*, 1979
——. *Charles II: Royal Politician*, 1987
Kishlansky, M. *A Monarchy Transformed: Britain 1603–1714*, 1996
Knights, Mark. *Politics and Opinion in Crisis, 1678–81*, Cambridge, 1994
Lee, Maurice Jnr. *Government by Pen: Scotland under James VI and I*, Urbana, Ill., 1980
Limon, Jerzy. *The Masque of Stuart Culture*, Newark, Del., 1990
Lindley, David. *The Court Masque*, 1984
—— (ed.). *Court Masques: Jacobean and Caroline Entertainments 1505–1640*, 1995
Lockyer, Roger. *Buckingham: The Life and Political Career of George Villiers, First Duke of Buckingham 1592–1628*, 1981
——. *The Early Stuarts: a Political History of England 1603–1642*, 1989
McCullough, Peter. *Sermons at Court: Politics and Religion in Elizabethan and Jacobean Preaching*, Cambridge, 1998
MacGregor, Arthur (ed.). *The Late King's Goods: Collections, Possessions and Patronage of Charles I in the Light of the Commonwealth Sale Inventories*, 1989
McIlwain, G.H. (ed.). *The Political Works of James I*, Cambridge, Mass., 1918
Macinnes, Allan I. *Charles I and the Making of the Covenanting Movement 1625–1641*, Edinburgh, 1991
Maguire, Nancy Klein. *Culture and Society in the Stuart Restoration*, 1995
Malekin, Peter. *Liberty and Love: English Literature and Society 1640–88*, 1981
Millar, O. *Tudor, Stuart and Early Georgian Pictures in the Collection of Her Majesty the Queen*, 2 vols, 1963
Miller, John. *James II: a Study in Kingship*, 1978
——. *Charles II*, 1991
Monod, Paul Kléber. *The Power of Kings: Monarchy and Religion in Europe 1589–1715*, 1999

Morrill, John, Slack, Paul and Woolf, Daniel (eds). *Public Duty and Private Conscience in Seventeenth Century England: Essays Presented to G.E. Aylmer*, Oxford, 1993

Mulryne, J.R. and Shewring, M. (eds). *Theatre and Government Under the Early Stuarts*, 1993

Nenner, Howard. *The Right to be King: The Succession to the Crown of England, 1602–1714*, Basingstoke, 1995

Nichols, J. (ed.). *The Progresses, Processions, and Magnificent Festivities of King James I the First*, 4 vols, New York, 1967

Ollard, Richard. *The Escape of Charles II after the Battle of Worcester*, 1966

——. *The Image of King Charles I and Charles II*, 1979

Orgel, Stephen. *The Jonsonian Masque*, Cambridge, Mass., 1965

—— and Strong, Roy (eds). *Inigo Jones: the Theatre of the Stuart Court*, 2 vols, 1973

——. *The Illusion of Power: Political Theater in the English Renaissance*, Berkeley, Calif., 1975

Parry, Graham. *The Golden Age Restor'd: the Culture of the Stuart Court 1603–42*, Manchester, 1981

Patterson, W.B. *King James VI and I and the Reunion of Christendom*, Cambridge, 1998

Peck, Linda Levy. *Northampton, Patronage and Policy at the Court of James I*, 1982

——. *Court, Patronage and Corruption in Early Stuart England*, 1990

Potter, Lois. *Secret Rites and Secret Writings: Royalist Literature 1641–1660*, Cambridge, 1989

Reeve, L.J. *Charles I and the Road to Personal Rule*, Cambridge, 1999

Roberts, Jane. *Royal Landscape: The Gardens and Park of Windsor*, New Haven, Co., 1997

——. *The King's Head: Charles I King and Martyr*, 1990

Russell, Conrad. *Parliaments and English Politics, 1621–29*, Oxford, 1979

——. *The Causes of the English Civil War*, Oxford, 1990

——. *The Fall of the British Monarchies 1637–42*, Oxford, 1991

Sainty, J.C. and Bucholz, R.O. *Officials of the Royal Household 1660–1837 Part I Department of the Lord Chamberlain and Associated Offices*, 1997

Seaward, P. *The Cavalier Parliament and the Reconstruction of the Old Regime, 1661–1667*, Cambridge, 1989

Sharpe, Kevin. *Faction and Parliament: Essays in Early Stuart History*, Oxford, 1978

——. *Criticism and Compliment: The Politics of Literature in the England of Charles I*, 1987

—— and Swicker, Steven (eds). *The Politics of Discourse: the Literature and History of Seventeenth Century England*, Berkeley, Calif., 1987

——. *The Personal Rule of Charles I*, New Haven, Co., 1992

—— and Locke, Peter (eds). *Culture and Politics in Early Stuart England*, Basingstoke, 1993

Shire, Helena Mennie. *Song, Dance and Poetry of the Court of Scotland Under King James VI*, 1969

Smith, David L. *The Stuart Parliaments 1603–1689*, 1999

Smuts, R. Malcom. *Court Culture and the Origins of a Royalist Tradition in Early Stuart England*, Philadelphia, 1987

——. *The Stuart Court and Europe: Essays in Politics and Political Culture*, Cambridge, 1996

Stafford, Helen Georgia. *James VI of Scotland and the Throne of England*, New York, 1940

Starkey, David, Morgan, D.A.L., Murphy, J., Wright, P., Cuddy, N. and Sharp, K. (eds). *The British Court from the Wars of the Roses to the Civil War*, 1987

Strong, Roy. *Van Dyck, Charles I on Horseback*, New York, 1972

——. *Britannia Triumphans: Inigo Jones, Rubens and Whitehall Palace*, 1980

——. *Henry, Prince of Wales and England's Lost Renaissance*, 1986

Stroud, Angus. *Stuart England*, 1999

Thurley, Simon. *The Royal Palaces of Tudor England*, New Haven, Co., 1993

Tomlinson, Howard (ed.). *Before the English Civil War*, 1983

Turner, F.C. *James II*, 1948

Tyacke, Nicholas. *Anti-Calvinists: The Rise of English Arminianism in the English Church from the Reformation to the English Civil War*, Cambridge, 1992

Veevers, Erica. *Images of Love and Religion: Queen Henrietta Maria and Court Entertainment*, 1989

Wedgwood, C.V. *A Coffin for King Charles: The Trial and Execution of Charles I*, New York, 1966

White, Peter. *Predestination, Policy and Polemic: Conflict and Consensus in the English Church from the Reformation to the Civil War*, Cambridge, 1992

Willson, D.H. *King James VI and I*, 1956

Young, Michael B. *Charles I*, Basingstoke, 1997

Zagorin, P. *The Court and the Country: the Beginning of the English Revolution*, New York, 1969

INDEX